ABIDE WITH US

DAILY HYMN DEVOTIONS

Richard C. Resch

Daniel Zager

CONCORDIA PUBLISHING HOUSE · SAINT LOUIS

ABOUT THE COVER

Artist Edward Riojas was commissioned to create the cover art for this devotional, *Abide with Us*, based on the Emmaus account from Luke 24:13–35. There, Jesus opened the Scriptures to disciples who had asked Him to stay, or abide, with them. Today, one of the beautiful and powerful ways the Scriptures continue to be opened to disciples of Jesus Christ is through the church's hymns. The daily devotions within this book are based on the theology of these hymns.

Published by Concordia Publishing House
3558 S. Jefferson Ave., St. Louis, MO 63118-3968
1-800-325-3040 • cph.org

1 2 3 4 5 6 7 8 9 10 34 33 32 31 30 29 28 27 26 25

CONTENTS

PREFACE

When we think of hymns, it is quite natural to think first and foremost of congregational singing of hymns during the Sunday Divine Service in our churches. Secondarily, we may think of hymn singing in the home, perhaps during evening devotions and children's bedtime. Or we might recall singing at the bedside of the saint about to enter eternal rest, perhaps the closing stanza of the hymn "Abide with Me":

> Hold Thou Thy cross before my closing eyes;
> Shine through the gloom, and point me to the skies.
> Heav'n's morning breaks, and earth's vain shadows flee;
> In life, in death, O Lord, abide with me. (*LSB* 878:6)

This single example of the richness of our hymnody suggests the premise of this book—that our hymnic heritage deserves to be used on a *daily* basis. Whether we sing, speak, or read silently these miniature sermons of the church, our faith is strengthened for daily living and in anticipation of the sure and certain hope of eternal life. Our hymns proclaim the Gospel by pointing us to Jesus. They help each of us to recall our Baptism and to anticipate with deep reverence and holy joy the presence of Jesus in the Sacrament of the Lord's Supper. Our hymns teach us, encourage us, and console us.

The book that you are holding in your hands provides a devotion for each day of the year. Each devotion begins with a hymn stanza followed by a brief devotional exposition of the hymn. A thematically linked closing hymn stanza follows, sometimes drawn from the same hymn as the opening stanza, sometimes drawn from a theologically complementary hymn. These closing texts provide an opportunity for prayer, though the reader will recognize that such poetic prayers sometimes differ from the type of prose prayers that are more customary in devotional books.

In addition to the daily devotions, this book provides a two-week series of devotions from Palm Sunday (Sunday of the Passion) through the Second Sunday of Easter, during which the reader is encouraged to depart from the daily devotional calendar to meditate on these high holy days.

Because most of the hymns can be found in *Lutheran Service Book* (which you will find abbreviated as *LSB*), we have used that hymnal to easily reference them. A few are from other hymnals, but all showcase the rich theology and comfort of the church's song. (If using *Lutheran Service Book* with this book, note that the Small Catechism can be found in that hymnal on pages 321–30.)

May these hymn-based devotions enrich the lives of God's saints as we live out our vocations here and look to eternal life in the presence of Christ.

The authors thank our editors at Concordia Publishing House—Jamie Moldenhauer, Lisa Clark, and Peter Reske—for their guidance and expertise in the editing and production of this book. Additionally, Richard Resch gives thanks to Concordia Theological Seminary in Fort Wayne, Indiana, where he learned confessional theology and where his vocation as Seminary Kantor was to immerse himself in Lutheran music and hymnody daily. Daniel Zager recalls with deep gratitude his loving parents, who provided him an elementary school education at St. Paul's Lutheran School in Wisconsin Rapids, Wisconsin, where he sang hymns on a daily basis and memorized and recited hymns every week.

Abide in Me, and I in you. (John 15:4)

JANUARY 1

This Jesus came to end sin's war;
This Name of names for us He bore.
Rejoice! Rejoice! With thanks embrace
Another year of grace. (*LSB* 896:3)

King David sings, "O God, save me by Your name" (Psalm 54:1). Jesus' name, the name above all other names, has been *on* you, *with* you, and *in* you since the day of your Baptism. There it has been, your abundant source of life and salvation. In David's troubles, he turned to the name that saves. May we follow his lead as we start the new year. Let the name of Jesus be our first thought in the morning and last thought at night. Let that name be on our lips for all needs, great and small, as we place our trust entirely in the One who saves. And may the only name that is omnipotent bless all our days.

Also, may His precious name always be hallowed, revered, and treated appropriately among us. As God's children, we know well from the Ten Commandments and the Lord's Prayer how much He cares about our use of His name. Unfortunately, we live in a time and a culture when the name of Jesus is being seriously abused around us; may we never be part of such misuse.

Jesus! Name of wondrous love,
Name all other names above,
Unto which must ev'ry knee
Bow in deep humility. (*LSB* 900:1)

Since there is no better way to start a new year than with Jesus' name on our lips, let us sing and rejoice and, with thanks, embrace another year of grace from the source of our life and salvation. "Blessed be the name of the Lord from this time forth and forevermore! From the rising of the sun to its setting, the name of the Lord is to be praised!" (Psalm 113:2–3).

"God, Father, Son, and Spirit, hear! To all our pleas incline Your ear; upon our lives rich blessing trace in this new year of grace." Amen. (LSB *896:7*)

JANUARY 2

**Wide open stand the gates adorned with pearl,
While round God's golden throne
The choirs of saints in endless circles curl,
And joyous praise the Son!
They watch Him now descending
To visit waiting earth.
The Lord of Life unending
Brings dying hope new birth! (*LSB* 639:1)**

W*IDE OPEN STAND THE GATES ADORNED WITH PEARL" IS A ONE*-of-a-kind sermon in hymn form on the blessed Sacrament of the Altar, written by the nineteenth-century pastor Wilhelm Loehe, who is commemorated today. In this hymn-sermon, Loehe gives all the clouds, smoke, and awe-filled profundity of the angels' "Holy, holy, holy" (Isaiah 6:2–4) in a congregational hymn, teaching hungry saints what is happening here.

And what is happening? The angels who first watched God descend to a manger now watch God descend to feed His people at the Table with His very body and blood! How can the Lord God of heaven and earth be coming down, so far down, to an altar as food? Yet, dear Christian, it is true! And He is doing it for you!

We are indeed the "waiting earth." We desperately need the gift of such heavenly food to live. This Bread of Life gives new birth, blessed forgiveness, health, and peace that passes all understanding. And that peace is Jesus Christ Himself. Now present on the altar for us are both host and meal—a glorious feast that binds us in unity and joins us with all the company of heaven.

Fellow saints, nothing like this happens in the rest of our lives. This overwhelming, beyond-belief beauty happens only in His Divine Service and at His Table. In these words, Pastor Loehe paints this stunning picture for you to sing—and you are in the picture!

"*O Christ, whom now beneath a veil we see, may what we thirst for soon our portion be: to gaze on Thee unveiled and see Thy face, the vision of Thy glory, and Thy grace." Amen.* (LSB 640:5)

JANUARY 3

Break forth, O beauteous heav'nly light,
And usher in the morning.
Ye shepherds, shrink not with affright,
The day of grace is dawning.
This Child, though weak in infancy,
Our confidence and joy shall be,
The pow'r of Satan breaking,
Our peace with God now making. (*LSB* 378:1)

BE NOT AFRAID, YE SHEPHERDS! A NEW MORNING HAS BEEN ushered in, and the day of grace has dawned! God has set in motion His mighty plan to save us. More joyous news has never been heard. Fear not! What an extraordinary new day dawned on this earth at Jesus' birth. Fear not!

And that new day reveals God's grace, mercy, and love for us as nothing else could. Grace is unearned, unmerited, yet freely given, for we have a God of grace who loves to give His gifts of grace lavishly and freely. And when God took on human flesh, we received grace upon grace in the highest gift possible: the gift of His Son.

Do not be deceived by what looks like a weak baby in infancy. This baby is God! Yes, He is a newborn in a manger among the animals, but—wonder of wonders—that baby can break Satan's power and save us.

In this sublime hymn from Bach's *Christmas Oratorio*, we pray that this dearest child from heaven may come, dwell, and be cradled in our hearts.

"O dearest Child, whom I adore, whose grace surpasses measure, my Brother, whom I cherish more than earth with all its treasure: Haste from Thy manger to depart, O come and dwell within my heart; with joy will I receive Thee, a cradle there will give Thee." Amen. (LSB *378:2*)

JANUARY 4

O Jesus Christ,
Thy manger is
My paradise at which my soul reclineth.
For there, O Lord,
Doth lie the Word
Made flesh for us; herein Thy grace forth shineth. (*LSB* 372:1)

WITH JUST ONE LINE, PAUL GERHARDT OFFERS A BEAUTIFUL picture of the extremes to which our God will go for us: "O Jesus Christ, Thy manger is my paradise at which my soul reclineth." Here, the awe and wonder of Jesus' incarnation becomes intensely personal, as the writer brings a glorious objective truth to the individual Christian. Our souls are given paradise because our God chooses such poverty as He starts His plan to save us.

"The angel host can never boast" about what is happening (st. 5). They are, without a doubt, the grandest possible soundtrack for any event, but they are not the ones who receive this glorious gift. God did not descend to a manger as a baby for His angels. Rather, God came for His dear children, for you and for me. His extreme coming down brings us bliss and gladness beyond measure! Oh, how greatly He must love us!

Other stanzas in the gorgeous tapestry of Gerhardt's hymn also display the extremes of our God in His incarnation. On the one hand, the sea and wind obey Him. On the other hand, He is coming to serve sinners in the greatest possible meekness as He joins them in their weakness. Oh, how greatly He must love us!

"Thy light and grace our guilt efface, Thy heav'nly riches all our loss retrieving. Immanuel, Thy birth doth quell the pow'r of hell and Satan's bold deceiving. Thou Christian heart, whoe'er thou art, be of good cheer and let no sorrow move thee! For God's own Child, in mercy mild, joins thee to Him; how greatly God must love thee!" Amen. (LSB *372:3–4*)

JANUARY 5

Come here, my friends, lift up your eyes,
And see what in the manger lies.
Who is this child, so young and fair?
It is the Christ Child lying there.

Welcome to earth, O noble Guest,
Through whom the sinful world is blest!
You came to share my misery
That You might share Your joy with me. (*LSB* 358:7–8)

SINGING, LIKE PRAYING, WAS A PART OF MARTIN LUTHER'S EVERY day. Perhaps you have seen the lovely painting of him playing the lute, surrounded by his family. That pictured Luther on a typical day, and at Christmastide especially, singing undoubtedly filled the air in Luther's home.

"From Heaven Above to Earth I Come," Luther's best-known hymn on the incarnation, is a marvelous example of his ability to bring great theological depth to even a young child. Luther tells of the Christmas miracle in a ballad form, like a story that unfolds. Therefore, here we have the most remarkable story ever told, now in the form of a cradlesong written by Luther, the Nightingale of Wittenberg.

Jesus Christ is this cradlesong, God's new song, come to earth to share our misery and bring us true joy for all eternity. This is nothing like the old song.

At this time of the year, our joy is boundless! The blessed saints could not be more filled with wonder, awe, and gratitude for this "new song" given to their hearts and lives—Jesus Christ. Sing for joy, O earth!

"My heart for very joy must leap; my lips no more can silence keep. I, too, must sing with joyful tongue that sweetest ancient cradlesong: Glory to God in highest heav'n, who unto us His Son has giv'n! While angels sing with pious mirth a glad new year to all the earth." Amen. (LSB *358:14–15*)

JANUARY 6

O Morning Star, how fair and bright!
You shine with God's own truth and light,
Aglow with grace and mercy!
Of Jacob's race, King David's son,
Our Lord and master, You have won
Our hearts to serve You only!
Lowly, holy!
Great and glorious,
All victorious,
Rich in blessing!
Rule and might o'er all possessing! (*LSB* 395:1)

I*N THE FINAL CHAPTER OF THE BIBLE, JESUS IDENTIFIES HIMSELF* as "the descendant of David, the bright morning star" (Revelation 22:16). Today, on the feast of the Epiphany, we join with the hymn writer, Philipp Nicolai, to address our Lord with this name that He gave Himself.

This Morning Star is fully divine, holy—shining with God's own truth and light. Simultaneously, He is fully human, lowly—living the perfect life that is impossible for us as fallen creatures before taking the weight of our sin on Himself and defeating death for us. Jesus, the Morning Star, is the visible manifestation of God, having come into this world for the sole purpose of our redemption.

This Morning Star is our merciful Lord and master, the one whose grace—undeserved love—makes all the difference as we live confidently here, knowing that His sacrifice has earned us an eternal home in His own presence. It is that confidence, rooted in Christ's saving work, that enables us to serve Him only, as the hymn says.

Thus, with Nicolai, we acclaim the Morning Star—great, glorious, victorious, ruler of all, rich in blessing! He is our Savior from sin and death.

"Almighty Father, in Your Son You loved us when not yet begun was this old earth's foundation! Your Son has ransomed us in love to live in Him here and above: This is Your great salvation. Alleluia! Christ the living, to us giving life forever, keeps us Yours and fails us never!" Amen. (LSB *395:4*)

JANUARY 7

Come, heav'nly Bridegroom,
Light divine,
And deep within our
hearts now shine;
There light a flame undying!
In Your one body let us be
As living branches of a tree,
Your life our lives supplying.
Now, though daily
Earth's deep sadness
May perplex us
And distress us,
Yet with heav'nly joy You
bless us. (*LSB* 395:2)

PHILIPP NICOLAI'S HYMN CONTINUES WITH A DIFFERENT NAME of Jesus: the heavenly Bridegroom. The church, as the Bride, awaits His coming, with the expectant, fervent prayer: "Come, Lord Jesus!" (Revelation 22:20). In His deep love, Jesus acts on behalf of His Bride. In the words of the hymn writer, Jesus is the "light divine." It is Jesus, the Bridegroom, who enters our hearts to light the flame of love, something we cannot do on our own. Indeed, Jesus is the life who supplies our lives, as a tree supplies life to its living branches. He is the vine; we are the branches (John 15:5).

Jesus comes to us in particular ways, that is, through His means of grace—summarized in a poetic economy of words by the hymn writer: "Your Word and Spirit, flesh and blood" (st. 3). That is all we need! We need the Word, read and preached. We need the Holy Spirit, who has called us by the Gospel and enlightened us with His gifts, as we read in Luther's Small Catechism. We need Christ's Holy Supper to receive His flesh and blood, given for thc forgiveness of sins. By these means the Bridegroom, "our dearest treasure" (st. 3), provides heavenly food to refresh our souls and assures us of the abundant life He has planned for us. Through Him, "God's own love . . . has reached us" (st. 3). That is the heavenly joy provided to us by our Bridegroom, Jesus.

"Lord, when You look on us in love, at once there falls from God above a ray of purest pleasure. Your Word and Spirit, flesh and blood refresh our souls with heav'nly food. You are our dearest treasure! Let Your mercy warm and cheer us! O draw near us! For You teach us God's own love through You has reached us." Amen. (LSB *395:3*)

JANUARY 8

What joy to know,
when life is past,
The Lord we love is
first and last,
The end and the beginning!
He will one day, oh,
glorious grace,
Transport us to that
happy place
Beyond all tears and sinning!
Amen! Amen!
Come, Lord Jesus!
Crown of gladness!
We are yearning
For the day of Your
returning! (*LSB* 395:6)

IN THE FINAL STANZA OF THIS GREAT HYMN, PHILIPP NICOLAI GIVES us words to sing and pray of the Christian's greatest joy. We know that when life here ends, our Lord will "transport us to that happy place beyond all tears and sinning!" Can you imagine an eternity without tears, sickness, disappointments, worries, and concerns? Can you imagine a time and a place where sin and death are forever absent?

Pastor Nicolai lived during a time of plague in the late sixteenth century, at one point having to contend with 170 deaths in his town during a single week—an unimaginable challenge to any pastor in ministering to his people by applying the comfort of the Gospel. Nevertheless, he wrote, "Christ goes with us all the way—today, tomorrow, ev'ry day! His love is never ending!" (st. 5). Jesus is "the Alpha and the Omega, the first and the last, the beginning and the end" (Revelation 22:13). That constant reality, which we grasp only by faith, enables us (with Pastor Nicolai) to look with confidence to our eternal future with Christ, regardless of our circumstances here. This is our certainty, and it is all we need when confronted with the tears and sins of our lives.

Thus, we pray, "Come, Lord Jesus! . . . We are yearning for the day of Your returning!"

"O let the harps break forth in sound! Our joy be all with music crowned, our voices gladly blending! For Christ goes with us all the way—today, tomorrow, ev'ry day! His love is never ending! Sing out! Ring out! Jubilation! Exultation! Tell the story! Great is He, the King of Glory!" Amen. (LSB *395:5*)

JANUARY 9

Why lies He in such mean estate
Where ox and ass are feeding?
Good Christian, fear; for sinners here
The silent Word is pleading.
Nails, spear shall pierce Him through,
The cross be borne for me, for you;
Hail, hail the Word made flesh,
The babe, the son of Mary! (*LSB* 370:2)

For some people, Christmas songs conjure images of snowflakes and goodwill. But many Christmas hymns do not shy away from key words like *sin*, *death*, *blood*, or *cross*—because those words are critical to the biblical story of what our God did. The writers of such hymns state what happened in Bethlehem and what was at stake in this birth, vividly telling of what God did, is doing, and will do.

William Dix's "What Child Is This" is a wonderful example. "Nails, spear shall pierce Him through, the cross be borne for me, for you." It is incredible that this carol is so popular when it is so raw and accurate concerning who Jesus is and that He came to die! Dix even dares to use the term *sinners*. Many people avoid words like *sin* and *sinners*, considering such words judgmental and off-putting, particularly to those who are not believers. But the world is filled with sinners, and thanks be to God that this birth happened to save sinners—to save *us*. God acted because we needed Him to act. "Hail, hail the Word made flesh, the babe, the son of Mary!"

"Come from on high to me; I cannot rise to Thee. Cheer my wearied spirit, O pure and holy Child; through Thy grace and merit, blest Jesus, Lord most mild, draw me unto Thee! Draw me unto Thee!" Amen. (LSB *386:2*)

JANUARY 10

The only Son from heaven,
Foretold by ancient seers,
By God the Father given,
In human form appears.
No sphere His light confining,
No star so brightly shining
As He, our Morning Star. (*LSB* 402:1)

ELISABETH CRUCIGER WAS A DEAR FRIEND OF MARTIN AND KATIE Luther, and she wrote this rich text about the brightly shining Morning Star now appearing in human form. Martin Luther realized, quite early on in the Reformation, that hymns in the vernacular gave Gospel truths directly to the hearts and minds of the saints. Therefore, he encouraged his friends to write these needed hymns, and Cruciger followed his advice.

All the hymns from the earliest days of the Reformation are filled with doctrine, including this one. They clearly and powerfully articulate the Gospel and thus could not be richer. And this was so needed! *What God has done* (Gospel) was in direct contrast and opposition to the dominant presence of *what we must do* (Law) that surrounded Luther at that time. The people had to be taught the difference! In the hymns that resulted, there were no throwaway words or ideas. Too much was at stake in churchly singing to waste time on fluff.

The light of Jesus Christ shines brightly in the days of Epiphany, and the light of the Gospel shined brightly in the days of the Reformation.

"O Lord, our hearts awaken to know and love You more, in faith to stand unshaken, in spirit to adore, that we, through this world moving, each glimpse of heaven proving, may reap its fullness there. O Father, here before You with God the Holy Ghost and Jesus, we adore You, O pride of angel host: before You mortals lowly cry, 'Holy, Holy, Holy, O blessed Trinity!'" Amen. (LSB 402:3–4)

JANUARY 11

Jesus, once with sinners numbered,
Had no blemish of His own;
In the waters of the Jordan
His true worth and work were shown:
Heaven opened and the Spirit
There descended like a dove,
As the Father's voice resounded,
"Hear My Son, the One I love." (*LSB* 404:1)

W***HEN JESUS CAME TO JOHN THE BAPTIST TO BE BAPTIZED IN*** the Jordan River, John understandably believed that the roles should be reversed: that he, a sinful man, should be baptized by Jesus, the sinless one. But Jesus said, "Let it be so now, for thus it is fitting for us to fulfill all righteousness" (Matthew 3:15). In that act, Jesus willingly numbered Himself with sinners, as prophesied in Isaiah 53:6.

Here in His Baptism, Jesus stood for the first time in the place of sinners: assuming our guilt, covering our sins, and providing us with His perfect righteousness. He would stand in our place again as He was mocked, scourged, and crucified—the sinless one sacrificed for the sinful ones.

In Jesus' Baptism, "the heavens were opened" (Matthew 3:16), and Holy Baptism does the same for us. Baptism "works forgiveness of sins, rescues from death and the devil, and gives eternal salvation to all who believe" (Small Catechism, Baptism, Second Part). The blessings of Baptism are boundless!

When Jesus came up out of the Jordan, an amazing confluence took place: The Holy Spirit rested on Jesus, and God the Father spoke. The entire Trinity was revealed at one time and in one place, marking this extraordinary moment when Jesus first stood in our place to open heaven for us!

"Jesus, once with sinners numbered, full obedience was Your path; You, by death, have consecrated water in this saving bath: dying to the sin of Adam, rising to a life of grace; we are counted with the righteous, over us the cross You trace." Amen. (LSB 404:4)

JANUARY 12

O Savior of our fallen race,
O Brightness of the Father's face,
O Son who shared the Father's might
Before the world knew day or night,
Alleluia!

O Jesus, very Light of Light,
Our constant star in sin's deep night:
Now hear the prayers Your people pray
Throughout the world this holy day.
Alleluia! (*LSB* 403:1–2)

THIS HYMN, ORIGINATING IN THE MEDIEVAL CHURCH, NAMES JESUS in various ways. In addition to being the Savior and the Son of the Father, He is the "Brightness of the Father's face" and the "Light of Light." The hymn writer draws on the magnificent opening verses of John's Gospel, where Jesus is clearly identified as being one with the Father named as "the true light, which gives light to everyone" (1:9).

This divine identity of Jesus—true God before creation—is essential to our redemption. Our fallen race could be redeemed only by the Son of God acting on our behalf. Yet equally important is that He "put our human vesture on and came to us as Mary's son," true man (st. 3).

As true God, Jesus lived the sinless life that God had intended for His creatures, willingly serving as our substitute and taking on Himself the sins of every human. As true man, He suffered the weight and pain of that sin, and He experienced something else that will never be true for us: being utterly abandoned by God the Father. Thanks be to God, Jesus' cry of abandonment—"My God, My God, why have You forsaken Me?" (Matthew 27:46)—will never be ours. Jesus came from His Father's throne to wash our guilt away, to redeem and reclaim us, to be our Savior.

"For from the Father's throne You came, His banished children to reclaim; and earth and sea and sky revere the love of Him who sent You here. O Christ, Redeemer virgin-born, let songs of praise Your name adorn, whom with the Father we adore and Holy Spirit evermore." Amen. (LSB *403:5, 7*)

JANUARY 13

And oh, what miracle divine,
When water reddened into wine!
He spoke the word, and forth it flowed
In streams that nature ne'er bestowed.

For this Thy glad epiphany
All glory, Jesus, be to Thee,
Whom with the Father we adore,
And Holy Spirit evermore. (*LSB* 399:4–5)

THE MIRACLES HAVE STARTED TO FLOW FROM THIS KING, WHOSE light has begun to shine as it awakens a darkened earth. Water to wine is impressive but perhaps not breathtaking, like feeding the five thousand and raising Lazarus from the dead—but miracles are miracles! Every one of them, from Jesus, reveals more about "God in man made manifest" (*LSB* 394), and they are all dazzling to behold.

From the Gospel account of the wedding at Cana, we learn from Mary what we are to do with our problems, concerns, and crises: "Do whatever He tells you" (John 2:5). Rather than hold on to our problems or crises, we give them to Jesus and then follow His will. We might even expect a miracle.

The days of miracles are not over. Jesus Christ is performing them constantly in His kingdom for His children. Knowing that He can *do* anything, we should pray and *ask Him* for anything. And if it is His will, He will make it happen in ways that might dazzle us.

He does this in the Divine Service by turning wine into life-giving blood at His Table. We receive one of the greatest miracles of all every time we come to the communion rail. "For this Thy glad epiphany all glory, Jesus, be to Thee"!

"Manifest at Jordan's stream, Prophet, Priest, and King supreme; and at Cana wedding guest in Thy Godhead manifest; manifest in pow'r divine, changing water into wine; anthems be to Thee addressed, God in man made manifest." Amen. (LSB *394:2*)

JANUARY 14

The world's remotest races,
Upon whose weary faces
The sun looks from the sky,
Shall run with zeal untiring,
With joy Your light desiring
That breaks upon them from on high.

Lift up your eyes in wonder—
See, nations gather yonder
From sin to be set free.
The world has heard Your story;
Her sons come to Your glory;
Her daughters haste Your light to see. (*LSB* 396:3–4)

THE MORNING STAR HAS COME DOWN INTO THIS WORLD TO SHINE His light on the *whole* world, sitting in darkness. *No one* is excluded from His bright and glorious saving light that desires to break "upon them from on high."

While the subject of missions is certainly not confined to one Church Year season, our Lord's Great Commission to His Bride to reach the lost with the Gospel naturally fits the themes of the Epiphany season. When the world hears Christ's story, "her sons come to Your glory; her daughters haste Your light to see." The Gospel message shines on weary faces longing to be free from sin, death, darkness, and all that is evil.

Nothing will be the same now that Morning Star has come, and the season of Epiphany unveils little by little what that means for each of us as members of the church, Christ's Bride. "Lift up your eyes in wonder—see, nations gather yonder." Yes, the Bride will, on that Last Day, witness a wonder—*all* people coming together because the Morning Star came not only for each of us but for *all.*

"Your heart will leap for gladness when from the realms of sadness they come from near and far. Your eyes will wake from slumber as people without number rejoice to see the Morning Star." Amen. (LSB *396:5*)

JANUARY 15

Abide with us, O Lord, we pray;
The gloom of darkness chase away;
Your work of healing, Lord, begin,
And take away the stain of sin.

Lord, once You came to earth's domain
And, we believe, shall come again;
Be with us on the battlefield,
From ev'ry harm Your people shield. (*LSB* 401:4–5)

ABIDE WITH US, O LORD, WE PRAY. . . . BE WITH US ON THE battlefield." These prayers reflect our need for our Lord's constant presence every passing hour—for we cannot journey alone. And our Lord Jesus Christ does not want us to be on this world's treacherous battlefield alone, so He bids us repeatedly, "Abide in Me, and I in you" (John 15:4).

We abide in Him when we allow His will to fill our lives, when we follow that will. How do we learn His will for us? We cannot begin to know any of it on our own, for God tells us, "My thoughts are not your thoughts, neither are your ways My ways" (Isaiah 55:8). But our gracious God has meticulously left His thoughts and ways for us in His Holy Word. As we read His Word, mark it, learn it, inwardly digest it, and pray that His will be done, He gives His will to us and then abides *in* us and *with* us.

Jesus Christ, our bright Morning Star, came to this earth's domain to "take away the stain of sin," chase away the darkness, heal us, shield us, and abide with us with His presence—especially in His Supper. There, we wondrously abide in Him.

Lord, "be with us on the battlefield, from ev'ry harm Your people shield. To You, O Lord, all glory be for this Your blest epiphany; to God, whom all His hosts adore, and Holy Spirit evermore." Amen. (LSB 401:5–6)

JANUARY 16

The people that in darkness sat
A glorious light have seen;
The light has shined on them who long
In shades of death have been,
In shades of death have been.

Lord Jesus, reign in us, we pray,
And make us Thine alone,
Who with the Father ever art
And Holy Spirit, one,
And Holy Spirit, one. (*LSB* 412:1, 6)

TODAY'S HYMN IS STRAIGHT FROM THE PROPHET ISAIAH: "THE people who walked in darkness have seen a great light; those who dwelt in a land of deep darkness, on them has light shone" (9:2). This is like many Epiphany hymns that begin in the deep darkness, gloom, and shades of death but very quickly move to the stunning, glorious light of our bright and shining Morning Star. Isaiah, too, hints that this darkness is temporary and will be resolved: "But there will be no gloom for her who was in anguish" (9:1). And as the hymn continues, we see how the gloom and anguish dissipate and have indeed been wonderfully replaced by resplendent joy!

Stanza 6 is a simple yet beautiful prayer appropriate for any day in the Church Year, for what it asks is always good, right, and beneficial. When we pray that Jesus Christ, our bright Morning Star, would reign in us—that He be first and foremost in our lives, be Himself the one thing needful in our lives—it is precisely what we all need to ask of our Morning Star. If the light of His Word and Sacraments is free to reign in us, then His will can reign in us, and this will be a good new year.

"O Father, here before You with God the Holy Ghost and Jesus, we adore You, O pride of angel host: Before You mortals lowly cry, 'Holy, holy, holy, O blessed Trinity!'" Amen. (LSB 402:4)

JANUARY 17

To Jordan came the Christ, our Lord,
To do His Father's pleasure;
Baptized by John, the Father's Word
Was given us to treasure.
This heav'nly washing now shall be
A cleansing from transgression
And by His blood and agony
Release from death's oppression.
A new life now awaits us. (*LSB* 406:1)

Jesus' Baptism is a pivotal moment, one worth examining in detail. When Jesus came to John to be baptized, John immediately perceived a profound disconnect and tried to prevent Jesus' request, saying, "I need to be baptized by You" (Matthew 3:14). John the Baptist knew that he was sinful, and that Jesus was the sinless one. Thus, John's logic understandably called for precisely the opposite of what Jesus asked of him.

Jesus' response to John frames this perceived disconnect not in human terms but in the divine plan of salvation. His words encapsulate all that He came to do: "Let it be so now, for thus it is fitting for us to fulfill all righteousness" (Matthew 3:15). There it is in a nutshell—Jesus came "to fulfill all righteousness." John the Baptist could not do so, and we cannot do so. God had to do it for us in the person and work of His Son, Jesus.

Jesus was baptized not because He was sinful but because He identified with sinners and came into this world for one purpose only—to save sinners. Jesus was baptized to show us in no uncertain terms that "Baptism now saves you" (1 Peter 3:21). As Luther wrote in this, his great Baptism hymn, "this heav'nly washing now shall be a cleansing from transgression." Indeed, in Baptism, "a new life now awaits us." This new life unites us with Christ and makes us participants in His resurrection. Thanks be to God—we *are* baptized!

"Within the Jordan's sacred flood the heav'nly Lamb in meekness stood that He, of whom no sin was known, might cleanse His people from their own." Amen. (LSB *399:3*)

JANUARY 18

These truths on Jordan's banks were shown
By mighty word and wonder.
The Father's voice from heav'n came down,
Which we do well to ponder:
"This man is My beloved Son,
In whom My heart has pleasure.
Him you must hear, and Him alone,
And trust in fullest measure
The word that He has spoken." (*LSB* 406:3)

WHAT HAPPENED IMMEDIATELY AFTER JESUS WAS BAPTIZED by John is stunning. God the Father spoke from heaven, declaring, "This is My beloved Son, with whom I am well pleased" (Matthew 3:17). The Holy Spirit also descended on Jesus in the form of a dove. These tangible revelations of the triune God are as significant for us today as they were for those who witnessed Jesus' Baptism.

In his Baptism hymn, Luther reminds us that Jesus—here declared and validated by God the Father as His very own beloved Son—is the one whom we must listen to and trust. Jesus' words give us life here on our earthly pilgrimage and there in an eternity of great joy shared with this Lamb of God baptized for us.

No voice of God the Father audibly speaks from heaven in our Baptism. Nevertheless, we are certain that, in Baptism, God acts to save us and makes us His beloved sons and daughters: "He saved us, not because of works done by us in righteousness, but according to His own mercy, by the washing of regeneration and renewal of the Holy Spirit, whom He poured out on us richly through Jesus Christ our Savior" (Titus 3:5–6).

This washing and renewal of the Holy Spirit, first revealed in Jesus' Baptism, is the saving action of our triune God for us "to comfort and sustain us" (st. 4).

"There stood the Son of God in love, His grace to us extending; the Holy Spirit like a dove upon the scene descending; the triune God assuring us, with promises compelling, that in our Baptism He will thus among us find a dwelling to comfort and sustain us." Amen. (LSB *406:4*)

JANUARY 19

Be still, my soul; your God will undertake
To guide the future as He has the past.
Your hope, your confidence let nothing shake;
All now mysterious shall be bright at last.
Be still, my soul; the waves and winds still know
His voice who ruled them while He dwelt below. (*LSB* 752:2)

W*HEN THE SEA WAS RAGING, JESUS' VOICE BROUGHT CALM TO* the wind and the waves. When Peter was sinking, the hand of Jesus reached out to save him. When the disciples were terrified, Jesus said to them, "Take heart; it is I. Do not be afraid" (Matthew 14:27). And so, "be still, my soul"—Jesus is in control!

"Be still, and know that I am God" (Psalm 46:10) is all the believer, the faithful saint, needs to know and cling to during the storms of life. Not only is God in control, but He also can and will bring good fruit out of the troubles and sufferings of His dear children. This is because such suffering is not happening outside of His loving, caring plan for us. In His compassionate love, He knows exactly what we need to make us totally dependent on Him. In His wisdom, He wants us to surrender our self-sufficient independence and instead cling to Him. Trust Him alone!

Then our soul, the heart of our faith, will be still and calm. It can rest and be filled with trusting peace as it believes Jesus when He says, "Take heart; it is I. Do not be afraid."

"Be still, my soul; the hour is hast'ning on when we shall be forever with the Lord, when disappointment, grief, and fear are gone, sorrow forgot, love's purest joys restored. Be still, my soul; when change and tears are past, all safe and blessed we shall meet at last." Amen. (LSB 752:4)

JANUARY 20

I know my faith is founded
On Jesus Christ, my God and Lord;
And this my faith confessing,
Unmoved I stand on His sure Word.
Our reason cannot fathom
The truth of God profound;
Who trusts in human wisdom
Relies on shifting ground.
God's Word is all-sufficient,
It makes divinely sure;
And trusting in its wisdom,
My faith shall rest secure. (*LSB* 587:1)

THE WRITER OF THE LETTER TO THE HEBREWS TELLS US THAT "the word of God is living and active" (4:12). Through the prophet Isaiah, God declares, "My word . . . shall not return to Me empty, but it shall accomplish that which I purpose" (55:11). God's Word is powerful and "all-sufficient," creating saving faith in Jesus Christ.

"Our reason cannot fathom the truth of God profound." Human reason cannot explain how water and the Word combine in Holy Baptism so that "Baptism . . . now saves you" (1 Peter 3:21). Human reason cannot explain how Jesus continues to feed us with His true body and blood in His Holy Supper for the forgiveness of sins. Indeed, human reason cannot explain the sheer power of God's Word, as the Holy Spirit works faith in our hearts. But faith is "the conviction of things not seen" (Hebrews 11:1).

The end of faith is eternal life in Christ, so we pray that He would increase our faith and keep us always in that saving faith. "In life and death, Lord, keep me until Your heav'n I gain, where I by Your great mercy the end of faith attain" (st. 3).

"Increase my faith, dear Savior, for Satan seeks by night and day to rob me of this treasure and take my hope of bliss away. But, Lord, with You beside me, I shall be undismayed; and led by Your good Spirit, I shall be unafraid. Abide with me, O Savior, a firmer faith bestow; then I shall bid defiance to ev'ry evil foe." Amen. (LSB 587:2)

JANUARY 21

Holy Spirit, ever dwelling
In the holiest realms of light;
Holy Spirit, ever brooding
O'er a world of gloom
and night;
Holy Spirit, ever raising
Those of earth to
thrones on high;
Living, life-imparting Spirit,
You we praise and magnify.

Holy Spirit, ever living
As the Church's very life;
Holy Spirit, ever striving
Through us in a ceaseless strife;
Holy Spirit, ever forming
In the Church the
mind of Christ:
You we praise with
endless worship
For Your gifts and fruits
unpriced. (*LSB* 650:1–2)

IN *HIS GREAT LOVE FOR HIS PEOPLE OF ALL TIMES AND ALL PLACES,* Jesus promised us the Holy Spirit: "But the Helper, the Holy Spirit, whom the Father will send in My name, He will teach you all things and bring to your remembrance all that I have said to you" (John 14:26). This Helper does for us what we could never do on our own: believe the Gospel. God the Holy Spirit works through the Word to teach and enlighten us. When we read the Word and hear it preached, the Holy Spirit works faith in our hearts to believe the good news of sins forgiven and eternal life won for us—"setting captive sinners free" (st. 3) and "raising those of earth to thrones on high."

The hymn writer also points us to the Holy Spirit as the one "ever forming in the Church the mind of Christ," echoing Paul in 1 Corinthians 2:16. Of course, that is true only because God the Holy Spirit has enlightened us with His "gifts and fruits unpriced."

The Holy Spirit is indeed "the Church's very life." Thus, we sing, "Living, life-imparting Spirit, You we praise and magnify."

"Holy Spirit, ever working through the Church's ministry; quick'ning, strength'ning, and absolving, setting captive sinners free; Holy Spirit, ever binding age to age and soul to soul in communion never ending, You we worship and extol." Amen. (LSB *650:3*)

JANUARY 22

He so cared for and esteemed me
That the Son He loved so well
He has given to redeem me
From the quenchless flames of hell.
O my Lord, the Spring of blessing,
Could somehow my finite mind
Of Your love the limit find
Though my efforts were unceasing?
All things else have but their day;
God's great love abides for aye. (*LSB* 977:2)

OUR FINITE MINDS CANNOT TAKE IN THE IMMENSITY OF GOD'S love. We cannot understand, measure, or adequately speak of it. However, our "finite" minds know this—His love is boundless, and "God's great love abides for aye." All things have their day and fade away, but not God's love. "His steadfast love endures forever!" (Psalm 118:1).

It is the Holy Spirit who enlightens our minds enough that we begin to understand what we learn and confess from the Small Catechism: "I believe that I cannot by my own reason or strength believe in Jesus Christ, my Lord, or come to Him; but the Holy Spirit has called me by the Gospel, enlightened me with His gifts, sanctified and kept me in the true faith" (Creed, Third Article).

This profound love was bestowed on us, God's children, at a tremendous cost. His only Son, whom He loved deeply, was given to redeem us. Such knowledge, wisdom, and insight are not within our grasp, but they begin to unfold on the day of our Baptism, even before many of us can speak, as the Holy Spirit starts to show us this love of the Father and the Son. He is our Helper. Thanks be to God!

"Jesus, Thy boundless love to me no thought can reach, no tongue declare; unite my thankful heart to Thee, and reign without a rival there! Thine wholly, Thine alone I am; be Thou alone my constant flame." Amen. (LSB *683:1*)

JANUARY 23

Let me be Thine forever,
My faithful God and Lord;
Let me forsake Thee never
Nor wander from Thy Word.
Lord, do not let me waver,
But give me steadfastness,
And for such grace forever
Thy holy name I'll bless.

Lord Jesus, my salvation,
My light, my life divine,
My only consolation,
O make me wholly Thine!
For Thou hast dearly bought me
With blood and bitter pain.
Let me, since Thou
hast sought me,
Eternal life obtain.
(*LSB* 689:1–2)

A*DDRESSING EACH PERSON OF THE* HOLY TRINITY, *TODAY'S HYMN*-prayer provides petitions for us to pray every day of our lives. "Let me be Thine forever." We pray that, as we walk through this life, we may never be separated from our "faithful God and Lord." Rather, may we be rooted continually in His Word, steadfastly believing that we belong to God by grace alone and that His grace is always sufficient for us (2 Corinthians 12:9).

Grounded in the Word by the power of the Holy Spirit, we know that Jesus is our light on life's path and our salvation. He won eternal life for us, but it cost Him everything. Through His bitter pain and death, His blood shed for us, and His glorious Easter resurrection, Jesus redeemed us from sin and death and made us His own, that we might "live under Him in His kingdom and serve Him in everlasting righteousness, innocence, and blessedness" (Small Catechism, Creed, Second Article).

The Holy Spirit guides us into believing the all-sufficient merit of Jesus' redeeming love for us. We pray that the Holy Spirit will keep us faithful to the end, confessing Jesus. May we be His forever!

"And Thou, O Holy Spirit, my comforter and guide, grant that in Jesus' merit I always may confide, Him to the end confessing whom I have known by faith. Give me Thy constant blessing and grant a Christian death." Amen. (LSB *689:3*)

JANUARY 24

**O God of mercy, God of might,
In love and pity infinite,
Teach us, as ever in Thy sight,
To live our lives in Thee.**

**Teach us the lesson Thou hast taught:
To feel for those Thy blood hath bought,
That ev'ry word and deed and thought
May work a work for Thee.**

**All are redeemed, both far and wide,
Since Thou, O Lord, for all hast died.
Grant us the will and grace provide
To love them all in Thee! (*LSB* 852:1, 3–4)**

T*EACH US, O LORD—WE HAVE SO MUCH TO LEARN. SHOW US YOUR* ways and lead us on Your paths by Your Word and Spirit, for we cannot begin to know Your thoughts and Your ways on our own (Isaiah 55:8). O Lord, we need Your wisdom to shape and govern our lives, and You have taught us that Jesus is wisdom. Therefore, fill us with Jesus and His love through Your Holy Word and Sacraments. Then may that Love shape our thoughts, words, and deeds as we serve Him and reach out to our neighbor in His kingdom.

This is the heart of today's hymn—a prayer for the grace to be there for our neighbor in need. It is a prayer that we might so live in Jesus that we live to shower His love on our neighbor. And so we pray, "Grant us the will and grace provide to love them all in Thee," so that wherever help is needed, we can there give help as unto our Lord (Matthew 25:40).

"In sickness, sorrow, want, or care, may we each other's burdens share; may we, where help is needed, there give help as unto Thee! And may Thy Holy Spirit move all those who live to live in love till Thou shalt greet in heav'n above all those who live in Thee." Amen. (LSB 852:5–6)

JANUARY 25

My sin and guilt are plaguing me;
O grant me true contrition
And by Your death upon the tree
Your pardon and remission.
Before the Father's throne above
Recall Your matchless deed of love
That He may lift my dreadful load,
O Son of God!
I plead the grace Your death bestowed. (*LSB* 972:2)

THE HYMN WRITER STATES IT BLUNTLY, WITH NO EXCUSES OR rationalizations: "My sin and guilt are plaguing me." When we feel that weight of sin, we confess our sins, believing that "a broken and contrite heart, O God, You will not despise" (Psalm 51:17). Christ's death on the cross was for one purpose only—the "pardon and remission" of our sins. We pray that Jesus would plead for us before God the Father, Christ's death being the only way to lift our "dreadful load" of sin. Scripture comforts us with that picture of Jesus pleading on our behalf: "But if anyone does sin, we have an advocate with the Father, Jesus Christ the righteous" (1 John 2:1).

As our prayer continues, the hymn writer provides petitions appropriate to our status as *forgiven* sinners. "Confirm in us Your Gospel, Lord, Your promise of salvation. And make us long to hear Your Word" (st. 3). Hearing God's Word—the Gospel of forgiveness and salvation unto eternal life—frees us from the worry and complete impossibility of addressing the "dreadful load" of sin on our own. Instead, we are freed to "follow our vocation" (st. 3), here succinctly and beautifully defined as spending "our lives in love for You and show[ing] Your love in all we do" (st. 3). Finally, we pray that, as the time of our death approaches, our Savior will bring us safely home to live forever in His presence.

"Confirm in us Your Gospel, Lord, Your promise of salvation. And make us long to hear Your Word and follow our vocation: to spend our lives in love for You and show Your love in all we do. And then, at last, when death shall loom, O Savior, come and bear Your loved ones safely home." Amen. (LSB 972:3)

JANUARY 26

"Come, follow Me," the Savior spake,
"All in My way abiding;
Deny yourselves, the world forsake,
Obey My call and guiding.
O bear the cross, whate'er betide,
Take My example for your guide.

"I am the light, I light the way,
A godly life displaying;
I bid you walk as in the day;
I keep your feet from straying.
I am the way, and well I show
How you must sojourn here below." (*LSB* 688:1–2)

JESUS WAS ABOUT TO SUFFER AND DIE FOR US. YET FIRST, HE TELLS His disciples, "If anyone would come after Me, let him deny himself and take up his cross and follow Me" (Matthew 16:24). The disciples learn the difficult lesson that they, too, will suffer as they follow this Messiah. This is also a lesson for us—there is a cost to follow Him.

Many hymns sing of that cost, but today's hymn perhaps does it best as it allows us to consider the path of following Him. He says, "Follow Me and abide in My ways." And we abide in His ways by hearing His voice, obeying His call, and letting His example be our guide.

That means Jesus comes first in all things—which is not easy, for we are used to putting ourselves first, thinking about ourselves first, and taking care of ourselves first. Our sinful nature, that old Adam, rebels against a directive to deny ourselves. Therefore, the biggest obstacle to being faithful disciples resides within. Nevertheless, the light who lights the way and who is Himself the way is with us every step of the way. "I show how you must sojourn here below," He promises. He leads, and we follow.

"Then let us follow Christ, our Lord, and take the cross appointed and, firmly clinging to His Word, in suff'ring be undaunted. For those who bear the battle's strain the crown of heav'nly life obtain." Amen. (LSB 688:5)

JANUARY 27

"My heart abounds in lowliness,
My soul with love is glowing;
And gracious words My lips express,
With meekness overflowing.
My heart, My mind, My strength, My all,
To God I yield, on Him I call.

"I teach you how to shun and flee
What harms your soul's salvation,
Your heart from ev'ry guile to free,
From sin and its temptation.
I am the refuge of the soul
And lead you to your heav'nly goal." (*LSB* 688:3–4)

TODAY WE CONSIDER MORE OF JESUS' INSTRUCTIONS TO HIS disciples. When Jesus comes first in the lives of His disciples, it looks like this: They yield to God their heart, mind, strength, and all, and on Him they call. Such a faithful path will undoubtedly be fraught with suffering, harm, and danger, for Satan hates that you are on this path of discipleship.

But despite Satan's fury, Jesus' disciples have all they need in their Lord's promises of protection, refuge, and safety every step of the way to their heavenly goal. Christ leads them, and they follow Him in God's plan for His children. They go forth clinging to His Word and Sacraments for the journey.

Such discipleship will be challenged, especially in our time of religious pluralism. For when we say there is only one way to the Father and only one way to salvation, we will likely be deemed intolerant for our exclusivity. Then we will taste what it was like for Jesus' first disciples and the early church to be rejected and hated for confessing that Jesus Christ *alone* is "the way, and the truth, and the life" (John 14:6). Such proclamation has always meant crosses—that is a part of being a disciple in Christ's kingdom.

"Then let us follow Christ, our Lord, and take the cross appointed and, firmly clinging to His Word, in suff'ring be undaunted. For those who bear the battle's strain the crown of heav'nly life obtain." Amen. (LSB 688:5)

JANUARY 28

All that for my soul is needful
He with loving care provides,
Nor of that is He unheedful
Which my body needs besides.
When my strength cannot avail me,
When my pow'rs can do no more,
Then will God His strength outpour;
In my need He will not fail me.
All things else have but their day;
God's great love abides for aye. **(*LSB* 977:3)**

MAY OUR PRAYERS ALWAYS ECHO WHAT PASTOR PAUL GERHARDT wrote at the beginning of this hymn: "For in all things I see traces of His tender love for me" (st. 1). But there may be times when we ask, "In *all* things? Really? Even in the face of death, sickness, loss of a job, or economic hardship?" Pastor Gerhardt experienced each of those circumstances in his lifetime and still concluded, "I will sing my Maker's praises and in Him most joyful be" (st. 1). In this beautiful hymn of faith and trust, he tells us more of seeing God's tender love during both joyous and challenging times.

God provides "all that for my soul is needful"—forgiveness of sins through Christ's atoning sacrifice and the promise of eternal life with Him. That blessing is the one thing "needful" amid life's greatest challenges. As God's baptized children, we know that in death our souls will rest in God's tender care. Moreover, God does not overlook our bodily needs in this life—daily, generously providing food, clothing, and home.

When our strength and power are seemingly stretched to the breaking point, God pours out His strength and love, renewing us in this life and filling us with the sure and certain hope of the life to come. His tender love surrounds us in all circumstances!

"I will sing my Maker's praises and in Him most joyful be, for in all things I see traces of His tender love for me. Nothing else than love could move Him with such deep and tender care evermore to raise and bear all who try to love and serve Him. All things else have but their day; God's great love abides for aye." Amen. (LSB 977:1)

JANUARY 29

As a father, ever yearning,
Longing to be reconciled,
Seeks the prodigal's returning,
Loving still the wayward child,
So my many sins and errors
Find a tender, pard'ning God,
Chast'ning frailty with His rod,
Not in vengeance with His terrors.
All things else have but their day;
God's great love abides for aye. (*LSB* 977:4)

OF ALL THE PARABLES JESUS TAUGHT DURING HIS EARTHLY ministry, few are more beautiful than that of the prodigal son. While the parable does tell the story of a son spending his inheritance in a prodigal, or recklessly extravagant, way, the true focus is on the loving father. The loving father grants the inheritance to his son even though the father is still alive, with the son showing a complete disdain for his father, desiring only his share of the father's wealth. But the father never stops loving his son, constantly yearning for his return to the family. Even while the son "was still a long way off, his father saw him and felt compassion, and ran and embraced him and kissed him" (Luke 15:20). The father goes to the wayward child, offering forgiveness and love even before they are sought. That is the truest picture of our heavenly Father's great love for us!

This hymn by Gerhardt is all about God's "tender love for me" (st. 1). Thus, it is no surprise that he devotes one stanza to this parable of the loving father. We are like the prodigal son, and our "many sins and errors find a tender, pard'ning God." Our heavenly Father may chasten us (Proverbs 3:11–12), but He does so always in His great love for His dear children.

"Since there's neither change nor coldness in God's love that on me smiled, I now lift my hands in boldness, coming to You as Your child. Grant me grace, O God, I pray You, that I may with all my might, all my lifetime, day and night, love and trust You and obey You and, when this brief life is o'er, praise and love You evermore." Amen. (LSB 977:5)

JANUARY 30

"Come unto Me, ye weary,
And I will give you rest."
O blessed voice of Jesus,
Which comes to
hearts oppressed!
It tells of benediction,
Of pardon, grace, and peace,
Of joy that hath no ending,
Of love that cannot cease.

"And whosoever cometh,
I will not cast him out."
O patient love of Jesus,
Which drives away our doubt,
Which, though we be unworthy
Of love so great and free,
Invites us very sinners
To come, dear Lord, to
Thee! (*LSB* 684:1, 4)

***O**NE OF MY SEMINARY PROFESSORS ADVISED HIS CLASSES THE* following: "When you wake up each morning, all your thoughts and concerns for the new day will try to rush at you like wild animals. Shove them all back! Listen instead to that other stronger, quieter voice, the voice of your Savior calling to you, 'Come unto Me, ye weary, and I will give you rest.' Listen to that voice and let that voice set the course for your day."

It may sound strange to talk about needing rest first thing in the morning, but waking up tired and troubled after a restless night filled with fretting over yesterday's problems happens all the time. If you tried to carry your troubles alone on your shoulders and failed yesterday, Jesus wants you to know that He is standing, ready to take them for you and carry them with you. "Come unto Me, ye weary, and I will give you rest."

"And whosoever cometh, I will not cast him out." The fact that the One now carrying your weaknesses, troubles, infirmities, and burdens can do anything and loves you means that you will receive His benediction of pardon, grace, and peace. He will give you rest.

"Let me be Thine forever, my faithful God and Lord; let me forsake Thee never nor wander from Thy Word. Lord, do not let me waver, but give me steadfastness, and for such grace forever Thy holy name I'll bless." Amen. (LSB *689:1*)

JANUARY 31

Evening and morning,
Sunset and dawning,
Wealth, peace, and gladness,
Comfort in sadness:
These are Thy works; all the glory be Thine!
Times without number,
Awake or in slumber,
Thine eye observes us,
From danger preserves us,
Causing Thy mercy upon us to shine. (*LSB* 726:1)

G*OD'S OMNISCIENT AND OMNIPRESENT EYE OBSERVES US AND* preserves us from danger. Fellow saints, this is enormous! God's eye is seeing everything and knowing everything—and all for our good! That kind of protection is hard to fathom. Furthermore, protection is but one aspect of God's wondrous plan of divine care and keeping for His dear children. This hymn by Paul Gerhardt helps us see these rich gifts of mercy shining on us.

Gerhardt often sounds like King David. Both writers excel in hymns that overflow with a rock-solid trust in the God of heaven and earth. And they both have saints singing hymns with confidence, hope, and trust that their God is there for them in all times and circumstances. "Trust in Him at all times, O people," David writes (Psalm 62:8). "Order my goings, direct all my doings," Gerhardt prays in his hymn (st. 2).

And this is our daily prayer as children in the kingdom to our gracious heavenly Father as we go forth. That Father-child relationship, established already in the "Our Father" of the Lord's Prayer, is a priceless treasure for us! We turn to that treasure day and night—"all I commit to Thy fatherly hand" (st. 2).

"Father, O hear me, pardon and spare me; calm all my terrors, blot out my errors that by Thine eyes they may no more be scanned. Order my goings, direct all my doings; as it may please Thee, retain or release me; all I commit to Thy fatherly hand." Amen. (LSB *726:2*)

FEBRUARY 1

Ills that still grieve me
Soon are to leave me;
Though billows tower,
And winds gain power,
After the storm the fair sun shows its face.
Joys e'er increasing
And peace never ceasing:
These shall I treasure
And share in full measure
When in His mansions God grants me a place. (*LSB* 726:3)

G*OD'S CHILDREN ARE NOT SPARED LIFE'S SADNESS, ILLS, AND* trials. Yet, when hard times happen, we know that what befalls us is never in the hands of fate. It would be terrifying to think that our hardships are left to chance and bad luck. Unfortunately, that is precisely how most people interpret challenging times.

But we, who love the Lord God of heaven and earth with all our heart, soul, and mind, know with absolute certainty that He controls everything in our lives. Our loving God has repeatedly told us, "My grace is sufficient for you, for My power is made perfect in weakness" (2 Corinthians 12:9). Here, He comforts us by saying, "When you are at your weakest, know that I am here for you with sufficient grace and power to bring you through anything." And by His grace, we know it, and we trust it!

We know God will work all things for our good—for we love Him and trust that He loves us with His promised boundless love. So even when ills still grieve, "billows tower, and winds gain power, after the storm the fair sun shows its face." Yes, God's love shows its face to the one who was hurting.

"To God in heaven all praise be given! Come, let us offer and gladly proffer to the Creator the gifts He doth prize. He well receiveth a heart that believeth; hymns that adore Him are precious before Him and to His throne like sweet incense arise." Amen. (LSB 726:4)

FEBRUARY 2

In peace and joy I now depart
Since God so wills it.
Serene and confident my heart;
Stillness fills it.
For the Lord has promised me
That death is but a slumber. (*LSB* 938:1)

TODAY WE REMEMBER THE PRESENTATION OF JESUS IN THE temple, when Simeon recognized Him as the Christ. Simeon responded with what we call the Nunc Dimittis, a joyful song in praise to God. This hymn by Martin Luther is a superb paraphrase of that song and a little sermon on what Jesus' presentation means.

Luther reveals the theological depth of Simeon's response to what God is doing in sending His Son. The Holy Spirit led the righteous and devout Simeon into the temple, and he saw what he had long been waiting for—the Messiah! Simeon then held God in his arms and said the inspired words of the Nunc Dimittis. Here Simeon confesses that his heart is serene, confident, and still. Now he can depart in peace and joy.

We can understand what Simeon was expressing. After our Lord has fed us with His own body and blood in His Supper, we, too, are confident and still and ready to depart in His peace for the week ahead, filled with His health and life for our days.

Luther ends this first stanza with our Lord's glorious promise: "Death is but a slumber." That is like no other promise ever heard on earth!

"Jesus, by Your presentation, when they blessed You, weak and poor, make us see Your great salvation, seal us with Your promise sure; and present us in Your glory to Your Father, cleansed and pure." Amen. (LSB *519:3*)

FEBRUARY 3

Christ Jesus brought this gift to me,
My faithful Savior,
Whom You have made my eyes to see
By Your favor.
Now I know He is my life,
My friend when I am dying. (*LSB* 938:2)

L*UTHER'S NUNC DIMITTIS* PARAPHRASE CONTINUES AND SINGS OF God bringing gifts to us in His Son. That's the Gospel—when God is doing it all, pure gift. Without His gifts, we are blind to who He is and what He wants us to have: His favor. But "Christ Jesus brought this gift to me, my faithful Savior."

A striking similarity between us and Simeon is our eyes of faith, beautiful eyes that see things nobody else can see. Simeon's canticle sings of this seeing: "My eyes have seen Your salvation" (Luke 2:30). Likewise, Luther's canticle sings, "You have made my eyes to see by Your favor."

In His Word, God Himself teaches us what these eyes of faith are: Abram "believed the Lord, and He counted it to him as righteousness" (Genesis 15:6). Simeon was righteous, and we are righteous because we believe as Abram believed. All this is because of the miraculous gift of Baptism. Through Baptism, we can sing, "I know He is my life, my friend when I am dying."

Luther ends the first two stanzas of his hymn with the subject of death. By doing so, he is being not morbid but wonderfully comforting. Seeing with our eyes of faith, we have no fear of death because our friend Jesus has removed death's sting and is with us through the valley of the shadow of death with His peace.

"Lo, on those who dwelt in darkness, dark as night and deep as death, broke the light of Thy salvation, breathed Thine own life-breathing breath. Alleluia, alleluia! Praise to Thee who light dost send! Alleluia, alleluia! Alleluia without end!" Amen. (LSB 578:2)

FEBRUARY 4

You sent the people of the earth
Their great salvation;
Your invitation summons forth
Ev'ry nation
By Your holy, precious Word,
In ev'ry place resounding. (*LSB* 938:3)

THE TIME OF EPIPHANY IS A NATURAL SEASON TO THINK ABOUT missions because, in one hymn and Scripture reading after another, it is revealed that Jesus Christ and His Gospel came to this earth for all people, every nation. And by grace, the church is given one of its first vital lessons in reaching all the world in Simeon's Nunc Dimittis: "My eyes have seen Your salvation that You have prepared in the presence of all peoples, a light for revelation to the Gentiles" (Luke 2:30–32).

In this third stanza of Luther's hymn paraphrase, he likewise includes a mission statement for Christ's church. Here and in his other hymns about mission, Luther gives all the credit for the church's reaching and growing to God. Any kingdom growth comes from God; we cannot do it.

Luther states how this great salvation comes to every nation: "by Your holy, precious Word, in ev'ry place resounding." So, the Word and the Spirit do the work! Our role in this crucial work is we witness it, teach and preach it, and are messengers of this excellent news to all. Our role is to reach out, and then we trust the Holy Spirit to take that powerful Word and carry it into the whole world.

"Fill with the radiance of Your grace the souls now lost in error's maze; enlighten those whose inmost minds some dark delusion haunts and blinds. O gently call those gone astray that they may find the saving way! Let ev'ry conscience sore oppressed in You find peace and heav'nly rest." Amen. (LSB *839:2–3*)

FEBRUARY 5

Thine over all shall be the praise
And thanks of ev'ry nation;
And all the world with joy shall raise
The voice of exultation.
For Thou shalt judge the earth, O Lord,
Nor suffer sin to flourish;
Thy people's pasture is Thy Word
Their souls to feed and nourish,
In righteous paths to keep them. (*LSB* 823:2)

TODAY'S HYMN, ALSO BY MARTIN LUTHER, CONTINUES YESTERDAY'S emphasis on mission work. Stanza 1 of this extraordinary text is today's final prayer.

God's grace, His will, His pleasure, His health, and His riches are for all peoples of every nation on earth. This second stanza is a fervent prayer that all may be converted and come to faith. Sin should not be allowed to continue and flourish, but Luther cries out here for God to bestow His grace and bring everyone to the verdant pastures of His Word, "their souls to feed and nourish, in righteous paths to keep them."

And where is the power for such conversion to become a reality? God's Word alone has all the power needed to bring the lost and wandering to the pastures, paths, and ways of blessed righteousness.

The final stanza is one of Christian hymnody's most excellent doxological stanzas. It raises one massive, exultant shout of praise to Father, Son, and Spirit and asks for "solemn awe [to] possess us" (st. 3). If Luther wanted an "Amen" at the end of his hymn, Luther put it there. And here is a grand example: "Now let our hearts say, 'Amen!'" (st. 3).

"May God bestow on us His grace, with blessings rich provide us; and may the brightness of His face to life eternal guide us, that we His saving health may know, His gracious will and pleasure, and also to the nations show Christ's riches without measure and unto God convert them." Amen. (LSB *823:1*)

FEBRUARY 6

Praise to the Lord, who o'er all things is wondrously reigning
And, as on wings of an eagle, uplifting, sustaining.
Have you not seen
All that is needful has been
Sent by His gracious ordaining? (*LSB* 790:2)

God acts. He provides for us, blessing us in countless ways as we live our earthly lives. We respond in thanks and praise, as Luther instructs in the Small Catechism in his explanation of the First Article of the Creed: "For all this it is my duty to thank and praise, serve and obey Him." Moreover, God acted to save us—through the atoning death and resurrection of His Son, Jesus Christ, thereby giving us the ultimate gift of eternal life! We can only respond in thanks and praise to the God who so richly acts on our behalf: "This is the Lord's doing; it is marvelous in our eyes" (Psalm 118:23).

The hymn writer fully understands this order of things and asks us to consider what should be obvious: Haven't you seen it in your lives, that everything we truly need has been given to us by our gracious God, even without our asking for it? "Surely His goodness and mercy shall daily attend you" (st. 4). With each new day, God gives us what we need—His goodness providing food and drink, house and home; His mercy providing forgiveness of sins, "for we daily sin much and surely deserve nothing but punishment" (Small Catechism, Lord's Prayer, Fifth Petition). As we go about our various vocations, it is God who acts to prosper our work and to defend us from the devil's attacks.

So, Christian, "ponder anew what the Almighty can do as with His love He befriends you" (st. 4). Our God is the friend of sinners, and His great love provides us everything we need in this life and in the life to come.

"Praise to the Lord, who will prosper your work and defend you; surely His goodness and mercy shall daily attend you. Ponder anew what the Almighty can do as with His love He befriends you." Amen. (LSB 790:4)

FEBRUARY 7

Jesus, Thy boundless love to me
No thought can reach, no tongue declare;
Unite my thankful heart to Thee,
And reign without a rival there!
Thine wholly, Thine alone I am;
Be Thou alone my constant flame. (*LSB* 683:1)

SOMETIMES, IT IS EASY TO FEEL INSIGNIFICANT IN GOD'S VAST universe—maybe even wonder how He could have time for me. At times like these, we should immediately open our Bible and learn again of His boundless love for each of us. From Genesis through Revelation, God tells His dear children of His love for them and that they are more precious to Him than sparrows, stars, and angels.

It is good for us to hear repeatedly that the almighty God of heaven and earth, the Lord of all things, has a boundless love *for us*! God's love knows no limits. This truly astonishing miracle is not easy to comprehend or describe, but Pastor Paul Gerhardt does so masterfully in his hymn. His words help us grasp—even be overwhelmed by—Jesus' "boundless love" for us. Rather than specks in the vast universe, we are like a pearl of great worth, a priceless treasure, and one wearing a crown in the eyes of our Lord.

Jesus is our joy, our treasure, and our crown! We want His boundless love to possess us whole, to dwell alone in our soul so that it may govern our every act, word, and thought to reflect His love in us and for us.

"O grant that nothing in my soul may dwell, but Thy pure love alone; Oh, may Thy love possess me whole, my joy, my treasure, and my crown! All coldness from my heart remove; my ev'ry act, word, thought be love." Amen. (LSB *683:2*)

FEBRUARY 8

This love unwearied I pursue
And dauntlessly to Thee aspire.
Oh, may Thy love my hope renew,
Burn in my soul like heav'nly fire!
And day and night, be all my care
To guard this sacred treasure there. (*LSB* 683:3)

JESUS LIVING IN US WITH HIS LOVE IS A SACRED AND PRICELESS treasure we guard as we carry it with us throughout our lives as baptized believers. There would be no baptismal life without His extraordinary love, which reached out and made us His own in Holy Baptism. And that baptismal life is kept alive and well by Jesus Himself in gifts of grace flowing from His Word, His Absolution, and His Holy Supper. These treasured gifts bestow *Jesus*—they fill us with Jesus and are gifts we cannot live without.

Our hymn today sings of a miraculous hope that fills us as the love of Jesus lives in us. It sings of how the Holy Spirit is always there, ready to renew our needy souls, like a heavenly fire! It sings of the true peace of Jesus that accompanies us in our suffering, our weakness, and the storms of life.

This cherished, treasured, and sacred Love—Jesus Christ—is our power and strength through every day of the baptismal life. In Him, we live safely in His love and we trust that He will be there in that final hour when He will be our rod, staff, and guide, drawing us safely to His side.

"In suff'ring be Thy love my peace, in weakness be Thy love my pow'r; and when the storms of life shall cease, O Jesus, in that final hour, be Thou my rod and staff and guide, and draw me safely to Thy side!" Amen. (LSB 683:4)

FEBRUARY 9

Thy holy body into death was given,
Life to win for us in heaven.
No greater love than this to Thee could bind us;
May this feast thereof remind us!
O Lord, have mercy!
Lord, Thy kindness did so constrain Thee
That Thy blood should bless and sustain me.
All our debt Thou hast paid;
Peace with God once more is made:
O Lord, have mercy! (*LSB* 617:2)

Martin Luther's hymn on the Lord's Supper has much to teach us. For those who have been instructed and receive the Holy Supper regularly, this hymn is a wonderful reminder of the great blessings God pours out on us through this Sacrament.

"All our debt Thou hast paid; peace with God once more is made." Jesus willingly gave His holy body into death on the cross. This was God's plan—life for us required death for Him. It is impossible to imagine a greater love than that of the Creator dying on behalf of His sinful creatures.

The death of Christ happened once for all (Hebrews 7:27). But Jesus instituted His Holy Supper so that we might receive His very body and blood for the forgiveness of our sins and, as Luther puts it, nourishment for "our weak souls that they may flourish" (st. 1). As we suffer trials, fears, and needs in this life, the body and blood of our Lord blesses and sustains us with the certainty of sins forgiven and eternal life won for us. For such rich gifts, we praise, bless, adore, and thank our Lord Jesus Christ!

"O Lord, we praise Thee, bless Thee, and adore Thee, in thanksgiving bow before Thee. Thou with Thy body and Thy blood didst nourish our weak souls that they may flourish: O Lord, have mercy! May Thy body, Lord, born of Mary, that our sins and sorrows did carry, and Thy blood for us plead in all trial, fear, and need: O Lord, have mercy!" Amen. (LSB 617:1)

FEBRUARY 10

I trust, O Christ, in You alone;
No earthly hope avails me.
You will not see me overthrown
When Satan's host assails me.
No human strength, no earthly pow'r
Can see me through the evil hour,
For You alone my strength renew.
I cry to You!
I trust, O Lord, Your promise true. (***LSB*** **972:1)**

TODAY'S HYMN IS ABOUT TRUST, HOPE, AND PROMISES—THREE defining pillars of baptismal life in Christ's kingdom. Our life as His baptized children is to be filled with confidence and hope in the beautiful promises given to us at our Baptism. We were promised the Helper, the Holy Spirit, who now lives in us and enables us to trust in God alone.

Learning where a person places their trust is understanding one of the most essential facts about a person—for it reveals their heart. So, when a Christian confesses with all their heart, soul, and mind that Jesus Christ alone is their hope, strength, and defender, they tell us who they are, and we now know where they will turn for everything.

This beautifully describes us as faithful saints in Christ's kingdom. Yet we are surrounded by souls who have no idea where to turn and who place their trust in all the wrong places. By God's grace, we know what they do not yet know: Jesus Christ is the answer to every possible question, challenge, danger, and need. And as our hymn today says, we can "spend our lives" showing Jesus' "love in all we do," especially to those who need to hear of that great "promise of salvation" (st. 3).

"I trust, O Lord, Your holy name; O let me not be put to shame nor let me be confounded. My faith, O Lord, be in Your Word forever firmly grounded. Bow down Your gracious ear to me and hear my cry, my prayer, my plea; make haste for my protection, for woes and fear surround me here. Help me in my affliction." Amen. (LSB *734:1–2*)

FEBRUARY 11

'Tis good, Lord, to be here!
Thy glory fills the night;
Thy face and garments, like the sun,
Shine with unborrowed light. (*LSB* 414:1)

OF JESUS' DISCIPLES, PETER WAS THE MOST IMPETUOUS, QUICK to speak and act. At Jesus' transfiguration, Peter had awakened from sleep just in time to witness the glory of Jesus speaking with Moses and Elijah. Peter blurted out, "'Master, it is good that we are here. Let us make three tents, one for You and one for Moses and one for Elijah'—not knowing what he said" (Luke 9:33). Understandably, he wanted to preserve the event by putting up tents for Jesus, Moses, and Elijah so that he could remain in that unique, glory-filled moment.

Peter was right—it is good to be where Jesus is. We know that Jesus' promise to the penitent criminal crucified beside Him—"Today you will be with Me in paradise" (Luke 23:43)—is also His promise to us. We will be with Jesus eternally, and we will know more than ever that it is "good, Lord, to be here!" But those words are also our words here and now, for when we are in God's house, receiving His Divine Service to us, He is bodily present on the altar. As we receive His true body and blood for the forgiveness of our sins, we can say, "It is good, Lord, to be here," to be where He is.

Peter also heard the words of the Father spoken at the transfiguration: "This is My Son, My Chosen One; listen to Him!" (Luke 9:35). That is also part of being where Jesus is—listening to His voice, hearing His life-giving words of grace. Truly, it is good to be where Jesus is!

"Yet, Savior, You are not confined to any habitation; but You are present even now here with Your congregation. Firm as a rock this truth shall stand, unmoved by any daring hand or subtle craft and cunning." Amen. (LSB 622:3)

FEBRUARY 12

O wondrous type! O vision fair
Of glory that the Church may share,
Which Christ upon the mountain shows,
Where brighter than the sun He glows!

With shining face and bright array
Christ deigns to manifest today
What glory shall be theirs above
Who joy in God with perfect love. (*LSB* 413:1, 3)

THE FIRST LINE OF THIS HYMN USES THE WORD TYPE IN A WAY that may be unfamiliar to us. *Type* can mean a "sort," "example," or "kind" of something. What happened that day on the Mount of Transfiguration overflows with types, and books could be written to reveal all the types shown on that mount.

Today's hymn is also filled with types, with the main one being glory. We read here of the radiant, dazzling glory in our Lord's appearance—"brighter than the sun He glows! With shining face and bright array," He manifests and foreshadows a type of future glory that will be ours on that Last Day, one that will last forever!

This type of glory certainly manifests on the Mount of Transfiguration. However, this is not our Lord's highest glory. No, He will leave the mount and walk the road to Calvary, where His highest glory will be on a cross and not easy to watch. Nevertheless, the glory we see with our Lord on a cross is the heart of the theology of the cross, which is the opposite of a theology of glory. Our Lord's glory is hidden in a suffering that took Him to the cross. Such a divine and paradoxical understanding of glory is foreign to this world: where humility is exalted and death is victory.

"And faithful hearts are raised on high by this great vision's mystery, for which in joyful strains we raise the voice of prayer, the hymn of praise. O Father, with th' eternal Son and Holy Spirit ever one, we pray Thee, bring us by Thy grace to see Thy glory face to face." Amen. (LSB *413:4–5*)

FEBRUARY 13

Lord Jesus Christ, You have prepared
This feast for our salvation;
It is Your body and Your blood,
And at Your invitation
As weary souls, with sin oppressed,
We come to You for needed rest,
For comfort, and for pardon. (*LSB* 622:1)

W***HEN WE FEEL THE WEIGHT OF SIN—WHAT WE HAVE DONE*** and what we have left undone—we come to the Lord's Supper. Christ has prepared this feast for our salvation, and He invites us to come and receive His true body and blood under the bread and wine. Christ Himself taught us that His blood "is poured out for many for the forgiveness of sins" (Matthew 26:28).

"We eat this bread and drink this cup, Your precious Word believing that Your true body and Your blood our lips are here receiving" (st. 4). As surely as the hymn writer states this truth, he also knows that human reason cannot fully comprehend it: "Though reason cannot understand, yet faith this truth embraces" (st. 5). Likewise, Hebrews 11:1 characterizes faith as "the conviction of things not seen." We cannot see Christ's body and blood; we see bread and wine. Yet faith enables us to say with the hymn writer, "I leave to You how this can be; Your Word alone suffices me; I trust its truth unfailing" (st. 5). The Holy Spirit works this faith in us to believe in Christ's promise: "Poured out for many for the forgiveness of sins."

As Luther reminds us, "where there is forgiveness of sins, there is also life and salvation" (Small Catechism, Sacrament of the Altar). In the Lord's Supper, we receive exactly what the hymn writer states: rest, comfort, and pardon for the sins that oppress us, the ultimate consolation both for our living and for our dying.

"For Your consoling supper, Lord, be praised throughout all ages! Preserve it, for in ev'ry place the world against it rages. Grant that this sacrament may be a blessed comfort unto me when living and when dying." Amen. (LSB 622:8)

FEBRUARY 14

On my heart imprint Your image,
Blessed Jesus, King of grace,
That life's riches, cares, and pleasures
Never may Your work erase;
Let the clear inscription be:
Jesus, crucified for me,
Is my life, my hope's foundation,
And my glory and salvation! (*LSB* 422)

SOME CONGREGATIONS SING THIS BEAUTIFUL HYMN-PRAYER EVERY week in Lent, and it is easy to understand why. This hymn by Thomas Kingo brings all that Lent is about together in one powerful stanza. Many people even have this beloved hymn memorized, and it often appears on worship service covers, newsletters, and bulletin boards.

The forty days of Lent are about the faithful repeatedly asking God for a clean heart. "Create in me a clean heart, O God, and renew a right spirit within me" (Psalm 51:10). The hymn asks Him to continually imprint Himself on our hearts. God grants it, but sadly, our need for it reappears within seconds. That is why the Kyrie—"Lord, have mercy"—immediately follows the Absolution in the Divine Service. Our need is *always* there.

The holy and solemn days of Lent prepare us for the summit of the church's year: the resurrection of our Lord. Meanwhile, for forty days, our readiness is about clean hearts, hearts imprinted with the image of Jesus, hearts inscribed with this truth: "Jesus, crucified for me, is my life, my hope's foundation, and my glory and salvation!"

"Do we pass that cross unheeding, breathing no repentant vow, though we see You wounded, bleeding, see Your thorn-encircled brow? Yet Your sinless death has brought us life eternal, peace, and rest; only what Your grace has taught us calms the sinner's deep distress. Jesus, may our hearts be burning with more fervent love for You; may our eyes be ever turning to behold Your cross anew till in glory, parted never from the blessed Savior's side, graven in our hearts forever, dwell the cross, the Crucified." Amen. (LSB *423:2–3*)

FEBRUARY 15

Lord Jesus, think on me
And purge away my sin;
From worldly passions
set me free
And make me pure within.

Lord Jesus, think on me,
By anxious thoughts oppressed;
Let me Your loving servant be
And taste Your promised rest.

Lord Jesus, think on me
Amid the battle's strife;
In all my pain and misery,
O be my health and
life! (*LSB* 610:1–3)

TODAY'S HYMN, WRITTEN IN THE FOURTH CENTURY, OFFERS A glimpse into how the early church expressed humanity's greatest problem—sin—and humanity's greatest need—forgiveness. These early Christians sang about it in a hymn that was a simple prayer, a penitential confession, and a fervent cry for God's gracious mercy.

Here, the singers list some of what is troubling them: anxious thoughts, worldly passions, darkness, perplexity, pain, and misery—all common in life's battle strife on this earth. Rather than keep this list to themselves, they seek to give it all to the One waiting to take it from them and make them clean.

They want to be made pure within, just as we all do. We all want health, life, and the peace that can only happen when sins are removed. So, we join them in singing this confident prayer that confesses sins to the One who removes sins.

The final part of this hymn-prayer looks to the next life. As forgiven children of our Lord, we pray that when this troubled life is past, we will see Jesus' "eternal brightness" and share His joy (st. 5). We ask to taste of His promised rest in forgiveness now and then forever rest in Him in the life to come.

"Lord Jesus, think on me nor let me go astray; through darkness and perplexity point out Your chosen way. Lord Jesus, think on me that, when this life is past, I may the eternal brightness see and share Your joy at last." Amen. (LSB *610:4–5*)

FEBRUARY 16

For me to live is Jesus,
To die is gain for me;
So when my Savior pleases,
I meet death willingly.

For Christ, my Lord, my brother,
I leave this world so dim
And gladly seek another,
Where I shall be with Him. (*LSB* 742:1–2)

The apostle Paul put it most memorably: "For me to live is Christ, and to die is gain" (Philippians 1:21). To die is *gain*! That sentiment is not readily accepted by the world in which we live. But the writer of today's hymn-prayer understands and mirrors Paul's words, writing that believers "meet death willingly" and "gladly seek" the world to come, the eternal world promised by our Savior. This hymn is a guide to a Christian death.

What is it that permits the Christian to be at peace with death? The hymn writer puts it succinctly: "My sin His merits cover, and I have peace with God" (st. 3). That is all that matters as death approaches. For our sins, we justly deserve God's present and eternal punishment. But Jesus lived the perfect life that we could not, and He died the death that our sins deserve—all of which is counted to us as righteousness (Romans 4:3). And that brings a peace that "surpasses all understanding" (Philippians 4:7), the peace that permits us to meet death willingly.

We pray that in our last hour God would grant us to be free of any doubts that would vex us, that He would grant us a firm faith in the certainty of sins forgiven through Jesus' blood. And we pray that we will "fall asleep believing" (st. 6) that we will awaken to life eternal in the presence of Jesus, who died to give us a blessed death and everlasting life.

"In my last hour, O grant me a slumber soft and still, no doubts to vex or haunt me, safe anchored in Thy will; and so to Thee still cleaving when death shall come to me, I fall asleep believing and wake in heav'n with Thee!" Amen. (LSB 742:5–6)

FEBRUARY 17

O perfect life of love!
All, all, is finished now,
All that He left His throne above
To do for us below.

No work is left undone
Of all the Father willed;
His toil, His sorrows, one by one,
The Scriptures have fulfilled. (*LSB* 452:1–2)

O ***PERFECT LIFE OF LOVE" SAYS IT ALL, AND YET DOES IT?*** **IT DOES** as far as words can, but words fail to describe *this* life and *this* love—one of perfection and love beyond all human thought and understanding. Our Lord Jesus Christ, You are that very life and love sent from the Father to this world for us.

"O perfect life of love!" It's a stunningly beautiful phrase, but it fails to reveal the anguish, pain, humiliation, and horror suffered during Your life as You carried the world's sins on Your shoulders for us.

"O perfect life of love!" Jesus Christ, Your perfect life accomplished all the Father willed for His Son as You fulfilled the Holy Scriptures for us.

"O perfect life of love!" Your love left nothing undone, dearest Lord Jesus, for Your life was one of extravagant love. In Your perfect life, O Lord, You lavished love on us and suffered for us.

"O perfect life of love!" With Your last words from the cross, "It is finished" (John 19:30), You, O blessed Jesus, crushed the serpent's head and accomplished what You descended to earth to do for us.

"Thousand, thousand thanks shall be, dearest Jesus, unto Thee" (*LSB* 420:1).

"Then, for all that wrought my pardon, for Thy sorrows deep and sore, for Thine anguish in the Garden, I will thank Thee evermore, thank Thee for Thy groaning, sighing, for Thy bleeding and Thy dying, for that last triumphant cry, and shall praise Thee, Lord, on high." Amen. (LSB *420:7*)

FEBRUARY 18

Triune God, be Thou our stay;
O let us perish never!
Cleanse us from our
sins, we pray,
And grant us life forever.
Keep us from the evil one;
Uphold our faith most holy,
And let us trust Thee solely
With humble hearts and lowly.
Let us put God's armor on,
With all true Christians running
Our heav'nly race and shunning
The devil's wiles and cunning.
Amen, amen! This be done;
So sing we, "Alleluia!"
(*LSB* 505:1)

ON THIS DAY, THE DATE OF HIS DEATH IN 1546, THE CHURCH remembers Martin Luther, reformer, teacher, hymn writer. Today's hymn, a single stanza but addressed successively to each person of the Trinity, is Luther's revision of an older hymn, now providing us petitions for daily prayer.

We ask the triune God to be with us always, keeping us unto eternal life, which comes to us by God's grace, as our sins are forgiven for the sake of Christ's suffering, death, and resurrection. Cleansed from our sins, we will live forever with our Savior.

We ask further that God would keep us from the assaults of the devil and that He would uphold and strengthen our faith so that we trust in Him to provide all that we need now and forever.

Luther knew well the truth of the apostle Peter's characterization of the devil: "Your adversary the devil prowls around like a roaring lion, seeking someone to devour" (1 Peter 5:8). Thus, we pray that God would help us to "put on the whole armor of God . . . to stand against the schemes of the devil" (Ephesians 6:11). We pray that we would, with God's help, resist the devil, keep the faith, finish the race, and receive the crown of righteousness (2 Timothy 4:7–8) for a blessed eternity in the presence of our triune God.

"Lord, help us ever to retain the Catechism's doctrine plain as Luther taught the Word of truth in simple style to tender youth." Amen. (LSB *865:1*)

FEBRUARY 19

Jesus, grant that balm
and healing
In Your holy wounds I find,
Ev'ry hour that I am feeling
Pains of body and of mind.
Should some evil
thought within
Tempt my treach'rous
heart to sin,
Show the peril, and
from sinning
Keep me from its
first beginning.

Should some lust or
sharp temptation
Fascinate my sinful mind,
Draw me to Your cross
and passion,
And new courage I shall find.
Or should Satan press me hard,
Let me then be on my guard,
Saying, "Christ for me
was wounded,"
That the tempter flee
confounded. (*LSB* 421:1–2)

TODAY'S HYMN HELPS US TO PRAY THAT WE MAY RESIST TEMPTATION. How? By focusing on the cross and Passion of our Lord.

The hymn writer bluntly describes our human condition, characterized by evil thoughts and lustful desires—the temptations that reside in our sinful minds. To fight against these temptations, we look to Jesus and what He endured on the cross for us. In His wounds we find "balm and healing" for hearts troubled by sin.

We also find the courage to address Satan, confounding him with the words "Christ for me was wounded." He doesn't know what more he can do when the Christian declares, "Christ died to save me—you have no power over me." All the devil can do is leave and await another opportunity for temptation. Jesus set the example for us when, at the conclusion of His temptations in the wilderness, He said, "Be gone, Satan!" (Matthew 4:10). As we resist the devil and his temptations, we invoke the name of Jesus and His once-for-all defeat of Satan at the cross: "It is finished" (John 19:30). "Your all-atoning passion has procured my soul's salvation" (st. 4).

"Ev'ry wound that pains or grieves me by Your wounds, Lord, is made whole; when I'm faint, Your cross revives me, granting new life to my soul. Yes, Your comfort renders sweet ev'ry bitter cup I meet; for Your all-atoning passion has procured my soul's salvation." Amen. (LSB 421:4)

FEBRUARY 20

Hail, Thou once despised Jesus!
Hail, Thou Galilean King!
Thou didst suffer to release us;
Thou didst free salvation bring.
Hail, Thou universal Savior,
Bearer of our sin and shame!
By Thy merit we find favor:
Life is given through Thy name.

Paschal Lamb, by God appointed,
All our sins on Thee were laid;
By almighty love anointed,
Thou hast full atonement made.
All Thy people are forgiven
Through the virtue of Thy blood;
Opened is the gate of heaven,
Reconciled are we with God. (*LSB* 531:1–2)

B*EFORE* H*E WAS CRUCIFIED*, J*ESUS WAS BEATEN BY* P*ILATE'S* soldiers, who placed a crown of thorns on His head and mocked Him, saying, "Hail, King of the Jews" (Matthew 27:29)—just as the prophet Isaiah had foretold. The innocent Son of God willingly suffered this abuse from the very people He came to save, including the ones who crucified Him. Worst of all, as He suffered on the cross, He was utterly abandoned by God the Father—complete separation—so that we will *never* experience that horrible deprivation.

In His great love for us, Jesus took on Himself the sin and shame of all who would ever live, paying the full price to atone for those sins and earning eternal life for all who believe in Him. Through His blood, we are forgiven and reconciled with God, and heaven is opened to us!

Even now, Jesus is at His Father's side, pleading and interceding on behalf of the sinners for whom He died. Moreover, He is preparing a place for us: "And if I go and prepare a place for you, I will come again and will take you to Myself, that where I am you may be also" (John 14:3).

"Jesus, hail! Enthroned in glory, there forever to abide; all the heav'nly hosts adore Thee, seated at Thy Father's side. There for sinners Thou art pleading; there Thou dost our place prepare, ever for us interceding till in glory we appear." Amen. (LSB *531:3*)

FEBRUARY 21

By Thy helpless infant years,
By Thy life of want and tears,
By Thy days of deep distress
In the savage wilderness,
By the dread, mysterious hour
Of the insulting tempter's pow'r,
Turn, O turn a fav'ring eye;
Hear our penitential cry!

By Thine hour of dire despair,
By Thine agony of prayer,
By the cross, the nail, the thorn,
Piercing spear, and torturing scorn,
By the gloom that veiled the skies
O'er the dreadful sacrifice,
Listen to our humble sigh;
Hear our penitential cry! (*LSB* 419:2–3)

"HEAR OUR PENITENTIAL CRY!" EACH STANZA OF THIS LENTEN hymn-prayer describes the awful cost of our redemption before turning us to our cry of repentance.

We repent of our sins, which caused Jesus to leave His exalted place at the right hand of the Father. He willingly gave it all up to become a helpless infant, living an earthly life of want and tears. We repent that Jesus had to go to the wilderness to be tempted by the devil, overcoming all of his insulting temptations, because we cannot.

We repent of our sins, which caused Jesus to plead with His Father in agony: "Let this cup pass from Me; nevertheless, not as I will, but as You will" (Matthew 26:39). We repent of our sins, which caused Jesus enormous physical pain—the crown of thorns, the nails in His hands and feet, the spear in His side, and the "torturing scorn" of those who knew not what they did (Luke 23:34). We repent that the sinless Creator had to die for us sinful creatures.

But thanks be to God that the grave could not hold our Savior! His redemptive work completed, He was restored to His throne on high, where He hears our penitential cry.

"By Thy deep expiring groan, by the sad sepulchral stone, by the vault whose dark abode held in vain the rising God, O, from earth to heav'n restored, mighty, reascended Lord, bending from Thy throne on high, hear our penitential cry!" Amen. (LSB *419:4*)

FEBRUARY 22

Thou hast suffered men to bruise Thee,
That from pain I might be free;
Falsely did Thy foes accuse Thee:
Thence I gain security;
Comfortless Thy soul did languish
Me to comfort in my anguish.
Thousand, thousand thanks shall be,
Dearest Jesus, unto Thee. (*LSB* 420:5)

"CHRIST, THE LIFE OF ALL THE LIVING, CHRIST, THE DEATH OF death, our foe" (st. 1). The opening line of today's hymn is a wonderful summary of what Jesus has done for us through His suffering, death, and resurrection. Jesus is the one who gives us life, and He does so by defeating death—our last enemy. The hymn writer helps us to understand precisely what it meant for Jesus, the innocent one, to willingly take the place of the guilty ones.

Jesus allowed men to "bruise" Him, to inflict harsh physical pain. Why? "That from pain I might be free." We confess every week in worship that we deserve God's punishment, but Jesus took the pain on Himself so that we would not suffer that just punishment. Jesus suffered the false accusations of His foes and tormentors. Why? So that we might have the "security" of knowing that Satan's accusations carry no weight before the judgment throne of God. When Jesus asked His Father to "let this cup pass," when He cried out, "My God, My God, why have You forsaken Me?" (Matthew 26:39; 27:46), He was "comfortless"; His "soul did languish." Why? So that we would never suffer such abandonment by God, so that in our soul's anguish we would be comforted.

The hymn writer summarizes Christ's vicarious atonement for us: "Thou didst choose to be tormented that my doom should be prevented" (st. 6). Our response can only be "thousand, thousand thanks" to Jesus for His great suffering on our behalf.

"Thou hast suffered great affliction and hast borne it patiently, even death by crucifixion, fully to atone for me; Thou didst choose to be tormented that my doom should be prevented. Thousand, thousand thanks shall be, dearest Jesus, unto Thee." Amen. (LSB 420:6)

FEBRUARY 23

From God can nothing
move me;
He will not step aside
But gently will reprove me
And be my constant guide.
He stretches out His hand
In evening and in morning,
My life with grace adorning
Wherever I may stand.

When those whom I regarded
As trustworthy and sure
Have long from me departed,
God's grace shall still endure.
He rescues me from sin
And breaks the chains
that bind me.
I leave death's fear behind me;
His peace I have within.
(*LSB* 713:1–2)

IT IS GOOD AND RIGHT FOR US TO BOLDLY SING THE TRUTH—THAT God will *never* leave or forsake us! *Nothing* can separate us from Him and His love for us. Living in that blessed certainty gives us His peace for all our days.

Our life is adorned with His grace that endures when all else around us disappoints and fails, a grace that is there from morning to evening as it puts away any fear of death. And it is His grace that rescues us from our sin as it breaks the chains of the old man seeking to bind us and blind us. We are *never* apart from that beautiful grace.

Yes, "the world's unpleasantness" may still surround us (st. 6), but it can never separate us from Him. Yes, some days may be rough and bring great distress, but we never face any of those days alone without Him. Praise be to Thee, O Three in One!

"Yet even though I suffer the world's unpleasantness, and though the days grow rougher and bring me great distress, that day of bliss divine, which knows no end or measure, and Christ, who is my pleasure, forever shall be mine. For thus the Father willed it, who fashioned us from clay; and His own Son fulfilled it and brought eternal day. The Spirit now has come, to us true faith has given; He leads us home to heaven. O praise the Three in One!" Amen. (LSB 713:6–7)

FEBRUARY 24

**The Lord my life arranges;
Who can His work destroy?
In His good time He changes
All sorrow into joy.
So let me then be still:
My body, soul, and spirit
His tender care inherit
According to His will.**

**Each day at His good pleasure
God's gracious will is done.
He sent His greatest treasure
In Jesus Christ, His Son.
He ev'ry gift imparts.
The bread of earth and heaven
Are by His kindness given.
Praise Him with thankful
hearts! (*LSB* 713:3–4)**

This hymn is a hidden gem, packed with Gospel goodness! These two stanzas mainly sing of two themes: God's will in our lives and God's abundant gifts. Both are central for life as His children.

We sing and pray here for a body, soul, and spirit that is calm and still, safely in God's tender care and keeping. This is what God's children inherit; we have an omniscient and omnipotent Father caring for all our needs. Come what may, this body, soul, and spirit can trust in God's gracious will in all things. Yes, sorrow may come, but here we express a confident trust that our God can and will turn it into joy.

Our Lord has arranged our lives; nothing can destroy His plan. We sing that "each day at His good pleasure God's gracious will is done" for us. And we trust that it is His will to lavish His gifts on us. "The bread of earth and heaven are by His kindness given." How can we help but "praise God with acclamation and in His gifts rejoice" (st. 5)?

"Praise God with acclamation and in His gifts rejoice. Each day finds its vocation responding to His voice. Soon years on earth are past; but time we spend expressing the love of God brings blessing that will forever last!" Amen. (LSB *713:5*)

FEBRUARY 25

I fall asleep in Jesus' wounds,
There pardon for my sins abounds;
Yea, Jesus' blood and righteousness
My jewels are, my glorious dress.
In these before my God I'll stand
When I shall reach the heav'nly land. (*TLH* 585:1)

TODAY'S HYMN PAINTS A BEAUTIFUL PICTURE OF THE CHRISTIAN'S death—"I fall asleep in Jesus' wounds." As baptized children of God, we confess with this hymn that we need fear the grave as little as our bed. We can be confident we will die in the promises of our Lord in peace and joy and without fear.

Until then, we live daily in the pardon and forgiveness won by Jesus' blood and are very well fed by His gracious gifts of Word and Sacraments, leading us to an abundant life as saints in His kingdom. This whole life became ours at our Baptism, as God washed away our sin and gave us Christ's righteousness in exchange. We now live in Jesus' blood and righteousness, with them as our "jewels" and "glorious dress."

For us, death is not to be feared, and we can even say, "I thank thee, Death, thou leadest me to that true life" (st. 2) in "the heavenly land." Like Simeon, we are ready to depart whenever God wills. His time is the best time; only He knows that exact time. We also know that when we stand before God, we will be dressed in a white robe of righteousness given to us by His own Son, Jesus Christ: "In these before my God I'll stand when I shall reach the heav'nly land."

"With peace and joy I now depart; God's child I am with all my heart. I thank thee, Death, thou leadest me to that true life where I would be. So cleansed by Christ, I fear not death. Lord Jesus, strengthen Thou my faith. Amen." (TLH 585:2)

FEBRUARY 26

I walk in danger all the way.
The thought shall never leave me
That Satan, who has marked his prey,
Is plotting to deceive me.
This foe with hidden snares
May seize me unawares
If I should fail to watch and pray.
I walk in danger all the way. (*LSB* 716:1)

JOHN BUNYAN'S THE PILGRIM'S PROGRESS *TELLS THE STORY OF A* man named Christian who travels a narrow road fraught with no end of dangers, perils, and obstacles on his way to heaven's gate. Christian's story is not all that different from ours, for we, too, "walk in danger all the way."

Peter warns, "There will be false teachers among you, who will secretly bring in destructive heresies, even denying the Master who bought them" (2 Peter 2:1). Yes, in these perilous end times, there are false teachers, wolves cunningly dressed as sheep, surrounding the faithful flock! Satan, the cruel enemy of the sheep, plots through clever deception, hidden snares, and harmless-sounding words to lure the sheep off the narrow path.

But like Bunyan's Christian, we are not alone on the narrow way that leads to heaven. No, Jesus and His angels walk with us. As baptized children of our Lord, we have nothing to fear, for His angel host will shield and befriend us as they hold Satan's power at bay. "Unharmed by foes, do what they may, I walk with angels all the way" (st. 4).

And the blessed road we are on leads to heaven's gate!

"I walk with Jesus all the way, His guidance never fails me; within His wounds I find a stay when Satan's pow'r assails me; and by His footsteps led, my path I safely tread. No evil leads my soul astray; I walk with Jesus all the way." Amen. (LSB 716:5)

FEBRUARY 27

Inscribed upon the cross we see
In shining letters, "God is love."
He bears our sins upon the tree;
He brings us mercy from above. (*LSB* 429:2)

THE CROSS WAS AN INSTRUMENT OF TORTURE IN THE ROMAN world. It was a painful, public, humiliating means of death. Yet this was the time, and the mode, God chose for His beloved Son to die for the sins of the world. But there was a significant difference in the crucifixion of Jesus: Jesus was guilty of nothing; He was sinless. He hung on the cross because of our guilt, our sins. He did so to save us from eternal death. "He brings us mercy from above."

While acknowledging the awful purpose of the cross as a means of punishment, we can look at the cross in another way: "Inscribed upon the cross we see in shining letters, 'God is love.'" The love that Jesus showed for us on the cross forever removes the possibility that we will be required to pay the full price for our sins. Jesus has already done that for us. Thus, the instrument of torture becomes for us the means of salvation and everlasting life.

For us the cross is the reminder of God's infinite love. Our churches have crosses inside and outside. We may wear crosses for the purpose of recalling Jesus' redeeming work. And we make the sign of the cross as a reminder of our Baptism into Christ's death (Romans 6:3).

Today's hymn-prayer puts the cross of Jesus into perspective. The cross "takes our guilt away," it "cheers with hope the gloomy day," and most important, it removes all terror from the grave (st. 3). Thanks be to God for the saving grace of Jesus' cross.

"The cross! It takes our guilt away; it holds the fainting spirit up; it cheers with hope the gloomy day and sweetens ev'ry bitter cup. It makes the coward spirit brave and nerves the feeble arm for fight; it takes the terror from the grave and gilds the bed of death with light." Amen. (LSB 429:3–4)

FEBRUARY 28

O child of woe:
Who struck the blow
That killed our gracious Master?
"It was I," thy conscience cries,
"I have wrought disaster!" (*LSB* 448:3)

As *we read the Gospel accounts of Jesus' Passion, it is* impossible to remove ourselves from that story. While we weren't there, the whole sordid mess of our sins was. There, Jesus took on Himself the sins of all the people who would ever live on this earth—the heaviest burden imaginable, one that could be carried only by the sinless Son of God. The hymn writer gets it exactly right: I was the one who "killed our gracious Master." I was the one who caused this "disaster."

Our consciences accuse us and tell us that we would have been like Peter—denying, more than once, that we even knew Jesus. We would have been part of the crowd crying for the release of the criminal Barabbas, while urging that the sinless Son of God be crucified. We might even have been one who jeered at the crucified Savior, mocking Him by saying, "If You are the Son of God, come down from the cross" (Matthew 27:40). There is simply no way to take ourselves out of this narrative, no way somehow to whitewash our role in Christ's Passion.

But here is the greatest news: The Gospel accounts don't stop at Calvary and Jesus' Passion; they continue on to the empty tomb and Jesus' resurrection. Jesus forgave Peter for his denials, and He also forgives you and me. The living Christ still comes to us today in His Word and Sacraments, giving us His very body and blood to eat and drink for the forgiveness of our sins—yes, for those sins that "killed our gracious Master."

"I caused Your grief and sighing by evils multiplying as countless as the sands. I caused the woes unnumbered with which Your soul is cumbered, Your sorrows raised by wicked hands." Amen. (LSB 453:4)

FEBRUARY 29

Drawn to the cross, which Thou hast blessed
With healing gifts for souls distressed,
To find in Thee my life, my rest,
Christ crucified, I come. (*LSB* 560:1)

THE CENTRAL SYMBOL OF THE CHRISTIAN CHURCH IS NOT CHRIST'S empty tomb but rather the cross. Of course, both are essential to the story of salvation—we can't have one without the other. Christ has died! Christ is risen! "If Christ has not been raised, your faith is futile and you are still in your sins" (1 Corinthians 15:17). But God's plan of salvation required that His beloved Son suffer the consequences of all human sins. The scales of divine justice would not balance if Jesus came into this world, preached and healed for a few years, died of natural causes, and then rose again three days later. No, the cross—with all its pain, humiliation, and suffering—was essential to God's plan of salvation. "Was it not necessary that the Christ should suffer these things and enter into His glory?" (Luke 24:26). The Sinless One had to suffer and die on behalf of the sinful many.

Paul, too, emphasizes the cross: "For the word of the cross is folly to those who are perishing, but to us who are being saved it is the power of God" (1 Corinthians 1:18). "Folly" and "foolishness"—Paul uses both words in this epistle to capture the world's thinking about God's Son having to suffer and die. The world's wisdom finds the cross to be an unnecessary stumbling block, making no sense. But God chose what is low and despised to be the means of our salvation. Thus, Paul can say with complete confidence, "I decided to know nothing among you except Jesus Christ and Him crucified" (2:2). Thanks be to God for the wisdom and power of the cross!

"In the cross of Christ I glory, tow'ring o'er the wrecks of time. All the light of sacred story gathers round its head sublime." Amen. (LSB 427:1)

MARCH 1

My song is love unknown,
My Savior's love to me,
Love to the loveless shown
That they might lovely be.
Oh, who am I
That for my sake
My Lord should take
Frail flesh and die? (*LSB* 430:1)

I*T'S A STRIKING, POETIC PHRASE: "LOVE TO THE LOVELESS SHOWN* that they might lovely be." This is the remarkable love "unknown"—that God, the Creator of the universe, would send His Son to die to redeem the very creatures He created. That kind of sacrificial love was previously unknown in human history, and it will never be equaled, nor does it need to be repeated. Paul caught the nature of this unique sacrificial love in Romans 5:7–8: "For one will scarcely die for a righteous person—though perhaps for a good person one would dare even to die—but God shows His love for us in that while we were still sinners, Christ died for us."

We might balk at being designated by the hymn writer as "loveless." After all, one might truthfully say, "I love my parents, spouse, and children." But our love for others does not make us loveable. Consider the proposition from Jesus' perspective: "If you love Me, you will keep My commandments" (John 14:15). What can we say to that? We can only join Paul in lamenting, "For I have the desire to do what is right, but not the ability to carry it out. For I do not do the good I want, but the evil I do not want is what I keep on doing" (Romans 7:18–19).

But God does not abandon us in our sins. The overwhelming love of God has rescued us from this dilemma; God's love for us in Christ changes the loveless to being lovely in His sight. Thanks be to God for His steadfast love!

"Can we fathom such deep mercy? Do we see what God has done? Who can grasp this great reversal: Love that gives His only Son? Christ, the sinless for the sinners, for the many dies the One." Amen. (LSB *446:4*)

MARCH 2

Your body and Your blood,
Once slain and shed for me,
Are taken at Your table, Lord,
In blest reality.

Search not how this takes place,
This wondrous mystery;
God can accomplish vastly more
Than what we think could be. (***LSB*** **628:3–4)**

The words of our Lord are clear: "Take, eat; this is My body." "Drink of it, all of you, for this is My blood" (Matthew 26:26, 27–28). This is the "blest reality" of which the hymn writer speaks. In this Sacrament, we receive Christ's very body and blood under the bread and wine for the forgiveness of sins. And yet the church has not always taken Jesus' clear words instituting His Holy Supper at face value, and they remain a source of division among Christians. Why is that?

In the words of today's hymn, "God can accomplish vastly more than what we think could be." Human wisdom has a difficult time trying to figure out how Christ's body and blood can be received by us. Human wisdom cannot fathom how this can happen time after time, for centuries and millennia of the Christian Church on earth. Human wisdom has this problem because it ignores God's clear words: "For My thoughts are not your thoughts, neither are your ways My ways, declares the Lord. For as the heavens are higher than the earth, so are My ways higher than your ways and My thoughts than your thoughts" (Isaiah 55:8–9). The God who created the universe, who worked salvation for the crown of His creation (Genesis 1:27), has no difficulty in providing the body and blood of Christ for us.

"God can accomplish vastly more than what we think could be." This is most certainly true—not only in His bodily presence in the Lord's Supper but also in bringing His dear children to the heavenly home that He has prepared for us.

"Oh, may I never fail to thank You day and night for Your true body and true blood, O God, my peace and light." Amen. (LSB *628:6*)

MARCH 3

A pilgrim and a stranger,
I journey here below;
Far distant is my country,
The home to which I go.
Here I must toil and travail,
Oft weary and opprest;
But there my God shall lead me
To everlasting rest.

Who would share
Abraham's blessing
Must Abraham's path pursue,
A stranger and a pilgrim,
Like him, must journey through.
The foes must be encountered,
The dangers must be passed;
A faithful soldier only
Receives the crown at
last. (*TLH* 586:1, 4)

Today's hymn, "A Pilgrim and a Stranger," from Paul Gerhardt is based on Psalm 39:12: "For I am a sojourner with You, a guest, like all my fathers." In other words, we are not home but on a journey, travelers bound for the far-distant country called heaven. This hymn teaches about the journey.

But the country at the end of our journey will be the beginning of a world in which everything has been made right. The pilgrim's new home in heaven will be the new creation, where new bodies are free from sin, sickness, fear, sadness, and tears. "But according to His promise we are waiting for new heavens and a new earth in which righteousness dwells" (2 Peter 3:13).

Throughout the hymn, we can sense the intense longing for this promised peace and rest. We are on Abraham's path, but we are ready whenever God wills to share Abraham's blessing and we say with Paul, "My desire is to depart and be with Christ, for that is far better" (Philippians 1:23).

"Despised and scorned, they sojourned here; but now, how glorious they appear! Those martyrs stand, a priestly band, God's throne forever near. On earth they wept through bitter years; now God has wiped away their tears, transformed their strife to heav'nly life, and freed them from their fears. They now enjoy the Sabbath rest, the heav'nly banquet of the blest; the Lamb, their Lord, at festive board Himself is host and guest." Amen. (LSB 676:2)

MARCH 4

I've met with storms and danger
E'en from my early years,
With enemies and conflicts,
With fightings and with fears.
There's nothing here
that tempts me
To wish a longer stay,
So I must hasten forward,
No halting or delay.

It is a well-worn pathway;
A host has gone before,
The holy saints and prophets,
The patriarchs of yore.
They trod the toilsome journey
In patience and in faith;
And them I fain would follow,
Like them in life and
death. (*TLH* 586:2–3)

TODAY WE CONSIDER AGAIN PAUL GERHARDT'S HYMN "A PILGRIM and a Stranger." These stanzas, which possibly stem from his personal experiences, give us insight into the steadfastness of the faithful believer. Pastor Gerhardt, his family, and his flock experienced plagues, famine, and the Thirty Years' War. Even though we do not face the same hardships and crosses, we, as saints in the church militant, face our own "storms and danger." We can readily relate to what he writes about our future and the often "toilsome journey" to that promised inheritance.

Gerhardt turns us to the example of those Christians who have "gone before," who in the face of storms, danger, enemies, and conflicts continued their journey with patience and unwavering faith in their Lord and Savior. Even when we feel, like Gerhardt, that nothing could tempt us to prolong this life, he encourages us to emulate the "holy saints and prophets . . . in patience and in faith." We have a sure hope in our Redeemer, who has gone before as the firstfruits in the resurrection and even now prepares a place for us in eternal joy (1 Corinthians 15:20; John 14:2–3).

"There shall we see in glory our dear Redeemer's face; the long-awaited story of heav'nly joy takes place: the patriarchs shall meet us, the prophets' holy band; apostles, martyrs greet us in that celestial land. There God shall from all evil forever make us free, from sin and from the devil, from all adversity, from sickness, pain, and sadness, from troubles, cares, and fears, and grant us heav'nly gladness and wipe away our tears." Amen. (LSB *514:2–3*)

MARCH 5

Cross of Jesus, cross of sorrow,
Where the blood of
Christ was shed,
Perfect man on thee did suffer,
Perfect God on thee has bled!

O mysterious condescending!
O abandonment sublime!
Very God Himself is bearing
All the sufferings of
time! (*LSB* 428:1, 3)

TODAY'S HYMN COMES FROM A LONGER WORK, A LIBRETTO BY William J. Sparrow Simpson from an oratorio called *The Crucifixion* by John Stainer. What a profound and solemn contemplation this hymn is, as we ponder the cross where God shed His blood for us—"very God Himself is bearing all the sufferings of time!"

In times of great sadness and sorrow, we may find it easier to speak than to sing, and even that can be difficult. Perhaps you have experienced this at funerals, memorial services, All Saints' services, and Good Friday services—the difficulty of maintaining the song in the face of deep sadness, when even a full sanctuary sounds more like an empty room. As much as we wish to sing, the words of these hymns can cause us to choke instead.

Nevertheless, part of our identity as Christians is to sing even while grieving and in tears. So, even if more liturgies are spoken during Lent, we continue to sing hymns. For it is good, right, and helpful to sing hymns of what happened on the "cross of Jesus," where "perfect man . . . did suffer" and "perfect God . . . has bled!"

"Do we pass that cross unheeding, breathing no repentant vow, though we see You wounded, bleeding, see Your thorn-encircled brow? Yet Your sinless death has brought us life eternal, peace, and rest; only what Your grace has taught us calms the sinner's deep distress. Jesus, may our hearts be burning with more fervent love for You; may our eyes be ever turning to behold Your cross anew till in glory, parted never from the blessed Savior's side, graven in our hearts forever, dwell the cross, the Crucified." Amen. (LSB *423:2–3*)

MARCH 6

Stricken, smitten, and afflicted,
See Him dying on the tree!
'Tis the Christ, by man rejected;
Yes, my soul, 'tis He, 'tis He!
'Tis the long-expected Prophet,
David's Son, yet David's Lord;
Proofs I see sufficient of it:
'Tis the true and faithful Word.

Tell me, ye who hear
Him groaning,
Was there ever grief like His?
Friends through fear His
cause disowning,
Foes insulting His distress;
Many hands were raised
to wound Him,
None would intervene to save;
But the deepest stroke
that pierced Him
Was the stroke that justice
gave. (*LSB* 451:1–2)

T***ODAY'S HYMN IS GRAPHIC AND INTENSELY PERSONAL, DESCRIBING*** the soul's horror at seeing "the true and faithful Word" dying on a tree. It sings of ultimate suffering, grief, and abandonment with no one stepping up to intervene; on the contrary, "the true and faithful Word" is rejected, disowned, and forsaken by all.

That true and faithful Word—"David's Son, yet David's Lord"—is Jesus Christ, the very Son of God, and it is He who is "stricken, smitten, and afflicted" for us. This hits home when we each know the bulk, weight, and putrid stench of our sins being carried by our Lord.

"But the deepest stroke that pierced Him was the stroke that justice gave." Jesus' coming to earth and what He had to suffer and endure on Calvary were necessary to satisfy what justice required to redeem those He loves with all His life. Yes, knowing that payment was needed *for me* is intensely personal.

"Where deep for us the spear was dyed, life's torrent rushing from His side, to wash us in the precious flood where flowed the water and the blood. Fulfilled is all that David told in sure prophetic song of old, that God the nations' king should be and reign in triumph from the tree." Amen. (LSB *455:2–3*)

MARCH 7

**Here we have a firm foundation,
Here the refuge of the lost:
Christ, the Rock of our salvation,
Is the name of which we boast;
Lamb of God, for sinners wounded,
Sacrifice to cancel guilt!
None shall ever be confounded
Who on Him their hope have built.** (*LSB* 451:4)

*"**Christ is faithful over God's house as a son. And we are*** His house, if indeed we hold fast our confidence and our boasting in our hope" (Hebrews 3:6). By God's grace, we live in that faithful house, a house built on the firm foundation of "Christ, the Rock of our salvation." In that name—and that name alone—may we boast. Or as Isaac Watts said, "Forbid it, Lord, that I should boast save in the death of Christ, my God" (*LSB* 425:2).

After suffering two strokes, Dr. Kenneth Korby, a beloved mentor of the church, was living in a nursing home when he received a visit from the Kantorei, the choir from Concordia Theological Seminary. His wife and daughter were there, and the staff gathered residents for the Kantorei to lead the service of Matins, so dearly loved by Kenneth. Sadly, Kenneth could no longer sing or speak the words. Yet when the choir came to the last line of the Te Deum, Dr. Korby shouted, "Never be confounded!" This was clear and from the depths of his soul as it powerfully proclaimed to everyone gathered the final words of the Te Deum: "O Lord, in You have I trusted; let me never be confounded" (*LSB*, p. 225).

"None shall ever be confounded who on Him their hope have built." Because Christ is faithful over God's house as a Son, we have hope in the very Lamb of God wounded for us sinners.

"In ev'ry time of need, before the judgment throne, Thy work, O Lamb of God, I'll plead, Thy merits, not mine own. Yet work, O Lord, in me as Thou for me hast wrought; and let my love the answer be to grace Thy love has brought." Amen. (LSB 452:6–7)

MARCH 8

Seek whom you may
To be your stay,
None can redeem his brother.
All helpers failed;
This man prevailed,
The God-man and none other,
Our Servant-King
Of whom we sing.
We're justified
Because He died,
The guilty being
guiltless. (*LSB* 557:2)

PAUL POSED THE QUESTION THIS WAY: "WHO WILL DELIVER ME from this body of death?" His answer: "Thanks be to God through Jesus Christ our Lord!" (Romans 7:24–25). Peter asked a similar question and provided the same answer: "Lord, to whom shall we go? You have the words of eternal life" (John 6:68). After Jesus' ascension into heaven, Peter would boldly confess Jesus in Jerusalem: "And there is salvation in no one else" (Acts 4:12). The answer is always Jesus.

Today's hymn invites us to "seek whom you may" and "seek where you may" (st. 1). It's not a cynical invitation, but the hymn writer knows that there can be only one answer. In the final analysis, we, like Paul and Peter, are drawn solely to Jesus as the solution to our seeking questions. The hymn writer puts it plainly: No human can redeem another human; no sinner can rescue a fellow sinner from eternal death. All such would-be helpers will fail. Only Jesus Christ, "the God-man," "our Servant-King," is up to the task. "We're justified because He died." Only Jesus can make the guilty guiltless.

So we build our lives—temporal and eternal—on Christ as the one solid foundation. His Word is sure and testifies to His redemptive work on our behalf, His dying and rising "once for all when He offered up Himself" (Hebrews 7:27). Thanks be to God, we are indeed "more than conquerors through Him who loved us" (Romans 8:37).

"Seek where you may to find a way that leads to your salvation. My heart is stilled, on Christ I build, He is the one foundation. His Word is sure, His works endure; He overthrows all evil foes; through Him I more than conquer." Amen. (LSB *557:1*)

MARCH 9

All for Christ I have forsaken
And have taken up my cross;
Worldly joy, its fame and fortune,
Now I count as worthless dross.

Who is sweeter than
Christ Jesus?
No good thing in Him I lack!
Hand to plow, at peace, I follow
Where He leads me . . . why
look back? (*LSB* 753:1–2)

DISCIPLES FOLLOW—THAT IS WHAT THEY DO. DISCIPLES LEARN this following from their kingdom's Lord in His own words: "If anyone would come after Me, let him deny himself and take up his cross daily and follow Me" (Luke 9:23). Following, then, becomes the disciple's blessed life in Christ's holy kingdom.

Yet these are not easy words to hear or live, as they describe how things work in the kingdom of Jesus Christ. Worldly joy, fame, and fortune are far from the path of Jesus' disciples, for we follow where He leads, learning to deny ourselves and take up our cross daily. Crosses are hard, but they are necessary in the kingdom for building up the saints!

Today's hymn asks a beautiful question: "Who is sweeter than Christ Jesus?" This question in hymnody hearkens to the twelfth-century Latin hymn writer Bernard of Clairvaux, who asked, "What sweeter love? What sweeter name?" In all cases, the answer is no love or name or lord is sweeter than Jesus Christ. These hymnists point us to such truths and believe this is all the disciple needs on the path of a faithful follower in the kingdom. There is no need to look back—it is a safe and blessed road ahead and grants abundant peace to the disciples of Jesus Christ.

"Then let us follow Christ, our Lord, and take the cross appointed and, firmly clinging to His Word, in suff'ring be undaunted. For those who bear the battle's strain the crown of heav'nly life obtain." Amen. (LSB 688:5)

MARCH 10

When God takes me
home to heaven,
Should this be the day I die,
God will keep my spouse
and children
As the apple of His eye.

Though the road
ahead be thorny,
Though dark clouds
all light obscure,
Though my cross-shaped
path grows steeper,
With the Lord, I am
secure. (*LSB* 753:4–5)

AS CHRIST'S DISCIPLES, OUR PATH MAY BE CROSS-SHAPED, THORNY, and steep. Yet it is always a path of rich blessing. On it, we tread every step in safety, for our heavenly Father is aware of and in control of even the smallest detail along the way. We are secure in His fatherly love and care. This is how Jesus Christ cares for each of His disciples—for you and me.

Our hymn today speaks of our complete trust in this gracious divine keeping, which extends from our days on earth through all our circumstances and even to eternity. Yet it is not only our paths that can test our trust. The hymn writer here acknowledges something that often goes unaddressed: concern for our family's welfare after our earthly departure. But with one line, the writer places that concern exactly where it should be—with God. "God will keep my spouse and children as the apple of His eye." We leave such matters with the One who will remain in control after He has taken us home to Him in heaven.

The same hymn writer who translated the text for the devotion wrote the hymn used for today's concluding prayer, which offers more wise advice about life as one of Christ's disciples.

"Be not afraid to suffer loss of all the things for which you pray, for He who faced for you the cross will give you strength to live each day. Seek first God's reign, His boundless grace, His holy name in all you do: Christ first and last in ev'ry place; all else will then be given you." Amen. (LSB *736:5–6*)

MARCH 11

Gone the past, unknown the future—
Grace supplies my daily breath;
Strong in Christ through death's dark valley,
Firm and faithful unto death. (*LSB* 753:3)

S*UBLIME GIFTS OF GRACE PERMEATE EVERY MOMENT OF LIFE FOR* a baptized child of God. Today's hymn resounds with a declaration that only one of His children could make—"grace supplies my daily breath." The flow of that grace commenced when God bestowed His strong name on us in Baptism, giving us a faith that transforms each breath into a gift of life by "grace."

I bind unto myself today
The strong name of the Trinity
By invocation of the same,
The Three in One and One in Three.

I bind unto myself today
The pow'r of God to hold and lead,
His eye to watch, His might to stay,
His ear to hearken to my need,
The wisdom of my God to teach,
His hand to guide, His shield to ward,
The Word of God to give me speech,
His heav'nly host to be my guard. (*LSB* 604:1, 3)

This baptismal grace is God's gift to us, His children. It is limitless, abounding in all things, even the unknown, and into the future. At all times, this beautiful baptismal life is richly sustained, nourished, and fed by Word and Sacraments. And this "Three in One and One in Three" promises to bring us safely "through death's dark valley, firm and faithful unto death."

"All who believe and are baptized shall see the Lord' salvation; baptized into the death of Christ, they are a new creation. Through Christ's redemption they shall stand among the glorious, heav'nly band of ev'ry tribe and nation. With one accord, O God, we pray: grant us Your Holy Spirit. Help us in our infirmity through Jesus' blood and merit. Grant us to grow in grace each day that by this sacrament we may eternal life inherit." Amen. (LSB *601*)

MARCH 12

O love, how deep, how broad, how high,
Beyond all thought and fantasy,
That God, the Son of God, should take
Our mortal form for mortals' sake! (*LSB* 544:1)

PAUL WRITES ABOUT "THE LOVE OF CHRIST THAT SURPASSES knowledge" (Ephesians 3:19), a love that in its fullness is simply beyond human understanding. In today's hymn, writer Thomas à Kempis not only ponders that love but emphasizes that it is a deeply personal love that Christ exercised "for us," that phrase occurring no less than thirteen times within four of its seven hymn stanzas! While we are unable fully to fathom God's great love—its depth, breadth, and height—we can be certain that it is for us and that it brings us eternal salvation.

God's plan of salvation was not relegated to an angel as some sort of heavenly representative or deputy. Instead, the Son of God took on human flesh and came Himself to save His beloved creatures. For us He was baptized. For us He overcame Satan's temptations, even after a forty-day period of fasting. For us He prayed, taught, and healed—and continues to do so *for us* today, as He pleads our case before His Father. For us He allowed Himself to be betrayed, to be mocked with a crown of thorns, to be nailed to a cross, to die a shameful death bearing our sins. "For us He gave His dying breath" (st. 5). He rose from death for us, ascended into heaven for us, and sent the Holy Spirit that He had promised, again for us, "to guide, to strengthen, and to cheer" (st. 6).

This hymn text gives us the blessed opportunity to rehearse the whole story of God's great love for us in His beloved Son, Jesus Christ. We have the assurance that His love for us is all that we need, now and in eternity.

"All glory to our Lord and God for love so deep, so high, so broad; the Trinity whom we adore forever and forevermore." Amen. (LSB 544:7)

MARCH 13

As rebels, Lord, who foolishly have wandered
Far from Your love—unfed, unclean, unclothed—
Dare we recall Your wealth so rashly squandered,
Dare hope to glean that bounty which we loathed? (*LSB* 612:1)

T***HE PRODIGAL SON IS ONE OF THE MOST FAMOUS REBELS EVER.*** And in his rebellion, he wandered far from his father's love; he rashly squandered what had been freely given to him and ended up unfed, unclean, and unclothed. This spoiled son was driven by all-consuming selfishness, greed, and lust, and he let that lust consume and push him down an utterly shameful path.

However, the heart of the parable of the prodigal son is not about the sins of the son—either son. Rather, it is about the boundless mercy and unconditional love of the father.

This parable is a master lesson by Jesus for us all. For we, too, have been given everything by our loving Father, who forgives and forgives and forgives us. Yet we, too, wander and squander the bounty of gifts from our Father. We, too, are foolish, sinful rebels gone astray.

But for the child of God, the story does not end there. No, our story ends with us in the arms of our loving and merciful Father. His loving arms are always open to receive us once again in forgiveness.

"Lord, to You I make confession: I have sinned and gone astray, I have multiplied transgression, chosen for myself my way. Led by You to see my errors, Lord, I tremble at Your terrors. Yet, though conscience's voice appall me, Father, I will seek Your face; though Your child I dare not call me, yet receive me in Your grace. Do not for my sins forsake me; let Your wrath not overtake me." Amen. (LSB *608:1–2*)

MARCH 14

Still we return, our contrite words rehearsing,
Speech, that within Your warm embrace soon dies;
All of our guilt, our shame, our pain reversing
As tears of joy and welcome fill Your eyes. (*LSB* 612:2)

IN THE PARABLE OF THE PRODIGAL SON, THE LOVING AND FORGIVING father greeted his contrite son with a warm embrace of genuine welcome and tears of gladness. Similarly, our heavenly Father waits to hear these words from us: "Father, I have sinned against heaven and before You" (see Luke 15:18). And by faith, we know that the arms of our heavenly Father are always open to receive us; to remove our guilt, shame, and pain; and to turn our remorse into a flood of joyful tears. For we were lost but are now found!

We are children who can now understand King David's song and gladly sing it with him: "You have turned for me my mourning into dancing; You have loosed my sackcloth and clothed me with gladness" (Psalm 30:11). Or as Martin Luther often explained, our repentance is a prelude to joy.

"I have sinned" are words that identify us as the blood-bought sons and daughters of God, the Father Almighty, Maker of heaven and earth. And as His sons and daughters, we rehearse these critically important words of contrition for a lifetime, for we are never free of our need for His mercy and forgiveness.

And we, together with God's children throughout the world, pray these beautiful, life-giving words in the Lord's Prayer: "Our Father, who art in heaven . . . forgive us our trespasses." A prelude to joy—Luther was so right!

"Lord, on You I cast my burden—sink it in the deepest sea! Let me know Your gracious pardon, cleanse me from iniquity. Let Your Spirit leave me never; make me only Yours forever." Amen. (LSB 608:4)

MARCH 15

A feast of love for us You are preparing;
We who were lost, You give an honored place!
"Come, eat; come, drink, and be no more despairing—
Here taste again the treasures of My grace." (*LSB* 612:3)

WE HAVE A FATHER WHO KNOWS THE SECRET AND DARKEST places of our minds. He knows our sordid wanderings and sinful past and our ungrateful hearts. Yes, He knows everything about us! Nevertheless, He runs out to embrace us with unconditional love, boundless mercy, and open arms. We do not deserve any of this, yet He is ready, even eager, to forgive us repeatedly, make us whole, and fill us with His peace.

The triune God does this for us every week in His Divine Service with His glorious Feast, filling us with the gifts we need for a new week, a week filled with Him. And each week we come again into His presence hungry, thirsty, weary, battered, and needy.

We say the words He wants to hear: "O God, be merciful to me." And He then speaks to us in return, "Come, eat; come drink, and be no more despairing—here taste again the treasures of My grace." So week after week, we are His guests at His Table, where His body and blood are given for us, and we emerge at peace with Him.

"O Lord, my God, to Thee I pray: O cast me not in wrath away! Let Thy good Spirit ne'er depart, but let Him draw to Thee my heart that truly penitent I be: O God, be merciful to me! O Jesus, let Thy precious blood be to my soul a cleansing flood. Turn not, O Lord, Thy guest away, but grant that justified I may go to my house at peace with Thee: O God, be merciful to me!" Amen. (LSB 613:2–3)

MARCH 16

To Thee, omniscient Lord of all,
In grief and shame I humbly call;
I see my sins against Thee, Lord,
The sins of thought and deed and word.
They press me sore; I cry to Thee:
O God, be merciful to me! (*LSB* 613:1)

EACH STANZA OF TODAY'S HYMN-PRAYER CONCLUDES WITH "O God, be merciful to me!" In grief and shame, we confess that we have sinned in "thought and deed and word." Our sins press on us. And we acknowledge that, because God is omniscient, He already knows the deepest sins of our inmost being—a terrifying thought! All we can do is cry to God for mercy. But the good news is that is all we need to do!

When Jesus told the parable of the Pharisee and the tax collector (Luke 18:9–14), He contrasted the proud Pharisee, who believed himself fully righteous, with the tax collector who "would not even lift up his eyes to heaven, but beat his breast, saying, 'God, be merciful to me, a sinner!'" Today's prayer places us right alongside that tax collector. Like him, we cannot bear to raise our eyes to heaven, for we know our sins. We join that tax collector in praying, "God, be merciful to me, a sinner."

And then we hear the sweet words of Jesus: "I tell you, this man went down to his house justified." How can this be? John provides an explanation: "If we say we have no sin, we deceive ourselves, and the truth is not in us. If we confess our sins, He is faithful and just to forgive our sins and to cleanse us from all unrighteousness" (1 John 1:8–9). God has had mercy on us for Jesus' sake!

"O Jesus, let Thy precious blood be to my soul a cleansing flood. Turn not, O Lord, Thy guest away, but grant that justified I may go to my house at peace with Thee: O God, be merciful to me!" Amen. (LSB *613:3*)

MARCH 17

I bind unto myself today
The strong name of the Trinity
By invocation of the same,
The Three in One and One in Three. (*LSB* 604:1)

FROM OUR BAPTISM, WE HAVE BEEN WEARING THE STRONG NAME of the Holy Trinity, which has marked us as God's own children and given us the baptismal life. It stands to reason that, as God's baptized children, we could not care more deeply about that strong name that planted faith in us and continues to give us life.

St. Patrick, whom we remember today, also cared deeply about that strong name. This is especially important because Patrick lived when the doctrine of the Holy Trinity was seriously challenged. Therefore, Patrick became a strong defender of the strong name. Statements spelling out the precise facts about God—Father, Son, and Holy Spirit—can be found everywhere in his writing and poetry.

The hymn "I Bind unto Myself Today" is perhaps Patrick's best-known example of this defense. One cannot miss the depth, breadth, and power manifest in the strong name of the Holy Trinity presented here. And here is Patrick's magnificent Christological stanza 8:

> Christ be with me, Christ within me,
> Christ behind me, Christ before me,
> Christ beside me, Christ to win me,
> Christ to comfort and restore me,
> Christ beneath me, Christ above me,
> Christ in quiet, Christ in danger,
> Christ in hearts of all that love me,
> Christ in mouth of friend and stranger.
> (*LSB Companion to the Hymns*, vol. 1, p. 695)

"I bind unto myself today the pow'r of God to hold and lead, His eye to watch, His might to stay, His ear to hearken to my need, the wisdom of my God to teach, His hand to guide, His shield to ward, the Word of God to give me speech, His heav'nly host to be my guard." Amen. (LSB *604:3*)

MARCH 18

**All men living are but mortal,
Yea, all flesh must fade as grass;
Only through death's
gloomy portal
To eternal life we pass.
This frail body here must perish
Ere the heav'nly joys it cherish,
Ere it gain the free reward
For the ransomed of the Lord.**

**There is joy beyond our telling,
Where so many saints
have gone;
Thousands, thousands,
there are dwelling,
Worshiping before the throne,
There the seraphim are shining,
Evermore in chorus joining:
"Holy, holy, holy, Lord!
Triune God, for aye
adored!"** (*TLH* 601:1, 4)

NOTHING PUTS THINGS INTO PERSPECTIVE FOR FLESH-AND-blood, breathing, living people like this passage: "All flesh is grass, and all its beauty is like the flower of the field" (Isaiah 40:6). We all know that the stunning flowers of summer in the fields have a fleeting life. Today's hymn, based on that passage, is a powerful reminder that all mortal flesh is like those flowers, frail and momentary, as is this earthly life, and *all* will fade as the grass.

Yet that fading and dying only signals a beginning for those who believe and are baptized—now, their souls can leave this earth, go through that gloomy portal, and go home to be with their Lord as one of His ransomed. This hymn paints a heavenly picture that could not be more splendid and breathtaking! Thousands upon thousands of saints and angels before the throne, raising their superb and exalted "Holy, holy, holy" to the triune God!

"O blessed saints in bright array now safely home in endless day, extol the Lord, who with His Word sustained you on the way. The steep and narrow path you trod; you toiled and sowed the Word abroad; rejoice and bring your fruits and sing before the throne of God. The myriad angels raise their song; O saints, sing with that happy throng! Lift up one voice; let heav'n rejoice in our Redeemer's song!" Amen. (LSB *676:3*)

MARCH 19

We sing our thanks for Joseph,
The guardian of our Lord,
Who faithfully taught Jesus
Through craft and deed and word.
Grant wisdom, Lord, and patience
To parents ev'rywhere
Who guide and teach the children
Entrusted to their care. (*LSB* 517:14)

On this day, the Church remembers Joseph, husband to Mary and guardian of our Lord, who has long been associated with caring fatherhood and skilled craftsmanship.

Joseph was a humble craftsman. Yet God gave him the highest honor of serving as our Lord's earthly father as Jesus grew up. And in Joseph's role, we see a stellar example of a father who "faithfully taught Jesus through craft and deed and word."

Earthly fatherhood is chiefly taught and modeled for the children of the heavenly Father in the relationship God has with us, His children, so clearly taught in the Introduction to the Lord's Prayer with two words: "Our Father." We treasure that relationship and use it every day, sometimes every hour. What a blessed relationship we have with our heavenly Father! In that relationship, God *always* wants us to turn to Him, to make Him the heart and center of our lives and our homes. And for those who are ourselves fathers, God calls us to faithfully raise our children, as Joseph did, to bring our children to Him in Holy Baptism, to bring our children to Him in the Divine Service, to bring our children to Him in catechesis, and to bring our children to Him for all life decisions.

"Our Father, who from heav'n above bids all of us to live in love as members of one family and pray to You in unity, teach us no thoughtless words to say but from our inmost hearts to pray." Amen. (LSB *766:1*)

MARCH 20

Sing, my tongue, the glorious battle;
Sing the ending of the fray.
Now above the cross, the trophy,
Sound the loud triumphant lay;
Tell how Christ, the world's redeemer,
As a victim won the day.

Tell how, when at length the fullness
Of the appointed time was come,
He, the Word, was born of woman,
Left for us His Father's home,
Blazed the path of true obedience,
Shone as light amidst the gloom. (*LSB* 454:1–2)

APART FROM THE HOLY SPIRIT, OUR TONGUES DO NOT KNOW WHAT to sing, but with Him, they can tell and sing glorious truths. We acknowledge our dependence on Him by speaking with David, "O Lord, open my lips" (Psalm 51:15). Yes, when our Lord opens our hearts and lips, our tongues have marvelous truths to confess.

Today's early Latin hymn is a treasure of those truths—a rich masterpiece on "Christ, the world's redeemer." In it, we sing the story of all time, starting at the divinely appointed time when God the Son left His Father's home to be born of a woman. What followed was a whole life of faithful obedience to the Father's will, of Christ saying, "Yes, Father, yes, most willingly I'll bear what You command Me. My will conforms to Your decree, I'll do what You have asked Me" (*LSB* 438:3).

"Sing, My Tongue, the Glorious Battle" is Latin hymnody at its best, for it is a rich, sung confession in which the church is able to rehearse again and again what Christ won for us on the cross, where He "as a victim won the day."

"Come, see these things and ponder, your soul will fill with wonder as blood streams from each pore. Through grief beyond all knowing from His great heart came flowing sighs welling from its deepest core." Amen. (LSB 453:2)

MARCH 21

Thus, with thirty years accomplished,
He went forth from Nazareth,
Destined, dedicated, willing,
Did His work, and met His death;
Like a lamb He humbly yielded
On the cross His dying breath.

Faithful cross, true sign of triumph,
Be for all the noblest tree;
None in foliage, none in blossom,
None in fruit thine equal be;
Symbol of the world's redemption,
For the weight that hung on thee! (*LSB* 454:3–4)

LUCAS CRANACH, THE SIXTEENTH-CENTURY PAINTER WHOSE works captured the heart of the Reformation, created an altarpiece that features Luther preaching from the pulpit *through a crucifix* to the people. This painting accurately illustrates the centrality of the Gospel of Jesus Christ in all of Luther's preaching. Luther could do no other, for he saw everything through the lens of what had happened on the cross of Jesus. Therefore, every word Luther spoke was seen through the lens of that crucifix.

"Symbol of the world's redemption, for the weight that hung on thee!" The faithful cross is the true sign of Christ's triumph. Everything in the life of the church, all preaching, teaching, and occasions, is to be seen through this blessed crucifix at the center of everything, just as Cranach portrayed. Another way of saying this is that, for the faithful in Christ, all is now seen through their beautiful eyes of faith. "Be for all the noblest tree; none in foliage, none in blossom, none in fruit thine equal be."

"O tree of beauty, tree most fair, ordained those holy limbs to bear: Gone is thy shame, each crimsoned bough proclaims the King of Glory now." Amen. (LSB 455:5)

MARCH 22

The royal banners forward go;
The cross shows forth redemption's flow,
Where He, by whom our flesh was made,
Our ransom in His flesh has paid:

Where deep for us the spear was dyed,
Life's torrent rushing from His side,
To wash us in the precious flood
Where flowed the water and the blood. (*LSB* 455:1–2)

S***OLEMN PROCESSIONS CAN BE BREATHTAKING, BUT NONE MORE*** than the royal one in today's hymn, where the royal banners of our King Jesus Christ move slowly on a path to His cross. As His children, we care deeply about what happened on that tree, through which we were washed clean as our King gave us life and where our ransom was won. There is no other procession, no other tree, and no other King like this!

What happened on our King's solemn path is vividly painted in this hymn sung on Holy Cross Day and during Holy Week. Hymns, like paintings and sermons, can powerfully proclaim truths of what happened throughout the precious life of our Lord and Savior and then apply those truths to our lives. And in this hymn, what happened on that day of days is strikingly preached in these words: "Where deep for us the spear was dyed, life's torrent rushing from His side, to wash us in the precious flood where flowed the water and the blood."

"Make me see Your great distress, anguish, and affliction, bonds and stripes and wretchedness and Your crucifixion; make me see how scourge and rod, spear and nails did wound You, how for them You died, O God, who with thorns had crowned You. Grant that I Your passion view with repentant grieving. Let me not bring shame to You by unholy living. How could I refuse to shun ev'ry sinful pleasure since for me God's only Son suffered without measure?" Amen. (LSB 440:2, 4)

MARCH 23

O tree of beauty, tree most fair,
Ordained those holy limbs to bear:
Gone is thy shame, each crimsoned bough
Proclaims the King of Glory now. (*LSB* 455:5)

TODAY WE PONDER THE TREE THAT BECAME OUR "TREE OF LIFE" in a beloved sixth-century Latin text by Venantius Fortunatus, a stunning work about the tree that means the most to each of us—because that tree gave us life!

Then, jumping centuries to the present, we can sing of that same tree in Pastor Stephen Starke's masterpiece "The Tree of Life":

Now from that tree of Jesus' shame
Flows life eternal in His name;
For all who trust and will believe,
Salvation's living fruit receive.
And of this fruit so pure and sweet
The Lord invites the world to eat,
To find within this cross of wood
The tree of life with ev'ry good. (*LSB* 561:4)

This tree is not a simple cross of wood, for it was ordained to bear the precious, dying limbs of God's own Son. And as a good and gracious result, the fruit of this tree is wonderfully pure and sweet, as it gives life and salvation to all who trust and believe.

In Luke 19, Zacchaeus climbed into what he thought was an ordinary tree to get a better look at Jesus. But then, by God's grace, that common tree became for him a tree of life, for Zacchaeus would never be the same after that. Because of Calvary's "tree of beauty, tree most fair," we, too, are never the same. Thanks be to God!

"Fulfilled is all that David told in sure prophetic song of old, that God the nations' king should be and reign in triumph from the tree, on whose hard arms, so widely flung, the weight of this world's ransom hung, the price of humankind to pay and spoil the spoiler of his prey." Amen. (LSB 455:3–4)

MARCH 24

Lamb of God, pure and holy,
Who on the cross didst suffer,
Ever patient and lowly,
Thyself to scorn didst offer.
All sins Thou borest for us,
Else had despair reigned o'er us:
Have mercy on us, O Jesus! O Jesus! (*LSB* 434:1)

"God will provide for Himself the lamb for a burnt offering" (Genesis 22:8). Abraham had wood and fire, but as Isaac alertly observed, there was no sacrificial lamb. There would soon come a point, however, when Isaac learned the awful truth: that at God's command, his father was about to sacrifice him. But God provided a substitute—a ram caught in a thicket by his horns—so that Isaac didn't have to die.

God will provide the lamb. The awful truth is that we all deserve to die eternally for our sins. But God provided a substitute—the Lamb of God, His Son, Jesus. While Abraham was spared from sacrificing his son, God the Father did not spare His only Son. He *could not* spare His Son if His rebellious creatures were to be saved and live forever in the presence of their Creator. Thus, the holy Son of God suffered on the cross, bearing all the sins of all people of all time. Now we live not in despair but in the confidence of eternal life, won for us by the Lamb of God.

Each week before receiving Christ's body and blood in His Holy Supper, we remember Jesus' sacrifice, confessing with John the Baptist that Jesus is "the Lamb of God, who takes away the sin of the world" (John 1:29). To Him we pray, "Have mercy on us. . . . Thy peace be with us" (sts. 2, 3).

"This Lamb is Christ, the soul's great friend, the Lamb of God, our Savior, whom God the Father chose to send to gain for us His favor. 'Go forth, My Son,' the Father said, 'and free My children from their dread of guilt and condemnation. The wrath and stripes are hard to bear, but by Your passion they will share the fruit of Your salvation.'" Amen. (LSB *438:2*)

MARCH 25

Then gentle Mary meekly bowed her head;
"To me be as it pleaseth God," she said.
"My soul shall laud and magnify God's holy name."
Most highly favored lady,
Gloria! (*LSB* 356:3)

TODAY WE REMEMBER THE ANNUNCIATION OF OUR LORD—WHEN the angel Gabriel announced to Mary that the time had come for God's plan that would change everything for all eternity. This stunning plan was necessary because of what happened long ago with another woman, Eve, in the Garden of Eden. Eve was approached not by a good angel like Gabriel but by the devil himself, and Eve believed him and conceived sin. What happened that day led to death for us all.

But God could not leave it there, for He loved us and announced His plan to rescue and save us already in Genesis 3:15. And since death had made its entrance through a woman, it is fitting that life be returned through a woman. Therefore, the opposite of Eve happens; by the Holy Spirit, Mary conceives the One who would rescue us.

We can learn much from this lowly yet "highly favored" maiden about responding to God's will and rescue plan. She humbly submits herself to His Word. The mother of our Lord is a model of hearing God's Word and having the trusting response of faith created by that Word.

Soon, Mary's response to this good news would explode in a song like no other—the Magnificat—as she sings, "My soul magnifies the Lord, and my Spirit rejoices in God my Savior, for He . . . has done great things for me" (Luke 1:46–48, 49). Her glorious canticle is the superb model for all our earthly singing, for it confesses what our God has done!

"We sing of Mary, mother, fair maiden, full of grace. She bore the Christ, our brother, who came to save our race. May we, with her, surrender ourselves to Your command and lay upon Your altar our gifts of heart and hand." Amen. (LSB 855:8)

MARCH 26

Sheep that from the fold did stray
No true shepherd e'er forsaketh;
Weary souls that lost their way
Christ, the Shepherd, gently taketh
In His arms that they may live:
Jesus sinners doth receive.

I, a sinner, come to Thee
With a penitent confession.
Savior, mercy show to me;
Grant for all my sins remission.
Let these words my soul relieve:
Jesus sinners doth receive. (*LSB* 609:3–4)

THE GOOD SHEPHERD LEAVES THE NINETY-NINE AND SEEKS THE lost one. He would not think of forsaking that one straying sheep. Then, upon finding His lost sheep, He rejoices greatly and carries it back to the fold (Matthew 18:12–13). "Weary souls that lost their way Christ, the Shepherd, gently taketh in His arms."

Not all shepherds are equal. Some would forsake their sheep, some lead them astray, and some care nothing about them. But our shepherd is the Good Shepherd, and He left heaven for the sake of His dear sheep. Yes, He came all the way down to this earth for His lost sheep, and eventually He had to die for them.

This Good Shepherd wants to hear the penitential cry of His sheep so that He can once again shower His mercy on them. He knows they are sinners, and He stands ready to grant sinners forgiveness, healing, and peace. "Let these words my soul relieve: Jesus sinners doth receive."

"Oh, how blest it is to know: were as scarlet my transgression, it shall be as white as snow by Thy blood and bitter passion; for these words I now believe: Jesus sinners doth receive. Now my conscience is at peace; from the Law I stand acquitted. Christ hath purchased my release and my ev'ry sin remitted. Naught remains my soul to grieve: Jesus sinners doth receive." Amen. (LSB *609:5–6*)

MARCH 27

It is Your work alone
That I am now converted;
O'er Satan's work in me
You have Your pow'r asserted.
Your mercy and Your grace
That rise afresh each morn
Have turned my stony heart
Into a heart newborn. (*LSB* 703:2)

JESUS TOLD NICODEMUS, "UNLESS ONE IS BORN AGAIN HE CANNOT see the kingdom of God" (John 3:3). How blessed we are that being born again is not something that we must achieve on our own. In fact, we *cannot* do so. Jesus went on to tell how one is born again: "Unless one is born of water and the Spirit, he cannot enter the kingdom of God" (John 3:5). In the Sacrament of Holy Baptism, water combined with the Word of God is a "new birth in the Holy Spirit" (Small Catechism, Baptism, Third Part). Paul writes, "He saved us, not because of works done by us in righteousness, but according to His own mercy, by the washing of regeneration and renewal of the Holy Spirit" (Titus 3:5).

In today's hymn, we acknowledge that it is God's work alone that we are converted, that our hearts are "newborn." And each new day finds God's mercy and grace richly poured out on us, as He continually keeps us in His care and defends us from the temptations and doubts with which the devil would afflict us.

Through water and the Word, God the Holy Spirit causes us to be born again—so that we *will* enter the kingdom of God. He is the faithful guide who shows us "the way that leads me to salvation" (st. 3). The hymn writer exclaims, "How can I thank You, Lord, for all Your loving-kindness" (st. 1)! God has accomplished salvation for us, and we will spend a blessed eternity in His presence giving thanks to Him for this great gift.

"Lord, You have raised me up to joy and exultation and clearly shown the way that leads me to salvation. My sins are washed away; for this I thank You, Lord. Now with my heart and soul all evil I abhor." Amen. (LSB 703:3)

MARCH 28

My Lord, You here have led me
To this most holy place
And with Yourself have fed me
The treasures of Your grace;
For You have freely given
What earth could never buy,
The bread of life from heaven,
That now I shall not die. (*LSB* 642:2)

TODAY'S HYMN-PRAYER CONCERNING THE LORD'S SUPPER provides an important perspective that we might otherwise miss: "My Lord, You here have led me." We know that our Lord gives us His true body and blood for the forgiveness of sins in His Holy Supper. But do we stop to think that—even before receiving that richness—it is the Lord who has led us to the Sacrament?

Think back to the night on which Jesus was betrayed, the night when He instituted His Holy Supper. The disciples weren't asking for or even contemplating such a rich gift; indeed, they must have been more than a little surprised at what was taking place as they shared that last meal with Jesus. But His words could not have been more clear: "This is My body. . . . This is My blood . . . poured out for many for the forgiveness of sins" (Matthew 26:26, 28).

Jesus provided what His disciples could not have imagined or asked for. He provided what His disciples—then and now—didn't even know that they needed. This is precisely the way our God proceeds: He acts, He provides, and we receive. He leads us to this sacred meal of everlasting life, where He feeds us "the bread of life from heaven, that now I shall not die."

"You gave me all I wanted; this food can death destroy. And You have freely granted the cup of endless joy. My Lord, I do not merit the favor You have shown, and all my soul and spirit bow down before Your throne." Amen. (LSB *642:3*)

MARCH 29

Thy works, not mine, O Christ,
Speak gladness to this heart;
They tell me all is done,
They bid my fear depart.
To whom save Thee,
Who canst alone
For sin atone,
Lord, shall I flee?

Thy cross, not mine, O Christ,
Has borne the crushing load
Of sins that none could bear
But the incarnate God.
To whom save Thee,
Who canst alone
For sin atone,
Lord, shall I flee? (*LSB* 565:1, 3)

TWO RECURRING WORDS IN THIS HYMN ARE VITAL TO understanding salvation and eternal life: "not mine." Our works do not and cannot bring us gladness of heart and peace of conscience in this life. Nor can they ever atone for our sins or bring us to the eternal life that God has always desired for the dear children that He Himself has created. It is not about us but about Christ, who became incarnate to save us.

Christ's works "tell me all is done," thus taking away all my fears about death. *Christ's death* "has paid the ransom due" (st. 4)—for all the sins of all the people who would ever live. *His wounds* "heal my bruised soul" (st. 2), and *His stripes* provide "the balm that makes me whole" (st. 2). Those painful torments inflicted on *Him* provide healing for me. It was *Christ's cross* where He bore the crushing load of sin. *Christ's righteousness* covers us and enables us finally to stand before God as redeemed sinners, worthy—only for Christ's sake—to inherit eternal life.

"To whom save Thee, who canst alone for sin atone, Lord, shall I flee?" Only to Christ!

"Thy death, not mine, O Christ, has paid the ransom due; ten thousand deaths like mine would have been all too few. To whom save Thee, who canst alone for sin atone, Lord, shall I flee? Thy righteousness, O Christ, alone can cover me; no righteousness avails save that which is of Thee. To whom save Thee, who canst alone for sin atone, Lord, shall I flee?" Amen. (LSB 565:4–5)

MARCH 30

Oh, how blest it is to know:
Were as scarlet my
transgression,
It shall be as white as snow
By Thy blood and bitter passion;
For these words I now believe:
Jesus sinners doth receive.

Now my conscience is at peace;
From the Law I stand acquitted.
Christ hath purchased
my release
And my ev'ry sin remitted.
Naught remains my
soul to grieve:
Jesus sinners doth
receive. (*LSB* 609:5–6)

I*N HIS VERY FIRST CHAPTER, THE PROPHET ISAIAH SPEAKS OF A* marvelous transformation: "Though your sins are like scarlet, they shall be as white as snow; though they are red like crimson, they shall become like wool" (v. 18). What a picture this is! Scarlet is transformed to a pure white, like newly fallen snow or a lamb's wool. How does this happen? The hymn writer makes clear that this transformation comes about through Jesus' "blood and bitter passion." Peter points to "the precious blood of Christ, like that of a lamb without blemish or spot" (1 Peter 1:19), while Paul summarizes, "Since, therefore, we have now been justified by His blood, much more shall we be saved by Him from the wrath of God" (Romans 5:9).

This transformation from the red stain of guilt to the pure white of innocence is accomplished purely through Jesus' atoning sacrifice. This transformation brings complete acquittal and innocence from the guilt of sin and a conscience at peace, with nothing to grieve our souls. We live our lives freed from guilt so that we can serve our Lord and our neighbors through our varied vocations.

"I have been forgiven; and when I this earth must leave, I shall find an open heaven" (st. 7). "Jesus sinners doth receive"—forgiving us and taking us to Himself for an eternity of the greatest joy. Thanks be to God!

"Jesus sinners doth receive; also I have been forgiven; and when I this earth must leave, I shall find an open heaven. Dying, still to Him I cleave: Jesus sinners doth receive." Amen. (LSB *609:7*)

MARCH 31

I am content! My
Jesus ever lives,
In whom my heart is pleased.
He has fulfilled the
Law of God for me,
God's wrath He has appeased.
Since He in death
could perish never,
I also shall not die forever.
I am content!
I am content!

I am content! My
Jesus is my light,
My radiant sun of grace.
His cheering rays beam
blessings forth for all,
Sweet comfort, hope, and peace.
This Easter sun has
brought salvation
And everlasting exultation.
I am content!
I am content! (*LSB* 468:1, 3)

PAUL WROTE TO TIMOTHY THAT "GODLINESS WITH CONTENTMENT is great gain, for we brought nothing into the world, and we cannot take anything out of the world" (1 Timothy 6:6–7). Today's hymn is a clear and beautiful statement of the *source* of the Christian's contentment.

We can join the hymn writer in his constant refrain "I am content!" solely because of what Jesus has done for us. He "fulfilled the Law of God" for us, thus appeasing God's wrath toward sin and balancing the divine scales of justice. Because Jesus defeated death through His glorious resurrection on Easter Sunday, we "also shall not die forever." No matter what our earthly means and possessions might be, in the final analysis, what ultimately matters is that eternal life is ours through the saving work of Jesus. His light provides us with "sweet comfort, hope, and peace" for all the days of our earthly lives. "I am content!"

But there is yet more! One day we shall all be "awakened from the dead, arising glorious" to live forever in the presence of our Savior (st. 4). On that great day, our bodies will rise, glorified and perfect, to be united with our immortal souls for an eternity of bliss and happiness. "I am content!"

"I am content! At length I shall be free, awakened from the dead, arising glorious evermore to be with You, my living head. The chains that hold my body, sever; then shall my soul rejoice forever. I am content! I am content!" Amen. (LSB 468:4)

APRIL 1

Banners of triumph, be unfurled!
Trumpets, sound throughout the world!
Crying and sighs, give way to singing:
Life from death, our Lord is bringing!
Let there begin the jubilee—
Christ has gained the victory! (*LSB* 481:3)

THE HYMNS OF THE TIME OF EASTER BRING US BEAUTIFUL, VIVID descriptions of the tremendous joy and blessing of the resurrection.

In today's hymn by Stephen Starke, we can all but see the grand, impressive, awe-filled procession with spectacular banners and festival trumpets sounding victory and triumph throughout the world. Such a procession is stunning to the point of being hard to imagine! Gone are darkness and gloom, crying and sighing. Now there is only a jubilee of joyous singing and music-making. "Life from death, our Lord is bringing! Let there begin the jubilee—Christ has gained the victory!"

The whole world changed with our Lord's victory. Nothing will ever be the same, and thanks be to God for that! It was the monumental change that God knew needed to happen after the fall into sin, but it meant death for His Son. Our joyful celebration in Eastertide must never forget the precious price paid for our victory. God gave His Son, His dearest possession, for our victory! Let all our days be filled with heartfelt thanks and praise that nothing will ever be the same through His Son's victory over sin, death, and the devil. "Banners of triumph, be unfurled!"

"He lives to silence all my fears; He lives to wipe away my tears; He lives to calm my troubled heart; He lives all blessings to impart. He lives and grants me daily breath; He lives, and I shall conquer death; He lives my mansion to prepare; He lives to bring me safely there." Amen. (LSB 461:5, 7)

APRIL 2

Scatter the darkness, break the gloom;
Sun, reveal an empty tomb
Shining with joy for all our sorrows,
Hope and peace for all tomorrows,
Life uneclipsed by doubt and dread:
Christ has risen from the dead! (*LSB* 481:1)

ON THE MOST SORROWFUL DAY, WHEN ADAM AND EVE CHOSE the serpent's voice over God's, the world was enveloped in profound darkness and sorrow. Thankfully, the God of heaven and earth did not abandon His creation. He had a plan that would disperse the darkness and shatter the gloom. It was a plan that would cost Him dearly.

Our hymn today concludes God's salvation plan by dissolving the deep darkness and breaking the gloom once and for all over creation with the words, "It is finished" (John 19:30). Now everything is new, bright white, and shining because of the most incredible news ever announced: Christ has risen from the dead! Alleluia! God paid the costly sacrifice of His Son and won the victory. Alleluia!

And now, in the wake of this glorious resurrection, hope, peace, joy, and gladness are ushered in for all our tomorrows. Easter's empty tomb scatters the darkness and breaks the gloom, banishing all doubt, fear, and dread like nothing else could. The most sorrowful day has been replaced with the most joyous one possible.

"This is a sight that gladdens—what peace it doth impart! Now nothing ever saddens the joy within my heart. No gloom shall ever shake, no foe shall ever take the hope which God's own Son in love for me has won. Now I will cling forever to Christ, my Savior true; my Lord will leave me never, whate'er He passes through. He rends death's iron chain; He breaks through sin and pain; He shatters hell's grim thrall; I follow Him through all." Amen. (LSB *467:3, 6*)

APRIL 3

Bearing the standard from on high
As the Lamb of God to die;
He who for us, so cruelly treated,
Lives again—our foes defeated!
Where is your sting, O death and grave?
Christ has shown His strength to save! (*LSB* 481:2)

THERE IS AN EXCELLENT REASON WHY THIS CORINTHIANS TEXT is included in most Christian funerals and memorial services: "O death, where is your victory? O death, where is your sting?" (1 Corinthians 15:55). These are precisely the words we need to hear when standing at the coffin of a loved one, for they put death in its proper context, which is *Alleluia! Christ is risen! He is risen indeed! Alleluia!* Now death has lost its sting.

When standing at the coffin of a Christian, it may look like death has won, and so it seemed when our Lord was buried in a tomb. *Not true!* Solely by God's grace, the opposite is true, for in the death of the Lamb of God, *death itself was defeated*! Now death is dead! And for the children of God, death is but a portal to an immortal life of endless bliss, and the children shout the glad, triumphant, and grateful news: "But thanks be to God, who gives us victory through our Lord Jesus Christ" (1 Corinthians 15:57).

"Christ has shown His strength to save," soundly defeating all foes seeking to harm and kill His dear children. Sin, death, and the devil will not have the last word with these baptized children of the heavenly Father. *Alleluia! Christ is risen! He is risen indeed! Alleluia!*

"O, where is your sting, death? We fear you no more; Christ rose, and now open is fair Eden's door. For all our transgressions His blood does atone; redeemed and forgiven, we now are His own." Amen. (LSB 480:4)

APRIL 4

Jesus lives! The vict'ry's won!
Death no longer can appall me;
Jesus lives! Death's reign is done!
From the grave will Christ recall me.
Brighter scenes will then commence;
This shall be my confidence. (*LSB* 490:1)

THE HYMN WRITER BEGINS EACH STANZA WITH THE GREAT TRUTH of Easter: "Jesus lives!" That fact allows the poet to close each stanza with the word "confidence." Because Jesus lives, we have confidence that His victory over death and the grave is also our victory. We are confident that Christ will call us out of our graves on the Last Day, and our glorified bodies will then be joined with our immortal souls: "I shall go where He is gone, live and reign with Him in heaven" (st. 2).

It is almost too much to take in. The perfection of eternal life in with Jesus is more than we can grasp here, but we may be absolutely and fully confident that Jesus suffered, died, and rose again for one purpose only—that we might share that perfection and live with Him forever.

Because Jesus lives, "death no longer can appall" us. Does death appall us? Or are we simply resigned to death, perhaps glibly dismissing it as one of life's realities? Actually, we should be appalled by death, for it was not what God intended when He created man and woman as the crown of His creation. But our first parents disobeyed His one command, sin entered the world, "and death through sin" (Romans 5:12). "Therefore, as one trespass led to condemnation for all men, so one act of righteousness leads to justification and life for all men" (v. 18). Through Adam's fall, we are all born sinful. But through Jesus' victory, we are all declared righteous. "Jesus lives! The vict'ry's won!" Consequently, we live—not in doubt but in full confidence of eternal life. Thanks be to God!

"Jesus lives! To Him the throne high above all things is given. I shall go where He is gone, live and reign with Him in heaven. God is faithful; doubtings, hence! This shall be my confidence." Amen. (LSB 490:2)

APRIL 5

Alleluia, alleluia, alleluia!

The strife is o'er, the battle done;
Now is the victor's triumph won;
Now be the song of praise begun.
Alleluia!

The pow'rs of death have done their worst,
But Christ their legions hath dispersed.
Let shouts of holy joy outburst.
Alleluia! (*LSB* 464:1–2)

The flower of Easter is the lily, the musical instrument is the trumpet, and the word is the ubiquitous Hebrew *Alleluia*, which means "praise the Lord." Today's hymn is another grand splash of alleluias—fitting for a joyful Eastertide. Let the whole earth praise the Lord that the strife and battle are over through His victory won on Calvary. Alleluia!

This hymn clearly states its chief meaning when it refers to strife and battle—Jesus Christ was victorious over "the age-bound chains" of death (st. 4). But in reality, sin and the devil fill the everyday lives of God's children with ongoing strife and battles. As we walk the disciple's path, we face vicious and unyielding attacks from the devil's wiles and cunning as we live surrounded by his evil.

There are times when that battle takes the form of a prolonged illness with a slow death. Immense relief is felt when God brings His saint home in His good time, and the battle ends. This is why today's hymn is often sung at funerals and memorial services. The departed saint's family and the congregation sing together of their relief that "the strife is o'er, the battle done." Their singing also confidently confesses that their loved one was brought safely through the battle and is now at peace with their victorious Lord Jesus Christ.

"Lord, by the stripes which wounded Thee, from death's dread sting Thy servants free that we may live and sing to Thee. Alleluia!" Amen. (LSB 464:5)

APRIL 6

Abide, O dearest Jesus,
Among us with Your grace
That Satan may not harm us
Nor we to sin give place.

Abide, O dear Redeemer,
Among us with Your Word,
And thus now and hereafter
True peace and joy afford. (*LSB* 919:1–2)

"ABIDE WITH US." PERHAPS THE FIRST TIME WE HEARD THOSE words was in the Eastertide reading of Luke's Gospel, as two followers of Jesus unknowingly encountered Him on their walk to Emmaus on the day of resurrection: "Stay with us, for it is toward evening, and the day is far spent" (Luke 24:29). We also pray that our Lord would abide with us, be a constant presence with us throughout our earthly lives, and ultimately take us to Himself. We will abide with our Savior in an eternity so perfect as to be beyond our human imaginings.

We pray first of all that Jesus would abide with His grace, His undeserved love for sinners. John declares that Jesus is "full of grace and truth" (1:14). His grace is what we need more than anything else, for "by grace you have been saved through faith" (Ephesians 2:8). Yes, Lord, stay among us with Your grace, for then "Satan may not harm us." Help us always to believe that Your grace is sufficient for us, as You told Paul (2 Corinthians 12:9).

We also pray that Jesus would abide among us with His Word, which brings us "true peace and joy" and, through the work of the Holy Spirit, provides daily growth "in grace and wisdom" (st. 4). Abide with Your protection, watching over us as we go about the daily tasks You have given us in our vocations and as we serve You and care for our neighbors. Finally, abide with Your love, for we know that "whoever abides in love abides in God, and God abides in him" (1 John 4:16).

"Abide, O faithful Savior, among us with Your love; grant steadfastness and help us to reach our home above." Amen. (LSB *919:6*)

APRIL 7

Now no more can death appall,
Now no more the grave enthrall;
You have opened paradise,
And Your saints in You shall rise.
Alleluia! (*LSB* 633:6)

APPALL ***IS A STRONG WORD, WITH IMPLICATIONS OF REVULSION,*** horror, and disgust. The translator of this early Latin hymn tells us that because Jesus shed His blood, because He took our place at Calvary, death is no longer appalling. And as our hymn text said a few days ago, "Jesus lives! The vict'ry's won! Death no longer can appall me" (*LSB* 490:1). Is death appalling? Yes . . . and no. Yes, because it is not what God intended for the crown of His creation, for the man and woman who were to live in perfect fellowship with Him in the perfect Garden of Eden that He created for them and their descendants. But we know that our first ancestors disobeyed God's one command. Their sin brought death into the world, claiming the lives of our first parents and each of us. That is appalling, based on what the Creator intended for His creatures.

But our Creator God planned for our redemption. His plan required His beloved Son to leave the perfection of heaven, take on human flesh, keep God's Law perfectly in a way that will always elude sinful humans, and then die a cruel, bloody death on our behalf. Jesus was our substitute in every way, except that He was sinless.

On Good Friday, at the very moment when Jesus cried, "It is finished" (John 19:30), death and the devil lost their power over us, lost the ability to be appalling! Death still stings, but because God "gives us the victory through our Lord Jesus Christ," we can say that death is no longer appalling (1 Corinthians 15:56–57). Rather, death has become for us the door to eternal life. For deliverance from death, we can only say, "Thanks be to God!"

"Easter triumph, Easter joy! This alone can sin destroy; from sin's pow'r, Lord, set us free, newborn souls in You to be. Alleluia!" Amen. (LSB *633:7*)

APRIL 8

He's risen, He's risen, Christ Jesus, the Lord;
He opened death's prison, the incarnate, true Word.
Break forth, hosts of heaven, in jubilant song
And earth, sea, and mountain their praises prolong.

The foe was triumphant when on Calvary
The Lord of creation was nailed to the tree.
In Satan's domain did the hosts shout and jeer,
For Jesus was slain, whom the evil ones fear. (*LSB* 480:1–2)

CHRIST IS RISEN! HE, THE INCARNATE WORD, OPENED DEATH'S prison for all time. We no longer fear death, for we know that Jesus' resurrection is our guarantee that we will live forever in His presence. He is risen indeed! Alleluia!

In today's hymn, C. F. W. Walther observes that the devil must have felt a sense of triumph when Jesus died, a Good Friday picture that we may not often think about: "In Satan's domain did the hosts shout and jeer." "But short was their triumph; the Savior arose" (st. 3)! And when He did so, Jesus defeated—for all time—death, hell, and Satan. When we confess in the Apostles' Creed that Jesus "descended into hell," we confess that Jesus demonstrated in no uncertain terms His complete victory over Satan.

The hymn writer makes another interesting observation: "Now open is fair Eden's door" (st. 4). When our first parents were banished from the Garden of Eden, God placed "the cherubim and a flaming sword" (Genesis 3:24) to prevent Adam from returning to the perfection of the Garden of Eden. But now Jesus, the Second Adam, has made all things new, and paradise is open forever! Christ is risen!

"But short was their triumph; the Savior arose, and death, hell, and Satan He vanquished, His foes. The conquering Lord lifts His banner on high; He lives, yes, He lives, and will nevermore die. O, where is your sting, death? We fear you no more; Christ rose, and now open is fair Eden's door. For all our transgressions His blood does atone; redeemed and forgiven, we now are His own." Amen. (LSB *480:3–4*)

APRIL 9

All you works of God, bless the Lord!
All you angels, now bless the Lord;
Come, you heavens and pow'rs that be,
Praise the Lord and His majesty.

Come, humanity, sing along,
Sing, you people of God, a song;
Priests and servants, your Lord now bless,
Join, you spirits and souls at rest:

Raise your voices high, praise and magnify,
All you works of God, bless the Lord! (*LSB* 930:1, 5)

O LORD, HOW MANIFOLD ARE YOUR WORKS! IN WISDOM HAVE YOU made them all; the earth is full of Your creatures" (Psalm 104:24). It is exceedingly good that all creation both recognizes and gives thanks and praise to its omnipotent, omniscient, and omnipresent Creator—the source of every molecule throughout this stunning universe.

In the First Article of the Creed, we confess that God the Father has not only given us all we have and see before our eyes, but He also preserves and defends us against all evil and misfortune. Therefore, we firmly believe and confidently trust that our Creator will also sustain us and all of His creation: "These all look to You, to give them their food in due season" (Psalm 104:27). And such boundless goodness from our Creator extends also to the critical, priceless, and lavish gifts of the Second and Third Articles of the Creed—called by the Gospel, enlightened with His gifts, and kept in the true faith.

With such an outpouring of divine gifts, how can we keep silent? Today's hymn is a fitting explosion of praise that magnifies the Creator of all things on the part of His whole creation—including His angels and His saints at rest. Naturally, this high praise is not simply a poem but is carried by one of the finest of all gifts—music!

"Bless the Lord, all you pure of heart; all you humble, His praise impart; God the Father and Son adore, bless the Spirit forevermore!" Amen. (LSB *930:6*)

APRIL 10

Abide with me, fast falls the eventide.
The darkness deepens; Lord, with me abide.
When other helpers fail and comforts flee,
Help of the helpless, O abide with me.

I need Thy presence ev'ry passing hour;
What but Thy grace can foil the tempter's pow'r?
Who like Thyself my guide and stay can be?
Through cloud and sunshine, O abide with me. (*LSB* 878:1–2)

IT WAS THE SUNDAY OF JESUS' RESURRECTION. TWO MEN WERE walking the seven miles from Jerusalem to the village of Emmaus. A stranger joined them and taught them—from Moses and all the prophets—that "the Christ should suffer these things and enter into His glory" (Luke 24:26). The travelers were kept from recognizing Jesus, but they knew that they didn't want this amazing teaching to end. So they pleaded with the stranger: "Stay with us" (v. 29).

We, too, plead with Jesus to abide with us. Every other possible helper or source of comfort will prove inadequate. In the helplessness of our sins, only Jesus can give the true comfort of full and free forgiveness. In our constant fight against temptation, only the grace of Jesus will help us to prevail. In our walk through this life—through both "cloud and sunshine"—only Jesus will prove to be a loving and trustworthy "guide and stay."

Even more important, we plead with Jesus to abide with us at the end of our earthly walk as death approaches. Only in Jesus can we fathom Paul's defiant exclamations: "O death, where is your victory? O death, where is your sting?" (1 Corinthians 15:55). Only in the abiding presence of Jesus do we gain the victory over death and the grave. Thus, we continually pray, "Abide with me."

"Hold Thou Thy cross before my closing eyes; shine through the gloom, and point me to the skies. Heav'n's morning breaks, and earth's vain shadows flee; in life, in death, O Lord, abide with me." Amen. (LSB *878:6*)

APRIL 11

Here, O my Lord, I see Thee face to face;
Here would I touch and handle things unseen;
Here grasp with firmer hand the eternal grace,
And all my weariness upon Thee lean.

Here would I feed upon the bread of God,
Here drink with Thee the royal wine of heav'n;
Here would I lay aside each earthly load,
Here taste afresh the calm of sin forgiv'n. (*LSB* 631:1–2)

OUR LORD MIRACULOUSLY FEEDS HIS WHOLE KINGDOM IN THE feast of His body and blood. In this Holy Supper, we always know we have the very Bread of Life to sustain us—He is there, present for us.

Today's hymn on the Lord's Supper is unique in that we hear what the child of God might think when approaching the altar to receive the Supper. Therefore, the first five stanzas are written in the first person and are personal. But the subject of the hymn text does not change—it's still about the Lord's Supper!

As we consider these thoughts about the Lord's glorious Supper, we also confess the real presence of Jesus' body and blood there. What happens at that Table could not be spelled out any clearer than in the words of the hymn itself: "Here, O my Lord, I see Thee face to face; here would I touch and handle things unseen." What a powerful confession to those who doubt the real bodily presence—in Communion, we are "face to face" with our Savior!

"Mine is the sin, but Thine the righteousness; mine is the guilt, but Thine the cleansing blood; here is my robe, my refuge, and my peace: Thy blood, Thy righteousness, O Lord my God." Amen. (LSB *631:5*)

APRIL 12

This is the hour of banquet and of song;
This is the heav'nly table spread for me;
Here let me feast and, feasting, still prolong
The brief bright hour of fellowship with Thee. (*LSB* 631:3)

O ***UR HYMN DESCRIBES A BRIEF BRIGHT HOUR IN WHICH JESUS IS*** everywhere as host and guest—a brief bright hour in which He both offers the feast and is Himself the feast. As His saints, we are not eager to have such a glorious feast end. It is hard for us to take in that such a heavenly banquet has been spread here for us. But God in His Word has proclaimed it and promised it, and we believe it.

Banquets often include music-making appropriate to the occasion. Today's hymn describes such an "hour of banquet and of song." This is grand music at a high feast! We want to sing; we cannot help but sing our heartfelt thanks, praise, laud, and honor for the gifts here given and received. Such joyous singing gives voice to what fills our hearts—overwhelming thanksgiving.

We give thanks because this Supper is the food we desperately need, and Jesus knows that. We need forgiveness; we leave forgiven. We need strength and refreshment, and the pastor leaves us with these words of thanksgiving to God for those very gifts: "You have refreshed us through this salutary gift, and we implore You that of Your mercy You would strengthen us through the same in faith toward You and in fervent love toward one another" (*LSB*, p. 166).

"I have no help but Thine; nor do I need another arm but Thine to lean upon. It is enough, my Lord, enough indeed; my strength is in Thy might, Thy might alone. Mine is the sin, but Thine the righteousness; mine is the guilt, but Thine the cleansing blood; here is my robe, my refuge, and my peace: Thy blood, Thy righteousness, O Lord my God." Amen. (LSB 631:4–5)

APRIL 13

Too soon we rise; the vessels disappear;
The feast, though not the love, is past and gone;
The bread and wine remove, but Thou art here;
Nearer than ever; still my shield and sun. (*LSB* 631:6)

"FEAST AFTER FEAST . . . COMES AND PASSES BY"* (ST. 7). *THERE are things we do not want to end, and this hymn poignantly speaks of one of those things—the Lord's Supper. "Too soon we rise; the vessels disappear." Yet the hymn is clear that not everything is past and gone. Yes, the vessels and the elements are covered, and we are back in the pew, but what happened at this Holy Table lives on—"the feast, though not the love, is past and gone."

Jesus is still present and nearer than ever, for He is, in fact, in us. "Thou art here." Jesus Christ is our "shield and sun" as we go forth to live in this troubled world in His strong name, and most important, we go forth forgiven and loved by that strong name—Jesus.

We have here received a "sweet foretaste of the festal joy, the Lamb's great marriage feast" (st. 7). Today's hymn also sings of our future, and oh, what a future we have! Today's feast points to the glad feast above—the ongoing, eternal "feast of bliss and love" (st. 7) in the place that our Lord Jesus has prepared for us. A sweet foretaste indeed!

"I have no help but Thine; nor do I need another arm but Thine to lean upon. It is enough, my Lord, enough indeed; my strength is in Thy might, Thy might alone. Feast after feast thus comes and passes by, yet, passing, points to that glad feast above, giving sweet foretaste of the festal joy, the Lamb's great marriage feast of bliss and love." Amen. (LSB *631:4, 7*)

APRIL 14

Jesus has come! Now see bonds rent asunder!
Fetters of death now dissolve, disappear.
See Him burst through with a voice as of thunder!
He sets us free from our guilt and our fear,
Lifts us from shame to the place of His honor.
Jesus has come! Hear the roll of God's thunder! (*LSB* 533:2)

JESUS HAS COME! HE HAS ACCOMPLISHED OUR SALVATION. BY defeating death and the devil, He has inaugurated a new reality in which we—despite our sins—now live "free from our guilt and our fear." Sin is a daily reality for us. With Luther we must confess that "we daily sin much and surely deserve nothing but punishment" (Small Catechism, Lord's Prayer, Fifth Petition). The hymn writer pictures "bonds" and "fetters," the restraints that keep prisoners shackled in their cells. But in our case, these shackles are worse than any earthly prison cell, for they are the bonds and fetters of eternal death, death being the "wages of sin" (Romans 6:23).

But Jesus has come! Now the bonds of death are "rent asunder." The fetters of death—those strong iron chains that would keep us in eternal bondage—"dissolve" and "disappear," along with our guilt and fear. We now grasp the full meaning of Jesus' own words: "So if the Son sets you free, you will be free indeed" (John 8:36).

Jesus "lifts us from shame to the place of His honor." The only way for Jesus to do so was to take our shame on Himself. He died in naked shame on the cross; He died *our* death. He gave up for a time His place of honor so that He could earn for us a place of honor in His kingdom that will last forever. "Jesus has come and brings pleasure eternal" (st. 1)!

"Jesus has come as the mighty Redeemer. See now the threatening strong one disarmed! Jesus breaks down all the walls of death's fortress, brings forth the pris'ners triumphant, unharmed. Satan, you wicked one, own now your master! Jesus has come! He, the mighty Redeemer!" Amen. (LSB *533:3*)

APRIL 15

Fruitful trees, the Spirit's sowing,
May we ripen and increase,
Fruit to life eternal growing,
Rich in love and joy and peace.

Laden branches freely bearing
Gifts the Giver loves to bless;
Here is fruit that grows by sharing,
Patience, kindness, gentleness. (***LSB*** 691:1–2)

FRUITFUL TREES IN GOD'S KINGDOM—WHAT DO THEY LOOK LIKE? We are given an accurate picture in today's hymn. And behold, these trees are a thing of very great beauty! And what stunning fruit is growing there, the fruit of patience, kindness, gentleness, goodness, self-control, love, joy, and peace.

What could be the reason for such magnificent trees so heavily laden with fruit? Jesus gives the answer: "I am the vine; you are the branches. Whoever abides in Me and I in him, he it is that bears much fruit, for apart from Me you can do nothing" (John 15:5). The fact that the magnificent trees are heavily laden with good fruit is completely the work of the Spirit's sowing and tending.

Abiding in Christ is the key to healthy, fruitful trees in the Kingdom. His Word and Sacraments keep the trees alive, healthy, and flourishing. That's the abiding that Jesus is talking about.

Sanctification, rightly understood, is Christ acting in us. His love is put there by Him, fed by Him, and nourished by Him. His love flows through us as He abides in us. That makes for good fruit because He is always the one doing the good. Others see Him in us as they see a fruitful tree.

"Rooted deep in Christ our Master, Christ our pattern and our goal, teach us as the years fly faster, goodness, faith, and self-control. Fruitful trees, the Spirit's tending, may we grow till harvests cease; till we taste, in life unending, heaven's love and joy and peace." Amen. (LSB *691:3–4*)

APRIL 16

Soul, adorn yourself with gladness,
Leave the gloomy haunts of sadness,
Come into the daylight's splendor,
There with joy your praises render.
Bless the One whose grace unbounded
This amazing banquet founded;
He, though heav'nly, high, and holy,
Deigns to dwell with you most lowly. (*LSB* 636:1)

J*UST AS A BRIDE ADORNS HERSELF WITH PRECIOUS JEWELS AND* fine clothing, so also, my soul, adorn yourself! As beautiful as those material goods may be, the soul is adorned with something even more beautiful: the sheer gladness of sins forgiven and the promise of eternal life. That is a very special kind of adornment, given freely by Jesus, the Bridegroom, for His Bride, the church. Our God, who dwells in the highest places, deigns to come near to us in a most intimate way, providing a lavish banquet that delivers this adornment of gladness for us.

"Soul, adorn yourself" with nothing less than this precious treasure from heaven, the priceless gifts that God gives us in His Holy Supper: "Christ's true body, for you riven, and His blood, for you once given" (st. 3). All the wealth of this world could never buy these magnificent gifts; they are given to us by the God who created us, the God who loved us so greatly that He gave His only begotten Son to save us. This adornment, coming from outside of us, presents us spotless and perfect before the Bridegroom, who loves us so greatly that He comes among us bodily in His Holy Supper. This adornment is given to us for the forgiveness of sins and the certainty of eternal life. Thanks be to our heavenly Bridegroom for so richly adorning His Bride!

"He who craves a precious treasure neither cost nor pain will measure; but the priceless gifts of heaven God to us has freely given. Though the wealth of earth were proffered, none could buy the gifts here offered: Christ's true body, for you riven, and His blood, for you once given." Amen. (LSB 636:3)

APRIL 17

Almighty God, Your Word is cast
Like seed into the ground;
Now let the dew of heav'n descend
And righteous fruits abound.

Let not the sly satanic foe
This holy seed remove,
But give it root in ev'ry heart
To bring forth fruits of love. (*LSB* 577:1–2)

ONE BEAUTIFUL AND BELOVED COLLECT—OR FORMULATED prayer—asks that we may hear, "read, mark, learn, and inwardly digest" the Holy Scriptures (Collect for Proper 10, Series A). We desperately need God's Word planted in us, sown in our hearts, where it gives us life! Through God's Word, we learn His ways and His thoughts and are given the Spirit of wisdom and truth for all our ways and days.

However, Satan is ready to pluck away and carry off God's precious planting. And this world's cares, riches, and busyness will try to outshine and overshadow the planting. But this is no ordinary planting—for God Himself is the Sower, and He declares, "So shall My Word be that goes out from My mouth; it shall not return to Me empty" (Isaiah 55:11).

In his hymn "Preach You the Word," Martin Franzmann calls this divine planting a "reckless love" and a "scattered plenteousness," for not all seeds take root and bear fruit (*LSB* 586:3, 5). It is a sad reality that some seed is wasted. Nevertheless, in His love, the Sower casts the seed, meant to take root in every heart, and sends "the dew of heav'n" to bring forth the fruits of love, peace, and joy, exactly as we pray in the collect and in this hymn.

"Let not the world's deceitful cares the rising plant destroy, but let it yield a hundredfold the fruits of peace and joy. So when the precious seed is sown, life-giving grace bestow that all whose souls the truth receive its saving pow'r may know." Amen. (LSB *577:3–4*)

APRIL 18

Draw us to Thee,
For then shall we
Walk in Thy steps forever
And hasten on
Where Thou art gone
To be with Thee, dear Savior.

Draw us to Thee,
Lord, lovingly;
Let us depart with gladness
That we may be
Forever free
From sorrow, grief, and sadness. (*LSB* 701:1–2)

THE CONSTANT PRAYER IN TODAY'S HYMN IS THAT THE LORD would "draw us" to Himself. Indeed, Jesus promised that God the Father does that work on behalf of His dear children: "No one can come to Me unless the Father who sent Me draws him" (John 6:44). Later in John's Gospel, Jesus said, "And I, when I am lifted up from the earth, will draw all people to Myself" (12:32). Scripture is always clear that it is God who graciously chooses us and draws us to Himself. Given our sinful human nature, we simply cannot draw ourselves to Him by our own intentions or efforts; we would always fall short.

The hymn writer is clear that drawing us to the Savior means nothing short of living eternally with Jesus—to go where He has already gone, to be with Him forever. Eternity with Jesus is the ultimate blessing, for it is where we will be "forever free from sorrow, grief, and sadness." Let those words sink in. No more grief, because there is no more death; no more sadness, because there is no more sin. Jesus has conquered sin and death, and He will draw us to Himself because His work of salvation is *for us*! His boundless love for us is for one purpose only—so that we may be joint heirs of the heavenly bliss that He already knows as we are numbered among the saints. Draw us to Thee!

"Draw us to Thee that also we Thy heav'nly bliss inherit and ever dwell where sin and hell no more can vex our spirit. Draw us to Thee unceasingly, into Thy kingdom take us; let us fore'er Thy glory share, Thy saints and joint heirs make us." Amen. (LSB 701:4–5)

APRIL 19

O Thou Physician blest,
Make clean my guilty soul
And me, by many a sin opprest,
Restore and keep me whole.

I know not how to praise
Thy mercy and Thy love;
But deign my soul from earth to raise
And learn from Thee above. (*TLH* 322:3–4)

THIS EARLY GREEK HYMN IS A TESTAMENT TO THE CHURCH'S understanding of confession and absolution and how they sang of it in those first centuries. It gives voice to what Jesus desires most from each of us: to recognize Him as the divine Physician who can grant us the ultimate gift of forgiveness.

We have a Lord of mercy and love who knows better than anyone the state of our sin-laden, guilty souls. Throughout Jesus' ministry, He repeatedly taught that He came for those in need of a physician, those who knew they were unworthy. Recognizing that need makes us worthy to sit at His Table, where that need is wonderfully met as He fills us with His love, mercy, forgiveness, and peace.

The hymn says, "I know not how to praise Thy mercy and Thy love." However, when we confess our sins to Him and come to His Table, we praise Him! This is precisely what Jesus wants most of us, and He can then say, "Your faith has saved you; go in peace" (Luke 7:50).

"Therefore my hope is in the Lord and not in mine own merit; it rests upon His faithful Word to them of contrite spirit that He is merciful and just; this is my comfort and my trust. His help I wait with patience. Though great our sins, yet greater still is God's abundant favor; His hand of mercy never will abandon us, nor waver. Our Shepherd good and true is He, who will at last His Israel free from all their sin and sorrow." Amen. (LSB *607:3, 5*)

APRIL 20

Entrust your days and burdens
To God's most loving hand;
He cares for you while ruling
The sky, the sea, the land.
For He who guides the tempests
Along their thund'rous ways
Will find for you a pathway
And guide you all your days. (*LSB* 754:1)

THERE MAY BE DAYS WHEN WE ACTUALLY DO PASS OUR TIME "in peace and quietness," as a classic prayer says (*LSB*, p. 313), and we thank God for such days. There are other days when we may feel particular burdens of life in this fallen world, and on those days, too, we go to our Lord in prayer. In this hymn, Pastor Paul Gerhardt encourages us to entrust *all* our days "to God's most loving hand." The God who rules and regulates the entire cosmos—"the sky, the sea, the land"—cares for each of His beloved sons and daughters. Our burdens are not inconsequential to our loving Father. He will find "a pathway" for each of us, and He will guide us all our days.

Jesus tells us very straightforwardly, "In the world you will have tribulation. But take heart; I have overcome the world" (John 16:33). The Christian's life is not without tribulation, trials, and sadness. Whatever our particular trials may be, we remember our Lord's words of encouragement and comfort. And we can indeed take heart, for the Lord who has overcome sin, death, and the devil cares for us, guides us, and finds exactly the right paths for us as we walk through this life. Moreover, we know that He will take us to Himself for an eternity of "peace and quietness" in His presence. This hope replaces our dismay, tempers our sadness and fears, and enables us to entrust all our days and burdens into the loving hands of our gracious Lord.

"Take heart, have hope, my spirit, and do not be dismayed; God helps in ev'ry trial and makes you unafraid. Await His time with patience through darkest hours of night until the sun you hoped for delights your eager sight." Amen. (LSB 754:3)

APRIL 21

Rely on God your Savior
And find your life secure.
Make His work your foundation
That your work may endure.
No anxious thought, no worry,
No self-tormenting care
Can win your Father's favor;
His heart is moved by prayer. (*LSB* 754:2)

TODAY WE LOOK AGAIN AT PASTOR GERHARDT'S HYMN AND RECEIVE more wise advice: "Rely on God your Savior." When we do so, we find that life is indeed secure. It may not always go the way we think it should, but life will always be secure in the sense that we know our gracious God cares for us on a daily basis, and we know that, in Christ, we have eternal life—come what may here on earth. Reliance on God, our Savior, is the means to work against our human tendencies toward anxiety, worry, and all manner of self-imposed cares.

Pastor Gerhardt also urges us to "make His work your foundation." The work of Christ, our Savior, was focused on His self-effacing love for His sinful, wayward children. It involved giving up the perfection of heaven, taking on human flesh, keeping the Law perfectly in our stead, and suffering and dying a painful death that should have been ours. To make His work our foundation means avoiding any kind of self-justifying tendencies on our part or pride in our own works as the basis for eternal salvation. Christ's work is sufficient; He has done it all for us. Whatever good we do is modeled on our Savior's work and directed toward our neighbors. *His work* is our foundation—both in life and in death.

Through His work, we are made blessed heirs of heaven. Christ Himself will crown us with life, and we will live forever in the perfection of His presence.

"Our hands and feet, Lord, strengthen; with joy our spirits bless until we see the ending of all our life's distress. And so throughout our lifetime keep us within Your care and at our end then bring us to heav'n to praise You there." Amen. (LSB 754:6)

APRIL 22

By grace I'm saved, grace free and boundless;
My soul, believe and doubt it not.
Why stagger at this word of promise?
Has Scripture ever falsehood taught?
No! Then this word must true remain:
By grace you too will life obtain. (*LSB* 566:1)

I ***HAD A DEAR COLLEAGUE WHO PEPPERED HIS SPEECH WITH THE*** phrase "by grace." These two words seemed everywhere, often prefacing his answer to a question: "Well, by grace . . ." One day, after I practiced a Bach fugue at the organ, I saw this colleague standing next to me with tears in his eyes, and he said, "By grace—Bach." I learned a great deal from this devout man who could not help but see everything through the eyes of faith.

By grace! The theme of today's hymn is a marvelous exposition of those two words in song. When we have been given everything truly important in this life freely and by grace, it can be difficult for us to take in all that this means for each of us unworthy sinners. But the hymn tells us—"my soul, believe and doubt it not."

In His Word, our Lord repeatedly makes such extraordinary promises to us. Therefore, nothing could be more faithful or trustworthy. As the hymn calls it, all of this is a staggering truth!

To preface our answer to any question and pepper our speech with "by grace" makes perfect sense for we who live "by grace." Like my colleague, we would do well to think that way as we live our days by grace!

"I trust in Him with all my heart; now all my sorrow ceases. His words abiding peace impart; His blood from guilt releases. Free grace through Him I now obtain; He washes me from ev'ry stain, and pure I stand before Him." Amen. (LSB *568:3*)

APRIL 23

By grace to timid hearts that tremble,
In tribulation's furnace tried,
By grace, in spite of fear and trouble,
The Father's heart is open wide.
Where could I help and strength secure
If grace were not my anchor sure? (*LSB* 566:5)

GRACE IN THE FACE OF CROSSES IS THE THEME OF TODAY'S HYMN stanza. Life in the kingdom as a disciple of Jesus Christ will have its share of trials and tribulations. We learn about this divine testing in the letter to the Hebrews, where it is revealed that we do not design it but God knows what is best for us and designs it. And this discipline is lovingly shaped by Him *specifically for us* (Hebrews 12:6–7).

It is a fatherly testing given in love for His dear child. And these trials are never suffered on our own; on the contrary, God's abundant grace surrounds and envelops us. Grace carries us through and, as the hymn puts it, is our help, strength, and anchor.

"Timid hearts that tremble" need help, strength, a stronghold, a fortress, something to hold on to. And the boundless grace that so wonderfully fills our lives in Word and Sacraments is that sure strength and stronghold. Those magnificent means of grace are a mighty fortress for all our days.

"For the moment all discipline seems painful rather than pleasant, but later it yields the peaceful fruit of righteousness to those who have been trained by it" (Hebrews 12:11). "The Father's heart is open wide."

"It was grace in Christ that called me, taught my darkened heart and mind; else the world had yet enthralled me, to Thy heav'nly glories blind. Now I worship none above Thee; for Thy grace alone I thirst, knowing well that, if I love Thee, Thou, O Lord, didst love me first." Amen. (LSB 573:2)

APRIL 24

In that fair home shall never
Be silent music's voice;
With hearts and lips forever
We shall in God rejoice,
While angel hosts are raising
With saints from great to least
A mighty hymn for praising
The Giver of the feast. (*LSB* 514:4)

CAN YOU IMAGINE IT? A TIME WHEN MUSIC IN PRAISE OF OUR triune God will never cease! A time when heavenly music unites all the saints and the angel hosts in a grand celestial song, incomparably greater than our foretaste of the feast to come here on earth in the Divine Service. What a stunning, glorious vision with music, the "new song" of the great revelation of Jesus to John (5:9), occupying a central place for all the redeemed saints.

This vision is given hymnic form by Johann Walter, the first Lutheran kantor, whom we commemorate today. Walter, a skilled composer and musician, worked closely with Martin Luther to assist the reformer in realizing his musical goals. Walter's hymn text reveals that the Lutheran kantor—leader of the church's song—was skilled not only in music but also in the biblical, confessional, liturgical, and sacramental theology of the church. In the Lutheran tradition, music is proclamation, the sung equivalent of preaching.

In the four stanzas of this hymn, part of a larger poetic project by Walter, we are given the privilege of proclaiming the end times and singing of the promise of life forever with Christ: "There shall we see in glory our dear Redeemer's face; the long-awaited story of heav'nly joy takes place" (st. 2). Thanks be to God for Walter and the long line of Lutheran kantors who enable us to sing the faith!

"Therefore in our hymns we pray Thee, grant us, blessed Trinity, at the last to keep Thine Easter with Thy faithful saints on high; there to Thee forever singing alleluia joyfully." Amen. (LSB 417:4)

APRIL 25

Christ is the world's Redeemer,
The lover of the pure,
The font of heav'nly wisdom,
Our trust and hope secure,
The armor of His soldiers,
The Lord of earth and sky,
Our health while we are living,
Our life when we shall die. (*LSB* 539:1)

"THE LOVER OF THE PURE" IS A LINE THAT ALMOST STOPS THE singer, wishing to pause and ponder these five words before moving on. These words are meant to describe us, but we do not recognize ourselves! A most remarkable line.

For good reason, we are not usually called "the pure"—hence why this line seems almost shocking to us. However, Jesus calls us "the pure" in the Sermon on the Mount, where He teaches what disciples look like in His kingdom: "Blessed are the pure in heart, for they shall see God" (Matthew 5:8).

The first line of this magnificent, early Latin hymn announces who made us "the pure." "Christ is the world's Redeemer." As our Redeemer, He has taken on our sins and therefore taken away our sins, making us pure. We contributed nothing! It is hard to believe how pure we are through what He won for us, but we are pure as the driven snow, dressed in the white robes of our Baptism, having been made right eternally with our heavenly Father.

This is all because Christ became the world's Redeemer! Our believing, forgiven hearts that trust in the world's Redeemer have made us one of "the pure," one of the "blessed" Jesus speaks of in His Beatitudes.

"Glory to God the Father, the unbegotten One, all honor be to Jesus, His sole-begotten Son, and to the Holy Spirit—the perfect Trinity. Let all the worlds give answer: Amen! So let it be." (LSB *539:4*)

APRIL 26

Christ has our host surrounded
With clouds of martyrs bright,
Who wave their palms
in triumph
And fire us for the fight.
Then Christ the cross ascended
To save a world undone
And, suff'ring for the sinful,
Our full redemption won.

Down through the
realm of darkness
He strode in victory,
And at the hour appointed
He rose triumphantly.
And now, to heav'n ascended,
He sits upon the throne
Whence He had ne'er departed,
His Father's and His
own. (*LSB* 539:2–3)

THIS IS OUR REDEMPTION STORY UNIQUELY TOLD IN TWO BRILLIANT stanzas of early Latin hymnody. Singers are placed by Christ within the glorious host of His saints—a magnificent cloud of martyrs—who surround them and inspire them with their lives and witness as they "wave their palms in triumph and fire us for the fight."

Next, we sing of how the very Son of God "the cross ascended to save a world undone." Then comes a part of the story that very few hymns mention: "Down through the realm of darkness He strode in victory." Here is an excellent example of how hymns teach doctrine to the saints. Many people assume Jesus' descent into hell, as we confess in the Apostles' Creed, was part of Jesus' suffering and death. Not true! When Jesus says, "It is finished" (John 19:30), this means that all He came to earth to accomplish is now completed, and it is time for Him to march victoriously through the realms of darkness before rising triumphantly on the third day.

The stanza ends when Jesus ascends and takes our human nature on the clouds to God's right hand, having won our redemption. Alleluia! Alleluia!

"Glory to God the Father, the unbegotten One, all honor be to Jesus, His sole-begotten Son, and to the Holy Spirit—the perfect Trinity. Let all the worlds give answer: Amen! So let it be." (LSB *539:4*)

APRIL 27

Glory to God the Father,
The unbegotten One,
All honor be to Jesus,
His sole-begotten Son,
And to the Holy Spirit—
The perfect Trinity.
Let all the worlds give answer:
Amen! So let it be. (*LSB* 539:4)

TODAY'S HYMN STANZA IS A GRAND AND GLORIOUS DOXOLOGY, A confident hymn of praise to the triune God. In the church's life of prayer, the Psalms, hymns, and prayers often end with a type of doxology that confesses and names the One who has the power to grant all that precedes the doxology.

"For Thine is the kingdom and the power and the glory forever and ever" is a type of doxology that concludes the Lord's Prayer. Some have even likened the book of Revelation to a doxology that concludes the Bible. From as early as the fifth century, many psalms and hymns have concluded with a type of doxology called the Gloria Patri or the Lesser Gloria: "Glory be to the Father and to the Son and to the Holy Spirit; as it was in the beginning, is now, and will be forever."

Such conclusions are creedal and reveal confidence in our Creator, Redeemer, and Sanctifier as the source and power of our lives. This type of high creedal thanksgiving and praise is a most fitting way to end our songs and prayers. These doxologies often include or conclude with "Amen," a Hebrew word meaning "it is true and reliable," affirming the truth and reliability of the words spoken and sung by the faithful at prayer.

"Praise, all you people, the name so holy of Him who does such wondrous things! All that has being, to praise Him solely, with happy heart its amen sings. Children of God, with angel host praise Father, Son, and Holy Ghost! Alleluia, alleluia!" Amen. (LSB *797:5*)

APRIL 28

I know that my Redeemer lives;
What comfort this sweet sentence gives!
He lives, He lives, who once was dead;
He lives, my ever-living head.

He lives to silence all my fears;
He lives to wipe away my tears;
He lives to calm my troubled heart;
He lives all blessings to impart. (*LSB* 461:1, 5)

JOB DECLARED, "FOR I KNOW THAT MY REDEEMER LIVES, AND AT the last He will stand upon the earth" (19:25). Job was certain that God would redeem sinners and that there would be a bodily resurrection to eternal life on the Last Day. We, who also have the eyewitness testimony of the Gospel writers, sing that same certainty: "I know that my Redeemer lives"! The hymn writer goes on to explore the blessings of that "sweet sentence," first spoken by Job.

What does it mean that Jesus, "who once was dead," now lives? "He lives to silence all my fears." Because Jesus lives, we don't fear the future, nor do we fear the time of our own death. We know that God holds our lives in His hands, granting to each of us days of service to Him and to our neighbors. While death is certain, we know that it will be in God's own time, and it will be akin to a sleep from which, on the Last Day, we will awaken to eternal life with our Redeemer. When we suffer the death of a near and dear loved one, the fact that "my Redeemer lives" makes all the difference. His resurrection calms our troubled hearts, and we have His promise that one day "He will wipe away every tear from their eyes, and death shall be no more" (Revelation 21:4). Jesus, our great Redeemer, has promised, "I go to prepare a place for you" (John 14:2). Our Redeemer lives and will bring us safely home!

"He lives and grants me daily breath; He lives, and I shall conquer death; He lives my mansion to prepare; He lives to bring me safely there." Amen. (LSB *461:7*)

APRIL 29

The Son obeyed His Father's will,
Was born of virgin mother;
And God's good pleasure to fulfill,
He came to be my brother.
His royal pow'r disguised He bore;
A servant's form, like mine, He wore
To lead the devil captive. (*LSB* 556:6)

MARTIN LUTHER SET OUT TO TEACH EVEN THE MOST PROFOUND theological truths and concepts in a way all could understand. "Dear Christians, One and All, Rejoice," which was the first hymn in the first Lutheran hymnal, provides an excellent example of this and is our focus for the next several devotions.

In this stanza, we learn what the incarnation meant for the Son of God—following His Father's will, coming down from heaven, being born in human flesh like ours, and taking on a servant's form. And such obedience by God's Son would make Jesus our Brother.

Luther's masterful incarnational teaching in this stanza is similar to Paul Gerhardt's in his Lenten hymn that tells of our Lord's obedience to His Father's will: "Yes, Father, yes, most willingly I'll bear what You command Me. My will conforms to Your decree, I'll do what You have asked Me" (*LSB* 438:3). And then, again, it is Gerhardt who expresses incarnational truths in our prayer for today, telling what caused this incarnation: Love caused it; "love brought You down to me" (*LSB* 334:4).

Luther and Gerhardt are two of a kind in crafting theological truths into beautiful and understandable words. What a monumental treasure and rich blessing the church has received in the hymnody of these two men as they teach us again and again from the Word of God.

"Love caused Your incarnation; love brought You down to me. Your thirst for my salvation procured my liberty. Oh, love beyond all telling, that led You to embrace in love, all love excelling, our lost and fallen race." Amen. (LSB *334:4*)

APRIL 30

To me He said: "Stay close to Me,
I am your rock and castle.
Your ransom I Myself will be;
For you I strive and wrestle.
For I am yours, and you are Mine,
And where I am you may remain;
The foe shall not divide us." (*LSB* 556:7)

T*HIS STANZA SHIFTS FROM DIALOGUE BETWEEN THE FATHER AND* Son to a striking dialogue between God the Son and those He came to ransom—you and me! Luther's writing here becomes personal. "For I am yours, and you are Mine," Jesus Himself tells us. He will be close to us, and we are to stay close to Him. We journey through this life knowing that our Lord is near—yes, He could not be closer!

As His children, we are safe, for we have a "rock and castle" in the very Son of God. In this safe place, we need never fear any foe, for we know with certainty that nothing can separate us from Him.

"Your ransom I Myself will be" is His breathtaking promise to us. He came to do what we could not. In Him, we have been ransomed—we are free! What else could we need? This beautiful, personal stanza teaches us that we have everything we need by grace!

"A mighty fortress is our God, a trusty shield and weapon; He helps us free from ev'ry need that hath us now o'ertaken. The old evil foe now means deadly woe; deep guile and great might are his dread arms in fight; on earth is not his equal. . . . But for us fights the valiant One, whom God Himself elected. Ask ye, Who is this? Jesus Christ it is, of Sabaoth Lord, and there's none other God; He holds the field forever." Amen. (LSB *656:1–2*)

MAY 1

"Though he will shed My precious blood,
Me of My life bereaving,
All this I suffer for your good;
Be steadfast and believing.
Life will from death the vict'ry win;
My innocence shall bear your sin,
And you are blest forever." (*LSB* 556:8)

TODAY WE PONDER THE ATONEMENT STANZA OF LUTHER'S masterful hymn. This is where the Son of God's coming to earth reaches its climax in the precious shed blood of our Savior. Though the foe will shed Christ's "precious blood," our Lord promises, "All this I suffer for your good."

This entire stanza is written in the voice of our Savior speaking to us, letting Him gently unfold what is happening, what He is doing, and the breathtaking fact that He is doing it all *for us.*

Then, our Savior, as a gentle, loving Shepherd, reveals our part when He asks that we "be steadfast and believing." This sounds like little in return on our part, but it is what He asks and precisely what He cares about most. The world consistently refuses to believe who He is. But the faithful children of God remain both steadfast and believing.

The stanza then reveals what was won for us: "Life will from death the vict'ry win." Victory! Life! For us! God was committed so that we could be acquitted and have life forever. Alleluia!

"The sinless Son of God must die in sadness; the sinful child of man may live in gladness; man forfeited his life and is acquitted; God is committed. O wondrous love, whose depth no heart hath sounded, that brought Thee here, by foes and thieves surrounded! All worldly pleasures, heedless, I was trying while Thou wert dying." Amen. (LSB *439:5, 7*)

MAY 2

"Now to My Father I depart,
From earth to heav'n ascending,
And, heav'nly wisdom to impart,
The Holy Spirit sending;
In trouble He will comfort you
And teach you always to be true
And into truth shall guide you." (*LSB* 556:9)

L*UTHER'S HYMN HAS MOVED FROM INCARNATION TO ATONEMENT* and now arrives at Jesus' ascension and Pentecost. Once again, the stanza is written in the voice of Jesus, talking to His people about His life and work.

The ascension is only briefly referenced on the way to the main subject of the stanza—the sending and work of the Holy Spirit. In sending the Holy Spirit, Jesus gives us heavenly wisdom, and since Jesus Himself is Wisdom, He is offering ways for us to receive Him and live in His truth and wisdom.

The Holy Spirit's sole purpose and work is to give Jesus, teach Jesus, and show the fullness of Jesus to His sheep. Therefore, the Spirit leads us into truth that guides all our ways and days and keeps us safe as it protects those from the evil one. And when we are filled with Jesus through His Word and Sacraments, we go forth comforted by the Comforter Himself.

Thanks be to God for His loving and fatherly gift of His Holy Spirit.

"Come, Holy Ghost, Creator blest, and make our hearts Your place of rest; come with Your grace and heav'nly aid, and fill the hearts which You have made. Teach us to know the Father, Son, and You, from both, as Three in One that we Your name may ever bless and in our lives the truth confess." Amen. (LSB *498:1, 6*)

MAY 3

"What I on earth have done and taught
Guide all your life and teaching;
So shall the kingdom's work be wrought
And honored in your preaching.
But watch lest foes with base alloy
The heav'nly treasure should destroy;
This final word I leave you." (*LSB* 556:10)

L*UTHER ENDS HIS HYMN WITH* J*ESUS' PARTING WORDS OF WISDOM* to His people. It is almost as if Jesus is going away, but He did not leave us even when He ascended, and He firmly promised *never* to leave us. He is near—He is as close as His Word and Sacraments.

What are His parting words for our life? He basically says, "Let everything in My life and work be the guide for your life and work, and in that way, the kingdom's work will be fulfilled." He wants His teachings to be honored and preached and lived. And in that way, His kingdom comes among us.

Jesus knows better than anyone that we will have a constant and devious enemy every step of our way. So He warns, "But watch lest foes with base alloy the heav'nly treasure should destroy." Yes, with all of his might, Satan will try to take and destroy the priceless treasure that Jesus won for us and now leaves with us. But that gracious life in Jesus' kingdom is ours forever!

"Since Christ returned to claim His throne, great gifts for me obtaining, my heart will rest in Him alone, no other rest remaining; for where my treasure went before, there all my thoughts will ever soar to still their deepest yearning. O grant, dear Lord, this grace to me, recalling Your ascension, that I may serve You faithfully in thanks for my redemption; and then, when all my days will cease, let me depart in joy and peace in answer to my pleading." Amen. (LSB 492:2–3)

MAY 4

All depends on our possessing
God's abundant grace and blessing,
Though all earthly wealth depart.
They who trust with faith unshaken
By their God are not forsaken
And will keep a dauntless heart.

When with sorrow I am stricken,
Hope anew my heart will quicken;
All my longing shall be stilled.
To His loving-kindness tender
Soul and body I surrender,
For on God alone I build. (*LSB* 732:1, 4)

SOMETIMES WE ANSWER QUESTIONS WITH A RESPONSE LIKE "Well, that all depends." The hymn writer here seems to be responding to a fundamental question, such as, "How shall I live my life?" His answer is that everything in life depends on God's grace and blessing, on His loving-kindness, on His wisdom. By faith, we trust that God will direct our lives according to His good and gracious will for us. We live fully dependent on Him.

Of course, that is not always an easy proposition for us to accept. The hymn writer readily acknowledges that sorrow is part of our lives. But when our lives depend on God's grace and blessing, we can live in hope, knowing that God will still the longings of our hearts and provide us an abundance of His tender love and kindness, even in the midst of sorrow. God makes it possible for us to bear sorrows, for we know that His grace has already provided us the certain promise of a perfect eternity with Him. Thus, everything in this life—and in the promised eternal life in God's presence—depends on His grace, freely given to us through our Lord Jesus. "All my trust in Him I place. . . . Safe I anchor in His grace" (st. 6).

"Well He knows what best to grant me; all the longing hopes that haunt me, joy and sorrow, have their day. I shall doubt His wisdom never; as God wills, so be it ever; I commit to Him my way." Amen. (LSB *732:5*)

MAY 5

All our knowledge, sense, and sight
Lie in deepest darkness shrouded
Till Your Spirit breaks our night
With the beams of truth unclouded.
You alone to God can win us;
You must work all good within us. (*LSB* 904:2)

THE PROPHET ISAIAH BOLDLY DECLARED, "THE WORD OF OUR GOD will stand forever" (40:8). Jesus Himself refuted the devil's temptation by pointing to God's Word and quoting from Deuteronomy: "Man shall not live by bread alone, but by every word that comes from the mouth of God" (Matthew 4:4). Peter then quoted Isaiah's text in his first epistle: "'The word of the Lord remains forever.' And this word is the good news that was preached to you" (1 Peter 1:24–25). This same assertion regarding the centrality and strength of God's Word, translated into Latin, became a motto for the Lutheran Reformation. Today's hymn, directing us to God's Word, is often sung at the beginning of the Divine Service: "Blessed Jesus, at Your Word we are gathered all to hear You" (st. 1).

Left to ourselves, however, we cannot believe God's Word. As Luther put it, "I believe that I cannot by own reason or strength believe in Jesus Christ, my Lord, or come to Him; but the Holy Spirit has called me by the Gospel" (Small Catechism, Creed, Third Article). Thus, the hymn writer proceeds in his second stanza to declare that it is the Spirit who "breaks our night with the beams of truth unclouded." It is the Spirit alone who "can win us" to God and "work all good within us." We may never boast of ourselves as believers. It is the Holy Spirit who helps us, who works faith within us to believe the precious promises of God's Word—"a light to my path" (Psalm 119:105).

"Gracious Savior, good and kind, Light of Light, from God proceeding, open now our heart and mind; help us by Your Spirit's pleading. Hear the cry Your Church now raises; hear and bless our prayers and praises." Amen. (LSB *904:3*)

MAY 6

Let us ever walk with Jesus,
Follow His example pure,
Through a world that would deceive us
And to sin our spirits lure.
Onward in His footsteps treading,
Pilgrims here, our home above,
Full of faith and hope and love,
Let us do the Father's bidding.
Faithful Lord, with me abide;
I shall follow where You guide. (*LSB* 685:1)

JESUS BIDS US NOT ONLY TO FOLLOW HIM BUT ALSO TO DENY ourselves and take up the cross (Matthew 16:24). That is not an easy proposition. It requires us to view ourselves as pilgrims in this world, temporary residents who realize that our lasting home is not yet realized. Yet, filled with faith, hope, and love, we wish to do the Father's bidding here through our various vocations. And so we pray that the Lord would abide with us so that we may follow Him as our guide through this life.

The hymn writer tells us that we will experience suffering and sadness, that annoying discomforts will come our way. That is simply a fact, given that we live in a fallen world. We know the sadness, for example, that comes with the death of a loved one.

But we also know that "joy will follow all our sadness" (st. 2), because where Jesus is, there can be only temporary loss. Indeed, the hymn writer points us to "celestial joy" (st. 2), that joy of heaven where we will experience the perfect life that God desires for us. The word *joy* appears three times in the second stanza of this hymn, emphasizing what God has in store for us pilgrims who walk with Jesus through this life, focused—by His grace—on the perfect life to come.

"Let us suffer here with Jesus and with patience bear our cross. Joy will follow all our sadness; where He is, there is no loss. Though today we sow no laughter, we shall reap celestial joy; all discomforts that annoy shall give way to mirth hereafter. Jesus, here I share Your woe; help me there Your joy to know." Amen. (LSB *685:2*)

MAY 7

Let us gladly die with Jesus.
Since by death He
conquered death,
He will free us from destruction,
Give to us immortal breath.
Let us mortify all passion
That would lead us into sin;
And the grave that shuts us in
Shall but prove the
gate to heaven.
Jesus, here with You I die,
There to live with You
on high. (*LSB* 685:3)

T***O THE WORLD, THE PHRASE "GLADLY DIE" MAKES LITTLE SENSE***—more common is to actively fight against death! The only way to perceive our death as something good, something we could "gladly" anticipate, is to connect it to Jesus' death. Just as His tomb could not hold Him, so also "the grave that shuts us in shall but prove the gate to heaven." Because of Christ's victory, death does not have the last word. For us, death is not a crushing, final blow; rather, it is the open door that leads us to heaven.

We live this earthly life with Jesus. He is our Head, and we are His "own living members" (st. 4). He comes to us in the ways He has promised—through His Word and Sacraments. As Paul wrote, "all of us who have been baptized into Christ Jesus were baptized into His death. . . . If we have been united with Him in a death like His, we shall certainly be united with Him in a resurrection like His" (Romans 6:3, 5). The hymn writer states it beautifully: "Where You live, there we shall be in Your presence constantly, living there with You forever." Thus, we pray, "Jesus, let me faithful be, life eternal grant to me" (st. 4).

"Let us also live with Jesus. He has risen from the dead that to life we may awaken. Jesus, You are now our head. We are Your own living members; where You live, there we shall be in Your presence constantly, living there with You forever. Jesus, let me faithful be, life eternal grant to me." Amen. (LSB 685:4)

MAY 8

Eternal Spirit of the living Christ,
I know not how to ask or what to say;
I only know my need, as deep as life,
And only You can teach me how to pray. (*LSB* 769:1)

Martin Luther gives priceless advice on how to pray: "I have often said how prayer must be formulated. We must not stipulate for God the measure, the term, the manner, the place, or the person. No, we must leave this to His knowledge of what He should give and what is useful for us" (*Luther's Works*, vol. 24, pp. 390–91).

Undoubtedly, we all could use some help in our praying, as today's hymn admits—"Only You can teach me how to pray." It also rightly confesses that we do not know "*how* to ask or *what* to say" (emphases added). Therefore, we call on the "eternal Spirit of the living Christ" for His help in this essential part of our life and our relationship with God.

We know that our God wants us to pray and knows our every need. So, all we have to do is come to Him, talk to Him, and ask Him. And in our coming, we trust that the Holy Spirit will intercede for us according to our needs. This is good and right, as it leaves all things to His will for us.

"Come, pray in me the prayer I need this day; help me to see Your purpose and Your will—where I have failed, what I have done amiss; held in forgiving love, let me be still. Come with the strength I lack, bring vision clear of human need; O give me eyes to see fulfillment of my life in love outpoured, my life in You, O Christ; Your love in me." Amen. (LSB 769:2–3)

MAY 9

He has raised our human nature
On the clouds to God's right hand;
There we sit in heav'nly places,
There with Him in glory stand.
Jesus reigns, adored by angels;
Man with God is on the throne.
By our mighty Lord's ascension
We by faith behold our own. (*LSB* 494:5)

THIS ASCENSION HYMN BY CHRISTOPHER WORDSWORTH IS A glorious feast of rich theology. And such a feast is particularly helpful in our understanding of Jesus' ascension. Many people assume that at His ascension to the Father's right hand, Jesus went to some faraway, unapproachable place, leaving us on our own. But Jesus has not left us!

On the contrary, Luther taught that the right hand of the Father is *everywhere*. Jesus has taken up the power and authority that were His since before time, but at the same time, He is with us, who remain bound by time and space. He is with us in Holy Baptism. He is with us in the preaching of His Word. And He is with us in His body and His blood on His altar. Jesus' presence could not be any closer to us, for we can taste and see that He is always good and near.

Because Jesus, the Second Person of the Trinity, has flesh and blood like us, His triumph is ours as well. The One who sits at the right hand of the Father is one of us, a human being. He "raised our human nature on the clouds to God's right hand; there we sit in heav'nly places, there with Him in glory stand"!

"O grant, dear Lord, this grace to me, recalling Your ascension, that I may serve You faithfully in thanks for my redemption; and then, when all my days will cease, let me depart in joy and peace in answer to my pleading." Amen. (LSB *492:3*)

MAY 10

To them the shining angels cry,
"Why stand and gaze
upon the sky?"
Alleluia, alleluia!
"This is the Savior,"
thus they say;
"This is His glorious
triumph day!"
Alleluia, alleluia! Alleluia,
alleluia, alleluia!

"You see Him now,
ascending high
Up to the portals of the sky."
Alleluia, alleluia!
"Hereafter Jesus you shall see
Returning in great majesty."
Alleluia, alleluia! Alleluia,
alleluia, alleluia! (*LSB* 493:3–4)

CHRISTMAS, GOOD FRIDAY, EASTER, AND ASCENSION ARE THE DAYS in the Church Year that mark the saving work of our Lord Jesus Christ. The Son of God became incarnate as a human, born into this world so that He could keep the Law on our behalf. He suffered death on our behalf, bearing the sins of the entire world. He rose from the dead, defeating death and the devil for us. His work completed, He ascended to His Father in heaven, having won eternal life for us. We rightly sing of His ascension, "This is His glorious triumph day!"

Christ's ascension presents us with an important truth, spoken to the disciples who witnessed this final act of triumph: "This Jesus, who was taken up from you into heaven, will come in the same way as you saw Him go into heaven" (Acts 1:11). What a comfort to those disciples and to us! We know that one day Jesus will return to earth "in great majesty" and take His redeemed people to live with Him in perfect happiness forever! We await that day with great longing, the day when "He will wipe away every tear from their eyes, and death shall be no more, neither shall there be mourning, nor crying, nor pain anymore" (Revelation 21:4). Jesus' ascension is the seal of this "future great reward" (st. 5). Knowing that He has earned such a blessed eternal life for us, we live even now in joyful expectation, singing alleluias to our Savior!

"Be now our joy on earth, O Lord, and be our future great reward. Alleluia, alleluia! Then, throned with You forever, we shall praise Your name eternally. Alleluia!" Amen. (LSB *493:5*)

MAY 11

Alleluia! Not as orphans
Are we left in sorrow now;
Alleluia! He is near us;
Faith believes, nor questions how.
Though the cloud from sight received Him
When the forty days were o'er,
Shall our hearts forget His promise:
"I am with you evermore"? (*LSB* 821:2)

FORTY DAYS AFTER HIS RESURRECTION—HIS REDEMPTIVE WORK completed—Jesus ascended into heaven. Luke tells us that Jesus led His disciples to Bethany, "and lifting up His hands He blessed them. While He blessed them, He parted from them and was carried up into heaven" (Luke 24:50–51). One could imagine the disciples being both sad and fearful after Jesus ascended, but Luke reports quite the opposite: "And they worshiped Him and returned to Jerusalem with great joy, and were continually in the temple blessing God" (vv. 52–53).

Perhaps the disciples reminded one another of words that Jesus had spoken to them earlier. Just days before, the disciples would have heard Jesus say, "And behold, I am with you always, to the end of the age" (Matthew 28:20). And the disciples may well have recalled Jesus' words spoken to them on the night of His betrayal: "I will not leave you as orphans; I will come to you" (John 14:18).

These words and promises of Jesus comfort us as well. The hymn writer declares, "Faith believes, nor questions how." The Holy Spirit works faith in our hearts to believe these precious promises of our Savior, promises that enable us—like the disciples—to live with great joy. And like the disciples, we continually bless God for His ongoing presence, as we hear Jesus' words and receive His true body and blood poured out for the forgiveness of our sins and the promise of eternal life with Him.

"Alleluia! Bread of heaven, here on earth our food, our stay; alleluia! Here the sinful flee to You from day to day. Intercessor, Friend of sinners, earth's Redeemer, hear our plea where the songs of all the sinless sweep across the crystal sea." Amen. (LSB 821:3)

MAY 12

On Christ's ascension I now build
The hope of my ascension;
This hope alone has always stilled
All doubt and apprehension;
For where the Head is, there as well
I know His members are to dwell
When Christ will come and call them. (*LSB* 492:1)

THIS HYMN, WHICH SINGS OF BUILDING AND GOING FORWARD IN hope because of Christ's ascension, explodes with confidence without a hint of doubt or apprehension. We, the joyful saints singing this hymn, know we were not left behind. We do not have to fend for ourselves but have been showered with great promises and gifts by our Lord and King. And we know what our eternity will be!

We are confident that Jesus is always with us as we go forward. We trust that His very body and blood will sustain us on our way, as He has promised to live in us. We also know that Jesus wants us to call on our Father at any time of the day or night for any and all needs. And finally, when our days on this earth cease, we know He has prepared a place for us.

Meanwhile, on our earthly pilgrimage, we go forth forgiven and sustained as we serve our Lord in our given vocations in His kingdom, always giving thanks and praise to Him for our life and salvation and for His inestimable promises and lavish gifts.

"O grant, dear Lord, this grace to me, recalling Your ascension, that I may serve You faithfully in thanks for my redemption; and then, when all my days will cease, let me depart in joy and peace in answer to my pleading." Amen. (LSB 492:3)

MAY 13

Christ sits at God's right hand,
His saving work complete,
To reign till ev'ry foe will lie
Beneath His feet—
All that the Father planned,
The Son sought to fulfill,
When first He said,
"Lord, here am I
To do Your will."

What costly sacrifice
To cover human sin!
Who but Christ Jesus
had the right
To enter in?
His blood, that sprinkled price,
So we might be assured
That our inheritance in light
Has been secured.
(*LSB* 564:1, 4)

A*LL THAT THE FATHER PLANNED" GOES BACK TO HIS WORDS IN* Genesis 3:15: "I will put enmity between you and the woman, and between your offspring and her offspring; He shall bruise your head, and you shall bruise His heel." "All that the Father planned" meant a costly sacrifice that only His Son could pay, and His Son willingly said, "Lord, here am I to do Your will."

Today's hymn speaks of a later point in "all that the Father planned"—for now His Son's saving work is complete, and He sits at God's right hand. Our "inheritance in light" has been secured, and sin, death, and the devil have been conquered! "Thanks be to God, who gives us the victory through our Lord Jesus Christ" (1 Corinthians 15:57).

"All that the Father planned" flows from a boundless, fatherly love for you and me. Another hymn writer said, "Love to the loveless shown that they might lovely be" (*LSB* 430:1). We were far from lovely, but the Father's love and the Father's plan made us lovely in His eyes, and that is where loveliness matters. While we await His return and our promised inheritance, His love surrounds us with gifts of grace.

"We thank You, Christ; new life is ours, new light, new hope, new strength, new pow'rs. This grace our ev'ry way attend until we reach our journey's end." Amen. (LSB *562:6*)

MAY 14

All praise to Christ we bring,
Our Lord who intercedes,
Our great High Priest enthroned above
Who knows our needs;
And to the Father sing
Our songs of thankful praise,
Who with the Spirit reigns in love
For endless days. (*LSB* 564:6)

HERE, WE RAISE A HYMN OF PROFOUND GRATITUDE AND PRAISE to the One who, in boundless love, has bestowed so much on us. This hymn is a testament to our great High Priest, who now sits at the Father's right hand, interceding on our behalf. He is our risen Lord and Savior, Jesus Christ, who understands and presents our needs to His Father. "Let us then with confidence draw near to the throne of grace, that we may receive mercy and find grace to help in time of need" (Hebrews 4:16).

One of the most treasured parts of living as God's children in His kingdom is knowing that we can always draw near the throne of grace for mercy and help. Repeatedly, Scripture gently tells us how much our heavenly Father wants us to come to Him with all that troubles us and see Him as the kind, gracious, and loving Father He is. And knowing that our blessed Jesus intercedes for us is an enormous comfort.

As God's children, we cannot help but explode in a hymn of thankfulness and praise, a high doxology to the Father, Son, and Holy Spirit, because the one who can meet our needs wants us to bring them to Him so that He can bless us, out of the abundance of His mercy and grace.

"Jesus, my great High Priest, offered His blood and died; my guilty conscience seeks no sacrifice beside. His pow'rful blood did once atone, and now it pleads before the Throne. My Advocate appears for my defense on high; the Father bows His ears and lays His thunder by. Not all that hell or sin can say shall turn His heart, His love, away." Amen. (TLH *220:1, 3*)

MAY 15

Rejoice, my heart, be glad and sing,
A cheerful trust maintain;
For God, the source of ev'rything,
Your portion shall remain.

Why spend the day in blank despair,
In restless thought the night?
On your Creator cast your care;
He makes your burdens light. (*LSB* 737:1, 3)

DAYS OF "BLANK DESPAIR," WHEN DEPRESSING THOUGHTS LEAD only to gloomy inaction. Nights of restless unease, when anxious thoughts keep us from sleep. Pastor Paul Gerhardt identifies human conditions that are just as real today as they were for him in the seventeenth century. But instead of lamenting such realities, he points to the solution: "Cast your burden on the LORD, and He will sustain you" (Psalm 55:22); cast "all your anxieties on Him, because He cares for you" (1 Peter 5:7).

To the one who is burdened, such advice may seem like wishful thinking. But Pastor Gerhardt expands on just who God, our Creator, is: our treasure, our joy, our "life and light and Lord," our shield, our great reward, our "counselor when doubts annoy" (st. 2). This God, described so expansively, invites us to place our burdens and anxieties on Him because He cares for us. It is both that simple and that profound.

God's ultimate care came when He saved us from the consequences of sin: All our "sins He casts aside in ocean depths to drown" (st. 5). The God who has accomplished our salvation will also be our help in days of blank despair and nights of restless thought. "He who did not spare His own Son but gave Him up for us all, how will He not also with Him graciously give us all things?" (Romans 8:32). Rejoice, be glad, and sing!

"He only will with patience chide, His rod falls gently down; and all your sins He casts aside in ocean depths to drown. Upon your lips, then, lay your hand, and trust His guiding love; then like a rock your peace shall stand here and in heav'n above." Amen. (LSB *737:5, 7*)

MAY 16

O gracious Lord, with love draw near
To these, Your children gathered here;
The Spirit's gift in them renew:
The gift of faith that clings to You.

Sustain the work You have begun
In these united to Your Son,
For in that pure baptismal flood
They have been cleansed by Jesus' blood. (*LSB* 599:1–2)

BAPTISM PLACES ON US THE NAME OF THE TRIUNE GOD AND begins its divine work of making a child of God. Then each child of God continues to grow in that good work through the Word and Spirit as we learn more deeply the truths of the faith. One way we grow in understanding that faith is through Luther's Small Catechism—a pedagogical masterpiece, presenting all the essential doctrines of the faith in the form of questions with answers.

Today's hymn was written by a pastor who knew what kind of singing would be most fitting upon completing such catechetical study. This beautiful prayer asks for the triune God's ongoing blessing for the baptized children of God kneeling and confessing their faith at His altar on this day. This is what we, as the church, fervently want for our dear ones who are young in the faith and have before them a whole life of Satan seeking to snatch them from this faithful path. Therefore, we pray:

Lord, keep them firm in their intent
To You, Your Word and Sacrament.
O make them bold, their faith to share
And make them strong, each cross to bear. (st. 4)

"Deliver them from ev'ry wile, from all that would their hearts beguile, from worldly ways and Satan's lies, that they may not Your Word despise. . . . O Father, grant that by Your grace they may Your will each day embrace; with fruits of faith their lives now bless, till they at death Your name confess." Amen. (LSB *599:3, 5*)

MAY 17

Come, my soul, with ev'ry care,
Jesus loves to answer prayer;
He Himself has bid thee pray,
Therefore will not turn away.

Thou art coming to a King,
Large petitions with thee bring;
For His grace and pow'r are such
None can ever ask too much. (*LSB* 779:1–2)

L*EARNING HOW TO PRAY MAY FEEL LIKE IT TAKES A LIFETIME TO* get it right. Even the apostles asked for help—"Lord, teach us to pray" (Luke 11:1)—and Jesus gave them the Lord's Prayer.

Prayer has been called an art form and has been compared to learning a new language—the heart's language. Such talk may make praying seem complex, but our Lord wishes it to be as easy as breathing for His children. We are simply talking to Him and bringing our needs to Him.

In these talks, we must remember two things: "Jesus loves to answer prayer" and we can never "ask too much." Today's hymn sings that we are coming to a King who loves to answer prayer and can grant anything. And this gracious King does not want the souls of His people to be burdened or troubled about anything, especially sin. He stands ready to hear petitions and grant His grace.

Nothing is too big to bring—no sin, no problem, no request. Absolutely no other king on earth can claim this and take such care of his people. But in Jesus' kingdom, we can come with every care to our omnipotent King, whose "grace and pow'r are such" that no one "can ever ask too much."

"With my burden I begin: Lord, remove this load of sin; let Thy blood, for sinners spilt, set my conscience free from guilt. Lord, Thy rest to me impart, take possession of my heart; there Thy blood-bought right maintain and without a rival reign." Amen. (LSB *779:3–4*)

MAY 18

While I am a pilgrim here,
Let Thy love my spirit cheer;
As my guide, my guard, my friend,
Lead me to my journey's end.

Show me what is mine to do;
Ev'ry hour my strength renew.
Let me live a life of faith;
Let me die Thy people's death. (*LSB* 779:5–6)

JESUS REGULARLY TOOK INTENTIONAL TIME FOR PRAYER AND meditation on the Word of God. If Jesus needed this prayer and meditation, how much more must we need it as we look to follow His example? We are pilgrims journeying to our true home and constantly need divine help as we travel.

We need a guide, a guard, and a friend—we need our Lord and Savior, Jesus Christ, to remove our sins and burdens. We know we, like Jesus, can come to our Father with every care and concern. So, we turn to Him constantly, which is precisely what He wants us to do.

We ask in this hymn that we might "live a life of faith." Such a life will start and end each day with prayer and will not stop there but have prayer almost constantly in the heart and on the lips. That is when prayer is right there for even a minor crisis and can grant comfort in a sleepless night.

In this life of faith, prayer will be like breathing. This breathing is hearing from Him and talking to Him constantly. We ask in the hymn, "Show me what is mine to do; ev'ry hour my strength renew." When our prayer is like breathing, He can do just that.

"With my burden I begin: Lord, remove this load of sin; let Thy blood, for sinners spilt, set my conscience free from guilt. Lord, Thy rest to me impart, take possession of my heart; there Thy blood-bought right maintain and without a rival reign." Amen. (LSB *779:3–4*)

MAY 19

To God the Holy Spirit let us pray
For the true faith needed on our way
That He may defend us when life is ending
And from exile home we are wending.
Lord, have mercy! (*LSB* 768:1)

JESUS PROMISED HIS DISCIPLES, "AND I WILL ASK THE FATHER, and He will give you another Helper, . . . the Spirit of truth" (John 14:16, 17). The Holy Spirit is our Helper—our Comforter, our Advocate who pleads before God on our behalf. He works faith in our hearts to believe the truth about God's gracious acts in Christ: "When the Spirit of truth comes, He will guide you into all the truth" (16:13).

Today's hymn teaches us something important about our prayer lives—namely, what do we ask of the Holy Spirit? Do we pray daily for true faith? Or do we take that for granted? As Luther wrote in this hymn, we pray for "true faith" so that the Holy Spirit may defend us—advocate on our behalf—when life here on earth is ending, when we are about to move from exile here to our true home, to live forever in the presence of Jesus, who redeemed us.

Do we pray that the Holy Spirit would teach us to know Jesus? Or do we take that for granted? One of the shortest and most pertinent requests in the Gospel accounts is put to the disciple Philip: "Sir, we wish to see Jesus" (John 12:21). That is our petition to the Holy Spirit as well, that we may know Jesus and "abide in the Lord who bought us, till to our true home He has brought us" (st. 4).

God wants us always to pray (Luke 18:1). Today's hymn teaches us to pray for the true faith, to pray that we would know Jesus Christ.

"Shine in our hearts, O Spirit, precious light; teach us Jesus Christ to know aright that we may abide in the Lord who bought us, till to our true home He has brought us. Lord, have mercy!" Amen. (LSB 768:4)

MAY 20

Come, Holy Ghost, God and Lord,
With all Your graces now outpoured
On each believer's mind and heart;
Your fervent love to them impart.
Lord, by the brightness of Your light
In holy faith Your Church unite;
From ev'ry land and ev'ry tongue
This to Your praise, O Lord, our God, be sung:
Alleluia, alleluia! (*LSB* 497:1)

MANY PENTECOST HYMNS ARE PRAYERS TO THE HOLY SPIRIT, of which today's Luther hymn is a splendid example. "Come, Holy Ghost, God and Lord" is often sung at call services at seminaries, at ordination or installation services, and on the Feast of Pentecost. All of these are times when the Holy Spirit's graces and power are prayed for—yes, fervently called on—to be "now outpoured."

In such services, the color red accompanies this hymn, for red is the churchly liturgical color signifying the work of the Holy Spirit. Therefore, the presence of red means something genuinely significant is happening in the life of Christ's church.

These are all signs of the divine at work, the work of the Holy Spirit, uniting Christ's church "from ev'ry land and ev'ry tongue" with the brightness of His light. Here the Holy Spirit is present as a holy fire bringing true comfort and strength as He gives Jesus Christ to His church. This is the only way we can contend, at times even bravely, through this earthly life.

"Come, holy Fire, comfort true, grant us the will Your work to do and in Your service to abide; let trials turn us not aside. Lord, by Your pow'r prepare each heart, and to our weakness strength impart that bravely here we may contend, through life and death to You, our Lord, ascend. Alleluia, alleluia!" Amen. (LSB *497:3*)

MAY 21

**Giver of grace, descend from high;
Your sev'nfold gifts to us supply;
Help us eternal truths receive
And practice all that we believe;
Give us Yourself that we may see
The glory of the Trinity. (*LSB* 500:3)**

PENTECOST ALWAYS BRINGS TO MIND THE WORK OF THE HOLY Spirit. As the Small Catechism explains, "the Holy Spirit has called me by the Gospel, enlightened me with His gifts, sanctified and kept me in the true faith" (Creed, Third Article.) The Holy Spirit is the one who works faith in us, and so we pray in today's hymn that the Holy Spirit would help us to receive eternal truths.

Sometimes we hear phrases like "I have decided to follow Jesus" or "I chose Jesus." While those sentiments may sound appealing, they neglect to understand rightly the work of the Holy Spirit in kindling our faith and keeping us with Jesus Christ in the one true faith. Jesus makes it clear in John 15:16: "You did not choose Me, but I chose you and appointed you that you should go and bear fruit." Similarly, John writes, "In this is love, not that we have loved God but that He loved us and sent His Son to be the propitiation for our sins" (1 John 4:10).

It is neither a trivial matter nor mere semantics; we need to understand the order of things: God *loved us* and sent His Son, Jesus, who *chose us* to be His beloved, redeemed children. God has acted on our behalf and accomplished our salvation. May the Holy Spirit always guide us to eternal truths.

"Lord, 'tis not that I did choose Thee; that, I know, could never be; for this heart would still refuse Thee had Thy grace not chosen me. Thou hast from the sin that stained me washed and cleansed and set me free and unto this end ordained me, that I ever live to Thee." Amen. (LSB 573:1)

MAY 22

Come down, O Love divine;
Seek Thou this soul of mine,
And visit it with Thine own ardor glowing;
O Comforter, draw near;
Within my heart appear,
And kindle it, Thy holy flame bestowing. (***LSB*** **501:1**)

IN TODAY'S HYMN, WE ASK THAT GOD THE HOLY SPIRIT WOULD COME to us, seeking our souls and enlightening us with His gifts. We know that we cannot of our own volition come to God; He must come to us. Jesus told His disciples, as He tells us, that He has already taken care of this problem: "But the Helper, the Holy Spirit, whom the Father will send in My name, He will teach you all things and bring to your remembrance all that I have said to you" (John 14:26). We desperately need this "Helper," this "Comforter," to work faith in our hearts! How? By teaching us all things and by bringing to our remembrance all that Jesus has said to us in His Word.

Why is this important? Jesus makes it clear in the next verse: "Let not your hearts be troubled, neither let them be afraid" (v. 27). As we walk through this life, with its share of troubles and fears, Jesus does not want our hearts to be troubled or fearful. Yes, we will have troubles in this world, but through the working of the Holy Spirit, we have the assurance that Jesus has overcome sin and death, thus quelling our deepest fears.

We pray that the "glorious light" of the Holy Spirit may "shine ever" on our sight (st. 2), comforting us by bringing to our remembrance all that Jesus has said to us, all that He has done to overcome the world.

"O let it freely burn, till worldly passions turn to dust and ashes in its heat consuming; and let Thy glorious light shine ever on my sight, and clothe me round, the while my path illuming." Amen. (LSB *501:2*)

MAY 23

Lord, Thee I love with all my heart;
I pray Thee, ne'er from me depart,
With tender mercy cheer me.
Earth has no pleasure I would share.
Yea, heav'n itself were void and bare
If Thou, Lord, wert not near me.
And should my heart for sorrow break,
My trust in Thee can nothing shake.
Thou art the portion I have sought;
Thy precious blood my soul has bought.
Lord Jesus Christ, my God and Lord, my God and Lord,
Forsake me not! I trust Thy Word. (*LSB* 708:1)

T***ODAY'S HYMN-PRAYER IS ONE OF THE MOST BELOVED HYMNS IN*** all of Lutheran hymnody. Here a saint's trusting voice seeks the tender mercy of their Lord Jesus Christ, whom they love with all their heart. Nothing can shake such trust, for Jesus Christ is first in their heart, soul, and mind.

And that is the place our Lord Jesus Christ wants to hold within each of us as our only and dearest treasure! Then, we will trust Him to be there for us no matter what trial, challenge, or sorrow may come our way. That is how it works in His kingdom.

Nothing on earth can compare with the most excellent treasure we have been given in our Lord Jesus Christ and His Word. Heaven itself would not be heaven if Jesus were not there, for His presence is heaven.

And we go forward knowing that He would never forsake us because His very precious blood bought us and made us His. Therefore, "Lord, Thee I love with all my heart."

"I build on this foundation, that Jesus and His blood alone are my salvation, my true, eternal good. Without Him all that pleases is valueless on earth; the gifts I have from Jesus alone have priceless worth." Amen. (LSB 724:2)

MAY 24

Yea, Lord, 'twas Thy rich bounty gave
My body, soul, and all I have
In this poor life of labor.
Lord, grant that I in ev'ry place
May glorify Thy lavish grace
And help and serve my neighbor.
Let no false doctrine me beguile;
Let Satan not my soul defile.
Give strength and patience unto me
To bear my cross and follow Thee.
Lord Jesus Christ, my God and Lord, my God and Lord,
In death Thy comfort still afford. (*LSB* 708:2)

WE LOOK AGAIN TODAY AT THE BELOVED HYMN-PRAYER "LORD, Thee I Love with All My Heart." Gifts of "body, soul, and all I have," plus a rich bounty of grace from the Giver of all good things—a cornucopia of magnificent blessings. That is what today's stanza recognizes with thanksgiving.

While we here have a life of labor, our faith is always richly fed by God's means of grace, filling us with His love. And that love lets us think about helping and serving our neighbor first. We cannot come to this way of thinking, giving, and acting on our own; that is His love in us.

The stanza continues with a prayer for protection from false doctrine and Satan's treachery while on our journey through this life of labor. It then asks for strength and patience to bear the crosses we will surely face on the blessed path of discipleship in God's kingdom, and finally it asks for the true comfort of Christ even at the time of death. What better gift than to know our Lord sustains each part of us in life and in death!

"O God, forsake me not! Lord, hear my supplication! In ev'ry evil hour help me resist temptation; and when the prince of hell my conscience seeks to blot, be then not far from me. . . . Lord, I am Yours forever. O keep me strong in faith that I may leave You never. Grant me a blessed end when my good fight is fought; help me in life and death—O God, forsake me not!" Amen. (LSB *731:3–4*)

MAY 25

Lord, let at last Thine angels come,
To Abr'ham's bosom bear me home,
That I may die unfearing;
And in its narrow chamber keep
My body safe in peaceful sleep
Until Thy reappearing.
And then from death awaken me,
That these mine eyes with joy may see,
O Son of God, Thy glorious face,
My Savior and my fount of grace.
Lord Jesus Christ, my prayer attend, my prayer attend,
And I will praise Thee without end. (*LSB* 708:3)

WE LOOK TODAY AT THE THIRD AND FINAL STANZA OF "LORD, Thee I Love with All My Heart." I have heard this text in many glorious musical settings, but perhaps the most beautiful rendering I have ever heard was at the deathbed of a 103-year-old man.

I was eager to begin ministering to him, but he held up one finger to stop me. Despite his labored and raspy breathing, he wished to speak. And speak he did. Slowly and with great effort, he said today's hymn one word at a time. And while one word at a time takes a long time, everyone in the room was in tears by the end.

What was happening here? A hymn etched in this man's memory was ministering to him as he died. Words memorized many decades ago confessed to him what was happening in that room as angels were ready to carry him to Abraham's bosom. As he sang these words in this unique and beautiful way, he was confessing to all that he was dying unfearing. Peace awaited him in the presence of Jesus, his Savior and his fount of grace, and so it awaits each of us, as our Lord's believing saints.

"Be still, my soul; the hour is hast'ning on when we shall be forever with the Lord, when disappointment, grief, and fear are gone, sorrow forgot, love's purest joys restored. Be still, my soul; when change and tears are past, all safe and blessed we shall meet at last." Amen. (LSB 752:4)

MAY 26

Our Father, who from heav'n above
Bids all of us to live in love
As members of one family
And pray to You in unity,
Teach us no thoughtless words to say
But from our inmost hearts to pray. (*LSB* 766:1)

GOD'S CHILDREN LEARN TO PRAY FROM JESUS CHRIST HIMSELF. And He teaches us to begin praying with the beautiful words, "Our Father." Martin Luther calls these words "friendly, sweet, . . . and warmhearted" (*Luther's Works*, vol. 42, p. 22). And in today's hymn, Luther offers this explanation of the Lord's Prayer to the church to sing.

The introduction to the Lord's Prayer—"Our Father who art in heaven"—is about a Father-child relationship that is almost beyond human comprehension in its beauty, simplicity, and greatness. The Small Catechism describes that relationship as one in which "with all boldness and confidence we may ask Him as dear children ask their dear father" (The Lord's Prayer, Introduction). And the "dear children" do this as members of one family praying in unity to our heavenly Father. Yes, we are all very different, but the differences come together in fellowship with this prayer, for here we are united as children of "our Father who art in heaven." Together, we pray to Him in unity "as members of one family."

And even more remarkable is that Jesus Christ Himself prays with this family, because His Father is our Father! Even when our bodies are tired and our words are weak, we place those tired, weak words in His hands and on His lips. He then prays them with us and for us.

"Amen, that is, so shall it be. Make strong our faith in You, that we may doubt not but with trust believe that what we ask we shall receive. Thus in Your name and at Your Word we say, 'Amen, O hear us, Lord!'" (LSB 766:9)

MAY 27

Your name be hallowed. Help us, Lord,
In purity to keep Your Word,
That to the glory of Your name
We walk before You free from blame.
Let no false teaching us pervert;
All poor deluded souls convert.

Your kingdom come. Guard your domain
And Your eternal righteous reign.
The Holy Ghost enrich our day
With gifts attendant on our way.
Break Satan's pow'r, defeat his rage;
Preserve Your Church from age to age. (*LSB* 766:2–3)

LUTHER'S HYMN ON THE LORD'S PRAYER CONTINUES TODAY BY looking at the first three petitions. These petitions teach God's children how to pray about their relationship with Him, specifically with regard to His name, His kingdom, and His will.

The First Petition—that God's name would be kept holy—is a worthy prayer, especially as we see His name and His Word being seriously misused rather than taught in truth and purity. But God cares very much about His name—so much so that He starts the Ten Commandments with the same directives. So we pray, "Help us, Lord, in purity to keep Your Word."

Likewise, we pray for God's kingdom to come and His will to be done. To today's minds in the world, and even sometimes in the church, God's will and authority are considered unacceptable, if they are considered at all. So we continue to pray for that kingdom and will, for His "eternal righteous reign," and we cannot help but add, "Lord, have mercy."

"Your gracious will on earth be done as it is done before Your throne, that patiently we may obey throughout our lives all that You say. Curb flesh and blood and ev'ry ill that sets itself against Your will." Amen. (LSB *766:4*)

MAY 28

Give us this day our daily bread,
And let us all be clothed and fed.
Save us from hardship, war, and strife;
In plague and famine, spare our life,
That we in honest peace may live,
To care and greed no entrance give. (*LSB* 766:5)

L*UTHER'S HYMN ON THE LORD'S PRAYER NOW TURNS TO "OUR"* petitions—when we ask for our needs, such as daily bread, bodily needs, health, family, government, weather, peace, neighbors, reputation, and so on in stanza 5. In stanza 6, our petitions continue with our greatest need: the forgiveness of sins. We also pray for the grace to forgive those who sin against us.

Stanza 7 asks for protection from the devil, the world, and our sinful nature. At times, it may seem like we are in the midst of a war, and so we pray for needed strength to overcome the devil's vicious attacks against us, that we may have victory over them.

And in stanza 8, we pray for rescue from any evil that may befall our body, soul, possessions, and reputation. We do have a great need for this protection all our days against this enemy, for as the hymn puts it, "the times and days are perilous" (st. 8). We also ask for a blessed end. As death draws near, we ask to be consoled and granted a calm and peaceful release as our souls are taken home to be with our Savior, Jesus.

Luther's final stanza brings the hymn to a close with a resounding amen, trusting "that what we ask we shall receive" from our Lord (st. 9).

"Forgive our sins, Lord, we implore, that they may trouble us no more; we, too, will gladly those forgive who hurt us by the way they live. Help us in our community to serve each other willingly. From evil, Lord, deliver us; the times and days are perilous. Redeem us from eternal death, and, when we yield our dying breath, console us, grant us calm release, and take our souls to You in peace." Amen. (LSB *766:6, 8*)

MAY 29

See, my soul, thy Savior chooses
Weakness here and poverty;
In such love He comes to thee.
Neither crib nor cross refuses;
All He suffers for thy good
To redeem thee by His blood. (*LSB* 897:2)

THE INCARNATION, PASSION, AND RESURRECTION OF JESUS—Christmas, Good Friday, and Easter—are inextricably intertwined. We don't often think of Good Friday during the Christmas season, though one of our best-loved carols confronts us with that harsh reality: "Nails, spear shall pierce Him through, the cross be borne for me, for you" (*LSB* 370:2). The Son of God obeyed His Father's will by coming as a baby, joining us in "weakness here and poverty" for one reason only: "to redeem thee by His blood."

Today's hymn provides a little poetic gem—namely, that Jesus refused "neither crib nor cross." Coming from the glory of the right hand of the Father, He was willing to be born as a helpless baby to live His infant years not in power but protected in a crib, still fully aware that ultimately He would die a painful death on a cross. As if the death of the Son of God on an instrument of torture was not in itself a sufficient penalty for the sins of the world, Jesus was forsaken by His Father—left to die utterly alone (Matthew 27:46)—so that we would never be alone, never be abandoned by God and left helpless in our sins.

To the contrary, when we die, we have the sweet comfort of knowing beyond any doubt that we are "saved eternally" (st. 3). How can we thank God for such a rich gift? The hymn writer asks this question and then tells us the answer: "I acknowledge that by Thee I am saved eternally" (st. 3). Faith in God's gift of redemption is our thankfulness to God.

"Lord, how shall I thank Thee rightly? I acknowledge that by Thee I am saved eternally. Let me not forget it lightly, but to Thee at all times cleave and my heart true peace receive." Amen. (LSB 897:3)

MAY 30

If Your beloved Son, O God,
Had not to earth descended
And in our mortal flesh and blood
Had not sin's power ended,
Then this poor, wretched soul of mine
In hell eternally would pine
Because of my transgression.

But now I find sweet peace and rest;
Despair no more reigns o'er me.
No more am I by sin oppressed,
For Christ has borne sin for me.
Upon the cross for me He died
That, reconciled, I might abide
With You, my God, forever. (*LSB* 568:1–2)

IF, THEN. *PAUL WRITES,* "*IF CHRIST HAS NOT BEEN RAISED,* THEN our preaching is in vain and your faith is in vain" (1 Corinthians 15:14, emphases added). Likewise, the hymn writer states that *if* Christ had not come to earth, taken human form, and ended the power of sin, *then* our souls would be consigned to hell eternally. Everything is dependent on Christ—His incarnation, His perfect life without sin, His willing obedience to go to the cross in our place, His death for us, and His glorious resurrection that defeated death once for all. He is the actor and the giver; we are the grateful recipients of His saving actions and His gracious gifts.

This makes all the difference for us not only eternally but even now. Instead of being oppressed by sin and despair, we "find sweet peace and rest." Instead of sorrow, we live anchored in the hope that only Christ can give, which He does through His Word and His Holy Supper, given freely and lavishly for us.

In fact, Christ *has* been raised from the dead! In fact, Christ Jesus *has* paid my debt "and gained for me God's favor" (st. 5). Thanks be to God!

"I trust in Him with all my heart; now all my sorrow ceases. His words abiding peace impart; His blood from guilt releases. Free grace through Him I now obtain; He washes me from ev'ry stain, and pure I stand before Him." Amen. (LSB *568:3*)

MAY 31

Behold, the world's
creator wears
The form and fashion of a slave;
Our very flesh our maker shares,
His fallen creatures all to save.

For this how wondrously
He wrought!
A maiden, in her lowly place,
Became, in ways
beyond all thought,
The chosen vessel of His grace.
(*LSB* 385:2–3)

On *May 31*, the church remembers and observes *Mary's* visitation to the home of Elizabeth and Zechariah. Upon Mary's entrance to their house, a miracle happened as John leaped for joy in Elizabeth's womb, and in this truly extraordinary way, John began his work as a forerunner of the Messiah. Mary's response is also extraordinary, for she erupts in song—not just any song but one of the church's treasured canticles, the Magnificat. In this visit, we see how the Holy Spirit works in those He has chosen for His dwelling. Just as John leaped for joy, Mary's heart overflowed with joy, and her spirit rejoiced greatly in God, her Savior, leading her to sing the glorious Magnificat. A similar thing occurs in us when Christ dwells in us and His Spirit makes its dwelling in us. We, too, cannot help but magnify the Lord. Paul writes about this in his admonition to the Ephesians: "Be filled with the Spirit, addressing one another in psalms and hymns and spiritual songs, singing and making melody to the Lord with your heart" (5:18–19). While we may not sing new and inspired canticles like Mary, our singing does express what our God has done for us and in us.

"My soul rejoices, my spirit voices—sing the greatness of the Lord! For God my Savior has shown me favor—sing the greatness of the Lord! With praise and blessing, join in confessing God, who is solely mighty and holy—O sing the greatness of God the Lord! His mercy surely shall rest securely on all who fear Him, love and revere Him—O sing the greatness of God the Lord!" Amen. (LSB *933:1*)

JUNE 1

If God Himself be for me,
I may a host defy;
For when I pray, before me
My foes, confounded, fly.
If Christ, my head and master,
Befriend me from above,
What foe or what disaster
Can drive me from His love? (*LSB* 724:1)

W*HILE* L*UTHER WROTE HYMNS THAT WERE SPLENDID TEACHING* sermons, Paul Gerhardt wrote hymns that were equally splendid devotional sermons. Very few other hymn writers begin to approach the greatness of what these two giants left for the church to sing.

Today's hymn stanza begins a Gerhardt masterpiece on trust, one of the finest devotions ever written on the subject, which will bless us for several days to follow. Pastor Gerhardt writes from the voice of one for whom trust means everything! This is because with Christ as Head and Master, God is on our side; we need to fear absolutely nothing!

Rock-solid trust comes from the unshakable belief that no matter what happens, we are covered by our Savior's gracious love and His plan for our life and we are never alone. "What foe or what disaster can drive me from His love?"

We know we belong to Jesus Christ, and nothing can separate us from His care, protection, and complete control over even the smallest detail in our lives. Nothing is left to fate, misfortune, or bad luck for the singing saint whose heart looks to and trusts Jesus Christ alone for everything.

"All depends on our possessing God's abundant grace and blessing, though all earthly wealth depart. They who trust with faith unshaken by their God are not forsaken and will keep a dauntless heart. If my days on earth He lengthen, God my weary soul will strengthen; all my trust in Him I place. Earthly wealth is not abiding, like a stream away is gliding; safe I anchor in His grace." Amen. (LSB *732:1, 6*)

JUNE 2

I build on this foundation,
That Jesus and His blood
Alone are my salvation,
My true, eternal good.
Without Him all that pleases
Is valueless on earth;
The gifts I have from Jesus
Alone have priceless worth. (*LSB* 724:2)

EVERY GIFT FROM JESUS IS PRICELESS! AND AS THE HYMN SAYS, "without Him all that pleases is valueless on earth." Nothing in this life can compare with His gracious and miraculous gifts to us. Without them, we have nothing; with them, we have everything!

Not all foundations in this world are equal—far from it. Today's hymn stanza confidently tells of the firmest possible foundation in the universe: "Jesus and His blood." And even though the singer of this hymn says, "I build," in reality, God begins to build our lives on this foundation at our Baptism and then continues to reinforce it through a lifetime of receiving His gifts of grace. Through these resplendent gifts, our foundation was first formed and then perfectly maintained. God's maintenance plan for His beloved children is like no other; it never fails and is good for all eternity.

This brilliant stanza seems to capture everything essential for life as God's child: our baptismal foundation, His ongoing gifts in His lavish means of grace, and of course, "Jesus and His blood," which alone are our salvation, our "true, eternal good." This is hard to take in, but as God's children, we want for nothing. Amen and amen!

"Jesus, Thy blood and righteousness my beauty are, my glorious dress; midst flaming worlds, in these arrayed, with joy shall I lift up my head. Bold shall I stand in that great day, cleansed and redeemed, no debt to pay; fully absolved through these I am from sin and fear, from guilt and shame." Amen. (LSB *563:1–2*)

JUNE 3

Christ Jesus is my splendor,
My sun, my light, alone;
Were He not my defender
Before God's judgment throne,
I never should find favor
And mercy in His sight,
But be destroyed forever
As darkness by the light.

He canceled my offenses,
Delivered me from death;
He is the Lord who cleanses
My soul from sin through faith.
In Him I can be cheerful,
Courageous on my way;
In Him I am not fearful
Of God's great Judgment
Day. (*LSB* 724:3–4)

PAUL GERHARDT'S TOWERING HYMN OF TRUST BRINGS TO MIND these words of Isaiah: "You keep him in perfect peace whose mind is stayed on You, because he trusts in You. Trust in the LORD forever, for the LORD GOD is an everlasting rock" (26:3–4). This text provides a wonderful meditation on that "perfect peace." We are kept in "perfect peace" with constant mercy and forgiveness, leading us to say, "Christ Jesus is my splendor, my sun, my light, alone." It is He who cancels all my offenses, He who delivers me from death, and He who brings me from darkness into the light. The word *alone* is the key here; "perfect peace" is not found in one of many places but in Christ Jesus *alone.*

Then Gerhardt answers the classic Small Catechism question "What does this mean?" It means that Christ Jesus "is the Lord who cleanses my soul from sin through faith. In Him I can be cheerful, courageous on my way; in Him I am not fearful of God's great Judgment Day." Perfect peace!

"You are my strength, my shield, my rock, my fortress that withstands each shock, my help, my life, my tower, my battle sword, almighty Lord—who can resist Your power?" Amen. (LSB 734:3)

JUNE 4

For no one can condemn me
Or set my hope aside;
Now hell no more can claim me:
Its fury I deride.
No sentence now reproves me,
No guilt destroys my peace;
For Christ, my Savior, loves me
And shields me with His grace. (*LSB* 724:5)

AS WE LIVE AND WALK DAILY WITH OUR SAVIOR, HE FEEDS US BY His Word and teaches us what love is and how He means for that love to shape our lives. Weekly, He welcomes us to His house and fills us with more of His love at His Table. With this, our Savior's love shields us with His grace and leads us to love our neighbor as we have first been loved. His love is our lifeblood.

Living in such love means "no one can condemn me or set my hope aside" and "no guilt destroys my peace." All fear is gone and is replaced with *true* peace when we walk in the love of Christ, our Savior. We are His, and He takes away all that could condemn us—we are set *free!*

Living His new commandment of love is impossible on our own; it requires Christ *in us*, and He stands ready to let His love shield and fill us with His grace. It bears repeating: His love is our lifeblood.

"Lord, Thee I love with all my heart; I pray Thee, ne'er from me depart, with tender mercy cheer me. Earth has no pleasure I would share. Yea, heav'n itself were void and bare if Thou, Lord, wert not near me. And should my heart for sorrow break, my trust in Thee can nothing shake. Thou art the portion I have sought; Thy precious blood my soul has bought. Lord Jesus Christ, my God and Lord, my God and Lord, forsake me not! I trust Thy Word." Amen. (LSB 708:1)

JUNE 5

Who clings with resolution
To Him whom Satan hates
Must look for persecution;
For him the burden waits
Of mock'ry, shame, and losses
Heaped on his blameless head;
A thousand plagues and crosses
Will be his daily bread. (*LSB* 724:6)

"***For the moment all discipline seems painful rather than*** pleasant, but later it yields the peaceful fruit of righteousness to those who have been trained by it" (Hebrews 12:11). That text, together with today's Gerhardt stanza, schools the disciple of Christ in precisely what to expect as a citizen of His kingdom.

"A thousand plagues and crosses will be his daily bread." One would think this statement outrageously brutal and cruel if one does not understand how our kind and wise heavenly Father cares for His children *in His love*. God's ways are not ours, and His thoughts are not ours; therefore, we may not understand what He is doing. But we can be assured His testing is for our good.

We are being disciplined, trained, and refined through these plagues and crosses. Our loving Father is building us up, pruning us, and strengthening us with trials designed *for us*. He knows what is best and exactly what we need.

Those trained by the Master in this way yield "the peaceful fruit of righteousness." This causes our faith to grow and bear fruit that would never have been possible before God's masterful pruning. His pruning causes us to cling to Him for everything, and we do such clinging grafted to Him—the healthiest place for us to be.

"God knows full well when times of gladness shall be the needful thing for thee. When He has tried thy soul with sadness and from all guile has found thee free, He comes to thee all unaware and makes thee own His loving care." Amen. (LSB 750:4)

JUNE 6

From me this is not hidden,
Yet I am not afraid;
I leave my cares, as bidden,
To whom my vows were paid.
Though life from me be taken
And ev'rything I own,
I trust in You unshaken
And cleave to You
alone. (*LSB* 724:7)

C***ARES AND TROUBLES, AS MENTIONED IN THE PREVIOUS STANZA*** and devotion, come to us all—that is a given. But what we do with them is not a given as it reveals something significant about us: where we are willing to place our trust. In today's hymn stanza, Pastor Paul Gerhardt demonstrates to his congregation faithful trust, thereby giving this wise advice: Give all your cares to the one who cares for you, your Lord and Savior, Jesus Christ. He is waiting to take your needs from you as He carries them for you. No one else loves you more than He does—so turn to Him.

Cleaving to Him with unshaken trust is healthy for us, even if we are in tears. As God's dear children, we know this is how things work in His kingdom, but our nature will fight it and tell us we should buck up and act independent.

Pastor Gerhardt's advice in this hymn teaches a theology of the cross, which will always strip us of our independence and bring us to a place of complete dependence. Meanwhile, everything around us shouts that this is foolishness and that it defies all good sense and reason. But we know crosses have always been seen as foolishness. "For the word of the cross is folly to those who are perishing, but to us who are being saved it is the power of God" (1 Corinthians 1:18). So we follow Gerhardt's example and embrace such "folly" with trust and peace.

"Father, O hear me, pardon and spare me; calm all my terrors, blot out my errors that by Thine eyes they may no more be scanned. Order my goings, direct all my doings; as it may please Thee, retain or release me; all I commit to Thy fatherly hand." Amen. (LSB *726:2*)

JUNE 7

No danger, thirst, or hunger,
No pain or poverty,
No earthly tyrant's anger
Shall ever vanquish me.
Though earth should
break asunder,
My fortress You shall be;
No fire or sword or thunder
Shall sever You from me.

No angel and no gladness,
No throne, no pomp, no show,
No love, no hate, no sadness,
No pain, no depth of woe,
No scheming, no contrivance,
No subtle thing or great
Shall draw me from
Your guidance
Nor from You separate.
(*LSB* 724:8–9)

WHAT RICH SINGING OF THE FAITH THIS IS! BLESSINGS ABOUND as we continue with this hymn, in which Pastor Gerhardt crafts the well-known Romans 8:31–39 passage by teaching what God's everlasting love means for His children.

"No" is the dominant word in these stanzas, but not a negative "no." On the contrary, it is repeated seventeen times for emphasis as it builds the robust case that *nothing* can separate us from Jesus Christ and His love for us. *Nothing* and *no one* in all of heaven and earth!

A man named Christian faced horrible obstacles on his road to heaven as God's child in John Bunyan's *The Pilgrim's Progress.* Yet, in the end, no obstacle of Satan was successful, and nothing separated Christian from God's plan to bring him safely home. Christian's story is our story. We know that even if the entire universe falls apart around us and Satan attacks us with all his might, God's love will be our mighty fortress and bring us safely home to Him. What immense strength and comfort this unshakable certainty brings as we, too, are pilgrims on our way home.

"From God can nothing move me; He will not step aside but gently will reprove me and be my constant guide. He stretches out His hand in evening and in morning, my life with grace adorning wherever I may stand." Amen. (LSB *713:1*)

JUNE 8

**My heart with joy is springing;
I am no longer sad.
My soul is filled with singing;
Your sunshine makes me glad.
The sun that cheers my spirit
Is Jesus Christ, my King;
The heav'n I shall inherit
Makes me rejoice and sing.** (*LSB* 724:10)

HOW CAN A PASTOR WRITE SUCH JOY-FILLED AND CHEERFUL words while serving amid unimaginable sorrow, grieving, and loss of the Thirty Years' War? And is it not puzzling that a stanza of exuberant rejoicing closes an intense hymn about the theology of the cross? No, this is unsurprising when the hymn writer is Pastor Paul Gerhardt.

The theology of the cross is not gloom and doom for those who understand it, believe it, and live it as Gerhardt did. As a pastor in very challenging times, he was living the glorious truths of Romans 8:31–39 and decided to write a hymn that let the whole church sing about how our God works.

Our hearts can be filled with joy and singing because nothing can separate us from our Lord, who loves us so much. A glad heart and a soaring spirit lead one to a joyously sung confession like this stanza. And for Pastor Gerhardt, this is how the big-picture story ends, so this is how he ends his hymn.

"There's nothing that can sever from this great love of God; no want, no pain whatever, no famine, peril, flood. Though thousand foes surround me, for slaughter mark His sheep, they never shall confound me, the vict'ry I shall reap. Nor any creature ever shall from the love of God this ransomed sinner sever; for in my Savior's blood this love has its foundation; God hears my faithful prayer and long before creation named me His child and heir." Amen. (LSB *746:2, 4*)

JUNE 9

We all believe in one true God,
Who created earth and heaven,
The Father, who to us in love
Has the right of children given.
He in soul and body feeds us;
All we need His hand
provides us;
Through all snares
and perils leads us,
Watching that no
harm betide us.
He cares for us by
day and night;
All things are governed by
His might. (*LSB* 954:1)

IN HIS *SMALL CATECHISM*, MARTIN LUTHER PROVIDED AN explanation of the Apostles' Creed in its three Articles devoted to God the Father, God the Son, and God the Holy Spirit. He also wrote this hymn, in which we sing and pray of the triune God—one stanza for each person of the Trinity.

In His great love for us, God the Father, Creator of heaven and earth, has made us His children, which makes us *coheirs* of God's riches through Christ: "We are children of God, and if children, then heirs—heirs of God and fellow heirs with Christ" (Romans 8:16–17). This is a remarkable truth that we may not often think of in quite this way. "The right of children" means that we *inherit* the riches that belong to Christ. We know that Christ sits at the right hand of the Father; by our inheritance, we, too, shall reside forever with Christ in the heavenly kingdom of His Father.

God the Father feeds us "in soul and body," giving us what we need for our souls—His Word and Sacraments—and for our bodies—food, drink, clothing, house, home, health, and safety. As our heavenly Father, He watches over us on our journey through this world and keeps us from harm and danger, both day and night.

We are in God the Father's care in this life, and we are heirs of His eternal riches in the heavenly world to come.

"We all believe in one true God, Father, Son, and Holy Ghost, ever-present help in need, praised by all the heav'nly host; all He made His love enfolds, all creation He upholds." Amen. (LSB *953:1*)

JUNE 10

**We all believe in Jesus Christ,
His own Son, our
Lord, possessing
An equal Godhead,
throne, and might,
Source of ev'ry grace
and blessing;
Born of Mary, virgin mother,
By the power of the Spirit,
Word made flesh, our
elder brother;
That the lost might life inherit,
Was crucified for all our sin
And raised by God to life
again. (*LSB* 954:2)**

JESUS CHRIST IS THE SON OF GOD THE FATHER AND AN EQUAL WITH the Father and the Holy Spirit as triune God, where "none is greater or less than another" (Athanasian Creed, *LSB*, p. 320). Jesus Christ is our Lord, who is the "source of ev'ry grace and blessing" *for us*—sinners redeemed by His blood.

Conceived by the power of the Holy Spirit, Jesus was born of the virgin Mary—thus without the curse of original sin that is the reality for every other human conceived (Psalm 51:5). The eternal Son of God lowered Himself and willingly became fully human, in Luther's words, "our elder brother." "The Word became flesh and dwelt among us" (John 1:14). But at the same time, Jesus was fully divine and able to keep God's Law perfectly on behalf of the sinful human race. He shed His blood on the cross to pay the price for all the sins of all people of all time. In His glorious resurrection, He defeated death; death will never have the last word for those who believe in Jesus.

In God's redemptive story, "the lost might life *inherit*" (emphasis added). This is the same truth that we pray in the first stanza of this hymn—that the Father has given us "the right of children" (st. 1), the right to be the children of God and to inherit the riches He longs to give us. Far greater than any earthly inheritance from parent to child, the redemptive work of Jesus Christ—Son of God and our Lord—gives us eternal life in His presence.

"We all believe in Jesus Christ, Son of God and Mary's son, who descended from His throne and for us salvation won; by whose cross and death are we rescued from all misery." Amen. (LSB *953:2*)

JUNE 11

We all confess the Holy Ghost,
Who, in highest heaven dwelling
With God the Father
and the Son,
Comforts us beyond all telling;
Who the Church, His
own creation,
Keeps in unity of spirit.
Here forgiveness and salvation
Daily come through Jesus' merit.
All flesh shall rise,
and we shall be
In bliss with God eternally.
Amen. (*LSB* 954:3)

JESUS PROMISED HIS DISCIPLES THAT HE WOULD SEND THE Comforter, the "Helper" (John 14:16), the Spirit of truth: "He will guide you into all the truth" (John 16:13). The Holy Spirit "called me by the Gospel, enlightened me with His gifts, sanctified and kept me in the true faith" (Small Catechism, Creed, Third Article). On our own, we cannot believe in Jesus Christ, but the Holy Spirit works faith in us to believe the good news of the Gospel. That is a comfort "beyond all telling."

Moreover, the entire Christian Church on earth is the work of the Holy Spirit—"His own creation." When Jesus told Peter, "I will build My church, and the gates of hell shall not prevail against it" (Matthew 16:18), that is the same promise. God builds His church; we do not. When we are tempted to bemoan the state of the church in our time, when we think it is somehow ineffective without our novel ideas, we must remember that the church is created and kept by the work of the Holy Spirit.

In this hymn stanza, Luther also teaches the purpose of the church: "Here forgiveness and salvation daily come through Jesus' merit." The church is where God's called and ordained pastors preach forgiveness and salvation through the atoning work of Jesus. The church is the place where Holy Baptism opens the door to heaven and where the Lord's Supper gives us Christ's body and blood for the forgiveness of sins. All this so that we may be "in bliss with God eternally"!

"We all confess the Holy Ghost, who from both in truth proceeds, who sustains and comforts us in all trials, fears, and needs. Blessed, holy Trinity, praise forever be to Thee!" Amen. (LSB *953:3*)

JUNE 12

Preach you the Word
and plant it home
To men who like or like it not,
The Word that shall
endure and stand
When flow'rs and men
shall be forgot.

The sower sows; his
reckless love
Scatters abroad the goodly seed,
Intent alone that all may have
The wholesome loaves that
all men need. (*LSB* 586:1, 3)

As a seminary professor, Martin Franzmann taught future pastors to sow and plant God's Word, and he was also an extraordinary hymn writer. In today's hymn, he crafts the "sower texts" of the Gospels into an ordination hymn, a masterpiece!

"Preach You the Word" is for preachers *and* hearers, as it is a hymn-homily on precisely what happens when God's Word is preached, planted, and sown—a master lesson for those in the pulpit and the pew. Why is this important for the hearer? Because it is crucial that the flock rightly understands the office of the ministry. God is sending a sower to them in the form of a pastor. They are receiving a great gift.

Franzmann's ordination hymn tells it like it is with zero sugarcoating. Therefore, on his first day, the ordinand hears a sanctuary filled with his new flock, family, friends, and clergy loudly singing and pointedly telling him that planting the Word in God's kingdom is a "hard . . . task" (st. 2)—and he should forget about praise and profit.

Instead, he is now to be about God's "scattered plenteousness" (st. 5), a "reckless love" of preaching, teaching, and planting His Word home. In His wisdom, God has placed this man in this specific place to do this miraculous planting.

In summation of his hymn, Franzmann writes, "Never faint; the Harvest Lord who gave the sower seed to sow will watch and tend His planted Word" (st. 6). Amen.

"Give us lips to sing Thy glory, tongues Thy mercy to proclaim, throats that shout the hope that fills us, mouths to speak Thy holy name. Alleluia, alleluia! May the light which Thou dost send fill our songs with alleluias, alleluias without end!" Amen. (LSB 578:5)

JUNE 13

Baptized into Your name most holy,
O Father, Son, and Holy Ghost,
I claim a place, though weak and lowly,
Among Your saints, Your chosen host.
Buried with Christ and dead to sin,
Your Spirit now shall live within. (*LSB* 590:1)

IN HIS LARGE CATECHISM, LUTHER WROTE THAT BAPTISM "IS SO full of consolation and grace that heaven and earth cannot understand it" (Part 4, paragraph 39). This lifelong consolation comes to us because God—not man—is the one who graciously works in and through Baptism. The benefits of Baptism—forgiveness of sins and eternal salvation—are ours not by virtue of human decision but by the grace of God, who gives us these priceless gifts out of sheer, undeserved love. God is the one who gives us a place among His saints, takes us to be His child and heir, and makes His Holy Spirit live within us.

The apostle Paul wrote that "all of us who have been baptized into Christ Jesus were baptized into His death" (Romans 6:3). The wonderful corollary of that statement comes next: "For if we have been united with Him in a death like His, we shall certainly be united with Him in a resurrection like His" (v. 5). So in Baptism, we get the dying over with, and we receive the ultimate gift of resurrection to eternal life with Christ, the one who works through water and the Word in Baptism.

That is the consolation that Luther wrote about, and the baptized children of God know with full certainty that however we may be afflicted on our walk through this life, we will be "united with Him in a resurrection like His." Thanks be to God for making us His children and heirs in Holy Baptism!

"My loving Father, here You take me to be henceforth Your child and heir. My faithful Savior, here You make me the fruit of all Your sorrows share. O Holy Spirit, comfort me when threat'ning clouds around I see." Amen. (LSB *590:2*)

JUNE 14

Jesus sat with His disciples
On a mountainside one day;
As the crowds of people gathered,
He began to teach and say:
"Blessed are the poor in spirit,
Heaven's kingdom they will share.
Blessed are the sad and mourning,
Joy and comfort will be theirs." (*LSB* 932:1)

J*OY AND COMFORT WILL BE THEIRS." REMEMBERING OUR LORD'S* birth, we often sing the refrain, "Oh, that we were there!" (e.g., *LSB* 386:4). Those words may also come to mind when we read Matthew's account of Jesus teaching on a mountainside. Oh, that we could have been there to hear Jesus Himself give a master class on His kingdom.

On that mountainside, Jesus gave a life lesson to the crowds—not just any life, but *life in His kingdom*. I wonder if the day Jesus presented it, the lesson was as misunderstood as it is today. For man's ears want to hear Law and are inclined to turn teaching like this into Law, but Jesus was giving pure Gospel.

The language of the Beatitudes is not demand and command—instead, it is a language describing God's children filled with Christ. And this is because there is not one part of these beautiful Beatitudes that the children could do on their own without Him living in them.

Starting with the first beatitude, we see that Jesus was the one who was truly poor in spirit, who mourns over sin, who is meek, who is humble, who is merciful, who is pure in heart, who makes peace between God and man, who suffers for righteousness.

There is only one way that "joy and comfort will be theirs"—if Jesus lives in them with His blessed means of grace.

"O Lord, let this Your little flock, Your name alone confessing, continue in Your loving care, true unity possessing. Your sacraments, O Lord, and Your saving Word to us, Lord, pure retain. Grant that they may remain our only strength and comfort." Amen. (LSB 647:2)

JUNE 15

"Blessed are the meek and humble,
All the earth to them is willed.
Those who hunger to be holy,
They are bless'd and will be filled.
Yes, the merciful are blessed,
Mercy will to them be shown.
And the pure in heart are blessed,
They have eyes for God alone." (*LSB* 932:2)

W***HAT A STRANGE KINGDOM THIS IS, WHERE THINGS SEEM TO*** be upside-down, inside-out, and backward from what we expect! Indeed, by reason, nothing makes sense in God's kingdom. Nevertheless, the crowds gathered to hear Jesus' message.

They learned that His disciples are poor, meek, humble, hungry, and could be persecuted, even to death. While this is true, their foremost identifying characteristic is that "they have eyes for God alone." And those beautiful eyes make them "pure in heart" and "blessed." That is Jesus' message to the gathered crowds.

The poor in spirit repent of their sins and are humbled like a child. They mourn their sins and the whole world's sins, and they seek blessed forgiveness. They hunger and thirst for righteousness and are willing to lose their life for it.

Then the Lord of this kingdom hears His blessed saints and gives them a pure heart as He takes away their sins. These blessed, forgiven, and righteous saints have been treated with extraordinary mercy—and they are now able to go forth in God's love, mercy, and forgiveness to give these beautiful gifts to their neighbors.

"Lord, give us faith to walk where You are sending, on paths unmarked, eyes blind as to their ending; not knowing where we go, but that You lead us—with grace precede us. You, Jesus, You alone deserve all glory! Our lives unfold, embraced within Your story; past, present, future—You, the same forever—You fail us never!" Amen (LSB 667:5–6)

JUNE 16

"Blessed are God's sons and daughters,
Making peace where there is strife.
Blessed are the persecuted,
Who for righteousness lose life;
Their reward is great in heaven,
In the kingdom up above—
So be glad to share My suff'ring
And rejoice to know My love." (*LSB* 932:3)

WHILE LIFE IN GOD'S KINGDOM IS A BLESSED ROAD, IT IS NOT easy and has often ended in martyrdom. With the prophets, martyrs, and a whole host of saints who have gone before, God's sons and daughters walk the kingdom road described in the Beatitudes—the path of discipleship. Oh, how blessed are these sons and daughters!

And yes, the discipleship path of the Beatitudes may include suffering and persecution. Nevertheless, this path is wonderfully different from all other paths because Jesus walks every step of the way with you. No one knows you better, and He has designed the right path for you as His beloved and dear disciple. And on your path, you will be richly fed, always protected, and never alone!

And it gets even better. Your "reward is great in heaven, in the kingdom up above"—an eternity of unspeakable joy and bliss awaits you. O redeemed saint and faithful disciple, you can trust with all your heart that there will be a glorious end to your earthly path. Pure joy, no tears, and a long-awaited rest for your soul. Oh, how "blessed are God's sons and daughters"!

"Christ has wiped away their tears forever; they have that for which we still endeavor. By them are chanted songs that ne'er to mortal ears were granted. Come, O Christ, and loose the chains that bind us; lead us forth and cast this world behind us. With You, the Anointed, finds the soul its joy and rest appointed." Amen. (LSB *679:4–5*)

JUNE 17

All praise to Thee, who safe hast kept
And hast refreshed me while I slept;
Grant, Lord, when I from death shall wake,
I may of endless light partake. (*LSB* 868:3)

WHAT ARE SOME OF OUR FIRST THOUGHTS WHEN WE AWAKEN each morning? Perhaps we recall a particularly vivid dream from the previous night. More likely, our minds move rather quickly to what is coming up on a new day—events, obligations, work, family plans. The hymn writer reminds us of something we are too apt to take for granted—namely, to praise and thank our gracious God for keeping us safe through the night. Luther's Morning Prayer begins in just such a way: "I thank You, my heavenly Father, through Jesus Christ, Your dear Son, that You have kept me this night from all harm and danger" (Small Catechism).

As we move into the new day, it is good to remember God's startling promise to us: "The steadfast love of the LORD never ceases; His mercies never come to an end; they are new every morning" (Lamentations 3:22–23). It is a remarkable gift—God's love and mercy come to us *anew* every day, each time we wake from sleep. Thus, we pray with the psalmist, "Satisfy us in the morning with Your steadfast love, that we may rejoice and be glad all our days" (Psalm 90:14).

The hymn writer reminds us of yet another important theme for morning prayer and devotion. One day we shall awaken from death; as we anticipate that blessed reality, we pray, "I may of endless light partake." Each day we wake to the tasks our God graciously gives us in our various vocations in life and we give thanks for sins forgiven, for the promise of eternal life in Christ, for the sure and certain hope of "endless light" in His presence.

"Direct, control, suggest this day all I design or do or say that all my pow'rs with all their might in Thy sole glory may unite." Amen. (LSB 868:5)

JUNE 18

Lord, support us all day long,
Guide and strengthen.
Evening comes, the
world is hushed,
Shadows lengthen,
Work is done, life's fevered pace
Now has ended;
Christ, to You, our final rest
Is commended.

Be our light in darkness, Lord,
Our defender;
In Your presence perils all
Must surrender.
Drive all dark satanic snares
From each dwelling;
Then, at peace, our
hearts Your praise
Will be telling. (*LSB* 884:1–2)

FOR THE FAITHFUL, ONE-ON-ONE CONVERSATIONS WITH GOD ARE the most essential part of every day. We, the saints, are hungry to hear from Him in His Word and to bring our needs to His throne. We have listened to our Lord's "Come to Me" (Matthew 11:28), and we come. The "when" of this devotional time may vary—morning for some, last thing at night for others, or grabbing a few quiet moments during the day.

These beautiful words in Pastor Stephen Starke's hymn, which we begin today, are just right for talking to God at the end of the day. It is a prayer recognizing the ongoing need for God's support, guidance, and strength in the fevered pace of life. But today's pace and work have ended, and we seek rest, peaceful sleep, and calm. And we pray for protection from "all dark satanic snares," for those forces never rest but continue their hideous work even as we sleep.

A peaceful night is one of life's most welcome blessings. For that, our minds must be quieted and our bodies calm and relaxed so that peaceful rest may overtake us. This happens when we have commended all things to our Lord and Savior, Jesus Christ.

"Gracious Lord, we give You thanks, praise and bless You, as the giver of all good we confess You. This past day we now commit to Your keeping and entrust to You the hours of our sleeping." Amen. (LSB 884:4)

JUNE 19

With Your presence,
Lord, draw near
Those who labor
Through the nighttime
on behalf
Of their neighbor.

Grant them courage
for each fear,
Faithful caring:
Your compassion and Your love
Truly sharing. (*LSB* 884:3)

F***IREFIGHTERS, POLICE, DOCTORS, NURSES, AND OTHERS*** selflessly dedicate their nights to serving their communities while we rest. They remain vigilant and ready to assist their neighbors, their selflessness shining through their actions. Yet we often sleep, unaware of their unwavering commitment to our safety and well-being.

Today's hymn is our prayer for them: "Grant them courage for each fear, faithful caring: Your compassion and Your love truly sharing." Our prayer today recognizes these laborers as divine messengers sent by God to care for us, His children. "For He will command His angels concerning you to guard you in all your ways" (Psalm 91:11). These nighttime workers who surround us are not just workers but laborers in His service.

They need our prayers and divine help in their tasks. We, as God's children, know they need His presence in their work. This hymn-prayer begins by asking for that blessed, divine presence for them as they labor. And then, with David, we can confidently say every night, "In peace I will both lie down and sleep; for You alone, O Lord, make me dwell in safety" (Psalm 4:8).

"Lord Jesus, since You love me, now spread Your wings above me and shield me from alarm. Though Satan would devour me, let angel guards sing o'er me: This child of God shall meet no harm. My loved ones, rest securely, for God this night will surely from peril guard your heads. Sweet slumbers may He send you and bid His hosts attend you and through the night watch o'er your beds." Amen. (LSB 880:4–5)

JUNE 20

Gracious Lord, we
give You thanks,
Praise and bless You,
As the giver of all good
We confess You.

This past day we now commit
To Your keeping
And entrust to You the hours
Of our sleeping. (*LSB* 884:4)

THIS IS THE EVENING PRAYER FOR THE CHILDREN OF GOD, FAITHFUL believers. The simple and beautiful prayer reveals that the saints who sing this

- come to their Lord at the end of the day.
- come with thanksgiving and praise to "the giver of all good."
- come confessing Him as the one who has blessed and kept them through the day now past.
- come to their Lord as night now approaches—in prayer.
- commit all that happened in the day now past to His keeping.
- entrust the coming hours of sleep and rest to His gracious care and keeping.

The saints rest securely and at peace, for they do not carry a day's labors and concerns to their beds and can sleep trustingly and peacefully. Moreover, the saints are deeply grateful for another day of gracious fatherly care and keeping. A heart filled with gratitude is a heart at peace; as saints, we are ready to commit and entrust the coming hours of night and darkness into the hands of our gracious heavenly Father, who sees, knows, and is in control of everything in our lives while He is also in control of the whole universe.

"Lord Jesus, since You love me, now spread Your wings above me and shield me from alarm. Though Satan would devour me, let angel guards sing o'er me: This child of God shall meet no harm. My loved ones, rest securely, for God this night will surely from peril guard your heads. Sweet slumbers may He send you and bid His hosts attend you and through the night watch o'er your beds." Amen. (LSB *880:4–5*)

JUNE 21

We walk by faith and
not by sight,
No gracious words we hear
From Him who spoke
as none e'er spoke,
But we believe Him near.

For You, O resurrected Lord,
Are found in means divine:
Beneath the water
and the Word,
Beneath the bread and
wine. (*LSB* 720:1, 4)

I REMEMBER ONCE BEING ASKED, "DOES GOD SPEAK TO YOU?" I replied that, yes, in His Word, God does indeed speak to me. But my questioner pressed me by asking whether I actually heard Jesus speaking—specifically, singularly to me. Again, I pointed to God's Word. Today's hymn suggests a more complete answer.

The apostle Paul wrote that "we walk by faith, not by sight" (2 Corinthians 5:7). By faith, which is solely the work of the Holy Spirit, we trust in the God that we do not *see* face to face this side of heaven. By faith, we believe the words of Jesus given to us in Holy Scripture, though we will not *hear* His voice until He awakens us from death on the Last Day. He tells us, "Blessed are those who have not seen and yet have believed" (John 20:29). And "Blessed rather are those who hear the word of God and keep it" (Luke 11:28).

God has graciously established means by which He comes to us—not private, privileged ways available to a chosen few, but means readily available to all in His church. He promises to be there in His Word, preached by His called pastors. His Word with the water of Holy Baptism "works forgiveness of sins, rescues from death and the devil, and gives eternal salvation to all who believe" (Small Catechism, Baptism, Second Part). In His Holy Supper, He give us His very body and blood "beneath the bread and wine" for the forgiveness of sins. These means of grace are ours by faith.

"Lord, when our life of faith is done, in realms of clearer light we may behold You as You are, with full and endless sight." Amen. (LSB 720:5)

JUNE 22

Father, hear my prayer,
Keep me safe today;
Sanctify my thoughts,
All I do and say:
As I teach the young
And esteem the old,
May Your bounteous grace
By my life be told.

Lord, I will today
On Your love rely;
Let no evil thought
Cloud the clear blue sky.
Joyful and content
With life's simpler things,
Knowing all I need
From Your kindness
springs. (*LSB* 871:2–3)

WHETHER YOU ARE A *FORTUNE* 500 CEO, A MIDDLE SCHOOL student, a farmer, a pastor, a pregnant mother, or a patient in assisted care, everyone needs their day to start "right"—and that means with God and not on your own. Today's hymn starts your day "right" with God as you immediately call upon Him as your Father.

At the dawn of each new day, we cannot begin to know our needs for that day but trust that our heavenly Father knows. So, we confidently come to Him and ask for His safety and blessing; in doing so, we rely on His promises of love and grace for us, His baptized children. Our baptismal life is filled with that kind of care and keeping.

This hymn contains a unique petition: May we be "joyful and content with life's simpler things," knowing that all we need "from Your kindness springs." Yes, it is good to embrace "life's simpler things" with joy and contentment and view them as a beautiful part of our heavenly Father's kind and gracious providence toward us. "Oh, how abundant is Your goodness, which You have stored up for those who fear You" (Psalm 31:19).

"The Father's love shield me this day; the Son's pure wisdom cheer my way; the Holy Spirit's joy and light drive from my heart the shades of night. Lord, bless and keep me as Your own; Lord, look in kindness from Your throne; Lord, shine unfailing peace on me by grace surrounded; set me free." Amen. (LSB *876:3, 5*)

JUNE 23

All Christians who have
been baptized,
Who know the God of heaven,
And in whose daily life is prized
The name of Christ once given:
Consider now what
God has done,
The gifts He gives to ev'ryone
Baptized into Christ Jesus!

You were before your
day of birth,
Indeed, from your conception,
Condemned and lost
with all the earth,
None good, without exception.
For like your parents'
flesh and blood,
Turned inward from
the highest good,
You constantly denied
Him. (*LSB* 596:1–2)

This is the one hymn Paul Gerhardt wrote on Baptism, and it is a gem. It is more Luther-like didactic and a bit of a departure from Gerhardt's usual devotional meditation hymn. Yet it is undoubtedly one of Lutheranism's finest hymns on the baptismal life. We will walk through this hymn over the next few days.

Our Baptism was God's work—pure grace, pure Gospel—when He placed His name on us at the font, making us His children. We go from the font to live in His gracious gifts and follow as His disciples, with the promise of an eternity with Him. This hymn's first stanza explodes with these miraculous Gospel truths.

But then, in Gerhardt's second stanza, we hear who we were before our Baptism, and these things are hard to hear. We were born into the deep sadness of what Adam and Eve left for us, as we were "turned inward from the highest good" and "constantly denied Him." We were "condemned and lost with all the earth." Everything was at stake! That is why the day of our Baptism is the most important day in our life. What other day can compare to the day when we were named His child and given *everything*?

"And thus I live in God contented and die without a thought of fear; my soul has to God's plans consented, for through His Son my faith is clear. O God, for Jesus' sake I pray Your peace may bless my dying day." Amen. (LSB 598:3)

JUNE 24

You, child, will go on before the Lord
As prophet, His way preparing;
To speak on behalf of God Most High,
His counsel of truth declaring:
Rich mercy and grace for all whereby
Iniquity is forgiven. (*LSB* 936:3)

LIKE MARY'S MAGNIFICAT, ZECHARIAH'S BENEDICTUS SPEAKS OF God's mighty deeds in the past, His intervention now, and His promises for the future. God, with His own Son, is stepping into history to redeem His people from their sins and accomplish their salvation. "Rich mercy and grace for all whereby iniquity is forgiven."

After nine months of silence, Zechariah is filled with the Holy Spirit and offers a hymn filled with prophecy about his son, John. It sets forth the eight-day-old John's purpose and path—to go on before the Lord as he prepares His way. John will "speak on behalf of God Most High," declaring His "counsel of truth." John will speak and be a lamp, going before and preparing the way for Christ.

This inspired hymn ends with the stark reality of our need for this bright, rising Sun and His illumination—"give light to those who sit in darkness and in the shadow of death, to guide our feet into the way of peace" (Luke 1:79). God had a plan of saving His children that would scatter the shades of sin and death and shatter their domination. His plan involved His dear Son and a child named John, who would go before Him to prepare His way, which would bring true peace to all of creation.

"O bright, rising Sun, now shine on us in need of illumination; come scatter the shades of sin and death and shatter their domination. Be guiding our footsteps on the path of peace, in Your presence dawning!" Amen. (LSB *936:4*)

JUNE 25

In Baptism we now put on Christ—
Our shame is fully covered
With all that He once sacrificed
And freely for us suffered.
For here the flood of His own blood
Now makes us holy, right, and good
Before our heav'nly Father. (*LSB* 596:4)

In Baptism, we are made holy, right, and good before our heavenly Father. Therefore, this blessed Sacrament is the highest and greatest miracle that can happen to us! A miracle was needed; before our Baptism, we were a sad and lost mess, but all of that was washed away when we "put on Christ." Baptism became our new daily garment.

What makes this even more astounding is that *He did it all* as a gift! He brings His treasure to newborns who cannot speak and names them His children. It is God's work in a gift like no other! For by His boundless grace, we are reborn as His children, and nothing can separate us from this priceless treasure.

This is all because of what Jesus Christ won for us in His resurrection—that is how He can bestow this gift upon us: "with all that He once sacrificed and freely for us suffered." It is this rebirth as His children in which we safely live all our days. Gerhardt's following words are the perfect conclusion to today's hymn devotion:

O Christian, firmly hold this gift
And give God thanks forever!
It gives the power to uplift
In all that you endeavor.
When nothing else revives your soul,
Your Baptism stands and makes you whole
And then in death completes you. (st. 5)

"My faithful God, You fail me never; Your promise surely will endure. O cast me not away forever if words and deeds become impure. Have mercy when I come defiled; forgive, lift up, restore Your child." Amen. (LSB *590:3*)

JUNE 26

So use it well! You are made new—
In Christ a new creation!
As faithful Christians, live and do
Within your own vocation,
Until that day when you possess
His glorious robe of righteousness
Bestowed on you forever! (*LSB* 596:6)

PASTOR PAUL GERHARDT OFFERS EXCELLENT PASTORAL ADVICE: Use your baptismal gift well! He wants you, dear baptized faithful child, to know that you are a new creation; your rebirth sees you through whatever your vocational or daily challenges may be. He wants you to see that every part of your life is *filled* with the blessings of baptismal grace. "Use it well!"

While this may seem obvious, pastors know that not everyone uses the day-to-day power available to them in their Baptism. Too often, even lifelong Christians think of Baptism as a one-time event that is over and done, so they believe it is up to them to live life on *their* strength and power from day to day. They see their Baptism as history, something marked by a big family celebration, something they cannot begin to remember, or something not relevant to their life now.

But this is tragically wrong! Your Baptism is a gift that you need, sorely need, daily for ongoing strength, power, and forgiveness in living your life—the *baptismal life*! You cannot and do not have to do it alone—for you are God's chosen and beloved child. So it makes sense that a pastor would, in his hymn writing, gently yet firmly nudge his flock toward using this extraordinary gift well.

"With one accord, O God, we pray: Grant us Your Holy Spirit. Help us in our infirmity through Jesus' blood and merit. Grant us to grow in grace each day that by this sacrament we may eternal life inherit." Amen. (LSB 601:2)

JUNE 27

All praise to Thee, my God, this night
For all the blessings of the light.
Keep me, O keep me, King of kings,
Beneath Thine own almighty wings.

Forgive me, Lord, for Thy dear Son,
The ill that I this day have done,
That with the world, myself, and Thee,
I, ere I sleep, at peace may be. (*LSB* 883:1–2)

HERE IS A MODEL PRAYER FOR THE CHILD OF GOD JUST BEFORE going to sleep at the end of the day. We begin by thanking God for all the blessings of the day. We ask God to forgive the sins we have committed this day, for we know—in the words of the Small Catechism—that "we daily sin much" (Lord's Prayer, Fifth Petition). We also know that, for Christ's sake, God forgives our sins. It is a great blessing—perhaps one we neglect to acknowledge—that at the end of each day, we fall asleep knowing that we are forgiven and at peace with God.

As we go to sleep each night, we are reminded that one day—according to the Lord's good and gracious will—our bodies will enter a sleep that will last until the great and glorious final day, when we will be awakened unto eternal life. Thus, we ask God in this simple but profound prayer that He would "teach me to . . . dread the grave as little as my bed" (st. 3). The child of God does not fear death, knowing that it is a temporary sleep before the Last Day—the great day of resurrection. This blessed reality allows us to pray for sweet "sleep that shall me more vig'rous make to serve my God when I awake!" (st. 4). Then tomorrow, by God's grace, will end with these same petitions.

"Teach me to live that I may dread the grave as little as my bed. Teach me to die that so I may rise glorious at the awe-full day. Oh, may my soul in Thee repose, and may sweet sleep mine eyelids close, sleep that shall me more vig'rous make to serve my God when I awake!" Amen. (LSB *883:3–4*)

JUNE 28

Water, blood, and Spirit crying,
By their witness testifying
To the One whose death-defying
Life has come, with life for all.

In a wat'ry grave are buried
All our sins that Jesus carried;
Christ, the Ark of Life, has ferried
Us across death's raging flood. (*LSB* 597:1–2)

JOHN'S FIRST EPISTLE INSPIRED THIS STRIKING "BAPTISMAL LIFE" hymn: "For there are three that testify: the Spirit and the water and the blood; and these three agree" (1 John 5:7–8). As God's children, we are given life through water, blood, and Spirit, as all three witness "to the One whose death-defying life has come, with life for all."

This powerful hymn text speaks of a new and different life from the one we were born into; yes, it is a rebirth by which we are made a new creation. Our new life is filled with abundant grace richly supplied in the waters of our Baptism, the blessed food at our Lord's Table, and the Spirit's working through God's Word as it is read and preached. In the church, we often refer to this witness of water, blood, and Spirit as the means of grace. The church's whole purpose is to give such means throughout the baptismal life, for it is these means that give Jesus Christ and fill God's children with His forgiveness, love, and peace.

Yet another way of describing this extraordinary baptismal life is to see it as the unending eighth day flowing from Christ's resurrection from the dead. Christ, the new Adam, has given us this eighth day, not limited to morning and evening, but as an endless baptismal life that leads to eternity.

"Dark the way, yet Christ precedes us, past the scowl of death He leads us; spreads a table where He feeds us with His body and His blood. Though around us death is seething, God, His two-edged sword unsheathing, by His Spirit life is breathing through the living, active Word." Amen. (LSB *597:3–4*)

JUNE 29

Christ is made the
sure foundation,
Christ, our head and
cornerstone,
Chosen of the Lord
and precious,
Binding all the Church in one;
Holy Zion's help forever
And our confidence alone.

To this temple, where
we call You,
Come, O Lord of
hosts, and stay;
Come with all Your
loving-kindness,
Hear Your people as they pray;
And Your fullest benediction
Shed within these walls
today. (*LSB* 909:1–2)

As the Bride of Christ, we cannot help but love this eighth-century Latin hymn that defines, guides, and comforts us so beautifully. In this sung confession, we lift our voices in a Peter-like confession that Jesus is "the Christ, the Son of the living God" (Matthew 16:16). In it, we sing that yes, He is our Head, He is our cornerstone, and He is our help forever, for He is the Son of the living God.

We regularly gather, and in that blessed gathering, we rejoice and give thanks for being the "chosen of the Lord and precious" as His beloved church. It is here that we receive gifts offered to us in His loving-kindness. It is here that we ask of Him, and receive of Him, one gift after another!

In this weekly Divine Service, we ask our Lord's "fullest benediction" with all confidence that we will receive it. Yes, we sorely need His divine blessing as we go forth into a godless world—for then Zion's help goes with us.

"Grant, we pray, to all Your faithful all the gifts they ask to gain; what they gain from You, forever with the blessed to retain; and hereafter in Your glory evermore with You to reign. Praise and honor to the Father, praise and honor to the Son, praise and honor to the Spirit, ever three and ever one: one in might and one in glory while unending ages run!" Amen. (LSB *909:3–4*)

JUNE 30

In Adam we have all been one,
One huge rebellious man;
We all have fled that evening voice
That sought us as we ran.

But Thy strong love, it sought us still
And sent Thine only Son
That we might hear His Shepherd's voice
And, hearing Him, be one. (*LSB* 569:1, 3)

AFTER ADAM AND EVE FELL INTO SIN BY DISOBEYING THE SINGLE command God had given them, they were immediately aware that they had separated themselves from God—hence the act of sewing fig leaves together to cover their nakedness. In the cool of the evening, God was walking in the Garden of Eden that He had given to the newly created man and wife. God called to them, "Where are you?" (Genesis 3:9). Even in the wake of this first—and costly—disobedience, God still "sought" His rebellious creatures, and even more, He gave the first promise of a Savior from sin.

We, too, are a part of this story, for "in Adam we have all been one." We are people who rebel against our Creator, having inherited sin down through the generations from those first parents in the garden. But we have also inherited that promise of a Savior, who would "bruise [the] head" of Satan—Christ defeating him at the cross through His substitutionary death on our behalf (Genesis 3:15). Thus, we are not only one with Adam in sin; through Christ, we have been made one with God—restored to the kind of loving companionship that our Creator always desired to have with His creatures.

May the Holy Spirit guide us into all truth and set us free from our "fancied wisdom, self-sought ways" (st. 5): our rationalizations and excuses, which are always sins against the First Commandment, placing our self-sought ways before those of our loving God. Thanks be to God that He still seeks us to make us one with Him!

"O Thou who, when we loved Thee not, didst love and save us all, Thou great Good Shepherd of mankind, O hear us when we call. Send us Thy Spirit, teach us truth; Thou Son, O set us free from fancied wisdom, self-sought ways, to make us one in Thee." Amen. (LSB *569:4–5*)

JULY 1

In God, my faithful God,
I trust when dark my road;
Great woes may overtake me,
Yet He will not forsake me.
My troubles He can alter;
His hand lets nothing falter.

If death my portion be,
It brings great gain to me;
It speeds my life's endeavor
To live with Christ forever.
He gives me joy in sorrow,
Come death now or
tomorrow. (*LSB* 745:1, 3)

IN TODAY'S MEDITATION, WE ACKNOWLEDGE RIGHT AT THE OUTSET that sometimes our walk through this life may involve traveling a dark road, with "great woes" and troubles of all sorts. But through it all, we trust in our faithful God; His loving hand still guides and directs every aspect of our lives. "His hand lets nothing falter," which is why the apostle Paul could state with such confidence, "And we know that for those who love God all things work together for good" (Romans 8:28). We indeed feel the pain that derives from the woes and troubles of this world, but by faith, we know that God's hand is still directing the lives of us, His dear children, and that God will bring us through all troubles and trials.

In the catalog of woes and troubles that may oppress us, there is one that looms largest for each of us: namely, death. But the hymn writer goes right to Paul's words: "For to me to live is Christ, and to die is gain" (Philippians 1:21). Death actually "speeds my life's endeavor to live with Christ forever." This perspective reminds us of our ultimate goal as we travel through life in this world: "to live with Christ forever." That premise places our woes, troubles, and even death in the context of eternal life—a gift of our faithful God!

"O Jesus Christ, my Lord, so meek in deed and word, You suffered death to save us because Your love would have us be heirs of heav'nly gladness when ends this life of sadness." Amen. (LSB 745:4)

JULY 2

Christ, mighty Savior, Light of all creation,
You make the daytime radiant with the sunlight
And to the night give glittering adornment,
Stars in the heavens.

Give heed, we pray You, to our supplication,
That You may grant us pardon for offenses,
Strength for our weak hearts, rest for aching bodies,
Soothing the weary. (*LSB* 881:1, 4)

ON THE FOURTH DAY OF CREATION, GOD CREATED THE HEAVENLY lights. While we may take the sun, moon, and stars for granted, we do well in recalling the Creator's wisdom to establish "lights in the expanse of the heavens to separate the day from the night . . . the light from the darkness" (Genesis 1:14, 18). The sun was to rule the day, the moon and the stars the night.

These differing kinds of light establish a rhythm for human life—work occurring primarily during the greater light of day, needed rest taking place during the lesser light of the night. The church established hours of prayer around this daily cycle of light and darkness, and our devotional lives often center on morning and evening prayer.

Our prayer at the close of the day, as in this ancient Latin hymn, appropriately seeks "pardon for offenses." With Luther's Evening Prayer, we say, "I pray that You would forgive me all my sins where I have done wrong." We also pray for strength in weakness, and "rest for aching bodies, soothing the weary" (Small Catechism).

The final stanza of this hymn takes us beyond this life to the eternity that will be ours when we rest forever in the light of Christ. Our bodies will indeed "slumber" in death even as our souls are "forever resting in the peace of Jesus" (st. 5). "In light or darkness," in this life or in the perfection of heaven, we worship our Savior "now and forever" (st. 5).

"Though bodies slumber, hearts shall keep their vigil, forever resting in the peace of Jesus, in light or darkness worshiping our Savior now and forever." Amen. (LSB *881:5*)

JULY 3

**Lord, help us ever to retain
The Catechism's doctrine plain
As Luther taught the Word of truth
In simple style to tender youth.**

**Help us Your holy Law to learn,
To mourn our sin and from it turn
In faith to You and to Your Son
And Holy Spirit, Three in One.** (*LSB* 865:1–2)

JESUS' DISCIPLES ARE FOOLISHLY DISCUSSING MATTERS OF greatness in His kingdom and ask the wrong question of Him: "Who is the greatest in the kingdom of heaven?" (Matthew 18:1). Jesus gave them a sharp response as He held high a little one and said, "Whoever humbles himself like this child is the greatest in the kingdom of heaven" (v. 4).

Martin Luther understood the importance of our little ones very well, so he gave the Word of truth in a simple style to tender youth in the Small Catechism. This was meant to bring to "the greatest in the kingdom" a wealth of what they need for life in the kingdom. Though simple, the Small Catechism does not "dumb it down" for kids. No, Luther gave them substance—for they need that.

His catechism treats the baptized children of God as "the greatest in the kingdom." He wants them to learn God's thoughts and ways now and for all their days.

Jesus' disciples needed to learn this lesson, and it is possible that we all need to learn this lesson too. Bringing up our children grounded in the faith is how we should train up "the greatest in the kingdom of heaven."

"Hear us, dear Father, when we pray for needed help from day to day that as Your children we may live, whom You baptized and so received. Lord, when we fall or go astray, absolve and lift us up, we pray; and through the Sacrament increase our faith till we depart in peace." Amen. (LSB *865:3–4*)

JULY 4

Lord Jesus Christ, the Church's head,
You are her one foundation;
In You she trusts, before You bows,
And waits for Your salvation.
Built on this rock secure,
Your Church shall endure
Though all the world decay
And all things pass away.
O hear, O hear us, Jesus! (*LSB* 647:1)

THIS HYMN IS A BEAUTIFULLY CRAFTED PICTURE OF A LITTLE BUT mighty "flock" (st. 2). And while this flock may be small and unimpressive to this world and its thinking, it is strong enough to "endure though all the world decay and all things pass away."

The church knows well that her strength and comfort is found in her Head and Cornerstone, the Lord Jesus Christ. She knows she cannot live for a moment without Him, for He is her rock and fortress. Therefore, these words are constantly on her lips: "O hear, O hear us, Jesus!"

Jesus hears her cry and makes her mighty in the ways that matter—ways the world will never understand. He has told her that He will do this through His Holy Word and blessed Sacraments—His beautiful means of grace. Through these means, she not only receives grace, but she also receives her strength and power to live.

This is His loving care for His dear Bride. She is sustained in these means and by these means as she confesses to all the world the truths contained therein. And along the way, she trusts these truths with all she has, for they are her wisdom for all her days.

"O Lord, let this Your little flock, Your name alone confessing, continue in Your loving care, true unity possessing. Your sacraments, O Lord, and Your saving Word to us, Lord, pure retain. Grant that they may remain our only strength and comfort." Amen. (LSB 647:2)

JULY 5

And for Your Gospel let us dare
To sacrifice all treasure;
Teach us to bear Your blessed cross,
To find in You all pleasure.
O grant us steadfastness
In joy and distress,
Lest we, Lord, You forsake.
Let us by grace partake
Of endless joy and gladness. (*LSB* 647:4)

T*ODAY'S HYMN IS OVERFLOWING WITH SOUND DOCTRINE AND* practice for Christ's church. The complete hymn is a mini course in what it means *to be the church* and offers this fervent plea: "O make us faithful Christians" (st. 3). Yes, doctrine and practice are essential to faithful Christians.

The hymn was written at a time when what it meant to be the church was being seriously challenged. For confessional pastors, steadfastness and faithfulness were their dominant themes out of necessity. They were living under severe crosses, yet by God's grace, these crosses were bearing fruit in some of our finest hymns, such as this one.

Therefore, we see here a strong emphasis on the theology of the cross. "Teach us to bear Your blessed cross" even if it means bearing a cross as Your disciple. "O grant us steadfastness in joy and distress" "for Your Gospel let us dare to sacrifice all treasure." These words were written by someone who knew the price of remaining steadfast under crosses.

In this hymn, we also have a beautiful, short prayer: "Help us to serve You evermore with hearts both pure and lowly" (st. 3). Only repentant hearts are able to serve the Lord Christ in His kingdom. Therefore, let Him make your heart pure—for service in His church.

"Help us to serve You evermore with hearts both pure and lowly; and may Your Word, that light divine, shine on in splendor holy that we repentance show, in faith ever grow; the pow'r of sin destroy and evils that annoy. O make us faithful Christians." Amen. (LSB 647:3)

JULY 6

Isaiah, mighty seer
in days of old,
The Lord of all in
spirit did behold
High on a lofty throne,
in splendor bright,
With robes that filled the
temple courts with light.
Above the throne were
flaming seraphim;
Six wings had they, these
messengers of Him.
With two they veiled their
faces as was right,
With two they humbly hid
their feet from sight,
And with the other two
aloft they soared;
One to the other called
and praised the Lord:
"Holy is God, the
Lord of Sabaoth!
Holy is God, the Lord
of Sabaoth!
Holy is God, the Lord
of Sabaoth!
His glory fills the heavens
and the earth!"
The beams and lintels
trembled at the cry,
And clouds of smoke enwrapped
the throne on high. (*LSB* 960)

On this day, the Church remembers Isaiah the prophet. The book of Isaiah is so rich with prophecies of Jesus that some have referred to this Old Testament book as a "Fifth Gospel." In chapter 9, for example, Isaiah prophesies the coming of the Savior: "For to us a child is born, to us a son is given" (v. 6). In chapter 53, we learn that this Son came into the world to be our substitute: "Surely He has borne our griefs and carried our sorrows. . . . He was pierced for our transgressions; He was crushed for our iniquities" (vv. 4–5).

Isaiah also gives us a picture of God's eternal glory, with the threefold acclamation "Holy is the Lord of hosts" (6:3). We are privileged to sing this acclamation (the Sanctus) in our Divine Service, as Jesus comes to us bodily in His Holy Supper. Luther paraphrased Isaiah's account in the hymn "Isaiah, Mighty Seer in Days of Old," providing us a powerful picture of God's holiness, which, one day, we will witness as we live forever in His presence.

"Isaiah 'twas foretold it, the rose I have in mind; with Mary we behold it, the virgin mother kind. To show God's love aright, she bore to us a Savior, when half-spent was the night." Amen. (LSB *359:2*)

JULY 7

I leave all things to
God's direction;
He loves me both
in joy and woe.
His will is good, sure
His affection;
His tender love is true, I know.
My fortress and my rock is He:
What pleases God,
that pleases me.

God knows what must
be done to save me;
His love for me will never cease.
Upon His hands He
did engrave me
With purest gold of loving grace.
His will supreme must ever be:
What pleases God, that
pleases me. (*LSB* 719:1–2)

AT THE OUTSET, THIS HYMN DECLARES IMPORTANT TRUTHS ABOUT God: "His will is good" and "His tender love is true." It also reminds us of a reality in our earthly lives—namely, that we will experience both "joy and woe." God's love for us is constant in *both* of these states—even, and perhaps especially, in the midst of woe, heartache, or grief. Thus, the hymn writer's refrain in each stanza is "What pleases God, that pleases me." He goes on to explain more fully *why* that is so.

"God knows what must be done to save me; His love for me will never cease." No matter how inexplicable life's circumstances may be, we know without doubt—by faith—that God has provided for our eternal salvation. "He who did not spare His own Son but gave Him up for us all, how will He not also with Him graciously give us all things?" (Romans 8:32). The hymn writer quotes the prophet Isaiah: "Behold, I have engraved you on the palms of My hands" (49:16). That is how closely God holds His beloved children, how we know with certainty that His tender love is ours in both joy *and woe*. The God who has provided for your soul's eternal salvation will—in His own way and in His own time—provide everything else, thus enabling us always to pray, "What pleases God, that pleases me."

"My God has all things in His keeping; He is the ever faithful friend. He gives me laughter after weeping, and all His ways in blessings end. His love endures eternally: what pleases God, that pleases me." Amen. (LSB 719:4)

JULY 8

Lord, to You I make confession;
I have sinned and gone astray,
I have multiplied transgression,
Chosen for myself my way.
Led by You to see my errors,
Lord, I tremble at Your terrors.

For Your Son has suffered for me,
Giv'n Himself to rescue me,
Died to save me and restore me,
Reconciled and set me free.
Jesus' cross alone can vanquish
These dark fears and soothe this anguish. (*LSB* 608:1, 3)

WE CANNOT ESCAPE SIN, FOR IT IS THERE FROM CONCEPTION and follows us all our days. But we can get rid of it—by giving it away and starting anew. That is what today's hymn is about—how to begin anew with the blessed confession of sins. We want and need to receive our Lord's mercy and to be set free. The confession of sins, either corporate or private, is how we receive God's grace and forgiveness as His children in His church.

When we sing this hymn, we freely confess our sinful state, which is of such *enormous* need that it sends us to our knees, pleading for mercy. And on our knees, clinging to Jesus, we are precisely where Jesus wants us to be. Yes, we may be in tears, yet this is a most blessed place as we are clinging to our Lord. For there we are stripped of any self-sufficient independence and instead become utterly dependent *on Him*—this is good and right and as it should be.

Jesus has been standing ready to forgive us all along—for *that* is what He does. We simply have to ask, and we will receive grace upon grace.

"Lord, on You I cast my burden—sink it in the deepest sea! Let me know Your gracious pardon, cleanse me from iniquity. Let Your Spirit leave me never; make me only Yours forever." Amen. (LSB 608:4)

JULY 9

Lord, 'tis not that I did choose Thee;
That, I know, could never be;
For this heart would still refuse Thee
Had Thy grace not chosen me.
Thou hast from the sin that stained me
Washed and cleansed and set me free
And unto this end ordained me,
That I ever live to Thee. (*LSB* 573:1)

JESUS COULD NOT BE MORE CLEAR: "YOU DID NOT CHOOSE ME, BUT I chose you" (John 15:16). The hymn writer alludes to our sinful nature, which precludes us from making that first move and actively choosing Jesus to be our Savior: "That, I know, could never be; for this heart would still refuse Thee." But why is that? Why can't we say that we choose Jesus as our Lord and Savior? Don't we play a part in salvation by accepting Jesus as our Savior? Scripture clearly teaches the exact opposite: "No one can say 'Jesus is Lord' except in the Holy Spirit" (1 Corinthians 12:3). In his Small Catechism, Luther expands on this biblical teaching: "I believe that I cannot by my own reason or strength believe in Jesus Christ, my Lord, or come to Him; but the Holy Spirit has called me by the Gospel, enlightened me with His gifts, sanctified and kept me in the true faith" (Creed, Third Article).

Eternal salvation is dependent not on us but solely on God's grace. And the Holy Spirit works through Word and Sacraments to *keep* us in the true faith, so that we don't have to constantly worry that we may be in danger of slipping away and therefore need to work harder. No! The good news of the Gospel is that Jesus chose us. He has done it all—for us and for our salvation!

"It was grace in Christ that called me, taught my darkened heart and mind; else the world had yet enthralled me, to Thy heav'nly glories blind. Now I worship none above Thee; for Thy grace alone I thirst, knowing well that, if I love Thee, Thou, O Lord, didst love me first." Amen. (LSB 573:2)

JULY 10

**My soul, now praise
your Maker!
Let all within me
bless His name
Who makes you full partaker
Of mercies more than
you dare claim.
Forget Him not whose
meekness
Still bears with all your sin,
Who heals your ev'ry weakness,
Renews your life within;
Whose grace and
care are endless
And saved you through the past;
Who leaves no suff'rer
friendless
But rights the wronged
at last. (*LSB* 820:1)**

A ***SINGING SAINT MEDITATES HERE ON AWE-INSPIRING GIFTS*** received, and then the saint's heart and soul explode with a grand text of high praise and thanksgiving. We begin meditating on this hymn, which paraphrases Psalm 103, one of David's finest, most beloved, and comforting texts.

It tells of a Maker who could not be closer to His children with His grace and mercy—good gifts they can trust and count on. He is a Maker ready to heal, comfort, and restore these children He loves so dearly. His beautiful grace and care are endless—all of this is true because our Maker *is our Father*.

Our Father is a merciful physician who heals our every weakness, starting with our greatest weakness—sinfulness. Then our forgiven soul is free to burst forth in song: "My soul, now praise your Maker!" He wants us to bless Him, thank Him, praise Him, and recognize that all good gifts and favors come from Him.

Such truly blessed children can go forth and live a restored life of thanksgiving, praise, and service as they "let all within" them "bless His name"!

"O bless the Lord, my soul! Let all within me join and aid my tongue to bless His name whose favors are divine. O bless the Lord, my soul, nor let His mercies lie forgotten in unthankfulness and without praises die!" Amen. (LSB *814:1–2*)

JULY 11

He offers all His treasure
Of justice, truth, and righteousness,
His love beyond all measure,
His yearning pity o'er distress;
Nor treats us as we merit
But sets His anger by.
The poor and contrite spirit
Finds His compassion nigh;
And high as heav'n above us,
As dawn from close of day,
So far, since He has loved us,
He puts our sins away. (*LSB* 820:2)

The omnipotence of our Maker, Father, and Physician is made known in this hymn-psalm essentially by David. Jesus said, "Those who are well have no need of a physician, but those who are sick" (Luke 5:31). Yes, Lord, we readily admit that we are sick and in need of Your healing, and by grace we see Your compassionate heart reaching out to us in love, granting the mercy we so need. "The poor and contrite spirit finds His compassion nigh."

You have not left us with our illness and need. "Since He has loved us, He puts our sins away." Forgiveness is the fulfillment of God's promises! Forgiveness has been the greatest need since the fall in the Garden of Eden. And this hymn sings beautifully of that need being met by our gracious God in a plan to save the world—even if it means the death of His Son.

What else is being sung here is undeserved mercy—what we receive in this exchange is certainly not what we in any way merit. "Nor treats us as we merit but sets His anger by." Bless the Lord, O my soul!

"'Tis He forgives thy sins; 'tis He relieves thy pain; 'tis He that heals thy sicknesses and makes thee young again. He crowns thy life with love when ransomed from the grave; He that redeemed my soul from hell hath sov'reign pow'r to save." Amen. (LSB 814:3–4)

JULY 12

For as a tender father
Has pity on his children here,
God in His arms will gather
All who are His in childlike fear.
He knows how frail our powers,
Who but from dust are made.
We flourish like the flowers,
And even so we fade;
The wind but through
them passes,
And all their bloom is o'er.
We wither like the grasses;
Our place knows us no more.

His grace remains forever,
And children's children
yet shall prove
That God forsakes them never
Who in true fear shall
seek His love.
In heav'n is fixed His dwelling,
His rule is over all.
(*LSB* 820:3, 4a)

THIS IS A BEAUTIFUL AND COMFORTING PHRASE: "FOR AS A TENDER father has pity on his children here"! The words *tender* and *pity* in this hymn context speak volumes about a father's love and even more who the heavenly Father is and what He is like—and He is *our Father*!

This Psalm 103 paraphrase lets us into David's meditation on man's weakness: "For He remembers our frame; He knows that we are dust" (Psalm 103:14). But David and the hymn move on quickly from our frail and needy state to the grace, goodness, and boundless compassion that our Father has for His children in their weakness.

God's children are never forsaken; quite the opposite. They are His *beloved* children who receive His abundant and lavish grace forever and ever. "God in His arms will gather all who are His in childlike fear." This includes even "the little ones" (Matthew 18:6) whom Jesus calls "the greatest" in His kingdom (v. 4). Yes, our tender Father has pity on His children. My soul, O praise the Lord!

"O hosts with might excelling, with praise before Him fall. Praise Him forever reigning, all you who hear His Word—our life and all sustaining. My soul, O praise the Lord!" Amen. (LSB *820:4b*)

JULY 13

Lord, let at last Thine
angels come,
To Abr'ham's bosom
bear me home,
That I may die unfearing;
And in its narrow chamber keep
My body safe in peaceful sleep
Until Thy reappearing.
And then from death
awaken me,
That these mine eyes
with joy may see,
O Son of God, Thy glorious face,
My Savior and my
fount of grace.
Lord Jesus Christ, my prayer
attend, my prayer attend,
And I will praise Thee
without end. (*LSB* 708:3)

WHEN JESUS TOLD THE STORY OF THE RICH MAN AND POOR Lazarus, He said that when Lazarus died, he "was carried by the angels to Abraham's side" (Luke 16:22). In Martin Schalling's magnificent hymn text, we, too, pray that at the time of death God's angels will bear our immortal souls to heaven. Thus, we die without fear, for we have Jesus' own promise: "Today you will be with Me in paradise" (Luke 23:43).

Our bodies, created by God, rest in peaceful sleep, which is the way Jesus spoke of death: "Our friend Lazarus has fallen asleep, but I go to awaken him" (John 11:11). Jesus Himself will awaken our bodies also from death—on that great and glorious day when He returns as judge of all people. Like Job of old (Job 19:25–27), we are absolutely certain that we will see Jesus with our very own eyes, as our glorified bodies rise to new and everlasting life.

That we will see the face of Jesus, our Redeemer, is an extraordinary thought. He is indeed our "fount of grace," and the depth of His love for us will be fully realized when we see Him face to face and bodily go to be with Him forever. In the paradise that He won for us, we will indeed "praise [Him] without end."

"Oh, that day when freed from sinning, I shall see Thy lovely face; clothed then in the blood-washed linen, how I'll sing Thy wondrous grace! Come, my Lord, no longer tarry; take my ransom'd soul away; send Thine angels soon to carry me to realms of endless day." Amen. (LSB 686:4)

JULY 14

For as rain and snow
from heaven
Water seeds in dusty soil,
Causing them to bud and flower,
Giving bread to those who toil;

So the Lord sends
forth His promise,
Words of life and
joy and peace—
Never void to Him returning,
Bearing fruit with great
increase. (*LSB* 827:3)

GOD'S WORD IS SO MUCH MORE THAN WORDS ON PRINTED PAGES! Pastor Stephen Starke tells us that God's Word is "life and joy and peace." God Himself declares the power of His Word, likening it to the rain and snow that come down from heaven, which are not random events but rather events that accomplish something specific—namely, watering the earth so that it can bring forth the wheat that becomes our daily bread. In a similar way, "So shall My word be that goes out from My mouth; it shall not return to Me empty, but it shall accomplish that which I purpose, and shall succeed in the thing for which I sent it" (Isaiah 55:11). The writer to the Hebrews echoes Isaiah when he states that "the word of God is living and active" (Hebrews 4:12).

God's Word—as it is read, preached, taught, studied—is living and active, accomplishing and succeeding in precisely the ways God intends. His Word is life-giving, stating with utmost confidence, "I shall not die, but I shall live" (Psalm 118:17). God's Word declares His salvation—from His promise after the fall into sin (Genesis 3:15); through the words of His prophets (for example, Isaiah 40); through the Gospel accounts of Christ's Passion, death, resurrection, and ascension; to the great vision of heaven in the revelation to the apostle John. His Word gives eternal life, and that great joy permits us, like Simeon of old, to go in peace.

"Hearken to the Lord whose coming marks the time when grace shall end, when with His angelic reapers He in glory shall descend. Soon the night, the final harvest; soon the time for work shall cease. Then the souls His grace has garnered shall enjoy His Sabbath peace." Amen. (LSB 827:4)

JULY 15

In Thee is gladness
Amid all sadness,
Jesus, sunshine of my heart.
By Thee are given
The gifts of heaven,
Thou the true Redeemer art.
Our souls Thou wakest,
Our bonds Thou breakest;
Who trusts Thee surely
Has built securely;
He stands forever:
Alleluia!
Our hearts are pining
To see Thy shining,
Dying or living
To Thee are cleaving;
Naught can us sever:
Alleluia! (*LSB* 818:1)

IN THIS HYMN, WE PROCLAIM THE ONE AND ONLY SOLUTION TO ALL sadness and to our worst imaginable distresses: Jesus, our Redeemer. Sin and death are powerful enemies; indeed, Scripture calls death "the last enemy" (1 Corinthians 15:26). But in that same chapter, the apostle Paul quotes the prophet Isaiah, writing, "Death is swallowed up in victory" (v. 54; see Isaiah 25:8). Jesus' victory over death is our victory, and it is the ultimate of "the gifts of heaven" cited in this hymn. Jesus willingly gave up heaven to become incarnate as our brother, redeeming us from sin and death so that the creature may share an eternity of happiness with the Creator. Jesus is the one who banishes sadness, replacing it with the gladness that only He can give.

Because of this ultimate gift from heaven, we live free from the fear of death. We are free to serve our neighbors by telling of salvation through Jesus and by loving and praising Him as long as He gives us breath to do so. In Christ, we "triumph o'er sadness" (st. 2). Nothing can separate us from Him: "dying or living to Thee are cleaving." Fear and sadness are gone; triumph and gladness are ours—now and forever!

"Since He is ours, we fear no powers, not of earth nor sin nor death. He sees and blesses in worst distresses; He can change them with a breath. Wherefore the story tell of His glory with hearts and voices; all heav'n rejoices in Him forever: alleluia! We shout for gladness, triumph o'er sadness, love Him and praise Him and still shall raise Him glad hymns forever: alleluia!" Amen. (LSB 818:2)

JULY 16

O gracious Lord, I firmly am believing
Your boundless love will bless each faithful soul,
As from this altar we are here receiving
Your body and Your blood to make us whole,
Your body and Your blood to make us whole.

Lord, I have sinned, a thousand times offending;
My thankless thoughts and words and deeds erase,
To me Your hand of mercy now extending,
O God, my Savior, I implore Your grace,
O God, my Savior, I implore Your grace. (*LSB* 635:1–2)

T***ODAY'S HYMN DESCRIBES LIFE AS A FAITHFUL SAINT IN CHRIST'S*** kingdom. We sin, confess our sins, receive absolution, and kneel at the altar to receive the only food able to forgive, sustain, strengthen, and refresh us for life. This is a beautiful pattern of living abundantly in the ongoing gifts of mercy and grace. We receive these boundless gifts every time we attend the Divine Service—gifts that, as the hymn puts it, "make us whole." And they make us whole by forgiving us repeatedly—even after our "thousand times offending" and our "thankless thoughts and words and deeds."

The opening line, "I firmly am believing," sets the tone for this hymn-prayer. Yes, we firmly believe with all our hearts that this is what our life of grace looks like, as it is filled with ongoing grace and blessings from the hand of our heavenly Father. Faith and belief are reinforced and built up each time we hear God's Word read and preached in the Divine Service. We can never get enough of these priceless gifts of grace offered in the ongoing feast of our Lord's Divine Service.

"But blest is each believing guest who in these promises finds rest; for Jesus shall in love remain with all who here His grace obtain. Help us sincerely to believe that we may worthily receive Your Supper and in You find rest. Amen! They who believe are blest." Amen. (LSB 634:7–8)

JULY 17

You see my sin yet seat me at Your table;
Lord, as a guest, I surely am the least:
Unclean, unfit, of worthy deeds unable—
My heart prepare for this most holy feast,
My heart prepare for this most holy feast.

O Lamb of God, my faithful, loving Savior,
You I embrace in faith and holy love;
Grant me the strength to show by my behavior
A life now hidden in Your reign above,
A life now hidden in Your reign above. (*LSB* 635:3–4)

WE BRING OUR SINS TO OUR LORD'S TABLE, KNOWING WE ARE unworthy. "You see my sin yet seat me at Your table." Nevertheless, we come because we know that our Lord instituted His Holy Supper for this very purpose—to invite sinners. He made this a feast for those who know their need for forgiveness. "I surely am the least: unclean, unfit, of worthy deeds unable." We come, and by His grace, we receive exactly what we need.

Being invited to and seated at this Holy Table has nothing to do with deserving, merit, or worthiness; this Table is for the unworthy. Such feasting is one of the most extraordinary parts of being God's child, for regardless of who we are, where we have been, or what we have done, we are given the finest food in all of heaven and earth—blessed divine food nourishing and reviving our hearts.

In receiving this sacred feast, Christ dwells within us, transforming us into healthy branches that can now bear fruit. This fruit, in turn, is love for our neighbor, a visible manifestation of the healing, change, and growth that Christ brings into our lives at His Table.

"Christ says: 'Come, all you that labor, and receive My grace and favor: those who feel no pain or ill need no physician's help or skill.' Let this food your faith so nourish that its fruit of love may flourish and your neighbor learn from you how much God's wondrous love can do." Amen. (LSB 627:7, 10)

JULY 18

Heavenly Bread, my life and benediction,
This cup You give can take away each ill.
Come and relieve my soul from all affliction;
Calm ev'ry sigh until my heart is still,
Calm ev'ry sigh until my heart is still. (*LSB* 635:5)

S***OME PEOPLE WILL SAY THEY EAT TO LIVE; OTHERS SAY THEY LIVE*** to eat—and the world is filled with both types. Yet only Christians know that they live because of *what they eat*—Jesus Christ in His Word, body, and blood. Jesus said, "I am the bread of life; whoever comes to Me shall not hunger, and whoever believes in Me shall never thirst" (John 6:35).

Not only do Jesus Christ's children know where to find the *only* food able to give them life, but they also know how this extraordinary food can take away ills, relieve troubled souls, calm trusting hearts, forgive sins, and give a divine benediction on their lives.

At Jesus' ascension, His disciples' last sight was His uplifted hands blessing them. The very Bread of Life granted His benediction to them and all His faithful children as they live in His name. His benediction tells us that we are not alone; He did not leave us but instead left His real presence with us in His body and His blood. And now, He sits at His Father's right hand as our Brother, Advocate, High Priest, and Intercessor. This is Bread—which is life and benediction. Oh, how blessed are we!

"Lord Jesus Christ, life-giving bread, may I in grace possess You. Let me with holy food be fed, in hunger I address You. Prepare me well for You, O Lord, and, humbly by my prayer implored, give me Your grace and mercy. O bread of heav'n, my soul's delight, for full and free remission I come with prayer before Your sight in sorrow and contrition. Your righteousness, Lord, cover me that I receive You worthily, assured of Your full pardon." Amen. (LSB 625:1, 3)

JULY 19

My hope is built on nothing less
Than Jesus' blood and righteousness;
No merit of my own I claim
But wholly lean on Jesus' name.
On Christ, the solid rock, I stand;
All other ground is sinking sand. (*LSB* 575:1)

AS RECORDED IN *MATTHEW 16:13–18,* JESUS ASKED HIS DISCIPLES an interesting question: "Who do people say that the Son of Man is?" They answered by reporting that some called Jesus a prophet, like Elijah or Jeremiah. But then came the really penetrating question, not only for those disciples but for us: "But who do you say that I am?" Peter gave the definitive answer: "You are the Christ, the Son of the living God." Jesus didn't praise Peter for somehow getting to this correct understanding on his own, but rather noted that Peter's answer came from the Father in heaven. So it is with us—our belief in Jesus as the Christ is a gift of the Holy Spirit, working faith in our hearts through the Word of God.

Jesus went on to say, "On this rock I will build My church." The "rock" is Peter's confession, that Jesus is "the Christ, the Son of the living God." The solid rock on which Jesus builds His church, the solid rock on which our faith is founded, is the confession that Jesus—true man and true God—is the long-awaited Christ, the Messiah, the Savior, the very Son of God, who came into this world for one reason only—to redeem His people from their sins, and to promise us that when we take our final breath, we will be with Jesus in paradise (Luke 23:43).

By grace, we stand on the solid rock of Christ's work, on the righteousness that Jesus earned for us by shedding His blood on the cross. Thanks be to God!

"When He shall come with trumpet sound, oh, may I then in Him be found, clothed in His righteousness alone, redeemed to stand before His throne! On Christ, the solid rock, I stand; all other ground is sinking sand." Amen. (LSB *575:4*)

JULY 20

My soul rejoices,
My spirit voices—
Sing the greatness of the Lord!
For God my Savior
Has shown me favor—
Sing the greatness of the Lord!
With praise and blessing,
Join in confessing
God, who is solely
Mighty and holy—
O Sing the greatness
of God the Lord!
His mercy surely
Shall rest securely
On all who fear Him,
Love and revere Him—
O Sing the greatness of God
the Lord! (*LSB* 933:1)

BECAUSE OF ITS PLACE IN THE OFFICE OF VESPERS, MARY'S great hymn of praise, the Magnificat, is regularly prayed throughout Christendom. Through the centuries, her hymn has inspired composers to write countless marvelous choral settings, and today's hymn is a fresh paraphrase for congregational singing. Singing this hymn with a group of faithful believers is a joy!

With two other Lukan canticles, the Benedictus and Nunc Dimittis, we have splendid models showing how God would have us sing of Him. The subject of these three hymns by Mary, Zechariah, and Simeon is *what God has done,* and that is the most important lesson we can learn from biblical hymns—that the subject is God. The singer confesses exalted truths about God in each of these hymns—but the singer is never the subject.

Mary has just learned how she fits into God's master plan and is awestruck that God chose her. She is humbled and cannot help but "sing the greatness of the Lord!" We, too, are awestruck that God chose us, and we cannot help but "sing the greatness of God the Lord!"

"His arm now baring, His strength declaring—sing the greatness of the Lord! The proud He scatters, their rule He shatters—sing the greatness of the Lord! Oppression halted; the meek exalted. Full are the hungry; empty, the wealthy—O sing the greatness of God the Lord! Here is the token all that was spoken to Abr'ham's offspring God is fulfilling—O sing the greatness of God the Lord!" Amen. (LSB *933:2*)

JULY 21

O blessed, holy Trinity,
Divine, eternal Unity,
O Father, Son, and Holy Ghost,
This day Your name
be uppermost.

The Father's love
shield me this day;
The Son's pure wisdom
cheer my way;
The Holy Spirit's joy and light
Drive from my heart the shades
of night. (*LSB* 876:1, 3)

THE HYMN TEXT FOR TODAY DOES NOT SEEK TO EXPLAIN THE three-in-one mystery of the Holy Trinity but simply, and more importantly, enables us to *pray* to our triune God. After praying that our triune God's name be "uppermost," we ask for the Father's love, the Son's wisdom, and the Holy Spirit's joy and light. The Father's love will shield us—soul and body—from all harm and danger, most especially from the assaults of the devil. The Son's wisdom cheers us on our way, not least by His promise that He will be with us "to the end of the age" (Matthew 28:20). The Holy Spirit sheds His joy and light on us as He enlightens us with His gifts and keeps us in the true faith.

In his fourth stanza, the hymn writer prays yet again to each person of the Trinity. May the Father, "my Maker, hold me in Your hand" (st. 4). May the Son, who won forgiveness through His suffering, death, and resurrection, "let me stand"—clothed in garments washed clean in His blood. May the Holy Spirit, the Comforter, never depart but rather "enrich my heart" (st. 4) with the faith that only He can provide, nourish, and sustain.

May these brief but meaningful petitions to our triune God—Father, Son, and Holy Spirit—be a part of our daily prayer life.

"My Maker, hold me in Your hand; O Christ, forgiven let me stand; blest Comforter, do not depart; with faith and love enrich my heart. Lord, bless and keep me as Your own; Lord, look in kindness from Your throne; Lord, shine unfailing peace on me by grace surrounded; set me free." Amen. (LSB *876:4–5*)

JULY 22

As silver tried by fire is pure
From all adulteration,
So through God's Word shall men endure
Each trial and temptation.
Its light beams brighter through the cross,
And, purified from human dross,
It shines through every nation. (*TLH* 260:5)

TODAY'S HYMN IS ONE OF LUTHER'S FIRST "THEOLOGY OF THE cross" statements and is a paraphrase of this psalm verse: "The words of the LORD are pure words, like silver refined in a furnace on the ground, purified seven times" (12:6).

As silver is refined by fire, God's children are refined by trials and crosses designed and sent *in love* by their heavenly Father. As His children cling to His Word through trials and temptations, they are given sufficient strength to endure. This theology of the cross is the "Master Pruner" at work building up and strengthening His dear children *in love*, and they can now bear fruit that was impossible before His chastening and testing.

Luther wrote this hymn in the earliest days of the Reformation when God's Word and those defending it as truth were being sorely challenged on every side. Life was life under the cross for these reformers, yet these stalwart theologians knew and firmly believed that God was in absolute control and His Word would endure. Life under the cross, with its trials and testing, shaped these men into giants of the faith who went on to write the Lutheran Confessions.

"Why should cross and trial grieve me? Christ is near with His cheer; never will He leave me. Who can rob me of the heaven that God's Son for me won when His life was given? When life's troubles rise to meet me, though their weight may be great, they will not defeat me. God, my loving Savior, sends them; He who knows all my woes knows how best to end them." Amen. (LSB *756:1–2*)

JULY 23

Defend Your truth, O God, and stay
This evil generation;
And from the error of its way
Keep Your own congregation.
The wicked everywhere abound
And would Your little flock confound;
But You are our Salvation! (*TLH* 260:6, alt.)

T*ODAY'S HYMN, A SIGNIFICANT PIECE OF RELIGIOUS HISTORY, IS* part of Martin Luther's prayer for the Bride of Christ in the earliest days of the Reformation. From the first Lutheran hymnal of 1524, this hymn text asks for God's defense and protection from an evil generation lost in the error of its way. In it, Luther fervently implores God to keep His dear Bride safe, for He is her salvation.

Remaining steadfast in God's truth has never been easy, but it was especially challenging at the Reformation because the Gospel truth of Jesus Christ was not what the "church" was about, nor was it given to others. However, this Gospel truth is precisely what Luther was about; it was probably why he was born. Therefore, in all his hymns, he gave a rich measure of the Gospel in Christ Jesus, and that was what was needed.

That is what is *always* needed—*what God has done for us in His Son.* We, too, do not live in easy times for Gospel truths, for every part of God's Word is being rewritten in our challenging times to fit enlightened thinking. "Did God really say that?" is what today's world asks. But that disastrous question goes back to the Garden of Eden, and the answer to anything found in God's Word will always be—Yes!

"May glorious truths that we have heard, the bright sword of Your mighty Word, spurn Satan that Your Church be strong, bold, unified in act and song. Stay with us, Lord, and keep us true; preserve our faith our whole life through—Your Word alone our heart's defense, the Church's glorious confidence." Amen. (LSB 585:4, 6)

JULY 24

Come, Thou bright
and Morning Star,
Light of Light without
beginning;
Shine upon us from afar
That we may be kept
from sinning.
Drive away by Thy clear light
Our dark night.

Ah! Thou Dayspring
from on high,
Grant that at Thy
next appearing
We who in the graves do lie
May arise, Thy
summons hearing,
And rejoice in our new life,
Far from strife. (*LSB* 872:1, 4)

TODAY'S HYMN SUGGESTS HOW WE MIGHT PRAY WHEN WE AWAKEN each morning. The hymn writer addresses Jesus as the "bright and Morning Star" (see Revelation 22:16) and as the "Light of Light," who was in the beginning with God (see John 1). The first petition in this morning prayer is "that we may be kept from sinning." Just as the rising sun drives away the darkness of the night and provides new light for each day's life and work, so also we pray that Jesus might be for us the "clear light" that saves us from the sins that constitute "our dark night." As in Luther's Morning Prayer, we ask "that You would keep me . . . from sin and every evil" (Small Catechism). We pray here that in each day's living we may resist sin and do the work of our varied vocations.

There will come a morning when we will wake to eternal life and our bodies will rise from the sleep of death. That longed-for event becomes the second petition in our morning prayer. We pray that when Jesus returns at the end of time, "we who in the graves do lie may arise, Thy summons hearing." For those who have died in Christ, this resurrection brings us to new life—eternal life that leaves the strife of this world far behind, exchanged for days of "purest joy, and perfect peace" (st. 5). For that new morning and that blessed end, we pray, "Come, Lord Jesus!"

"Light us to those heav'nly spheres, Sun of grace, in glory shrouded; lead us through this vale of tears to the land where days unclouded, purest joy, and perfect peace never cease." Amen. (LSB 872:5)

JULY 25

In the shattered bliss of Eden
Dawned the day of sacrifice,
As our primal parents shuddered—
Sin had caused this dreadful price!
Faith embarked with this discernment:
Only God can cover sin,
As He took their leafy garments
And He clothed their shame with skin. (*LSB* 572:1)

W*HEN OUR FIRST PARENTS DISOBEYED* GOD *BY EATING FRUIT* from the one tree He had forbidden to them, sin entered what God intended to be perfection—man and woman, the crown of His creation, living in harmony with God in the blissful Paradise He had created. Prior to the fall, "the man and his wife were both naked and were not ashamed" (Genesis 2:25). When they disobeyed God, "they knew that they were naked. And they sewed fig leaves together and made themselves loincloths" (Genesis 3:7). In His great mercy and love, God not only promised the One who would forever defeat the devil and his lies; He also made garments of skins and clothed Adam and Eve. In this very first instance of sin, God showed His love for His fallen children.

That promised One who would defeat the devil is God's Son, Jesus. Though He was present at creation, He willingly entered the sinful world, lived the perfect life that original sin precluded for us, and in naked shame died on the cross, giving His blood as the once-for-all sacrifice required to balance the scales of divine justice. Now He gives us His very body and blood in His Holy Supper, thereby *covering* our sins. The skins that God provided Adam and Eve were a *temporary* covering for their bodies. The body and blood of Christ provide us robes of righteousness for *eternal* life!

"Gone the bliss of Eden's garden, gone the age of sacrifice; ours the time of grace and favor, ours the call to paradise! Ever, Lord, impress upon us: only You can cover sin—take our worthless, self-made garments; clothe our shame and cleanse within." Amen. (LSB 572:6)

JULY 26

**Alleluia! Let praises ring!
Unto the Lamb of God we sing,
In whom we are elected.
He bought His Church
with His own blood,
He cleansed her in
that blessed flood,
And as His bride selected.
Holy, holy
Is our union
And communion.
His befriending
Gives us joy and peace
unending.** (*LSB* 822:2)

JESUS IS THE BRIDEGROOM; THE CHURCH IS HIS BRIDE. WHEN husband and wife are joined together in holy matrimony, the love between bridegroom and bride is readily apparent for all to see. But that love between husband and wife is patterned after a far greater love—that of Christ for His church. Christ as Bridegroom had to die for His Bride. He bought her with His own blood, thereby cleansing her for an eternal union, an everlasting and intimate communion, between Bridegroom and Bride. This is the *divine love*, the holy love, that is given to us by Christ, our Bridegroom. It makes all the difference in our lives, the hymn writer stating, "His befriending gives us joy and peace unending."

The Holy Spirit works faith in our hearts to believe this good news of the Gospel. Jesus promised His disciples that He would send the Holy Spirit to "guide you into all the truth" (John 16:13). The hymn writer declares the Spirit's work in this way: "The saving faith in us He wrought and us unto the Bridegroom brought" (st. 3). We didn't choose the Bridegroom; He chose us as His Bride, and God the Holy Spirit gives us this saving faith in Jesus, the church's Bridegroom.

Jesus' love for His church gives us "joy eternal, bliss supernal . . . and an endless glad hosanna" (st. 3). For such great love, "let praises ring!"

"Alleluia! Let praises ring! Unto the Holy Ghost we sing for our regeneration. The saving faith in us He wrought and us unto the Bridegroom brought, made us His chosen nation. Glory! Glory! Joy eternal, bliss supernal; there is manna and an endless, glad hosanna." Amen. (LSB *822:3*)

JULY 27

A multitude comes from
the east and the west
To sit at the feast of salvation
With Abraham, Isaac,
and Jacob, the blest,
Obeying the Lord's invitation.
Have mercy upon us, O Jesus!

All trials shall be like a
dream that is past,
Forgotten all trouble
and mourning.
All questions and doubts
have been answered at last,
When rises the light
of that morning.
Have mercy upon us, O
Jesus! (*LSB* 510:1, 3)

WE LEARN IN *MATTHEW* 8 THAT SAINTS FROM EVERY AGE AND part of the world will sit with the patriarchs at the final resurrection banquet feast. And who will these privileged saints be in attendance? Those who on earth feared, loved, and trusted in their Lord Jesus Christ above all things will have a place at this magnificent banquet that will be beyond all human comprehension.

Trials, troubles, mourning, questions, and doubts will all be things of the past at that festive table. We will no longer even remember such things, for we will finally be free from Satan, sinning, sadness, and tears. Oh, how we have longed for this as we pray, "Come, Lord Jesus, come quickly!"

We also look forward to music-making like we have never heard on earth. The heavens will ring with an explosion of angelic singing to the Lamb who sits upon the throne, *and we will be there to hear it!* As Johann Walter, the first Lutheran kantor, wrote, "In that fair home shall never be silent music's voice; with hearts and lips forever we shall in God rejoice, while angel hosts are raising with saints from great to least a mighty hymn for praising the Giver of the feast" (*LSB* 514:4).

"O God, let us hear when our Shepherd shall call in accents persuasive and tender, that while there is time we make haste, one and all, and find Him, our mighty defender. Have mercy upon us, O Jesus!" Amen. (LSB *510:2*)

JULY 28

O let the harps break forth in sound!
Our joy be all with music crowned,
Our voices gladly blending!
For Christ goes with us all the way—
Today, tomorrow, ev'ry day!
His love is never ending!
Sing out! Ring out!
Jubilation!
Exultation!
Tell the story!
Great is He, the King of Glory! (*LSB* 395:5)

TODAY, THE CHURCH REMEMBERS THE GREAT LUTHERAN KANTOR Johann Sebastian Bach, who died on this day in 1750. His sacred cantatas, Passion settings, and organ chorale preludes continue to proclaim the Gospel today just as surely as they did during his lifetime.

Bach was formed in part by the hymnal used during his elementary school days at the Lutheran parish school of St. George in Eisenach. In that hymnal, Bach first encountered the great Lutheran chorales, some dating back to the time of Martin Luther, who, coincidentally, attended that very same school in Eisenach some two hundred years earlier. One of the hymns in this hymnal was Philipp Nicolai's "O Morning Star, How Fair and Bright."

Bach's thinking about music in the Divine Service could have been shaped by Nicolai's fifth stanza, where the poet speaks of "music" as crowning our Christian joy. But more than that, the poet states the reason for that joy: "Christ goes with us all the way!" He consoles, helps, and cheers us in our daily lives—"today, tomorrow, ev'ry day," and He promises us an eternity with Himself in heaven: "His love is never ending!" Bach's music proclaims that blessed reality.

"What joy to know, when life is past, the Lord we love is first and last, the end and the beginning! He will one day, oh, glorious grace, transport us to that happy place beyond all tears and sinning! Amen! Amen! Come, Lord Jesus! Crown of gladness! We are yearning for the day of Your returning!" Amen. (LSB *395:6*)

JULY 29

If thou but trust in God to guide thee
And hope in Him through all thy ways,
He'll give thee strength, whate'er betide thee,
And bear thee through the evil days.
Who trusts in God's unchanging love
Builds on the rock that naught can move. (*LSB* 750:1)

JESUS TELLS US VERY FRANKLY THAT "IN THE WORLD YOU WILL have tribulation." But with that warning comes His comforting promise: "But take heart; I have overcome the world" (John 16:33). He doesn't promise that Christians will somehow be immune from troubles—quite the opposite. We *will* experience periods of trial and tribulations, whether sickness, disease, addiction, unemployment, family or marital problems, or other ramifications of life in this fallen world. But in the midst of whatever difficulties we may suffer, we know beyond any doubt that Jesus has *overcome* the world. That means that He has defeated our greatest enemies in this world—sin and death. Thus, we "take heart" as we suffer, for we know that our sufferings are temporary, and we look to the sure and certain hope of eternal life with Christ. The apostle Paul put it this way: "For I consider that the sufferings of this present time are not worth comparing with the glory that is to be revealed to us" (Romans 8:18).

Today's hymn-prayer encourages us to trust and hope in Jesus' firm promise—He has overcome the world. And in the midst of our tribulations, He will give strength to bear us "through the evil days." We pray for patience and a "cheerful hope, with heart content" to take whatever God in His wisdom and "discerning love" may send us (st. 3). After all, He "chose us for His own" (st. 3) and will never cease to care for us in this world before He takes us to Himself.

"Be patient and await His leisure in cheerful hope, with heart content to take whate'er thy Father's pleasure and His discerning love hath sent, nor doubt our inmost wants are known to Him who chose us for His own." Amen. (LSB *750:3*)

JULY 30

Forth in Thy name, O Lord, I go,
My daily labor to pursue,
Thee, only Thee,
resolved to know
In all I think or speak or do.

The task Thy wisdom
has assigned,
O let me cheerfully fulfill;
In all my works Thy
presence find,
And prove Thy good and
perfect will. (*LSB* 854:1–2)

W***HEN WE THINK OF "DAILY LABOR," WE MAY BE QUICK TO LIMIT*** those considerations to the employment situations God has graciously given. But the hymn writer would have us expand the concept of labor to include all vocations, not only those working situations in which some are paid. It is akin to Luther's Small Catechism explanation of the Fourth Petition of the Lord's Prayer, where he provides an expansive definition of "daily bread," including not only the items that support our physical lives but also the human relationships of husbands and wives, parents and children, and employers and workers.

The tasks God's "wisdom has assigned" include such works as a husband and wife serving each other, parents lovingly caring for their children, children learning to obey their parents, students respecting their teachers, neighbors caring for one another, and church members honoring the called pastor God has provided to care for their souls. Such relationships are also vocations at which we work, just as surely as the God-given jobs and professions that occupy our lives and enable us to enjoy those gifts of food, clothing, house, money, and goods that constitute our "daily bread."

Thus, as the hymn writer notes, in "all [our] works [may we] Thy presence find." Each of our vocations is a gift from God, and we go forth daily to run our course here even as we focus on our ultimate call to heaven.

"Give me to bear Thine easy yoke, and ev'ry moment watch and pray, and still to things eternal look, and hasten to Thy glorious day." Amen. (LSB *854:4*)

JULY 31

Shepherd of tender youth,
Guiding in love and truth
Through devious ways;
Christ, our triumphant king,
We come Your name to sing
And here our children bring
To join Your praise.

O ever be our guide,
Our shepherd, and our pride,
Our staff and song.
Jesus, O Christ of God,
By Your enduring Word
Lead us where You have trod;
Make our faith strong.
(*LSB* 864:1, 4)

TODAY'S TEXT BY CLEMENT OF ALEXANDRIA IS ONE OF THE earliest hymns in Christendom written outside of Scripture. Clement placed it at the end of his work called *The Instructor*, which was meant to help mentor the young and newly converted Christians to the faith. Jesus Christ, the Good Shepherd, cares deeply about these vulnerable lambs, His "tender youth." "Unless you turn and become like children, you will never enter the kingdom of heaven" (Matthew 18:3).

Regardless of our role as parents, pastors, or teachers, it is both our joy and responsibility to bring His tender youth, His babes in Christ, to His "enduring Word," where He promises to shape them in His love. Then, their Teacher will be their Shepherd as He is found in His Word, where He fills them with His wisdom, knowledge, and truth.

Regardless of age, we are all lifelong students in the faith; our catechesis never ends. We cannot know God's commands, thoughts, and ways on our own; we need His help! And He wants to "be our guide, our shepherd, and our pride, our staff and song" as He strengthens our faith.

"O teach them with all diligence the truths of God's own Word, to place in Him their confidence, to fear and trust their Lord, to learn that in our God alone their hope securely stands, that they may never doubt His love but walk in His commands." Amen. (LSB 867:4–5)

AUGUST 1

All mankind fell in Adam's fall;
One common sin infects us all.
From one to all the curse descends,
And over all God's wrath impends.

Through all our pow'rs corruption creeps
And us in dreadful bondage keeps;
In guilt we draw our infant breath
And reap its fruits of woe and death. (*LSB* 562:1–2)

In Psalm 51, David writes, "*Behold, I was brought forth in* iniquity, and in sin did my mother conceive me" (v. 5). The hymn writer adds, "In guilt we draw our infant breath." We are guilty from the moment of birth. Original sin may be defined in this way: "One common sin infects us all." Why would we sing about, or pray about, the biblical teaching of original sin? First, it keeps us from ever thinking that maybe, just maybe, one could lead an exemplary life and thereby gain an eternity in heaven. No! Sin is deeply rooted in our very nature—since conception and birth. Second, this biblical teaching shows us our utter dependence on God's grace in Jesus Christ.

Jesus is, as the hymn writer states, the "second Adam," who "came to bear our sin," to become "our only hope, our only stay" (st. 4). In Romans 5, Paul contrasts Adam—the one man by whose *disobedience* sin entered the world—with Jesus—the one man by whose *obedience* many are made righteous.

Original sin is the recognition that we cannot ever live up to or keep God's Law; rather, we look to the Gospel, which is "our life, our light, our way" (st. 4).

"But Christ, the second Adam, came to bear our sin and woe and shame, to be our life, our light, our way, our only hope, our only stay. As by one man all mankind fell and, born in sin, was doomed to hell, so by one Man, who took our place, we all were justified by grace. We thank You, Christ; new life is ours, new light, new hope, new strength, new pow'rs. This grace our ev'ry way attend until we reach our journey's end." Amen. (LSB 562:4–6)

AUGUST 2

Speak, O Lord, Your servant listens,
Let Your Word to me come near;
Newborn life and spirit give me,
Let each promise still my fear.
Death's dread pow'r, its inward strife,
Wars against Your Word of life;
Fill me, Lord, with love's strong fervor
That I cling to You forever! (***LSB*** **589:1**)

JESUS IS ALWAYS THE ONE WHO SEARCHES AND FINDS, AND HE IS the one who bids us come, see, and follow. And this is as it should be, for we are lost, blind, and in need of His direction. When Jesus said, "Follow Me," to Matthew, it was easy for us to understand (Matthew 9:9). But do we know what Jesus means for us when He says, "Follow Me"?

Today's hymn is a lesson with the answer—and it is all about listening and hearing Him. As Jesus leads, we follow Him through His Word day by day. Such listening and hearing distinguish today's faithful saints following their Master. "Hear instruction and be wise, and do not neglect it. Blessed is the one who listens to me, watching daily at my gates, waiting beside my doors" (Proverbs 8:33–34).

Jesus wants to talk *to* and *with* us every day. He knows how much we need His food, strength, counsel, wisdom, guidance, peace, and forgiveness. The Holy Spirit gives us Jesus, and our lives can bear the abundant fruit that marks us as disciples who follow Jesus. That is the blessed life of discipleship in His kingdom.

"As I pray, dear Jesus, hear me; let Your words in me take root. May Your Spirit e'er be near me that I bear abundant fruit. May I daily sing Your praise, from my heart glad anthems raise, till my highest praise is given in the endless joy of heaven." Amen. (LSB *589:4*)

AUGUST 3

From depths of woe
I cry to Thee,
In trial and tribulation;
Bend down Thy
gracious ear to me,
Lord, hear my supplication.
If Thou remb'rest ev'ry sin,
Who then could
heaven ever win
Or stand before Thy presence?

Thy love and grace alone avail
To blot out my transgression;
The best and holiest
deeds must fail
To break sin's dread oppression.
Before Thee none can
boasting stand,
But all must fear Thy
strict demand
And live alone by mercy.
(*LSB* 607:1–2)

THIS HYMN, A PARAPHRASE OF PSALM 130, IS ONE OF THE FIRST and finest written by Luther. The psalmist's cry for mercy and deliverance from sin is matched by his confidence that, with the Lord, there is forgiveness, steadfast love, and plentiful redemption.

Likewise, Luther is crystal clear about sin, which separates us from God and precludes us from standing before God boasting of our good works and hoping thereby to enter heaven. Even our "best and holiest deeds" are completely inadequate "to break sin's dread oppression." It is the blood of Jesus Christ that blots out our transgressions. God's "love and grace alone" provide the plentiful redemption sought by the psalmist.

We place our hope in the Lord and not in our own merits. Such hope "rests upon His faithful Word" (st. 3). As Paul wrote, "Where sin increased, grace abounded all the more" (Romans 5:20). God's Word assures us that our cries for grace and mercy are heard and that we are able to go to the Lord day after day seeking His mercy and forgiveness, certain that He hears and forgives—richly and daily—for Christ's sake.

"Though great our sins, yet greater still is God's abundant favor; His hand of mercy never will abandon us, nor waver. Our shepherd good and true is He, who will at last His Israel free from all their sin and sorrow." Amen. (LSB 607:5)

AUGUST 4

God, who made the earth and heaven,
Darkness and light:
You the day for work have given,
For rest the night.
May Your angel guards defend us,
Slumber sweet Your mercy send us,
Holy dreams and hopes attend us
All through the night. (*LSB* 877:1)

SLEEPLESSNESS IS A HUMAN CONDITION FOR WHICH THERE IS NO shortage of suggested remedies, from sleep aids available at the drugstore to the proverbial "counting of sheep." For the Christian, we are also blessed with the beautiful traditions of evening prayer, whether offered in the context of the church's Daily Office hours of Vespers or Compline, or in private evening devotions. We pray that the Lord would guard us from all harm and danger through the night and graciously grant to us the sleep that rejuvenates the body for another day of service in our Christian vocations.

Our evening hymns frequently link overnight sleep for our bodies to the sleep of death. Jesus often referred to death as sleep (John 11:11). For Jesus, death is but a sleep. By the power of His Word, He awakened Lazarus from the sleep of death, foreshadowing Jesus' own resurrection on the third day. When we die, we will sleep for a time, but, like Jesus before us, we will awaken to life—*eternal life*—with the one who has conquered death forever.

May our evening prayers always serve as a reminder that the sleep of death is but a brief interval that will on the Last Day give way to a new and eternal morning in the presence of Christ.

"Guard us waking, guard us sleeping, and when we die, may we in Your mighty keeping all peaceful lie. When the last dread call shall wake us, then, O Lord, do not forsake us, but to reign in glory take us with You on high." Amen. (LSB 877:3)

AUGUST 5

The Church's one foundation
Is Jesus Christ, her Lord;
She is His new creation
By water and the Word.
From heav'n He came
and sought her
To be His holy bride;
With His own blood
He bought her,
And for her life He died.

Elect from ev'ry nation,
Yet one o'er all the earth;
Her charter of salvation:
One Lord, one faith, one birth.
One holy name she blesses,
Partakes one holy food,
And to one hope she presses
With ev'ry grace endued.
(*LSB* 644:1–2)

THIS BELOVED HYMN CUTS ACROSS DENOMINATIONAL LINES TO sing an accurate and beautiful biblical picture of Christ's Bride. These words have found a home in virtually every hymnal in Christendom and, interestingly, even in some churches that do not believe all of what is confessed.

What is here confessed about the Bride/church? This Bride has one and only one foundation: Jesus Christ, her Lord, who came from heaven to purchase her with His blood. That means that this Bridegroom died for His Bride.

"She is His new creation by water and the Word." The Bride's whole identity is found in the Bridegroom's Holy Word and Sacraments. His Word is her life and food; in other words, she lives on them. The Bride/church comprises God's children, who have been washed in the waters of Holy Baptism, making them members, from every nation from all over the earth.

The Bride gathers regularly in the Bridegroom's real presence and "partakes one holy food," His Supper. This food keeps her wonderfully healthy as it feeds her with His grace upon grace and gift upon gift.

"Yet she on earth has union with God, the Three in One, and mystic sweet communion with those whose rest is won. O blessed heav'nly chorus! Lord, save us by Your grace that we, like saints before us, may see You face to face." Amen. (LSB 644:5)

AUGUST 6

Though with a scornful wonder
The world sees her oppressed,
By schisms rent asunder,
By heresies distressed,
Yet saints their watch
are keeping;
Their cry goes up, "How long?"
And soon the night of weeping
Shall be the morn of song.

Through toil and tribulation
And tumult of her war
She waits the consummation
Of peace forevermore
Till with the vision glorious
Her longing eyes are blest,
And the great Church victorious
Shall be the Church at
rest. (*LSB* 644:3–4)

LIFE IN THIS WORLD IS NOT EASY FOR THE BRIDE OF CHRIST. AND the world is all too ready to observe the church's tumult, tribulation, oppression, division, and procession of heretics "with a scornful wonder." The world asks, "This is the Bride of Christ? All we can see is a profoundly flawed organization overflowing with sinners that Satan loves to torment."

Well, what the world sees and what the true church *is* are very different things. Yes, the Bride is waiting for her Bridegroom to return with "longing eyes." Yes, she sometimes cries, "How long?" But the Bride has *every* confidence that her Bridegroom will return for her, for He promised, "Surely I am coming soon" (Revelation 22:20).

And the Bride can trust her Bridegroom's promises because He loves her so much that He shed His blood to save her. He loves her so much that He continues to give His body, blood, and Word so that He can live in union with her while she waits for Him to return. The Bride of Christ lives in the care and keeping of the triune God, who blesses, feeds, sustains, and preserves her "till with the vision glorious her longing eyes are blest."

And the world will never see or understand any of this.

"Yet she on earth has union with God, the Three in One, and mystic sweet communion with those whose rest is won. O blessed heav'nly chorus! Lord, save us by Your grace that we, like saints before us, may see You face to face." Amen. (LSB 644:5)

AUGUST 7

Satan, hear this proclamation:
I am baptized into Christ!
Drop your ugly accusation,
I am not so soon enticed.
Now that to the font
I've traveled,
All your might has
come unraveled,
And, against your tyranny,
God, my Lord, unites
with me! (*LSB* 594:3)

I AM BAPTIZED INTO CHRIST! IN HIS LARGE CATECHISM, LUTHER states a first-person, present-tense proposition: "Nevertheless, I am baptized! And if I am baptized, it is promised to me that I shall be saved and have eternal life, both in soul and body" (Part 4, paragraph 44). It's personal; it's now; it's a *daily* reality. Your Baptism gives you the daily assurance that God has done His work in you and you are safely held by Him forever.

Baptism gives the power to confront Satan and to say in no uncertain terms that his accusations—with which he would terrify you—were dissolved already in the waters of your Baptism. Daily remember your Baptism and know beyond any doubt that God has claimed you as His own!

Baptism gives you the power to confront the certainty of death and to say with the hymn writer, "Death, you cannot end my gladness. . . . Baptism has the strength divine to make life immortal mine" (st. 4). Through your Baptism, you can look death in the eye and say, "You cannot have me—I belong to Christ, who has saved me."

Luther was right to say that Baptism is "so full of consolation and grace that heaven and earth cannot understand it" (Large Catechism, Part 4, paragraph 39). While we may not fully comprehend the grace of God in the sacrament of Baptism, by faith, we take comfort—every day—in the sure and certain promises of Baptism. "Baptism . . . now saves you" (1 Peter 3:21).

"Death, you cannot end my gladness: I am baptized into Christ! When I die, I leave all sadness to inherit paradise! Though I lie in dust and ashes faith's assurance brightly flashes: Baptism has the strength divine to make life immortal mine." Amen. (LSB 594:4)

AUGUST 8

The gifts Christ freely gives
He gives to you and me
To be His Church, His bride,
His chosen, saved and free!
Saints blest with these rich gifts
Are children who proclaim
That they were won by Christ
And cling to His strong name. (*LSB* 602:1)

SCHOLAR AND SEMINARY PROFESSOR NORMAN NAGEL SAW GOD'S good gifts everywhere and could not help but fill his preaching, teaching, and writing with "the gifts." Many know that Professor Nagel inspired today's hymn text about "the gifts."

God's gifts are indeed everywhere! Our gracious God, in His boundless mercy, loves to shower His lavish grace on His dear children from the moment of their Baptism throughout their lives. His church calls *how* He does this "the means of grace."

Today's hymn and concluding prayer stanza summarize those means of grace in the lives of the saints. The hymn describes what it is like to be His children living together as His Bride, His church, constantly being fed by His grace in all the ways His Word has promised. And the final prayer stanza is one of high thanksgiving and praise for the blessed means by which He gives us His grace.

God's gifts are not earned, deserved, or even rewarded for good behavior; this is not how things work in God's kingdom. No, His gifts are *free* and undeserved. The triune God loves to shower His love, grace, and gifts in an extravagant way on the children He loves—so much that He died for them.

"All glory to the One who lavishes such love; the triune God in love assures our life above. His means of grace for us are gifts He loves to give; all thanks and praise for His great love by which we live!" Amen. (LSB 602:6)

AUGUST 9

The gifts flow from the font
Where He calls us His own;
New life He gives that makes
Us His and His alone.
Here He forgives our sins
With water and His Word;
The triune God Himself
Gives pow'r to call Him Lord. (*LSB* 602:2)

YOUR BAPTISM IS THE MOST IMPORTANT DAY OF YOUR LIFE. Yet it is amazing that most would be surprised, or even shocked, by that statement and would easily have a list of days more important to them.

But what could possibly be more important than the day when God put His name on you and called you *His child*? From that day on, you have not been the same, and nothing will ever be the same in your life. No other significant day will be able to compare.

For those most blessed waters sprinkled on you that day gave you *new life*—the baptismal life! God's miraculous means of grace, which may look like simple water and words, are in reality *power* for all your days. For even at a tender age, you already needed the forgiveness of sins—and you received it. You desperately needed a loving and compassionate heavenly Father—and you received Him. And you needed His divine gifts for all your days—and you will receive them.

These are the waters that revive your soul when you are weary, refresh you when thirsty, wash you when soiled, and sustain you through life's trials and crosses. Your Baptism is not a one-time event that happened and is over and done. No, your Baptism is a *life,* the baptismal life. And it is filled with ongoing gifts.

"O Christian, firmly hold this gift and give God thanks forever! It gives the power to uplift in all that you endeavor. When nothing else revives your soul, your Baptism stands and makes you whole and then in death completes you." Amen. (LSB 596:5)

AUGUST 10

The gifts of grace and peace
From absolution flow;
The pastor's words are Christ's
For us to trust and know.
Forgiveness that we need
Is granted to us there;
The Lord of mercy sends
Us forth in His blest care. (*LSB* 602:3)

THE BLESSED GIFT OF ABSOLUTION IS LIKE NO OTHER GIFT ON earth, for this gift addresses our greatest need—the forgiveness of sins. The Small Catechism teaches us at an early age that our pastor's words are Christ's words for us to trust and know as he speaks the Absolution following our Confession.

It is good and right that the glorious words of Absolution begin each Divine Service. For in these beautiful and miraculous words, God removes our sins from us as far as the east is from the west. Forgiven saints then joyfully continue to sing and pray the Divine Service filled with one gift after another. This is the very best way possible to start a week—forgiven and richly fed by the gifts.

This is the Lord of mercy sending His children "forth in His blest care." It is His plan to do this, again and again, in His Divine Service as His children start their week according to His plan—as He pardons, cleanses, makes them healthy, and fills them with His grace and peace.

Why would anyone choose to start their week without "the gifts"!

"Lord, to You I make confession: I have sinned and gone astray, I have multiplied transgression, chosen for myself my way. Led by You to see my errors, Lord, I tremble at Your terrors. Lord, on You I cast my burden—sink it in the deepest sea! Let me know Your gracious pardon, cleanse me from iniquity. Let Your Spirit leave me never; make me only Yours forever." Amen. (LSB *608:1, 4*)

AUGUST 11

The gifts are there each day
The holy Word is read;
God's children listen, hear,
Receive, and they are fed.
Christ fills them with Himself,
Blest words that give them life,
Restoring and refreshing
Them for this world's strife. (***LSB*** **602:4)**

HEARING GOD'S WORD READ AND PREACHED BESTOWS THE forgiveness of sins on those hearing it. Gifts upon gifts. What? Does this mean we don't have to do something? Right, miracle of miracles, these *means* are how God wishes to bestow His grace. Yet we are doing something; we are hearing—and "faith comes from hearing and hearing through the word of Christ" (Romans 10:17).

It *is* an extraordinary fact! A fact that properly understands the means of grace, but unfortunately, this understanding is a foreign concept to most Christians. They are uncomfortable with gifts all the time and, by nature, want *to do* something. But that is the realm of Law.

However, the means of grace bestow pure Gospel, and Gospel is God's gift. This is how it works in the realm of Gospel—God is the actor, and we are the recipients. It is His wish that His Holy Word read and preached will be a gift for us as food that restores and refreshes us "for this world's strife."

As we hear His precious Word, we are given armor for Satan's daily attack. We are given Wisdom that is Jesus Christ Himself *in us*. And we are being given extraordinary power because His Words are not ordinary words.

"Lord, Your words are waters living when my thirsting spirit pleads. Lord, Your words are bread life-giving; on Your words my spirit feeds. Lord, Your words will be my light through death's cold and dreary night; yes, they are my sword prevailing and my cup of joy unfailing!" Amen. (LSB *589:3*)

AUGUST 12

The gifts are in the feast,
Gifts far more than we see;
Beneath the bread and wine
Is food from Calvary.
The body and the blood
Remove our ev'ry sin;
We leave His presence in
His peace, renewed again. (*LSB* 602:5)

THE SACRAMENT OF THE ALTAR IS FOOD FOR SIN-PARCHED SOULS and is spread simply on an altar, but make no mistake: this is *not* simple food. Instead, it is the very bodily presence of our Lord and Savior, Jesus Christ, who died on a cross at Calvary *for us*—His body and His blood *for us.*

Therefore, this precious food was purchased at a very great price and is another beautiful means of grace full of forgiveness, mercy, and peace *for us.* Indeed, these are "gifts far more than we see" for our healing, our tasting, our refreshment, and our health. "Oh, what transport of delight from Thy pure chalice floweth!" (*LSB* 709:5).

The whole Divine Service moves very carefully to a summit of receiving this divine food in these gifts. The blessed saints are here involved in *great* feasting that leaves them filled with Christ. Without a doubt, this is the high point of their week.

They leave the Divine Service to begin a week in a troubled world where Satan will yet again surely torment them. But now the saints do not face Satan and the troubles of this world on their own—for they have been made strong and filled with Jesus Christ and His peace that passes all understanding, a constant source of comfort and strength.

"By faith Your Word has made us bold to seize the gift of love retold; all that You are we here receive, and all we are to You we give. Lord Jesus Christ, we humbly pray: O keep us steadfast till that day when each will be Your welcomed guest in heaven's high and holy feast." Amen. (LSB *623:3, 5*)

AUGUST 13

Why should cross and
trial grieve me?
Christ is near
With His cheer;
Never will He leave me.

Who can rob me of the heaven
That God's Son
For me won
When His life was
given? (*LSB* 756:1)

THE CROSS IS, OF COURSE, CENTRAL TO THE GOSPEL—JESUS allowed Himself to be crucified on a cross to pay the price for our sins. But prior to willingly dying for us on the cross, Jesus made this striking statement: "If anyone would come after Me, let him deny himself and take up his cross and follow Me" (Mark 8:34). For the Christian, a cross is a consequence of following Christ, a corollary of discipleship.

The theology of the cross acknowledges that the Christian's life is *never* without pain and burdens—crosses. This is in contradistinction to a false theology of glory, which mistakenly posits that the Christian will enjoy a carefree life of health, wealth, and happiness, as evidence of God's favor.

Pastor Paul Gerhardt reminds us that "God, my loving Savior," is the one who *sends* crosses into our lives—in the form of "life's troubles" (st. 2). But the crosses He sends will "not defeat me" (st. 2), for throughout our cross-bearing, Christ remains near and will never leave us. His love sends our crosses, and His love sustains us as we bear our crosses. Through this process, Jesus draws us closer to Himself, strengthening our faith and clarifying again and again that He alone is our ultimate hope and salvation.

With Pastor Gerhardt, we can be confident that crosses and trials will *not* defeat us. Christ has sent them and knows how and when to end them. Most important of all, we know that no one can "rob me of the heaven that God's Son for me won." That sure and certain promise of eternal life sustains us in the midst of cross and trial.

"When life's troubles rise to meet me, though their weight may be great, they will not defeat me. God, my loving Savior, sends them; He who knows all my woes knows how best to end them." Amen. (LSB 756:2)

AUGUST 14

God gives me my days of gladness,
And I will
Trust Him still
When He sends me sadness.
God is good; His love attends me
Day by day,
Come what may,
Guides me and defends me. (*LSB* 756:3)

In his explanation of the First Article of the Creed in the Small Catechism, Luther teaches us that God "*daily* provides me with all that I need to support this body and life" (emphasis added). Our heavenly Father cares for us *every* day of our lives. In the words of Pastor Paul Gerhardt, "His love attends me day by day, come what may, guides me and defends me." We have "days of gladness," when perhaps we are a bit more likely to take God's rich daily blessings for granted. But we also experience days of sadness, which are the crosses and trials *sent* by God to draw His dear children ever closer to Him. Pastor Gerhardt suffered the loss of three of his four children in their infancies, the death of his wife after thirteen years of marriage, and the loss of his position as pastor in Berlin because he refused to compromise his commitment to confessional Lutheran teaching. Through all such crosses and trials, he still wrote, "I will trust Him still when He sends me sadness."

In his explanation of the Third Article, Luther wrote that God "*daily* and richly forgives all my sins" (emphasis added). Of His daily blessings to us, this is the greatest of all, for it means that come what may in this earthly life, we have the certainty of eternal life with Christ. "Death cannot slay me" (st. 5). For the Christian, death never has the last word. "Christ has made my death a portal from the strife of this life to His joy immortal!" (st. 5). Death is our door to paradise, to life with Christ forever.

"Now in Christ, death cannot slay me, though it might, day and night, trouble and dismay me. Christ has made my death a portal from the strife of this life to His joy immortal!" Amen. (LSB *756:5*)

AUGUST 15

Not what these hands
have done
Can save this guilty soul;
Not what this toiling
flesh has borne
Can make my spirit whole.

Not what I feel or do
Can give me peace with God;
Not all my prayers and
sighs and tears
Can bear my awful load.

Thy work alone, O Christ,
Can ease this weight of sin;
Thy blood alone, O
Lamb of God,
Can give me peace
within. (*LSB* 567:1–3)

THE HUMAN PROBLEM IS THE "WEIGHT OF SIN," ITS "AWFUL LOAD," the guilt that we experience deep in our souls. God's Law shows us that we sin daily in our thoughts, words, and actions.

In the world around us, we see inadequate approaches to the problem of sin. Perhaps it's the suggestion just to get to work and become a better person. Or perhaps it's just a matter of praying more or feeling sufficiently bad for sins. But the hymn writer identifies the common inadequacy in all such "solutions"—they depend on *us*! He spells it out clearly: "Not what I feel or do can give me peace with God."

The solution to sin always comes from our merciful and loving God, not from our inward longings. Christ alone "can ease this weight of sin." Only Christ the Lamb of God can give the inner peace that we need to live our lives in service to the neighbor in full assurance of eternal life in the presence of the Lamb.

We are saved by God's grace alone, poured out to us richly in Holy Baptism, His Holy Supper, and His life-giving Word. He is the giver; we are the recipients of His lavish gifts. The solution: "Thy love to me, O God, not mine, O Lord, to Thee" (st. 4).

"Thy love to me, O God, not mine, O Lord, to Thee, can rid me of this dark unrest and set my spirit free. Thy grace alone, O God, to me can pardon speak; Thy pow'r alone, O Son of God, can this sore bondage break." Amen. (LSB *567:4–5*)

AUGUST 16

The tree of life with ev'ry good
In Eden's holy orchard stood,
And of its fruit so pure and sweet
God let the man and woman eat.
Yet in this garden also grew
Another tree, of which they knew;
Its lovely limbs with fruit adorned
Against whose eating God had warned. (*LSB* 561:1)

THE GARDEN OF EDEN WAS THE PICTURE OF ABSOLUTE perfection—what could go wrong? Yet something went *very* wrong. Why? Perhaps this is the most frequently asked question in confirmation class—*how* and *why* could this happen?

It happened because God, in His wisdom, did not want His excellent creation to be mere puppets, all programmed to say "yes" and automatically do His will. Instead, He bestowed upon His new creation a precious gift—free will. The first to exercise this free will was an angel who desired to sit next to God and be His equal. This rebellious angel was the first to decide, "I'm not going to obey," leading the world into such disobedience. This was the devil, the leader of "the angels who did not stay within their own position of authority, but left their proper dwelling" (Jude 6).

This devil moved immediately to lead Adam and Eve into an act of disobedience to eat "fruit adorned against whose eating God had warned." This devil was successful in the disobedience that plunged the world into darkness, sin, and death—but God steps in immediately to tell how this story will end. "I will put enmity between you and the woman, and between your offspring and her offspring; He shall bruise your head, and you shall bruise His heel" (Genesis 3:15). God's resolution would be costly to Him, but with this one verse, He sets His plan into motion.

"But Christ, the second Adam, came to bear our sin and woe and shame, to be our life, our light, our way, our only hope, our only stay." Amen. (LSB *562:4*)

AUGUST 17

The stillness of that sacred grove
Was broken, as the serpent strove
With tempting voice Eve to beguile
And Adam too by sin defile.
O day of sadness when the breath
Of fear and darkness, doubt and death,
Its awful poison first displayed
Within the world so newly made. (*LSB* 561:2)

O DAY OF SADNESS"! NOTHING WOULD EVER BE THE SAME AGAIN—for on that day, God's pristine new creation was plunged into the depths of darkness, evil, sin, and death. This saddest of all days poisoned every bit of the whole world, and it started to decay and die that day. Immediately, God acted, and in His love and mercy, He planned to save the world at tremendous cost to Himself.

We sing of that cost in the Good Friday hymn "O Darkest Woe." This hymn brings the reality of that first day of profound sadness to the day when God in His Son said, "It is finished" (John 19:30).

O darkest woe!
Ye tears, forth flow!
Has earth so sad
  a wonder?
God the Father's only Son
Now is buried yonder.

O sorrow dread!
Our God is dead,
Upon the cross extended.
There His love
  enlivened us
As His life was ended.
(*LSB* 448:1–2)

God's plan for our salvation has the last word—*thanks be to God*! He turns all our sadness into the highest gladness, for within hours after singing these heavy words on Good Friday, we are back in His house, but this time with gold and white, lilies and trumpets, and we sing, "Awake, my heart, with gladness" (*LSB* 467:1).

"This is a sight that gladdens—what peace it doth impart! Now nothing ever saddens the joy within my heart. No gloom shall ever shake, no foe shall ever take the hope which God's own Son in love for me has won." Amen. (LSB *467:3*)

AUGUST 18

Now from that tree of Jesus' shame
Flows life eternal in His name;
For all who trust and will believe,
Salvation's living fruit receive.
And of this fruit so pure and sweet
The Lord invites the world to eat,
To find within this cross of wood
The tree of life with ev'ry good. (*LSB* 561:4)

G. ***K. Chesterton wrote a poem about the honored donkey*** who was privileged to carry Jesus on Palm Sunday into Jerusalem. His poetry shows that not all donkeys are equal, and today's hymn shows that not all wood is equal.

The wood in today's hymn formed a cross that carried the world's sin and shame—as it was placed on *the very Son of God*! There cannot be any more significant wood in history than the wood of Jesus' cross. This wood became an instrument of excruciating and humiliating execution, seemingly the most pitiful wood of all.

Herein lies the greatest paradox of all time—our Lord's lowest point was also His highest point. In His dying words, "It is finished" (John 19:30), we see His highest glory. The work of salvation that He came to earth to accomplish was finished, and now His cross of wood becomes our tree of life with every good. Gone is the shame, as "each crimsoned bough proclaims the King of Glory now" (*LSB* 455:5).

All who trust and believe what Jesus' death accomplished for them on His cross of wood receive the pure and sweet fruit from this tree of beauty—and it becomes their *tree of life*.

"O tree of beauty, tree most fair, ordained those holy limbs to bear: gone is thy shame, each crimsoned bough proclaims the King of Glory now. To Thee, eternal Three in One, let homage meet by all be done; as by the cross Thou dost restore, so guide and keep us evermore. Amen." (LSB *455:5–6*)

AUGUST 19

Jesus Christ, my sure defense
And my Savior, now is living!
Knowing this, my confidence
Rests upon the hope here given,
Though the night of death be fraught
Still with many an anxious thought. (*LSB* 741:1)

AMONG THE BLESSINGS THAT GOD HAS GIVEN HIS CHILDREN IS "confidence." The child of God is confident that God wants us to pray and hears our prayers and confident that God watches over us and cares for us throughout our earthly lives, confident especially that He has accomplished salvation for us and promised us life with Him forever. Our confidence of eternal life is rooted in the resurrection of Christ: "Because I live, you also will live" (John 14:19). That confidence changes the way we live our lives here and now. Because we are confident that God directs our lives and will always provide for us, we are free to live out our vocations and love and serve our neighbors. Because we are confident that, at the time of death, God will take us to Himself, we can live without doubts and fears concerning our own death or the death of our loved ones. "So we have come to know and to believe the love that God has for us. God is love, and whoever abides in love abides in God, and God abides in him. By this is love perfected with us, so that we may have confidence for the day of judgment" (1 John 4:16–17).

While the hymn writer acknowledges "many an anxious thought" at the time of death, he immediately addresses that concern with confidence: "Jesus, my Redeemer, lives; likewise I to life shall waken. He will bring me where He is" (st. 2). Our confidence is never found in ourselves or our deeds; rather, it is always the work of Christ on our behalf. We live—and die—confidently, believing God's loving promises.

"Laugh to scorn the gloomy grave and at death no longer tremble; He, the Lord, who came to save will at last His own assemble. They will go their Lord to meet, treading death beneath their feet." Amen. (LSB *741:7*)

AUGUST 20

I am flesh and must return
To the dust, whence I am taken;
But by faith I now discern
That from death I shall awaken
With my Savior to abide
In His glory, at His side. (*LSB* 741:4)

We hear these words on Ash Wednesday: "Remember that you are dust, and to dust you shall return" (*LSB Altar Book*, p. 486). But even as we hear those words and consider the enormity of that scriptural truth (Genesis 3:19), we also know that those words are not the end of the story—as we look ahead to the glorious resurrection of Jesus on Easter Day. The hymn writer points to our own resurrection: "That from death I shall awaken" to live forever with Jesus. What is the source of that confidence? "By *faith* I now discern" (emphasis added). The Holy Spirit has worked faith in us to believe that the resurrection promise is *for us*.

The bodies that God created uniquely for each of us—"For You formed my inward parts; You knitted me together in my mother's womb" (Psalm 139:13)—will indeed return to dust, even as our immortal souls live with Christ: "Today you will be with Me in paradise" (Luke 23:43). At the resurrection, the body that God created for you will rise from death and be glorified, perfected for a life without end in the presence of Christ. The prophet Job spoke words that give us great joy and assurance for the resurrection: "And after my skin has been thus destroyed, yet in my flesh I shall see God, whom I shall see for myself, and my eyes shall behold, and not another" (Job 19:26–27). God will restore your flesh, your body, and when you see Him for the first time it will be with your own eyes. Thanks be to God for these resurrection promises. May He come soon to make all things new!

"Glorified, I shall anew with this flesh then be enshrouded; in this body I shall view God, my Lord, with eyes unclouded; in this flesh I then shall see Jesus Christ eternally." Amen. (LSB 741:5)

AUGUST 21

Then take comfort and rejoice,
For His members Christ will cherish.
Fear not, they will hear His voice;
Dying, they will never perish;
For the very grave is stirred
When the trumpet's blast is heard. (***LSB*** **741:6**)

I*N JOHN 11,* WE READ THE DETAILED ACCOUNT OF *LAZARUS—HIS* death and his resurrection at Jesus' command. Lazarus and his sisters, Mary and Martha, were among Jesus' closest friends; John noted that indeed "Jesus wept" as Mary told Him of her brother's death (v. 35). Jesus used this occasion for a definitive proof that He is master over death, declaring, "I am the resurrection and the life. Whoever believes in Me, though he die, yet shall he live, and everyone who lives and believes in Me shall never die" (John 11:25–26). In Christ, death does not have the last word.

Yet death is a very real consequence of sin, and death still exacts its toll. The tears we cry at the death of a loved one are real, just as Jesus wept over His friend's death. Yet when we grieve the death of a loved one, we do not "grieve as others do who have no hope" (1 Thessalonians 4:13). We have a sure and certain hope through those words Jesus spoke to Mary and Martha, through His Word preached into our hearts and minds, and through His body and blood given into death *for us* on the cross and received by us in His Holy Supper for the forgiveness of our sins.

Jesus raised Lazarus from the dead, but Lazarus would die again, his body awaiting the resurrection of all flesh on the Last Day. Not long after Jesus called Lazarus from the grave, Jesus was crucified, died, and was buried. But the grave could not and did not hold Him. His resurrection—the once-and-for-all defeat of death—assures us that we "shall never die."

"Jesus lives! The vict'ry's won! Death no longer can appall me; Jesus lives! Death's reign is done! From the grave will Christ recall me. Brighter scenes will then commence; this shall be my confidence." Amen. (LSB 490:1)

AUGUST 22

See this wonder in the making:
God Himself this child is taking
As a lamb safe in His keeping,
His to be, awake or sleeping.

Here we bring a child of nature;
Home we take a newborn creature,
Now God's precious son or daughter,
Born again by Word and water. (*LSB* 593:1, 4)

WHEN JESUS SAID, "UNLESS ONE IS BORN AGAIN HE CANNOT see the kingdom of God," Nicodemus took Him literally: "How can a man be born when he is old? Can he enter a second time into his mother's womb and be born?" Jesus' answer may not have provided him with immediate understanding: "Unless one is born of water and the Spirit, he cannot enter the kingdom of God" (John 3:3–5).

We, too, may need some assistance in understanding the miracle of Baptism. Luther clarifies, "The word of God in and with the water does these things. . . . With the word of God it is a Baptism, that is, a life-giving water, rich in grace, and a washing of the new birth in the Holy Spirit" (Small Catechism, Baptism, Third Part).

Today's hymn rightly calls Baptism a *wonder*! In Baptism, God takes a "child of nature"—that is, a sinful human being—and makes that child a "newborn creature." Baptism is not a mere ceremony of naming. No, it is so much more! "All of us who have been baptized into Christ Jesus were baptized into His death. . . . If we have been united with Him in a death like His, we shall certainly be united with Him in a resurrection like His" (Romans 6:3, 5). In Christ, through Baptism, it is all about *eternal life*; His resurrection is made our resurrection!

Our hymn writer states it so beautifully: "Miracle each time it happens as the door to heaven opens" (st. 2). Yes, in Baptism, the door to heaven opens, and in God's time, we shall enter heaven through that open door.

"Miracle each time it happens as the door to heaven opens and the Father beams, 'Beloved, heir of gifts a king would covet!'" Amen. (LSB 593:2)

AUGUST 23

The will of God is always best
And shall be done forever;
And they who trust in Him are blest;
He will forsake them never.
He helps indeed
In time of need;
He chastens with forbearing.
They who depend
On God, their friend,
Shall not be left despairing. (*LSB* 758:1)

O*NE NIGHT IN FORT WAYNE, INDIANA, A CATASTROPHIC FIRE* destroyed a downtown paper company owned by a member of St. Paul's Lutheran Church. The newspaper interviewed the owner, and she was quoted in a headline above a picture of her company in flames: "The Will of God Is Always Best."

I have always remembered her words spoken after she lost everything. What a towering witness to her faith for the whole community. She essentially said, "I am God's child, and He sees and knows what is best for me. His will is of the greatest importance to me, for His will is always best."

She was living under God's grace and mercy, and she trusted when her Lord said, "My grace is sufficient" (2 Corinthians 12:9). Therefore, she was also essentially saying that this fire was in God's control and a part of His plan for her life. She certainly was not viewing it as "bad luck." No, God was in control!

This true story also shows powerfully how the words of hymns we rehearse through a lifetime of singing will be there for us when we need them. "They who depend on God, their friend, shall not be left despairing."

"Lord, this I ask, O hear my plea, deny me not this favor: when Satan sorely troubles me, then do not let me waver. O guard me well, my fear dispel, fulfill Your faithful saying: All who believe by grace receive an answer to their praying." Amen. (LSB *758:3*)

AUGUST 24

What is the world to me
With all its vaunted pleasure
When You, and You alone,
Lord Jesus, are my treasure!
You only, dearest Lord, my soul's delight shall be;
You are my peace, my rest.
What is the world to me! (*LSB* 730:1)

IT IS NOT SO MUCH A QUESTION AS IT IS A BOLD RETORT BY THE Christian: "What is the world to me!" It is the child of God emphasizing a truth from Jesus' High Priestly Prayer to His Father: "They are not of the world, just as I am not of the world" (John 17:16). Jesus clarifies that He is not asking His Father to take His children out of the world but rather to "keep them from the evil one" (v. 15) and to "sanctify them in the truth; Your word is truth" (v. 17).

The hymn writer observes that in contrast to seeking the truth of God's Word, "the world seeks to be praised and honored" (st. 2). Accomplishments and achievements leading to ever greater power and prestige are valued above all else. In contrast to valuing the truth of God's Word, "the world seeks after wealth" (st. 3). The hymn writer makes an astute comment about the world's seeking: "Yet never is content though gold should fill its coffers" (st. 3). The world's truism is that one can never have enough wealth, or power and prestige; it is a never-ending quest for more.

In contrast to the values of the world, the child of God focuses on Jesus. He is "my treasure," "my soul's delight," "my peace, my rest." He is "my joy, my crown, my all, my bliss eternally" (st. 4). Jesus provides true wealth—all the money in the world cannot purchase the incomparable riches of eternal life. So we live content with the abundant blessings God gives us in this world, knowing that the greatest blessing is yet to come!

"What is the world to me! My Jesus is my treasure, my life, my health, my wealth, my friend, my love, my pleasure, my joy, my crown, my all, my bliss eternally. Once more, then, I declare: what is the world to me!" Amen. (LSB *730:4*)

AUGUST 25

But all of that was washed away—
Immersed and drowned forever.
The water of your Baptism day
Restored again whatever
Old Adam and his sin destroyed
And all our sinful selves employed
According to our nature. (*LSB* 596:3)

WHAT WAS WASHED AWAY ON THE DAY OF OUR BAPTISM? Everything that "old Adam and his sin destroyed." Everything that "all our sinful selves employed according to our nature." Quite a day indeed! And what happened was not simply a washing, drowning, or immersing; it was a *rebirth* that, by grace, made us God's own children.

The water of our Baptism is different from all other water. Yes, it is natural water, but it becomes divine and blessed because God's Word is attached, making it holy, set apart, the most extraordinary water on earth. God's act of rescue happened for us at this font as He showered His baptismal grace on His new child.

We do nothing except receive the gift—we bring no virtue, decision, or worthiness to this lavish washing. We come only in need of being rescued. Then, God acts through this blessed sacrament, and grace is bestowed as a pure gift, *and we are rescued.* He places His name on us, claims us, restores us, and forgives us. We go forth from that font to live a rich baptismal life filled with the Holy Spirit and faith. And as His new children, we are now members of His kingdom and joint heirs with Him in eternal life.

"The gifts flow from the font where He calls us His own; new life He gives that makes us His and His alone. Here He forgives our sins with water and His Word; the triune God Himself gives pow'r to call Him Lord." Amen. (LSB 602:2)

AUGUST 26

Come, very Sun of truth and love;
Pour down Thy radiance from above
And shed the Holy Spirit's ray
On all we think or do or say.
Alleluia!

On Christ, the true bread, let us feed;
Let Him to us be drink indeed;
And let us taste with joyfulness
The Holy Spirit's plenteousness.
Alleluia! (*LSB* 874:2, 5)

THIS FOURTH-CENTURY HYMN BY AMBROSE OF MILAN SERVES AS a salutary reminder of the rich—and lengthy—traditions of the church, which we are privileged to inherit. Like our Christian forebears, we, too, address petitions to the Holy Trinity.

We ask God the Father to guide all our undertakings in life, to give us a full measure of His grace and power so that we might overcome temptation and love rather than envy our neighbors, and "to give us grace our wrongs to bear" (st. 4). This grace allows us to confess our sins, knowing that in Christ we receive free and full forgiveness.

We ask Christ—the "very Sun of truth and love"—to pour down upon us exactly what He promised: "the Helper, the Holy Spirit" (John 14:26), who teaches us all things, informing "all we think or do or say." This is indeed "the Holy Spirit's plenteousness," daily bringing to our remembrance all that Jesus said and taught.

We also pray that we may receive Christ in precisely the place He has promised to be—receiving His true body and blood in the Holy Supper that He instituted for the forgiveness of our sins and the strengthening of our faith. May Christ always be our "true bread" and our "drink indeed."

"O Father, glorious evermore, we plead with Thee for grace and pow'r to conquer in temptation's hour, to guide whate'er we nobly do, with love all envy to subdue, to give us grace our wrongs to bear, to make ill fortune turn to fair." Amen. (LSB 874:3–4)

AUGUST 27

Hold me ever in Your keeping;
Comfort me in pain and strife.
In my laughter and my weeping
Be with me throughout my life.
Give me greater love for You,
And my faith and hope renew
In Your birth, Your life, and passion,
In Your death and resurrection. (*LSB* 692:2)

FROM CHILDHOOD, I HAVE A DISTINCT MEMORY OF A FEW TIMES when my brother and I stayed for a night with our grandparents. Around 9:00 in the evening was their regular time "to read prayers"—silently, each from their own books. My grandmother usually read her prayers from *The Lutheran Hymnal*. Today's hymn is yet another example of just how rich our hymns are as a source of prayer, with stanza 2 above being one that we might pray daily.

We ask Jesus to be with us always, throughout our lives. Whether in times of laughter or in times of weeping—hold and keep us close to You, O Lord. We ask for comfort in times of pain and illness, strife, and uncertainty—hold and keep us close to You, O Lord. Fix our eyes on You, O Lord, and give us a greater love for You. Above all else, strengthen our faith in You, for it is Your birth, life, Passion, death, and resurrection that are the sole basis of our sure and certain hope of eternal life with You!

Jesus, the Son of God, was there at creation, when man was formed from the dust of the ground. In the fullness of time, Jesus became fully human, taking on flesh and blood to save His creatures from sin and death. That saving act prompts our praise and adoration! May we follow where His steps are leading—through this life and unto the next.

"Praise to You and adoration, blessed Jesus, Son of God, who, to serve Your own creation, came to share our flesh and blood. Guide me that I never may from Your fold or pastures stray, but with zeal and joy exceeding follow where Your steps are leading." Amen. (LSB *692:1*)

AUGUST 28

May Christ our intercessor be
And through His
blood and merit
Read from His book
that we are free
With all who life inherit.
Then we shall see
Him face to face,
With all His saints in
that blest place
Which He has purchased
for us. (*LSB* 508:6)

EVERY YEAR, AS THE CHURCH YEAR CLOSES, THE LECTIONARY reviews all we need to know about the end times. Our dear Lord wants us to be ready. He tells us what we need to hear: "Now when these things begin to take place, straighten up and raise your heads, because your redemption is drawing near" (Luke 21:28). As His beloved saints, we long for that day and will have nothing to fear on that day, for our names are written in His book where His blood and merit *have made us free*!

On the other hand, the unbelieving world is terrified of that day, and with good reason. For them, there will be no hope left. They have chosen to be the master of their lives and go it on their own. And they will be left alone as everything comes crashing down around them. It will happen as the Creed says: "He will come to judge the living and the dead."

In these days, while we wait, we pray fervently for these lost souls that they will wake up to the life and salvation that could be theirs. For them, it is not too late until it is too late. Christ wants to be their intercessor and patiently waits.

We, however, long to "see Him face to face, with all His saints in that blest place." Lord, come quickly. Amen.

"O Jesus Christ, do not delay, but hasten our salvation; we often tremble on our way in fear and tribulation. O hear and grant our fervent plea: come, mighty judge, and set us free from death and ev'ry evil." Amen. (LSB *508:7*)

AUGUST 29

Create in me a new heart, Lord,
That gladly I obey Your Word.
Let what You will be my desire,
And with new life my soul inspire. (*LSB* 704:3)

W***HEN WE REGARD OURSELVES HONESTLY—IN THE LIGHT OF*** God's Law—we see the stain of our sins, the many shortcomings in our lives, our continuing failures to live and act as God desires. We acknowledge our sinfulness, for "if we say we have no sin, we deceive ourselves, and the truth is not in us." And then comes the great good news of the Gospel: "If we confess our sins, He is faithful and just to forgive us our sins and to cleanse us from all unrighteousness" (1 John 1:8–9).

When Jesus met a woman caught in the act of adultery, He said to her, "Neither do I condemn you; go, and from now on sin no more" (John 8:11). But how do we "sin no more"? Is it just a matter of trying harder to keep God's Law? If that were true—if we could through our own efforts keep the Law—then Jesus would not have been required by His Father to suffer and die for us.

In Psalm 51, David makes it clear: We were born sinful. "Behold, I was brought forth in iniquity, and in sin did my mother conceive me" (v. 5). Instead of "trying harder" to keep God's Law, which will always fail because it depends on us and our works, we ask God for *His salvation*: "Create in me a clean heart, O God, and renew a right spirit within me" (v. 10). Such a "clean heart" believes that God has already saved us. David asks God to "restore to me the joy of Your salvation" (v. 12). That is the renewal that we need. In Christ, God has already done it all for us! His salvation is our greatest joy.

"Grant that I only You may love and seek those things which are above till I behold You face to face, O Light eternal, through Your grace." Amen. (LSB 704:4)

AUGUST 30

Tell how God the Father's will
Made the world, upholds it still,
How His own dear Son He gave
Us from sin and death to save.

Tell of our Redeemer's grace,
Who, to save our human race
And to pay rebellion's price,
Gave Himself as sacrifice.

Tell of God the Spirit giv'n
Now to guide us on to heav'n,
Strong and holy, just and true,
Working both to will and
do. (*LSB* 830:2–4)

NEAR THE END OF *MARK'S GOSPEL*, JESUS COMMANDS US: "GO into all the world and proclaim the gospel to the whole creation" (v. 15). "Go, proclaim," or in the repeated word in today's hymn, "tell." We are to *tell* the world of the Good News rooted in the person and work of Jesus Christ. This hymn provides a marvelously succinct summary of the Gospel, articulated via the three persons of the triune God.

God the Father, the Creator of the world, sent His own dear Son to save the human race from the rebellion initiated by the sin of our first parents. God's Son was the only one who could pay the full price—by living the perfect life that will always elude us and then by sacrificing Himself for our sins. This act of love *for us* occurred purely through God's grace; it is not a gift we could ever merit.

God the Holy Spirit is the one who works faith in our hearts to believe in Jesus Christ and His saving acts. Indeed, the Spirit is "giv'n now to guide us on to heav'n." Before His ascension into heaven, Jesus told His disciples, "You will receive power when the Holy Spirit has come upon you, and you will be My witnesses" (Acts 1:8). God the Holy Spirit works faith in our hearts to believe, and He is the one who gives us the means to *tell* the story of God's grace in Jesus Christ.

"Lord of harvest, great and kind, rouse to action heart and mind; let the gath'ring nations all see Your light and heed Your call." Amen. (LSB *830:6*)

AUGUST 31

One thing's needful; Lord, this treasure
Teach me highly to regard.
All else, though it first give pleasure,
Is a yoke that presses hard!
Beneath it the heart is still fretting and striving,
No true, lasting happiness ever deriving.
This one thing is needful; all others are vain—
I count all but loss that I Christ may obtain! (***LSB*** **536:1**)

When Jesus visits Mary and Martha's home, they learn a critical kingdom lesson. The heart of that lesson is Mary's sitting at our Lord's feet and receiving from Him. Mary is hearing and being taught what our Lord knows she needs most. He is giving, and she is receiving. But Martha has things backward as she is giving and He is receiving. It is not what Martha was doing that was wrong; instead, she chose not to sit at Jesus' feet. This is a lesson in putting "first things first."

Our striving and fretting, our anxiety and troubles, our doing over our receiving of His gifts is the heart of the problem for Martha and us. Our Lord says, "Martha, Martha, you are anxious and troubled about many things, but one thing is necessary. Mary has chosen the good portion, which will not be taken away from her" (Luke 10:41–42). Like Mary, we are blessed to receive the gifts Christ wants to give, which are abundantly given in His Divine Service.

Today's hymn sums it up this way: "Lord, this treasure teach me highly to regard." Christ is our treasure, and He freely gives Himself to us!

"Wisdom's highest, noblest treasure, Jesus, is revealed in You. Let me find in You my pleasure, and my wayward will subdue, humility there and simplicity reigning, in paths of true wisdom my steps ever training. If I learn from Jesus this knowledge divine, the blessing of heavenly wisdom is mine." Amen. (LSB *536:3*)

SEPTEMBER 1

Nothing have I, Christ, to offer,
You alone, my highest good.
Nothing have I, Lord, to proffer
But Your crimson-colored blood.
Your death on the cross has death wholly defeated
And thereby my righteousness fully completed;
Salvation's white raiments I there did obtain,
And in them in glory with You I shall reign. (*LSB* 536:4)

TODAY'S ***HYMN STANZA TELLS IT LIKE IT IS—WE HAVE*** **NOTHING** to offer or proffer, and all our best efforts are not worth much. In other words, we can't do it! Despair not, dear child of Christ, for we do not have to do it; *it has been done*! We have Jesus Christ; He alone is our highest good, and He has done it *for us*! We have the one thing needful, Jesus Christ, our treasure. "I count all but loss that I Christ may obtain!" (sts. 1, 5).

When Jesus visited Mary and Martha, Mary's, not Martha's, thoughts were devoted to where true eternal joys are found. She sat at her Savior's feet and let Him reveal His ways and wisdom. And as she did, she forgot earthly concerns and found contentment in receiving what He knew she needed to hear—His Words for her life.

This is a masterful lesson in what happens when the faithful come to the Divine Service. In coming, they leave behind or set aside earthly troubles and concerns and, for a time, sit at Jesus' feet to receive His beautiful gifts of grace for their lives. There, He feeds them exactly what they need.

"Therefore You alone, my Savior, shall be all in all to me; search my heart and my behavior, root out all hypocrisy. Through all my life's pilgrimage, guard and uphold me, in loving forgiveness, O Jesus, enfold me. This one thing is needful; all others are vain—I count all but loss that I Christ may obtain!" Amen. (LSB 536:5)

SEPTEMBER 2

"As surely as I live," God said,
"I would not see the sinner dead.
I want him turned
from error's ways,
Repentant, living endless days."

And so our Lord gave
this command:
"Go forth and preach
in ev'ry land;
Bestow on all My
pard'ning grace
Who will repent and
mend their ways.

"All those whose sins
you thus remit
I truly pardon and acquit,
And those whose sins
you will retain
Condemned and guilty shall
remain." (*LSB* 614:1–3)

GOD DECLARES, "*I HAVE NO PLEASURE IN THE DEATH OF THE* wicked, but that the wicked turn from his way and live" (Ezekiel 33:11). He wants *life*—not death—for everyone. God desires repentance. God has given to His church the Office of the Keys, meaning "the keys are giv'n to open, close the gates of heav'n" (st. 4). As Jesus told His disciples, "If you forgive the sins of any, they are forgiven them; if you withhold forgiveness from any, it is withheld" (John 20:23).

It is a wonderful gift to the church—Jesus Himself gives His pastors the authority to forgive sins "in the stead and by the command of my Lord Jesus Christ" (*LSB*, p. 291). Thus, Christ's forgiveness is readily available to repentant sinners—immediately. It is as if Christ Himself sits with us, hears our deepest confession, then places His hands on us, looks us in the eye, and says, "I died for you. On this your confession I forgive you your sins and heaven is open to you. Go and sin no more." "All praise to You, O Christ, shall be for absolution full and free" (st. 7)!

"The words which absolution give are His who died that we might live; the minister whom Christ has sent is but His humble instrument. When ministers lay on their hands, absolved by Christ the sinner stands; he who by grace the Word believes the purchase of His blood receives." Amen. (LSB *614:5–6*)

SEPTEMBER 3

How vast Your mercy to accept
The burden of our sin
And bow Your head in cruel death
To make us clean within. (*LSB* 553:2)

"LORD, HAVE MERCY; CHRIST, HAVE MERCY; LORD, HAVE MERCY." We sing that prayer at the beginning of each Divine Service, echoing Bartimaeus, who pleaded with Jesus to restore his sight: "Jesus, Son of David, have mercy on me" (Mark 10:47). In our spiritual blindness, we, too, stand in desperate need of our Lord's mercy—His undeserved love for us, the sinners He came to redeem.

Today's hymn confronts us with two realities: the burden of human sin and the vastness of God's mercy. Jesus, the perfect one, was willing to suffer a cruel death to atone for His imperfect creatures—to "make us clean within." Paul writes, "God, being rich in mercy, because of the great love with which He loved us, even when we were dead in our trespasses, made us alive together with Christ—by grace you have been saved" (Ephesians 2:4–5). That is the very nature of our God: "rich in mercy," filled with "great love," making us "alive together with Christ," so that we may live with Him forever in His perfect heavenly kingdom.

Today's hymn also bears another important reminder, as we ask God to "purge us of our pride" (st. 4). Human pride would like very much for us to play some role in salvation, to share in God's saving work, perhaps "making a choice for Jesus" or making God's salvation at least partially contingent on our obedience and love for Him. No! God's *mercy* and *grace* consist in His all-sufficient work on our behalf and His undeserved love for us. We are saved by God's great *mercy*! As the hymn writer states, "Our only glory, may it be to glory in the Lord!" (st. 5).

"O let Your mighty love prevail to purge us of our pride that we may stand before Your throne by mercy purified. Christ Jesus, be our present joy, our future great reward; our only glory, may it be to glory in the Lord!" Amen. (LSB 553:4–5)

SEPTEMBER 4

Sing praise to God, the highest good,
The author of creation,
The God of love who understood
Our need for His salvation.
With healing balm our souls He fills
And ev'ry faithless murmur stills:
To God all praise and glory!

We sought the Lord in our distress;
O God, in mercy hear us.
Our Savior saw our helplessness
And came with peace to cheer us.
For this we thank and praise the Lord,
Who is by one and all adored:
To God all praise and glory! (*LSB* 819:1, 3)

ONE OF THE SHORTEST PETITIONS WE PRAY IS "LORD, HAVE mercy." It is such a brief, pointed cry, but one that speaks to all our needs in this life and on our way to the life to come. The hymn writer recognizes this petition as one that arises out of our "distress." Distress, for any one of us, could refer to needs of the body—food, shelter, clothing—perhaps after a weather-related disaster. Distress could be our need for healing, or that of a loved one who suffers from disease or illness. For such temporal needs, we pray, "Lord, have mercy."

When we examine our lives, we recognize our sins of thought, word, and deed. Here, too, we can only plead, "Lord, have mercy." Like the tax collector who "would not even lift up his eyes to heaven," we pray, "God, be merciful to me, a sinner" (Luke 18:13). What a comfort it is for us to know that God "understood our need for His salvation," that He "saw our helplessness and came with peace to cheer us." He has already provided what we need the most—forgiveness of sins, life, and salvation.

God wants us to pray, to ask for His mercy. He knows our needs and will never forsake us. For such a great blessing "to God all praise and glory!"

"He never shall forsake His flock, His chosen generation; He is their refuge and their rock, their peace and their salvation. As with a mother's tender hand, He leads His own, His chosen band: To God all praise and glory!" Amen. (LSB *819:4*)

SEPTEMBER 5

Thou hast died for my
transgression,
All my sins on Thee were laid;
Thou hast won for me salvation,
On the cross my debt was paid.
From the grave I shall arise
And shall meet Thee in the skies.
Death itself is transitory;
I shall lift my head in glory.

For the joy Thine
advent gave me,
For Thy holy, precious Word;
For Thy Baptism, which
doth save me,
For Thy blest
Communion board;
For Thy death, the bitter scorn,
For Thy resurrection morn,
Lord, I thank Thee
and extol Thee,
And in heav'n I shall behold
Thee. (*LSB* 548:2–3)

A ***WISE FRIEND OBSERVED THAT A GOOD HYMN TEXT*** **ACTUALLY** *tells the story* of salvation. Today's hymn does just that, the poet requiring only three stanzas to summarize what God has accomplished for His people and to remind us of how God comes to us here and now to forgive our sins and save us.

Does it seem somehow just too elementary to proclaim that Christ took all our sins on Himself, died for us, thereby paying our debt, and then rose from the dead? May it never be so among us! That act of love for fallen humanity is what enables us with all confidence to say that death does not have the last word, that on the Last Day we, too, will rise from death and join our Savior in heaven.

How do we know this story of salvation? How do we know what to *tell* through our singing and speaking? With an economy of words, the hymn writer beautifully summarizes the means of grace: "For Thy holy, precious Word; for Thy Baptism, which doth save me, for Thy blest Communion." God comes to us in His Word and Sacraments, giving us forgiveness of sins, life, and salvation. Thanks be to God!

"Thanks to Thee, O Christ, victorious! Thanks to Thee, O Lord of Life! Death hath now no power o'er us, Thou hast conquered in the strife. Thanks because Thou didst arise and hast opened paradise! None can fully sing the glory of the resurrection story." Amen. (LSB 548:1)

SEPTEMBER 6

Rise! To arms! With prayer employ you,
O Christians, lest the foe destroy you;
For Satan has designed your fall.
Wield God's Word, the weapon glorious;
Against all foes be thus victorious,
For God protects you from them all.
Fear not the hordes of hell,
Here is Emmanuel.
Hail the Savior!
The strong foes yield
To Christ our shield,
And we, the victors, hold the field. (*LSB* 668:1)

WHY IS THERE A "CHURCH MILITANT" SECTION IN MOST hymnals? Because the Bride of Christ *is at war*! In these dark and latter days, she faces fierce and unending attacks by the ever-devious and cunning Satan. Hymns for such times of warfare are of enormous comfort to the Bride as they help her understand what is happening and let her sing of divine comfort in the battle.

When Michael and his angels threw Satan and his angels to earth, there was with it a terrifying pronouncement: "Woe to you, O earth and sea, for the devil has come down to you in great wrath, because he knows that his time is short" (Revelation 12:12). In the face of this "woe pronouncement," today's hymn is one of those comforting texts that let the Bride sing of protection in God's Word, a weapon glorious. Christ is our shield, and "we, the victors, hold the field."

It matters not that Satan has designed our fall; we have a Savior protecting us every step of the way. The theme of today's hymn is stated in the first line: "With prayer employ you." We desperately need to use our daily conversation with God for the daily battle we face. Talk to Him and ask for help in the war.

"Lord, give us faith to walk where You are sending, on paths unmarked, eyes blind as to their ending; not knowing where we go, but that You lead us—with grace precede us." Amen. (LSB 667:5)

SEPTEMBER 7

Cast afar this world's
vain pleasure
And boldly strive for
heav'nly treasure.
Be steadfast in the
Savior's might.
Trust the Lord, who
stands beside you,
For Jesus from all
harm will hide you.
By faith you conquer in the fight.
Take courage, weary soul!
Look forward to the goal!
Joy awaits you.
The race well run,
Your long war won,
Your crown shines splendid
as the sun. (*LSB* 668:2)

THESE TWO SENTENCES EXPRESS THE HEART AND MESSAGE OF today's hymn stanza: "By faith you conquer in the fight. Take courage, weary soul!" Yes, God's saints live safely and abundantly in the miraculous faith He planted in them. And living in that beautiful faith, they are filled with might, strength, and courage as He graciously sustains them by Word and Sacraments. Through those powerful means, He gives His dear saints all they need for every step of their heavenly race.

The race may cause them to be weary and bloodied at times, but they are never alone, for He is always standing beside them. They will run their race well if they remain steadfast in faith, trust solely in Him, and cling to His promises. For He will give courage to their weary souls while running, ever onward, striving for heavenly treasure and their promised inheritance. "Your long war won, your crown shines splendid as the sun."

"Triune God, be Thou our stay; O let us perish never! Cleanse us from our sins, we pray, and grant us life forever. Keep us from the evil one; uphold our faith most holy, and let us trust Thee solely with humble hearts and lowly. Let us put God's armor on, with all true Christians running our heav'nly race and shunning the devil's wiles and cunning. Amen, amen! This be done; so sing we, 'Alleluia!'" Amen. (LSB 505)

SEPTEMBER 8

Wisely fight, for time is fleeting;
The hours of grace are
fast retreating;
Short, short is this
our earthly way.
When the Lord the
dead will waken
And sinners all by
fear are shaken,
The saints with joy
will greet that day.
Praise God, our triumph's sure.
We need not long endure
Scorn and trial.
Our Savior King
His own will bring
To that great glory which
we sing. (*LSB* 668:3)

T***HE HOURS OF GRACE ARE FAST RETREATING," GIVING THIS RICH*** hymn context. While God's time of grace may seem endless, it will not last forever, and it lasts only now through His patience and mercy for the lost. Christ's beloved Bride has been waiting for His return since her earliest days. "The saints with joy will greet that day."

Today's hymn offers a wise warning to all in this fleeting time: "Short, short is this our earthly way." But both sheep and goats, believers and unbelievers, wheat and weeds hear such wise words, with starkly different reactions. What believers long for, unbelievers dread. Believers cannot wait to greet that day, but unbelievers know that day is to be feared as the final day of reckoning when they will be judged and found wanting. That day will be their ultimate day of sorrow and weeping.

But for the believing saints, it will be the day they have longed for when the church's Bridegroom calls them to His wedding feast. Johann Walter describes it this way: "There shall we see in glory our dear Redeemer's face; the long-awaited story of heav'nly joy takes place: The patriarchs shall meet us, the prophets' holy band; apostles, martyrs greet us in that celestial land" (*LSB* 514:2).

"Our hope and expectation, O Jesus, now appear; arise, O Sun so longed for, o'er this benighted sphere. With hearts and hands uplifted, we plead, O Lord, to see the day of earth's redemption that sets Your people free!" Amen. (LSB *515:4*)

SEPTEMBER 9

This is a sight that gladdens—
What peace it doth impart!
Now nothing ever saddens
The joy within my heart.
No gloom shall ever shake,
No foe shall ever take
The hope which God's own Son
In love for me has
won. (*LSB* 467:3)

EVEN IN CHILDHOOD, PAUL GERHARDT WITNESSED AND experienced troubles related to theological conflict and outright war. These formative years may have prepared him for additional hardships into his adulthood. So when we read today's prayers, drawn from his Easter hymn "Awake, My Heart, with Gladness," we might wonder how he could have such a positive outlook. The answer is that this deep faith is not his own doing but rather the work of God the Holy Spirit, who nurtures and sustains faith in our hearts through the means of grace.

Why is it that Gerhardt could say that nothing saddens the joy within his heart, that no gloom in this world can shake his faith in God, that his heart is free from cares, that "no trouble troubles me" (st. 5)? A twenty-first-century reader might well dismiss him as simply being a "Pollyanna," as having an irrepressible optimism unanchored in reality!

But, in fact, Gerhardt's—and our—optimism is indeed anchored in something very specific: "the hope which God's own Son in love for me has won." That hope is based on the resurrection of Jesus from the dead. Our last enemy—death—has been defeated! Alleluia! Christ is risen! He is risen indeed! Alleluia! And we, too, will rise from death on the Last Day to live forever with our Savior. That reality—grasped by faith—allows us, with Gerhardt, to put into perspective the gloom, sorrows, and troubles of this life. Such troubles are finite; we look to an infinite, perfect eternity in heaven with Jesus.

"The world against me rages, its fury I disdain; though bitter war it wages, its work is all in vain. My heart from care is free, no trouble troubles me. Misfortune now is play, and night is bright as day." Amen. (LSB 467:5)

SEPTEMBER 10

O Word of God incarnate,
O Wisdom from on high,
O Truth unchanged, unchanging,
O Light of our dark sky:
We praise You for the radiance
That from the hallowed page,
A lantern to our footsteps,
Shines on from age to age. (*LSB* 523:1)

IN THE BEGINNING WAS THE WORD, AND THE WORD WAS WITH GOD, and the Word was God" (John 1:1). The opening of John's Gospel, appointed as the Holy Gospel for Christmas Day, is so striking, for John refers to Jesus as "the Word." At Jesus' incarnation, "the Word became flesh and dwelt among us, and we have seen His glory, glory as of the only Son from the Father, full of grace and truth" (v. 14). Jesus is the incarnate Word of God—true God and true man. We are saved by His *grace*; we are enlightened by His *truth*. Later in John's Gospel, in Jesus' High Priestly Prayer, Jesus asks the Father to "sanctify them in the truth; Your word is truth" (John 17:17). Jesus, the Word of God, is truth; the Word of God, recorded in the Scriptures, is truth. Jesus Himself made this clear: "You search the Scriptures because you think that in them you have eternal life; and it is they that bear witness about Me" (John 5:39).

Today's hymn sings of these interrelated aspects of the Word of God. The hymn writer speaks of Jesus—the incarnate Word of God—as our Wisdom from on high, our unchanging Truth, and the Light in our darkness. At the same time, the Word of God, "from the hallowed page" of Scripture, is the "lantern to our footsteps" and the chart and compass that guides us "all life's voyage through" (st. 2). God's Word "guides, O Christ, to You" (st. 2), the incarnate Word of God.

"The Church from You, dear Master, received the gift divine; and still that light is lifted o'er all the earth to shine. It is the chart and compass that, all life's voyage through, mid mists and rocks and quicksands still guides, O Christ, to You." Amen. (LSB *523:2*)

SEPTEMBER 11

Christ is our cornerstone,
On Him alone we build;
With His true saints alone
The courts of heav'n are filled.

On His great love
Our hopes we place
Of present grace
And joys above. (*LSB* 912:1)

I ***HAVE VIVID BOYHOOD MEMORIES OF DEDICATION SUNDAY FOR OUR*** newly built church and school complex. Before entering the building for the first of three worship services that day, we took part in an outdoor ceremony, which included inserting copies of historical documents into a metal box that would be permanently contained within the cornerstone—a foundational feature joining together two walls.

Today's hymn proclaims, "Christ is our cornerstone, on Him alone we build." The apostle Paul calls us "fellow citizens with the saints and members of the household of God, built on the foundation of the apostles and prophets, Christ Jesus Himself being the cornerstone" (Ephesians 2:19–20). Jesus joins us together in His church, anchoring us in the foundation of His Word as it has been proclaimed to us by the prophets and apostles. That Jesus Himself is the cornerstone of this structure means that He is the foundation of all that we do, of all that we hope for—the very foundation of our lives!

It is "His great love" for us that forms the basis of our hopes for "present grace and joys above." God's grace in Christ is ours every day. His undeserved love provides "all that I need to support this body and life" (Small Catechism, Creed, First Article). By His grace, we have forgiveness of sins and the promise of eternal life, "when all the blest to endless rest are called away" (st. 2). Christ is our cornerstone, through His grace providing foundational support for all that we need—in this life and in the life to come.

"Here may we gain from heav'n the grace which we implore, and may that grace, once giv'n, be with us evermore until that day when all the blest to endless rest are called away." Amen. (LSB 912:2)

SEPTEMBER 12

Once in the blest
baptismal waters
I put on Christ and
made Him mine;
Now numbered with God's
sons and daughters,
I share His peace
and love divine.
O God, for Jesus' sake I pray
Your peace may bless
my dying day.

His body and His
blood I've taken
In His blest Supper, feast divine;
Now I shall never be forsaken,
For I am His, and He is mine.
O God, for Jesus' sake I pray
Your peace may bless my
dying day. (*LSB* 598:1–2)

This hymn beautifully summarizes Baptism and the Lord's Supper, through which we receive God's gifts. These gifts provide us with eternal life with Christ. That is the peace we pray for in this hymn: "Your peace may bless my dying day." That petition is not only the constant refrain to these hymn stanzas; it is also the confident refrain for each day here on earth, living our lives with no fears for eternity.

Paul teaches us that in Baptism we "put on Christ" (Galatians 3:27). That means that, through Baptism, we are united with Christ, and His righteousness becomes our righteousness. Instead of seeing our sins, God sees us in the "white garments" (Revelation 3:4–5) of Christ's righteousness. Baptism is a present-tense reality, as Luther stresses in his Large Catechism: "I am baptized. . . . It is promised to me that I shall be saved and have eternal life" (Part 4, paragraph 44). But there is yet more! In His Holy Supper, Christ gives us His very body and blood, a "feast divine," freely providing us forgiveness of sins, life, and salvation.

The final stanza of this hymn states the ultimate benefits of the Sacraments: "I live in God contented and die without a thought of fear" (st. 3). What blessings God has given us in the Sacraments—that we may sing and pray in such contentment and confidence!

"And thus I live in God contented and die without a thought of fear; my soul has to God's plans consented, for through His Son my faith is clear. O God, for Jesus' sake I pray Your peace may bless my dying day." Amen. (LSB *598:3*)

SEPTEMBER 13

Before the throne of God above
I have a strong, a perfect plea:
A great High Priest, whose name is Love,
Who ever lives and pleads for me.

When Satan tempts me to despair,
And tells me of the guilt within,
Upward I look, and see Him there
Who made an end of all my sin. (*LSB* 574:1, 3)

W*HEN WE THINK OF JESUS' GREAT LOVE FOR US, WE MAY DO* so—quite naturally—in the *past* tense. He was born of Mary, lived the perfect life that would never be possible for us, suffered for us, died, rose from the dead, and ascended into heaven. Past events—more than two thousand years ago.

While His great work of salvation has been accomplished once for all, His love for us and His work on our behalf continues. The writer of the epistle to the Hebrews tells us that, as our great High Priest, Jesus "always lives to make intercession" for us (Hebrews 7:25).

The hymn writer helps us to understand this wonderful reality of Christ's continuing work on our behalf. Think of what it means that Jesus "pleads for me" before His Father. In Jesus' High Priestly Prayer to the Father, He prays, "I do not ask that You take them out of the world, but that You keep them from the evil one" (John 17:15). That petition is a great comfort. Jesus' love continues as He *pleads* for us before God the Father.

Knowing this continuing love of Jesus, this continuing plea for our eternal welfare, keeps us from despair. It is a blessed reality: Jesus "ever lives and pleads for me"!

"Because the sinless Savior died, my sinful soul is counted free; for God, the just, is satisfied to look on Him and pardon me. At one with Him, I cannot die, my soul is purchased by His blood; my life is hid with Christ on high, with Christ, my Savior and my God." Amen. (LSB 574:4, 6)

SEPTEMBER 14

Grant me the strength to do
With ready heart and willing
Whatever You command,
My calling here fulfilling;
That I do what I should
While trusting You to bless
The outcome for my good,
For You must give success. (*LSB* 696:2)

PAUL WRITES, "WHETHER WE LIVE OR WHETHER WE DIE, WE ARE the Lord's" (Romans 14:8). In today's hymn, we pray for God's blessings in both our living and in our dying.

God gives each of us vocations in this life, and we pray that we might willingly fulfill whatever God gives us to do—all the while trusting Him to bless our work and bring it to the outcome He deems best. We pray that our words may always be appropriate, asking the Lord for a gracious way of speaking rather than uttering hurtful words that we later regret. We ask that our interactions with others—including those with whom we disagree—might be filled with "kindly words and actions" (st. 4), for that is how the Christian might win over those who are opposed to the Lord. Finally, we pray that—with the Spirit's help—we might "live in peace with all" (st. 4).

When we leave this life, we ask that we do so "confiding in [our] Savior" to care for both soul and body (st. 5). We pray that God would receive our souls into eternal life, even while our bodies sleep in peace in their temporary resting places. On the Last Day, God will awaken our bodies from sleep and take us to Himself forever. That is the ultimate blessing of our faithful God!

"Let me depart this life confiding in my Savior; by grace receive my soul that it may live forever; and let my body have a quiet resting place within a Christian grave; and let it sleep in peace. And on that final day when all the dead are waking, stretch out Your mighty hand, my deathly slumber breaking. Then let me hear Your voice, redeem this earthly frame, and bid me to rejoice with those who love Your name." Amen. (LSB *696:5–6*)

SEPTEMBER 15

We thank Thee that Thy Church, unsleeping
While earth rolls onward into light,
Through all the world her watch is keeping,
And never rests by day or night. (*LSB* 886:2)

THIS EVENING HYMN BEAUTIFULLY PICTURES THE CHURCH AT prayer. We are reminded that the church, established by God the Holy Spirit, exists throughout this world on each earthly continent and island. While we conclude our evening prayers and sleep under the cover of darkness, there are Christians elsewhere in the world who are greeting the dawn and daylight with their morning prayers. This cycle of daylight and darkness, morning and evening across the globe means that Christ's church is "unsleeping" and "never rests by day or night."

The apostle Paul encourages Christians to "pray without ceasing" (1 Thessalonians 5:17). While we cannot engage in constant verbal prayer, what a comfort it is to realize that "the voice of prayer is never silent" (st. 3), that within the twenty-four-hour span of a single day, Christ's church is always at prayer—praying that the Gospel may always be preached in its truth and purity throughout the world, praying that our heavenly Father may keep all in His church in His tender, protective care at all times and in all places.

Jesus has promised, "I will build My church, and the gates of hell shall not prevail against it" (Matthew 16:18). We should always treasure that word of assurance, for there are times when we despair about the church on earth, doubting that it is equal to the task of preaching the Gospel and expanding His kingdom. What a blessing to be reminded in today's hymn, "Thy kingdom stands and grows forever" (st. 5).

"As o'er each continent and island the dawn leads on another day, the voice of prayer is never silent, nor dies the strain of praise away." Amen. (LSB 886:3)

SEPTEMBER 16

For Christ bore our sins, and not His own,
When He on the cross was hanging;
And then He arose and moved the stone
That we, unto Him belonging,
Might join with angelic hosts to raise
Our voices in endless singing. (*LSB* 503:3)

"YOU ARE FOUND INNOCENT OF ALL CHARGES; YOU ARE FREE TO go." Those are the sweetest, most welcome words that a defendant in a court of justice could ever hear. Because Christ bore our sins on the cross, died in our place, and then rose from the dead, the verdict of "innocent" is ours. His innocence is transferred to us, and we now belong to Him forever. The hymn writer notes that our response is one of "endless singing," as we join the angelic hosts of heaven in their songs of praise to the One who has redeemed His people from their sins. But we don't wait until Christ takes us to Himself in heaven at the time of our death. No, "with angels and archangels and with all the company of heaven we laud and magnify Your glorious name, evermore praising You and saying: Holy, holy, holy Lord God of pow'r and might" (*LSB* Divine Service, Setting One, Proper Preface and Sanctus). Even here and now we join with angels and all the saints, including our departed loved ones, in the heavenly Sanctus, praising the God who rescued us from sin and death.

Yet we await with great expectation "that final journey" taking us home to Jesus (st. 5). We have His wonderful words of promise: "I go to prepare a place for you. And if I go and prepare a place for you, I will come again and will take you to Myself, that where I am you may be also" (John 14:2–3). Those are among the sweetest, most welcome words that Jesus has spoken to us!

"When we on that final journey go that Christ is for us preparing, we'll gather in song, our hearts aglow, all joy of the heavens sharing, and walk in the light of God's own place, with angels His name adoring." Amen. (LSB *503:5*)

SEPTEMBER 17

Consider how the birds above
Feed day by day with carefree ease—
Does God not keep them in His love?
Are we not worth much more than these?

The lilies grow, they do not toil;
How fair is their fragility—
If God clothes these, which quickly spoil,
Will He not clothe both you and me? (*LSB* 736:1–2)

***D*O NOT BE ANXIOUS ABOUT YOUR LIFE" (MATTHEW 6:25). JESUS** points particularly to anxieties over what we eat, drink, and wear. But if we are honest, we can point to so many other concerns in our lives—health, housing, employment, and money among them. We must admit that we worry about much—on a daily basis.

In verses 26 through 33, Jesus reminds us that our Father in heaven provides food for the birds. "Are we not worth much more than these?" He clothes the fields with the beauty of flowers. "Will He not much more clothe you, O you of little faith?" Jesus tells us what should be obvious: "Your heavenly Father knows that you need them all." But precisely there we prefer worry to assurance, and we neglect to believe the clear promise of Jesus: "Seek first the kingdom of God and His righteousness, and all these things will be added to you."

The hymn text for today encourages us not to be "weighed down by worldly care" (st. 3), to guard against greed, and, perhaps most difficult of all, "be not afraid to suffer loss of all the things for which you pray" (st. 5). But how do we overcome sins of worry and fear concerning earthly possessions? The hymn writer states it succinctly: Jesus, who endured the cross for us, "will give [us] strength to live each day" (st. 5), as well as the faith to trust in Him who has already seen to our ultimate need—eternal life!

"Seek first God's reign, His boundless grace, His holy name in all you do: Christ first and last in ev'ry place; all else will then be given you." Amen. (LSB *736:6*)

SEPTEMBER 18

Oh, blest the house,
whate'er befall,
Where Jesus Christ is all in all!
A home that is not wholly His—
How sad and poor and dark it is!

Oh, blest that house
where faith is found
And all in hope and
love abound;
They trust their God
and serve Him still
And do in all His holy
will! (*LSB* 862:1–2)

"WHERE JESUS CHRIST IS ALL IN ALL!" THAT PHRASE IS THE recipe for a blessed home and family life, where husband and wife, parents and children, multiple generations, live together in the peace and harmony that comes only from mutual faith and trust in Jesus Christ. Without Christ at the center, "how sad and poor and dark" home and family life would be.

Does this mean that the Christian household will never experience sadness, want, or the darkness caused by life in a fallen world? No, the Christian is not somehow immune from those aspects of life. To the contrary, Jesus told us, "In the world you will have tribulation. But take heart; I have overcome the world" (John 16:33). Illness, disease, disappointment, unemployment, poverty, death—such aspects of life will also afflict Christian homes. But when such things take place, the Christian takes refuge in Jesus, for He has overcome the world. The Christian household has the privilege of prayer to the God who assures us, "Call upon Me in the day of trouble; I will deliver you, and you shall glorify Me" (Psalm 50:15).

Jesus doesn't promise us prosperity or a life free from illness, disappointment, or want. He gives us something greater—the sure and certain hope of eternal life. His pledge of everlasting love gives us the hope and trust that we need to serve Him in this world and to live in peace and joy in our Christian homes and families.

"Then here will I and mine today a solemn promise make and say: Though all the world forsake His Word, I and my house will serve the Lord!" Amen. (LSB *862:5*)

SEPTEMBER 19

With the Lord begin your task;
Jesus will direct it.
For His aid and counsel ask;
Jesus will perfect it.
Ev'ry morn with Jesus rise,
And when day is ended,
In His name then close your eyes;
Be to Him commended.

Let each day begin with prayer,
Praise, and adoration.
On the Lord cast ev'ry care;
He is your salvation.
Morning, evening, and at night
Jesus will be near you,
Save you from the tempter's might,
With His presence cheer you. (*LSB* 869:1–2)

IN THE LUTHERAN GRADE SCHOOL I WAS PRIVILEGED TO ATTEND, each new school year began with all eight grades gathered together in church singing this hymn as our opening prayer. It was predictable and consistent; year after year, we always sang the same opening hymn. That is akin to beginning each day with Luther's Morning Prayer and then, as he suggests, going "joyfully to your work" (Small Catechism). That kind of repetitive consistency is a salutary practice in the Christian life.

No matter the tasks we might face on a given day, we ask Jesus for His direction, aid, and counsel. If we awake knowing that we will face particular problems, ills, or challenges, we heed the words of Peter to cast "all your anxieties on Him, because He cares for you" (1 Peter 5:7). As the hymn writer points out, Jesus is our *salvation*. That means God has already taken care of our greatest need and surely will provide all else. "He who did not spare His own Son but gave Him up for us all, how will He not also with Him graciously give us all things?" (Romans 8:32).

When we begin our tasks with the Lord Jesus, we do not fear the devil, earthly foes, ills, or disaster; rather, we trust His promises and take great cheer in His constant presence.

"With your Savior at your side, foes need not alarm you; in His promises confide, and no ill can harm you. All your trust and hope repose in the mighty Master, who in wisdom truly knows how to stem disaster." Amen. (LSB *869:3*)

SEPTEMBER 20

Come, you faithful, raise the strain
Of triumphant gladness!
God has brought His Israel
Into joy from sadness,
Loosed from Pharaoh's bitter yoke
Jacob's sons and daughters,
Led them with unmoistened foot
Through the Red Sea waters. (*LSB* 487:1)

For 430 years, the people of Israel lived in slavery in Egypt (Exodus 12:40). When God delivered His people from this bondage, He used the blood of a lamb to spare His chosen people from the final plague—the death of all the firstborn in Egypt. Then He led the people on dry ground through the Red Sea while drowning Pharaoh and his armies. These words of Moses to Israel could not have been more true: "Fear not, stand firm, and see the salvation of the Lord, *which He will work for you today*" (Exodus 14:13, emphasis added). It was the Lord who worked salvation for the Israelites.

Those words of Moses proved to be true yet again—when it was the Lord who worked salvation at Calvary. He did so for all people of all times and places. This time, the blood of *the Lamb* was required. Jesus, the very Son of God, shed His holy, precious blood on the wood of the cross. That blood, which we receive in His Holy Supper for the forgiveness of our sins, marks us as people who will not die eternally! Our loving God provides us a way through the waters that would drown us, a way through the deep waters of our sins, a way of escape from the bondage of sin that enslaves us. "See the salvation of the Lord, which He will work for you today."

We "raise the strain of triumphant gladness" (st. 5), for Christ has defeated death by rising from the tomb. His resurrection will be our resurrection, and we will live with Him forever. He has worked salvation *for us*!

"Alleluia! Now we cry to our King immortal, who, triumphant, burst the bars of the tomb's dark portal. Come, you faithful, raise the strain of triumphant gladness! God has brought His Israel into joy from sadness!" Amen. (LSB 487:5)

SEPTEMBER 21

Stay with us, till night has come:
Our praise to You
this day be sung.
Bless our bread,
Open our eyes:
Jesus, be our great surprise.

Talk with us, till we behold
A joyful life You will unfold:
Heal our eyes
To see the prize:
Jesus, take us to the
light. (*LSB* 879:1, 4)

S*TAY WITH US." TWO FOLLOWERS OF JESUS SPOKE THOSE WORDS* to the traveling companion then unknown to them (Luke 24:29). What they did know is that this stranger taught them about Christ by opening the Scriptures. After Jesus made Himself known in the breaking of the bread at table, they put it all together and said, "Did not our hearts burn within us while He talked to us on the road, while He opened to us the Scriptures?" (v. 32). God's Word has that power for us too, as the Holy Spirit works faith in our hearts to believe the good news of the resurrection.

Stay with us: Continue to teach us through Your Word. *Stay with us*: Continue to feed us with Your body and blood in the Supper that You instituted that Thursday evening before Your crucifixion. *Stay with us.* Indeed, all of this is *for us*—for the forgiveness of sins and an eternity in the presence of the Risen One.

"Stay with us, for it is toward evening and the day is now far spent" (v. 29). Perhaps we most long for the companionship of Jesus at those times when darkness approaches in our lives. Whether it is illness, affliction, fear, or despair, we pray: *Stay with us.* At the time of the death of a loved one, we pray: *Stay with us.* As our own death approaches, may we have the blessing of praying this same prayer.

Jesus has already answered this prayer: "I am with you always, to the end of the age" (Matthew 28:20). Thanks be to God for the gift of His presence!

"Stay with us, till day is done: no tears nor dark shall dim the sun. Cheer the heart, Your grace impart: Jesus, bring eternal life." Amen. (LSB 879:5)

SEPTEMBER 22

Now that the daylight fills the sky,
We lift our hearts to God on high,
That He, in all we do or say,
Would keep us free from harm today;

Would guard our hearts and tongues from strife;
From anger's din would shield our life;
From evil sights would turn our eyes,
And close our ears to vanities. (*LSB* 870:1–2)

*M**ORNING, AND EVENING—THE DAWNING OF THE LIGHT, AND*** then the passing of the light as it gives way to the darkness of the night. These times of the day have long been occasions for the Christian to pray. Indeed, the psalmist tells us, "It is good to give thanks to the LORD, to sing praises to Your name, O Most High; to declare Your steadfast love in the morning, and Your faithfulness by night" (92:1–2). Today's hymn provides thoughts and words for prayer as one awakens to another day of grace.

We pray that God would keep us from all harm and bodily danger as we begin a new day and go about our daily tasks. We pray that God "would guard our hearts and tongues from strife." Strife, bickering, and arguing are all around us—perhaps in personal interactions but certainly in the broader arena of the day's national and international news. We pray that our hearts and tongues would be kept from participating in such strife and that we may be shielded from "anger's din." The world around us is filled with evil sights; we pray that God would help us to avert our eyes from such sin and instead focus on His cross, where He redeemed us. The world around us is also filled with "vanities," including careless, self-aggrandizing speech that all too often focuses on self instead of Savior. May God keep us from all such vain speech and instead point us to the treasures of His Word.

"So we, when this new day is gone and night in turn is drawing on, with conscience by the world unstained shall praise His name for vict'ry gained." Amen. (LSB *870:3*)

SEPTEMBER 23

**Dear Christians, one and all, rejoice,
With exultation springing,
And with united heart and voice
And holy rapture singing,
Proclaim the wonders God has done,
How His right arm the vict'ry won.
What price our ransom cost Him! (*LSB* 556:1)**

CHRISTIANS, REJOICE! EXULT! UNITE YOUR VOICES AND SING IN rapture as you have never sung before! And *proclaim*—to each other, to all who will listen—the *wonders* that our God has done. So writes Martin Luther in one of his earliest hymns—in fact, the first hymn printed in the first Lutheran hymnal, dating from 1524.

After these exhortations to rejoicing and proclamation, Luther provides the reason *why* we do so. It is because of what God has done for us. He has won the victory over sin, death, and the devil. He has ransomed us—bought us back after we defied Him through willful, sinful disobedience to His Law.

Luther goes on in nine more hymn stanzas to tell the full story of our redemption, expanding on and explaining the implications of that ominous last line of this first stanza: "What price our ransom cost Him!" Yes, winning the victory for sinful humanity cost God the Father "His dearest treasure," His beloved Son, Jesus Christ (st. 4). The Father had to ask His Son to become incarnate as a human being, to keep the Law on our behalf, to assume all the sins of all people of all time, and to die in our place. The Son had to be willing to serve as the substitute for us, knowing full well that it would mean the hatred and scorn of His own creatures and a painful death, including being forsaken by His Father.

All of this He willingly suffered so that we will *never* be forsaken by God. "He planned for my salvation" (st. 4).

"But God had seen my wretched state before the world's foundation, and mindful of His mercies great, He planned for my salvation. He turned to me a father's heart; He did not choose the easy part but gave His dearest treasure." Amen. (LSB 556:4)

SEPTEMBER 24

God said to His beloved Son:
"It's time to have compassion.
Then go, bright jewel of My crown,
And bring to all salvation.
From sin and sorrow set them free;
Slay bitter death for them that they
May live with You forever." (*LSB* 556:5)

FROM THE TIME OF THE FALL INTO SIN IN THE GARDEN OF EDEN, God had a plan of salvation for the sinful human race. The apostle Paul wrote, "But when the fullness of time had come, God sent forth His Son, born of woman, born under the law" (Galatians 4:4). Jesus—true God and true man—was the only one who could free us from sin and sorrow. "So if the Son sets you free, you will be free indeed" (John 8:36). While we still suffer times of sorrow, especially at the death of a loved one, Jesus provides us the only real remedy for that sorrow. Because He has defeated death, we are comforted even in our times of great sorrow, knowing that we will live forever with Him in those holy and perfect realms that He willingly surrendered for a time.

"And being found in human form, He humbled Himself by becoming obedient to the point of death, even death on a cross" (Philippians 2:8). Jesus humbled Himself, His "royal pow'r" being "disguised" (st. 6) so that He could take on the form of a servant, living and dying for us. "The Son obeyed His Father's will" (st. 6). That act of obedience, flowing from divine love, makes all the difference for us in how we live our lives and in how we understand the crosses and sorrows that God allows to enter our lives. We rest in the Gospel truth that the Father has had compassion on us and His beloved Son has earned salvation for us.

"The Son obeyed His Father's will, was born of virgin mother; and God's good pleasure to fulfill, He came to be my brother. His royal pow'r disguised He bore; a servant's form, like mine, He wore to lead the devil captive." Amen. (LSB *556:6*)

SEPTEMBER 25

O Christ, who art the light and day,
Thou drivest night and gloom away;
O Light of Light, whose Word doth show
The light of heav'n to us below.

All-holy Lord, in humble prayer
We ask tonight Thy watchful care.
O grant us calm repose in Thee,
A quiet night, from perils free. (*LSB* 882:1–2)

Jesus said, "I am the light of the world. Whoever follows Me will not walk in darkness, but will have the light of life" (John 8:12). In Baptism, we are brought into the light of Christ—our sins are forgiven, we are rescued from death and the devil, and we are given eternal salvation. The light of Christ is our life and salvation!

Today's hymn-prayer speaks of Christ as "the light and day." He is the "Light of Light" who drives away all darkness. Paul observed, "At one time you were darkness, but now you are light in the Lord" (Ephesians 5:8). It is Jesus' work on our behalf—His perfect life, death, and resurrection—that takes us out of the realm of darkness into the realm of light. That is not something we can do on our own; Christ did it for us. As His beloved children, living in His light, it is our privilege to bring our evening petitions to our merciful and loving Lord.

We pray that He would keep us in His Word, which shows us "the light of heav'n," His light directing us as we journey through this life toward the life to come. We pray that each night of our lives would find us in His care and keeping, free from all perils and dangers, "that the evil foe may have no power over me" (Small Catechism, Evening Prayer). Finally, we pray that our Savior would "be with us even to the end" (st. 6), bringing us to that eternal home where "the Lord God will be their light" (Revelation 22:5).

"O Lord, remember us who bear the burden of the flesh we wear; Thou who dost e'er our souls defend, be with us even to the end." Amen. (LSB *882:6*)

SEPTEMBER 26

O God, forsake me not!
Your gracious presence lend me;
Lord, lead Your helpless child;
Your Holy Spirit send me
That I my course may run.
O be my light, my lot,
My staff, my rock, my shield—
O God, forsake me not! (*LSB* 731:1)

O GOD, FORSAKE ME NOT!" THE POET OPENS AND CLOSES EACH stanza of his hymn with that petition, which becomes our constant prayer as well. The child of God prays especially for the gift of the Holy Spirit, that the Spirit may constantly lead and guide us through the course of earthly life. It is the Holy Spirit who not only kindles our faith through Holy Baptism but continually increases and nurtures that faith through God's Word and His Holy Supper. Thus, we pray, "Increase my feeble faith, which You alone have wrought" (st. 2). We also pray that God would not forsake us in times of temptation but that He would help us to resist temptation and retain a clean conscience.

"O God, forsake me not!" We can rest in the certainty that God never will forsake or leave His dear children. How do we know that? We recall that haunting, painful, final cry of Jesus from the cross: "My God, My God, why have You forsaken Me?" (Matthew 27:46). That Jesus was completely abandoned by God—left utterly alone, with no access to His God and Father—is a stark reminder of what He suffered for us. He experienced that torment so that we will *never* be abandoned or forsaken by God. He will hear our prayers for deliverance from hardship, harm, and danger; for deliverance from temptation; and for the continuing gift of His Holy Spirit. Thanks be to God that He hears this petition: "O God, forsake me not!"

"O God, forsake me not! Lord, I am Yours forever. O keep me strong in faith that I may leave You never. Grant me a blessed end when my good fight is fought; help me in life and death—O God, forsake me not!" Amen. (LSB *731:4*)

SEPTEMBER 27

Thy body, giv'n for me, O Savior,
Thy blood which Thou for me didst shed,
These are my life and strength forever,
By them my hungry soul is fed.
Lord, may Thy body and Thy blood
Be for my soul the highest good! (***LSB*** **619:1**)

IN HIS "CHRISTIAN QUESTIONS WITH THEIR ANSWERS," DR. MARTIN Luther, ever the clear teacher, asks and answers, "What has Christ done for you that you trust in Him? He died for me and shed His blood for me on the cross for the forgiveness of sins" (Small Catechism, Christian Question 9). That one-time event accomplished our salvation. By instituting His Holy Supper on the night when He was betrayed, Jesus gives us still more. He comes to us bodily in His Sacrament of the Altar, giving us His very body and blood "for the forgiveness of sins" (Matthew 26:28). He shed His blood once for our salvation; now He gives us His body and blood again and again in this Sacrament—for the forgiveness of sins and for the strengthening of our faith. Today's hymn states it beautifully: Christ's body and blood "are my life and strength forever, by them my hungry soul is fed."

In considering the eternal, "forever," implications of this blessed Sacrament, the hymn writer repeats Paul's defiant question: "Who is to condemn? Christ Jesus is the one who died—more than that, who was raised—who is at the right hand of God, who indeed is interceding for us" (Romans 8:34). Jesus died and rose *for us*. Jesus is bodily present in His Supper, giving His true body and blood *for us*. Thus, we do not fear hell, for in death we will rest securely with Jesus, and on the Last Day rise to heaven. Christ's body and blood are indeed "for my soul the highest good!"

"Who can condemn me now? For surely the Lord is nigh, who justifies. No hell I fear, and thus securely with Jesus I to heaven rise. Lord, may Thy body and Thy blood be for my soul the highest good!" Amen. (LSB *619:3*)

SEPTEMBER 28

**Oh, how great is Your compassion,
Faithful Father, God of grace,
That with all our fallen race
In our depth of degradation
You had mercy so that we
Might be saved eternally!**

**Your great love for this has striven
That we may, from sin made free,
Live with You eternally.
Your dear Son Himself has given
And extends His gracious call,
To His supper leads us all. (*LSB* 559:1–2)**

Sometimes important matters are left unsaid or only implied. *False* teaching is not the only potential problem. *Incomplete* teaching—crucial matters that might be overlooked, ignored, or neglected—can be problematic as well. Today's hymn tells the whole story of sin and grace in an almost catechetical way.

"In our depth of degradation," used in both the opening and closing stanzas, does not allow us to escape the reality of our sinful nature. But God the Father in His great compassion, mercy, and love has freed us from sin that we might live with Him eternally. *How* did He do that? His dear Son, Jesus Christ, gave Himself for us. *Why* did He do that? Purely out of grace—undeserved love. *How* does this grace come to us? "In Your Sacraments and Word. There He sends true consolation, giving us the gift of faith" (st. 3). Moreover, the hymn writer points us to the ultimate result—eternal salvation: "Since Your Word cannot deceive me, my salvation is to me safe and sure eternally" (st. 4).

Praying this hymn gives us the opportunity to recall that in the person and work of Jesus Christ, we are saved by God's grace, which comes to us through *means*—Word and Sacraments—by which God the Holy Spirit works saving faith within us.

"Firmly to our soul's salvation witnesses Your Spirit, Lord, in Your Sacraments and Word. There He sends true consolation, giving us the gift of faith that we fear not hell nor death. Lord, Your mercy will not leave me; ever will Your truth abide. Then in You I will confide. Since Your Word cannot deceive me, my salvation is to me safe and sure eternally." Amen. (LSB *559:3–4*)

SEPTEMBER 29

**Michael fought the
heav'nly battle,
Godly angels by his side;
Warred against the
ancient serpent,
Foiled the beast, so full of pride,
Cast him earthbound
with his angels;
Now he prowls, unsatisfied.**

**Swift as lightning
falls the tyrant
From his heav'nly perch on high,
As the word of Jesus' vict'ry
Floods the earth
and fills the sky.
Wounded by a wound eternal
Now his judgment has drawn
nigh! (*LSB* 521:2, 5)**

THERE WAS A WAR IN HEAVEN! LEADING UP TO THIS WAR, SATAN was in heaven, accusing God's saints of their sins. He claimed to be their true leader because they loved to sin and follow him. It is as if Satan was a prosecuting attorney in the heavenly court. And his accusations against God's people were ugly! But God had a plan to send His Son to a cross that would "bruise [the] head" of the serpent (Genesis 3:15). Then, Satan would no longer be able to bring charges against God's children in that heavenly court.

The archangel Michael defeated Satan in that heavenly war and threw him and his legions to earth. John records a loud voice from heaven saying, "Therefore, rejoice, O heavens and you who dwell in them! But woe to you, O earth and sea, for the devil has come down to you in great wrath, because he knows that his time is short!" (Revelation 12:12).

Today is St. Michael and All Angels Day, which begins a period when the church looks at what it means to be the church militant. Yes, we are militant because *we are at war with Satan*! He attacks us day and night, brutally and mercilessly. We feel his wrath. But thanks be to God, that is not the end of the story for God's beloved children, for "Jesus' vict'ry floods the earth and fills the sky"!

"Jesus, send Your angel legions when the foe would us enslave. Hold us fast when sin assaults us; come, then, Lord, Your people save. Overthrow at last the dragon; send him to his fiery grave." Amen. (LSB 521:6)

SEPTEMBER 30

They shine with light and heav'nly grace
And constantly behold Thy face;
They heed Thy voice, they know it well,
In godly wisdom they excel.

But watchful is the angel band
That follows Christ on ev'ry hand
To guard His people where they go
And break the counsel of the foe. (*LSB* 522:2, 7)

P*SALM 91 PROMISES, "HE WILL COMMAND HIS ANGELS* concerning you to guard you in all your ways" (v. 11). The doctrine of angels is wonderfully comforting. But to understand this doctrine correctly, we must set aside all we know about angels from the Hallmark store. Instead, we look at God's Word concerning these magnificent creatures and learn how vital angels are for life as the church militant.

They excel in strength and are infinitely more powerful than the strongest humans. They can do things that we cannot even begin to imagine. But above all, they do the will of God. They have no independent action or work apart from Him; in this work, they never rest nor sleep. They are His ministers at all times, and He sends them to be the guardians of His beloved children, "where they go and break the counsel of the foe." This is a true comfort for us.

Yes, we walk in danger all the way, but we "walk with angels all the way" (*LSB* 716:4). And we know they are with us until our last moments on this earth, when they will carry us out of the battle to our home in heaven.

"Lord God, to Thee we give all praise, with grateful hearts our voices raise, that angel hosts Thou didst create around Thy glorious throne to wait. They never rest nor sleep as we; their whole delight is but to be with Thee, Lord Jesus, and to keep Thy little flock, Thy lambs and sheep." Amen. (LSB *522:1, 3*)

OCTOBER 1

Stars of the morning, so gloriously bright,
Angels in heaven, resplendent in light,
These, where no darkness the glory can dim,
Praise the Thrice Holy One, serving but Him.

These are Your ministers, these are Your own,
Lord God of Sabaoth, nearest Your throne;
These are Your messengers, these whom You send,
Helping Your helpless ones, Helper and Friend. (*LSB* 520:1–2)

"HELPING YOUR HELPLESS ONES" IS A TENDER AND PASTORAL way for today's hymn to speak of what God's angels do for us. Divine, angelic help always surrounds each child of God—even when they do not know they need it. These magnificent creatures serve God day and night; they are His ministers and messengers working for us as they follow His command. And they do not sleep.

They aid us, fight for us, protect us, and help the "helpless ones" in myriad ways we will never know. "For He will command His angels concerning you to guard you in all your ways" (Psalm 91:11). Luther's Morning Prayer has us pray these words every morning: "Let Your holy angel be with me, that the evil foe may have no power over me" (Small Catechism). We pray for protection for our day going forward when we do not know how much we will begin to need it.

What a splendid gift we have from our gracious heavenly Father in His gift of guardian angels for us! We hardly know where to start in acknowledging, thanking, and praising Him for guarding us in all our ways.

"Still let them aid us and still let them fight, Lord of angelic hosts, battling for right, till, where their anthems they ceaselessly pour, we with the angels may bow and adore. For this, now and in days to be, our praise shall rise, O Lord, to Thee, whom all the angel hosts adore with grateful songs forevermore." Amen. (LSB 520:4; 522:8)

OCTOBER 2

Fight the good fight with all your might;
Christ is your strength, and Christ your right.
Lay hold on life, and it shall be
Your joy and crown eternally.

Run the straight race through God's good grace;
Lift up your eyes, and seek His face.
Life with its way before us lies;
Christ is the path, and Christ the prize. (*LSB* 664:1–2)

TIMOTHY WAS BLESSED TO HAVE PAUL AS HIS MENTOR IN THE faith. In both of his letters to Timothy, Paul focuses his young colleague (and us) on Christ—pointing to His purpose for coming into the world and His life-giving words of salvation. Early in his first letter to Timothy, Paul writes, "Christ Jesus came into the world to save sinners" (1:15). Toward the end of that letter, Paul points us to "the sound words of our Lord Jesus Christ" (6:3), the foundation on which we "fight the good fight of the faith" (v. 12).

Today's hymn similarly focuses on Christ, referring to Him as our strength, our path, our prize, our very life, and our love. Moreover, "He changes not" (st. 4). The letter to the Hebrews puts it this way: "Jesus Christ is the same yesterday and today and forever" (13:8). What a comfort that is to us! The unchangeable, eternal Christ came into the world to save us, still provides for us out of His boundless mercy, and holds us in His loving arms eternally.

Thus, in Christ, we "cast care aside" (st. 3), certain that He will give us what we need to fight the good fight, finish the race, and keep the faith (2 Timothy 4:7). We do none of that on our own; it is the gracious work of Christ—our "joy and crown eternally."

"Cast care aside, lean on your guide; His boundless mercy will provide. Trust, and enduring faith shall prove Christ is your life and Christ your love. Faint not nor fear, His arms are near; He changes not who holds you dear; only believe, and you will see that Christ is all eternally." Amen. (LSB *664:3–4*)

OCTOBER 3

Salvation unto us has come
By God's free grace and favor;
Good works cannot avert our doom,
They help and save us never.
Faith looks to Jesus Christ alone,
Who did for all the world atone;
He is our one Redeemer. (*LSB* 555:1)

W*ORKS HAVE ALWAYS BEEN A STUMBLING BLOCK IN* CHRIST'S church. That is because the Law written in our hearts can easily mislead us to think that if we do certain things and try hard enough, we can keep the Law and please God! This hymn calls such thinking nonsense—"a false, misleading dream" (st. 3)!

Luther and his friends set out to expose such lies, and one of the ways was through hymns filled with correct teaching, such as this one by Paul Speratus. Singing hymns with Gospel truth was able to reach the young and old of Wittenberg very directly: "Good works cannot avert our doom, they help and save us never." But then the hymn moves on to tell what Christ has done for us.

Gloriously, the first line of this hymn states the heart of the Reformation—"salvation unto us has come by God's free grace and favor." This stunning statement of pure joy lets Christ's church live freely in Gospel truth! And it could not be stated any more clearly than at the end of this first stanza: "Faith looks to Jesus Christ alone, who did for all the world atone; He is our one Redeemer."

Salvation is not about us, but Jesus Christ has done it all for us! We have a Savior and a Redeemer! Thanks be to God!

"Let me not doubt, but truly see Your Word cannot be broken; Your call rings out, 'Come unto Me!' No falsehood have You spoken. Baptized into Your precious name, my faith cannot be put to shame, and I shall never perish." Amen. (LSB *555:7*)

OCTOBER 4

Since Christ has full atonement made
And brought to us salvation,
Each Christian therefore may be glad
And build on this foundation.
Your grace alone, dear Lord, I plead,
Your death is now my life indeed,
For You have paid my ransom. (***LSB*** **555:6**)

TODAY'S HYMN PROCLAIMS THE FOUNDATION FOR OUR WHOLE LIFE with simple clarity—Jesus Christ won our salvation. We receive it as a *gift*! Therefore, we confidently build our lives on the priceless truths presented in this stanza. What a rock-solid foundation we have for all our days, knowing that our ransom, our salvation, *could not* be more secure.

"Each Christian therefore may be glad"! We cannot help but be glad for miraculous gifts that define our lives as His baptized children in His kingdom. And while our days here on earth may include suffering, challenges, hardships, and crosses, the end of our days has already been determined—we are His forever! Christ's death has become our life now and for eternity.

Therefore, we trust that His Word cannot be broken—and we doubt it not! And along the way, we hear His compassionate voice calling us, "Come unto Me!" (st. 7). Our firm foundation, Jesus Christ, shows us the way and is "the way" for every step through our baptismal life.

Being baptized into that strong name of the Holy Trinity means that we are His! "Each Christian therefore may be glad"! We are His, and He is ours! We "build on this foundation."

"Let me not doubt, but truly see Your Word cannot be broken; Your call rings out, 'Come unto Me!' No falsehood have You spoken. Baptized into Your precious name, my faith cannot be put to shame, and I shall never perish." Amen. (LSB *555:7*)

OCTOBER 5

Faith clings to Jesus' cross alone
And rests in Him unceasing;
And by its fruits true faith is known,
With love and hope increasing.
For faith alone can justify;
Works serve our neighbor and supply
The proof that faith is living. (*LSB* 555:9)

T*HIS COULD BE CALLED THE "FAITH" STANZA OF THIS MONUMENTAL* Reformation hymn. The previous stanzas defined the work of the Law but then separated that from the glorious truths of the Gospel. Now, the hymn answers the catechism's ubiquitous question: "What does this mean?"

It means that Law and Gospel each has a distinct role in the miraculous gift of our faith given at Baptism. It is a faith that "clings to Jesus' cross alone," and that clinging faith is where we live out the delicate balance of Law and Gospel. Luther often simplified this blessed life by reducing it to two words: *faith* and *love*. Therefore, this is the "faith and love" stanza, as it speaks of the fruits of our faith. "And by its fruits true faith is known, with love and hope increasing."

Our baptismal life continually fills us with Christ's love through His means of grace. Then we are to reach out and give that love to our neighbor. And who is my neighbor? Anyone I can reach with my service. Yes, my neighbor and his needs are all around me. And this is how our works rightly fit into our life as saints in Christ's kingdom. "Works serve our neighbor and supply the proof that faith is living."

"All blessing, honor, thanks, and praise to Father, Son, and Spirit, the God who saved us by His grace; all glory to His merit. O triune God in heav'n above, You have revealed Your saving love; Your blessed name we hallow." Amen. (LSB 555:10)

OCTOBER 6

God loved the world
so that He gave
His only Son the lost to save,
That all who would
in Him believe
Should everlasting life receive.

Christ Jesus is the
ground of faith,
Who was made flesh
and suffered death;
All then who trust in Him alone
Are built on this chief
cornerstone. (*LSB* 571:1–2)

"THE GOSPEL IN A NUTSHELL" IS A PHRASE SOMETIMES USED TO refer to John 3:16. The first stanza of today's hymn is a close paraphrase of that beautiful text, which does indeed encapsulate the Gospel—in His great love for the world, God gave His only Son to die in our place and then rise from the dead so that we, too, may have eternal life. The Holy Spirit works faith in our hearts to *believe* in Jesus' redemptive work. Jesus Himself bids us, "Believe in God; believe also in Me" (14:1), for "whoever believes in Him should not perish but have eternal life" (3:16). Our triune God does *everything* to bring us to eternal life: The Father gave His Son, the Son obeyed His Father's will, and the Son sends the Holy Spirit to "guide you into all the truth" (16:13), including *believing* the Gospel promise.

Jesus is the "ground" of this Spirit-worked faith, the "chief cornerstone" on which God's plan of salvation is founded. From the moment of our first parents' fall into sin, God formed a plan of salvation so that we might have *life*. The prophet Ezekiel records God's words: "I have no pleasure in the death of the wicked, but that the wicked turn from his way and live" (33:11). Today's hymn declares that truth: "God would not have the sinner die" (st. 3). To the contrary, by God's grace, we are "heaven's heirs" (st. 3)!

"God would not have the sinner die; His Son with saving grace is nigh; His Spirit in the Word declares how we in Christ are heaven's heirs. Be of good cheer, for God's own Son forgives all sins which you have done; and, justified by Jesus' blood, your Baptism grants the highest good." Amen. (LSB *571:3–4*)

OCTOBER 7

Go, My children, with
My blessing,
Never alone.
Waking, sleeping, I am with you;
You are My own.
In My love's baptismal river
I have made you Mine forever.
Go, My children, with
My blessing—
You are My own. (*LSB* 922:1)

At the close of each Divine Service, your pastor speaks words of blessing: "The Lord bless you and keep you" (Numbers 6:24). In today's hymn, Pastor Jaroslav Vajda provides a beautiful text for meditation on the Lord's blessings to us.

First and foremost, in Baptism, God has made us His own. We say, "I *am* baptized," for Baptism is a present-tense reality throughout our lives. Because God made us His own in Baptism, we are never alone; "I have made you Mine forever." That is a blessing for us to remember every day of our lives.

In his Small Catechism, Martin Luther names the blessings of Baptism: "It works forgiveness of sins, rescues from death and the devil, and gives eternal salvation to all who believe" (Second Part). Thus, Vajda writes: "Go, My children, sins forgiven, at peace and pure" (st. 2). We are "at peace," knowing that our sins are forgiven and that Christ Himself will one day welcome us to our eternal home in heaven. That blessing allows us to live here in peace, without fear, so that we might love and serve our neighbors through our varied vocations.

Pastor Vajda imagines words from God the Father reminding us of the blessings of the Divine Service: "Here you heard My dear Son's story; here you touched Him" (st. 2). God blesses us as we hear the Gospel and as we receive Christ's very body and blood for the forgiveness of sins. God's blessings in Word and Sacraments are rich indeed, and we do well to meditate on what it means to go forth in life with those blessings.

"Go, My children, sins forgiven, at peace and pure. Here you learned how much I love you, what I can cure. Here you heard My dear Son's story; here you touched Him, saw His glory. Go, My children, sins forgiven, at peace and pure." Amen. (LSB 922:2)

OCTOBER 8

Jesus sinners doth receive;
Oh, may all this saying ponder
Who in sin's delusions live
And from God and heaven wander!
Here is hope for all who grieve:
Jesus sinners doth receive.

Sheep that from the fold did stray
No true shepherd e'er forsaketh;
Weary souls that lost their way
Christ, the Shepherd, gently taketh
In His arms that they may live:
Jesus sinners doth receive. (*LSB* 609:1, 3)

THE PHARISEES DIDN'T LIKE WHAT THEY SAW, SO THEY ASKED Jesus' disciples, "Why does your teacher eat with tax collectors and sinners?" After all, for the Pharisees, that very act made Jesus unclean. But Jesus immediately clarified the matter: "I came not to call the righteous, but sinners" (Matthew 9:11, 13). From His birth to His suffering, crucifixion, death, and resurrection, Jesus came into this world for the purpose of saving sinners—including each of us. During His earthly ministry, Jesus received sinners and ate with them. Jesus still receives sinners today, hearing our penitential prayers and graciously giving us full and free forgiveness.

Again, we read in Luke's Gospel that "the Pharisees and the scribes grumbled, saying, 'This man receives sinners and eats with them'" (Luke 15:2). Jesus responded with the beautiful parable of the lost sheep (vv. 1–7). The one sheep that wanders away is so loved by the shepherd that he leaves the others to find the wanderer and bring it back—and then throws a celebration with friends and neighbors: "Rejoice with me, for I have found my sheep that was lost."

Jesus, the Good Shepherd, cares that much for each of us. He claimed us in our Baptism and will not let us go. His love for us is so great that there is joy in heaven when we repent of our sins. When we grieve over our sins, the Good Shepherd takes us in His arms that we may live! "Jesus sinners doth receive."

"I, a sinner, come to Thee with a penitent confession. Savior, mercy show to me; grant for all my sins remission. Let these words my soul relieve: Jesus sinners doth receive." Amen. (LSB 609:4)

OCTOBER 9

Chief of sinners though I be,
Jesus shed His blood for me,
Died that I might live on high,
Lives that I might never die.
As the branch is to the vine,
I am His, and He is mine. (*LSB* 611:1)

IT IS A STRIKING STATEMENT BY PAUL, IDENTIFYING HIMSELF AS the *chief* of sinners: "The saying is trustworthy and deserving of full acceptance, that Christ Jesus came into the world to save sinners, *of whom I am the foremost*" (1 Timothy 1:15, emphasis added). He said this because in his former life he had actively persecuted Christians: "I was a blasphemer, persecutor, and insolent opponent" (v. 13). But, of course, Paul is not alone—each of us justifiably lays claim to being "chief" among sinners. God's Law convicts us, allowing no excuses for our sinful actions, thoughts, and desires.

But, as Paul makes clear, Jesus came into our world for one reason only—to save sinners. He kept the Law perfectly on our behalf. By shedding His blood on the cross, He *died* so that we may *live* eternally. Now He lives—as our "advocate with the Father" (1 John 2:1)—so that we will not suffer eternal death. We hold fast to Jesus' life-giving promise: "Whoever believes in Me, though he die, yet shall he live, and everyone who lives and believes in Me shall never die" (John 11:25–26).

Today's hymn-prayer provides yet another precious truth: "Love that found me—wondrous thought! Found me when I sought Him not" (st. 2). We don't seek Jesus—our sinful nature precludes that action on our part. We are not the actors; rather, Jesus, our Good Shepherd, seeks His lost sheep, finds us, and rescues us.

In His great love for us, Jesus came into the world to save each of us, "chief of sinners though I be."

"Oh, the height of Jesus' love, higher than the heav'ns above, deeper than the depths of sea, lasting as eternity! Love that found me—wondrous thought! Found me when I sought Him not." Amen. (LSB 611:2)

OCTOBER 10

Jesus, lead Thou on
Till our rest is won;
And although the way be cheerless,
We will follow calm and fearless.
Guide us by Thy hand
To our fatherland. (*LSB* 718:1)

HAVE YOU EVER WONDERED JUST HOW MUCH YOUR HEAVENLY Father loves you? You know that His love is so vast that He sent His beloved Son to suffer and die in your place, and then to rise from death on the third day—thereby defeating sin and death *for you*. His love for His fallen creatures—all of us—gives us eternal life in His kingdom. But there is yet more love from our heavenly Father!

One of the most amazing pictures—and promises—in all of God's Holy Word is that of God wiping away all tears from the faces of His beloved children. Think about that for a moment. How much more personal does it get—God Himself wiping away tears from my face and yours? In the great book of Revelation, John spells it out for us: "He will wipe away every tear from their eyes, and death shall be no more, neither shall there be mourning, nor crying, nor pain anymore, for the former things have passed away" (Revelation 21:4). Think about that when you ponder how much God loves you. He has won eternal life for you. And the day is coming when He Himself will wipe away all tears from our eyes—the last vestiges of sin and death in this world.

Jesus will indeed lead us on "till our rest is won" and we arrive in the heavenly home that He is preparing for us. There He will tenderly and lovingly dry our tears. "Show us that bright shore where we weep no more" (st. 3).

"When we seek relief from a long-felt grief, when temptations come alluring, make us patient and enduring. Show us that bright shore where we weep no more. Jesus, lead Thou on till our rest is won. Heav'nly leader, still direct us, still support, console, protect us, till we safely stand in our fatherland." Amen. (LSB *718:3–4*)

OCTOBER 11

In Thine arms I rest me;
Foes who would molest me
Cannot reach me here.
Though the earth be shaking,
Ev'ry heart be quaking,
Jesus calms my fear.
Lightnings flash
And thunders crash;
Yet, though sin and
hell assail me,
Jesus will not fail
me. (*LSB* 743:2)

Jesus is our "priceless treasure," our "truest friend" (st. 1), the one who shields us from all who would harm us, who protects us from all dangers, who calms all our fears. He watches over us in the literal storms of life, when thunder and lightning, tornadoes and hurricanes cause us to fear for our personal safety. But beyond such earthly events, Jesus is our protection from an even more dangerous set of foes, which Luther identifies as sin, death, and the power of the devil (Small Catechism, Creed, Second Article). Those enemies are our worst adversaries, for they affect far more than our safety and our earthly dwellings; they threaten our eternal well-being.

The hymn writer tells us that "though sin and hell assail me, Jesus will not fail me." When our sins—past and present—haunt us, Jesus is present where He has promised to be—in His Word and Sacraments, assuring us of pardon for our sins. As He said before He healed a paralyzed man, so He says to us: "Take heart, My son; your sins are forgiven" (Matthew 9:2). As He said to the disciples on the night when He was betrayed, so He says to us: "Drink of it, all of you, for this is My blood of the covenant, which is poured out for many for the forgiveness of sins" (26:28).

Because of what Jesus has done for us, we can join the hymn writer in saying, "Satan, I defy thee; death, I now decry thee; fear, I bid thee cease" (st. 3). We rest in the arms of Jesus, our "priceless treasure" (st. 6).

"Hence, all fear and sadness! For the Lord of gladness, Jesus, enters in. Those who love the Father, though the storms may gather, still have peace within. Yea, whate'er I here must bear, Thou art still my purest pleasure, Jesus, priceless treasure!" Amen. (LSB 743:6)

OCTOBER 12

Light of Light, O Sole-Begotten
Radiance of the Father's face,
Word made flesh, who lived among us
Full of truth and full of grace,
Shine upon our human darkness;
Pierce the night that shrouds our race. (*LSB* 914:1)

JOHN 1:1–14 IS A MOST GLORIOUS TEXT, REVEALING IN BEAUTIFUL, striking language just who Jesus is. Pastor Stephen Starke's hymn similarly focuses on Jesus—present at the creation of light, and now our light in the darkness of sin.

Jesus is *light*. John identifies Him as "the true light, which gives light to everyone" (John 1:9). Later in John's Gospel, Jesus refers to Himself in the same way: "I am the light of the world. Whoever follows Me will not walk in darkness, but will have the light of life" (John 8:12). The first words of today's hymn refer to Jesus as "Light of Light." We pray that He would "shine upon our human darkness," that He would "pierce the night that shrouds our race." Jesus is the only light that can penetrate the darkness of human sinfulness. As the Word made flesh, Jesus redeemed us from the darkness and won for us the eternal light of heaven, where "night will be no more," where "the Lord God will be their light" (Revelation 22:5).

John emphasizes that Jesus was present when God the Father spoke light into creation. Then—in God's appointed time—Jesus, present "in the beginning" (John 1:1), is Himself "the *light* of men" (v. 4, emphasis added). Jesus is indeed "Light of Light," the "Sole-Begotten Radiance of the Father's face, Word made flesh." Now the same Spirit who at creation hovered "over the face of the waters" (Genesis 1:2) comes to us with the assurance that "Christ the Lord will shine upon you and from death your soul shall keep" (st. 3). Jesus is our light—unto eternal life.

"Come, Lord Jesus, by Your Spirit in our hearts Your work begin, bring the healing restoration of Your image lost by sin; from Your fullness all receiving grace on grace, new life within!" Amen. (LSB 914:4)

OCTOBER 13

Lord, it belongs not to my care
Whether I die or live;
To love and serve Thee is my share,
And this Thy grace must give.

If life be long, I will be glad
That I may long obey;
If short, yet why should I be sad
To soar to endless day? (*LSB* 757:1–2)

As children of God, we are truly privileged to pray and sing these words and to believe beyond any doubt that death is not the last word for the Christian. It is not a matter of fatalism, or indifference to the life God grants. Rather, it is a Spirit-worked faith, enabling us to pray that "whether I die or live" is neither our care nor our worry. If we live a long life, may we faithfully serve God in our various vocations. But if in God's wisdom we live a short life, "why should I be sad to soar to endless day?"

To be sure, death hurts, but we do "not grieve as others do who have no hope" (1 Thessalonians 4:13). We know that we belong to Christ, who leads us "through no darker rooms than He went through before" (st. 3). He entered the darkness of the tomb and overcame it in His glorious resurrection. His victory is now our victory. Thus, we are not consumed by fear or worry concerning our lives here, because we have the certainty of *eternal* life with Christ in heaven. With Paul, we believe that "to live is Christ, and to die is gain" (Philippians 1:21).

It is enough that Christ knows all, that we are in His care and keeping, and that we most certainly will be with Him forever!

"Christ leads me through no darker rooms than He went through before; he that unto God's kingdom comes must enter by this door. My knowledge of that life is small, the eye of faith is dim; but 'tis enough that Christ knows all, and I shall be with Him." Amen. (LSB *757:3, 6*)

OCTOBER 14

Now rest beneath
night's shadow
The woodland, field,
and meadow;
The world in slumber lies.
But you, my heart, awaking
And prayer and music making,
Let praise to your Creator rise.

The radiant sun has vanished,
Its golden rays are banished
From dark'ning skies of night;
But Christ, the Sun of gladness,
Dispelling all our sadness,
Shines down on us in warmest
light. (*LSB* 880:1–2)

A***S SUMMER GIVES WAY TO AUTUMN AND TIMES OF DAYLIGHT GROW*** shorter, we find ourselves turning lights on earlier in the evening to ward off the darkness. Brightly illuminated homes of our day stand in marked contrast to earlier times, when the darkness of the evening was profound, as, for example, during the seventeenth-century times of Pastor Paul Gerhardt. His evening hymn is a prayer for God's care and keeping through the darkness of the night.

Christ is the one who makes all the difference in the darkness, whether the darkness of a single night or the darkness of a sinful life. He is "the Sun of gladness," who alone can dispel our sadness, doubts, apprehensions, and fears. In the dark shadows of the evening, He "shines down on us in warmest light." His promise, "I am with you always, to the end of the age" (Matthew 28:20), provides the reassurance that we need in moments of darkness. We pray that Christ would shield us from all harm and danger and that He would send His angels to guard us against the power of the devil.

The evening is also an appropriate time for us to pray for those who are nearest to us, the family members who are among God's most precious gifts to each of us. Gerhardt also gives us beautiful words to pray for our loved ones. Each evening, we commend ourselves and our loved ones to the merciful care of our loving God.

"My loved ones, rest securely, for God this night will surely from peril guard your heads. Sweet slumbers may He send you and bid His hosts attend you and through the night watch o'er your beds." Amen. (LSB 880:5)

OCTOBER 15

The death of Jesus
Christ, our Lord,
We celebrate with one accord;
It is our comfort in distress,
Our heart's sweet joy
and happiness.

He blotted out with
His own blood
The judgment that
against us stood;
For us He full atonement made,
And all our debt He fully
paid. (*LSB* 634:1–2)

PAUL WRITES THAT "WE WERE RECONCILED TO GOD BY THE death of His Son" (Romans 5:10). The hymn writer calls Christ's death "our comfort in distress, our heart's sweet joy and happiness." Why is it that we *celebrate* the death of God's only Son? That is the way God the Father chose to balance the scales of justice for mankind's sin. The death of Jesus paid the full price for our sins. The shedding of His blood on our behalf blots out all the sins we have ever committed and will ever commit. There is no more glorious truth than that of redemption through the blood of Christ!

But Christ has provided far more than this most welcome, objective theological truth. In His Holy Supper, instituted the night before He died, He promises us that when we receive the bread and wine of the Supper, we receive His true body and blood for the forgiveness of sins, for our salvation. The hymn writer notes that "we taste His love so sweet, so near" (st. 3). In this most intimate way, we receive Christ and the forgiveness He won for us. And we receive it again and again—throughout our lives!

Christ is present bodily on the altars of our churches. While we cannot explain the real presence of Christ in His Holy Supper, we don't need to. The Holy Spirit works faith in our hearts to believe Christ's promises and to receive His life-giving food unto eternal life.

"His Word proclaims and we believe that in this Supper we receive His very body, as He said, His very blood for sinners shed. We dare not ask how this can be, but simply hold the mystery and trust this word where life begins: 'Given and shed for all your sins.'" Amen. (LSB *634:4–5*)

OCTOBER 16

The Gospel shows the Father's grace,
Who sent His Son to save our race,
Proclaims how Jesus lived and died
That we might thus be justified.

It sets the Lamb before our eyes,
Who made the atoning sacrifice,
And calls the souls with guilt oppressed
To come and find eternal rest. (*LSB* 580:1–2)

PAUL MEMORABLY DEFINES THE GOSPEL AS "THE POWER OF GOD for salvation to everyone who believes," noting further that, in the Gospel, "the righteousness of God is revealed" (Romans 1:16–17). The Gospel is so much more than words on a page! Through the Gospel, the Holy Spirit actively works faith in us, bringing us salvation unto eternal life. Today's hymn is a beautiful meditation on the Gospel, like a shimmering jewel offering us multiple perspectives on God's great gift.

"The Gospel shows the Father's grace," the free, unmerited love that caused the Father to send His Son into this world to save us. The Gospel proclaims Jesus' willingness to enter our sinful world, live the perfect life that will always elude us, and then suffer and die for our salvation—the Lamb sacrificed for us. The Gospel "brings the Savior's righteousness to robe our souls in royal dress" (st. 3). Jesus' saving work means that we are dressed not in the stained clothing of our sins but rather in the pure white robes of Christ's righteousness. The prophet Isaiah proclaimed that same Gospel: "He has clothed me with the garments of salvation; He has covered me with the robe of righteousness" (61:10).

Clothed in Christ's righteousness, we have been released from the power of sin, from guilt, from a troubled conscience, from fear of death and the grave. Through the Gospel, we have eternal rest!

"It brings the Savior's righteousness to robe our souls in royal dress; from all our guilt it brings release and gives the troubled conscience peace. It is the pow'r of God to save from sin and Satan and the grave; it works the faith which firmly clings to all the treasures which it brings." Amen. (LSB *580:3–4*)

OCTOBER 17

The Lord, my God, be praised,
My light, my life from heaven;
My maker, who to me
Has soul and body given;
My Father, who will shield
And keep me day by day
And make each moment yield
New blessings on my way.

The Lord, my God, be praised,
My trust, my life from heaven,
The Father's own dear Son,
Whose life for me was given,
Who for my sin atoned
With His most precious blood
And gives to me by faith
The highest heav'nly
good. (*LSB* 794:1–2)

MARTIN LUTHER OBSERVED THAT THE WAY WE PRAISE GOD IS by proclaiming the Word of God (*Luther's Works*, vol. 53, p. 323). Here, the hymn writer praises God by declaring what the Father, Son, and Holy Spirit have done *for us*.

God the Father made us—soul and body. He graciously watches over us each day, not only shielding us from all harm and danger but also providing "new blessings on my way." God the Son gave His life for us, atoning for our sins by shedding His precious blood on the cross. He gives to us "the highest heav'nly good"—eternal life in His very presence. God the Holy Spirit, the Comforter, provides "support in sorrow's gloomy hour" (st. 3). As we declare what God has done for us, we praise Him for these rich gifts.

This generous, loving, eternal God is indeed our light, our trust, our hope, our very life from heaven! As the heavenly host give Him their laud and praise, we, too, praise Him—by recalling all that He has done for us, by declaring His "mighty acts" (Psalm 145:4).

"The Lord, my God, be praised, my hope, my life from heaven, the Spirit, whom the Son in love to me has given. His grace revives my heart and gives my spirit pow'r, help, comfort, and support in sorrow's gloomy hour." Amen. (LSB *794:3*)

OCTOBER 18

What mercy God showed to our race,
A plan of rescue by His grace:
In sending One from woman's seed,
The One to fill our greatest need—
For on a tree uplifted high
His only Son for sin would die,
Would drink the cup of scorn and dread
To crush the ancient serpent's head! (*LSB* 561:3)

T*REES AND WOOD—IN THIS HYMN,* PASTOR STEPHEN STARKE USES those images to tell the story of sin and salvation. God told Adam that he could eat of every tree in the beautiful garden that was his to tend, except for "the tree of the knowledge of good and evil" (Genesis 2:17).

But—as he still does—Satan cast doubt on God's clear commands, and our first parents fell into sin, unleashing the "awful poison" of "fear and darkness, doubt and death" into our world (st. 2). These results of their sinful disobedience would affect not only Adam and Eve but also everyone born into this world.

In His great love for humankind, God had "a plan of rescue by His grace." The one and only human who would ever be born into this world *without sin*—Jesus, Son of God—would bring salvation to all by willingly being nailed to a different tree, the tree of the cross. This rescue from sin and death is ours purely by the grace of God; we cannot earn it.

Thus, while the fruit of a tree brought sin into the world, the tree on which the Son of God died brought eternal life and salvation "for all who trust and will believe" (st. 4). Thanks be to God for the tree of Jesus' cross.

"*O tree of beauty, tree most fair, ordained those holy limbs to bear: gone is thy shame, each crimson bough proclaims the King of Glory now." Amen.* (LSB 455:5)

OCTOBER 19

God is my comfort and my trust,
My hope and life abiding;
And to His counsel, wise and just,
I yield, in Him confiding.
The very hairs, His Word declares,
Upon my head He numbers.
By night and day God is my stay;
He never sleeps nor slumbers. (***LSB*** **758:2**)

IT WAS A PARTICULARLY HAUNTING SCENE ON THE MOUNT OF OLIVES the night before Jesus was crucified. Jesus, knowing what was to come the next day, was in agony and prayed: "Father, if You are willing, remove this cup from Me. Nevertheless, not My will, but Yours, be done" (Luke 22:42). Jesus' prayer is a model for us, as we often conclude our own petitions with "Your will be done," words Jesus also taught us.

Today's hymn-prayer asserts that "the will of God is always best" (st. 1), and that we who trust in and depend on God will be blessed. That sounds good, doesn't it? We simply depend on God, and all will be well—*and that is true*! But the hymn writer also asserts "to His counsel, wise and just, I yield, in Him confiding." What does that mean?

When we pray to God that His will be done, we realize that we may not like what comes next. For Jesus, that meant unspeakable suffering and an agonizing death. Are we willing to yield to the Father's wise counsel as the Son did? We thank our Savior that He obeyed His Father's will. If He had not, we would be lost forever! But He did, and we are redeemed.

Thus, when we pray "God's will be done," we know that it may not aways accord with our wishes, but we also know that God does only what is best for His children's eternal welfare.

"When life's brief course on earth is run and I this world am leaving, grant me to say, 'Your will be done,' Your faithful Word believing. My dearest Friend, I now commend my soul into Your keeping; from sin and hell, and death as well, by You the vict'ry reaping." Amen. (LSB *758:4*)

OCTOBER 20

There is a time for ev'rything,
A time for all that
life may bring:
A time to plant, a time to reap,
A time to laugh, a time to weep,
A time to heal, a time to slay,
A time to build where rubble lay,
A time to die, a time to mourn,
A time for joy and to be born,

A time to hold, then be alone,
A time to gather scattered stone,
A time to break, a time to mend,
A time to search and
then to end,
A time to keep, then throw away,
A time to speak, then
nothing say,
A time for war till hatreds cease,
A time for love, a time for
peace. (*LSB* 762:1–2)

ECCLESIASTES 3 GIVES A LENGTHY LIST OF OPPOSITES, PREFACED by "For everything there is a season, and a time for every matter under heaven" (v. 1). In today's hymn, Pastor Stephen Starke paraphrases this list before providing pastoral comfort.

God understands the tragedies that affect our lives. In sadness, we are comforted that even out of evil He can "bring great good" (st. 3). We acknowledge we now see only dimly, but one day we shall see Him face to face (1 Corinthians 13:12).

"There is a time for ev'rything" is *not* a surrender to unknown forces. It is the recognition that Christ has redeemed us, and we always stand safely beneath His cross. There is a time for everything, and our times are always in the hands of our Father.

"Eternal Lord, Your wisdom sees and fathoms all life's tragedies; You know our grief, You hear our sighs—in mercy, dry our tear-stained eyes. From evil times, You bring great good; beneath the cross, we've safely stood. Though dimly now life's path we trace, one day we shall see face to face. Before all time had yet begun, You, Father, planned to give Your Son; Lord Jesus Christ, with timeless grace, You have redeemed our time-bound race; O Holy Spirit, Paraclete, Your timely work in us complete; blest Trinity, Your praise we sing—there is a time for ev'rything!" Amen. (LSB *762:3–4*)

OCTOBER 21

Through Jesus' blood and merit
I am at peace with God.
What, then, can daunt my spirit,
However dark my road?
My courage shall not fail me,
For God is on my side;
Though hell itself assail me,
Its rage I may deride.
(*LSB* 746:1)

ROMANS 8 CONCLUDES WITH A MAGNIFICENT CRESCENDO OF assurance and certainty that the Christian is never ever separated from the love of God in Christ Jesus. No matter what tragic event might occur, the believer has the ultimate victory. Today's hymn is a beautiful paraphrase of Paul's words.

In our earthly lives, there can be darkness and tragedy. The hymn writer mentions famine, peril, and flood. We are all too familiar with the events chronicled in each day's broadcast and printed news: weather-related catastrophes, wars, and humankind's cruelty to fellow humans.

Beyond such events in the world, there are the assaults of the devil and his temptations. But we know that "God is on my side," that He has given us the ultimate victory through the blood of His Son, Jesus Christ. The devil will not win; death will not have the last word. "We are more than conquerors through Him who loved us" (Romans 8:37).

The hymn writer concludes with the remarkable truth that "long before creation," God "named me His child and heir" (st. 4). God "chose us in Him before the foundation of the world" (Ephesians 1:4). His eternal love provides us the assurance that nothing in all creation "will be able to separate us from the love of God in Christ Jesus our Lord" (Romans 8:39).

"For neither life's temptation nor death's most trying hour nor angels of high station nor any other pow'r nor things that now are present nor things that are to come nor height, however pleasant, nor darkest depths of gloom nor any creature ever shall from the love of God this ransomed sinner sever; for in my Savior's blood this love has its foundation; God hears my faithful prayer and long before creation named me His child and heir." Amen. (LSB *746:3–4*)

OCTOBER 22

Thy strong word did cleave the darkness;
At Thy speaking it was done.
For created light we thank Thee,
While Thine ordered seasons run.
Alleluia, alleluia!
Praise to Thee who light dost send!
Alleluia, alleluia!
Alleluia without end! (*LSB* 578:1)

IN THE BEGINNING." THE BOOK OF GENESIS OPENS WITH THOSE words. God's first act in the beginning was to create *light*. He used words to speak light into existence and then separated it from darkness.

The Gospel of John begins with those same three words. John tells us that the *Word*—Christ—was present at creation. Then, in God's time, that Word became incarnate and entered this world as "the true light" (John 1:9). He came because we—the crown of His creation—live in the darkness of sin. We desperately need the light of His salvation.

This Word "bespeaks us righteous" (st. 3), making us bright with His holiness. Thus, when God looks at us, He sees not the darkness of our sin but the brightness that is ours through the light of Christ. From His "cross forever beameth all Thy bright redeeming light" (st. 4). That light saves us.

God has sent the true light that accomplishes our salvation. Our response is to *proclaim* this mercy by speaking His holy name, shouting the hope that fills us, and singing His glory.

"Give us lips to sing Thy glory, tongues Thy mercy to proclaim, throats that shout the hope that fills us, mouths to speak Thy holy name. Alleluia, alleluia! May the light which Thou dost send fill our songs with alleluias, alleluias without end!" Amen. (LSB *578:5*)

OCTOBER 23

All that the mortal eye beholds
Is water as we pour it.
Before the eye of faith unfolds
The pow'r of Jesus' merit.
For here it sees the crimson flood
To all our ills bring healing;
The wonders of His precious blood
The love of God revealing,
Assuring His own pardon. (***LSB*** **406:7)**

O*F THE VARIOUS FIGURES THAT WE ENCOUNTER SURROUNDING* the birth of Jesus, Simeon is one of the most fascinating. The Holy Spirit had revealed that "he would not see death before he had seen the Lord's Christ" (Luke 2:26). We can only imagine how he might have waited year after year, wondering if this day might be the one where he would see the fulfillment of God's promise. Forty days after Jesus' birth, Mary and Joseph brought Jesus to the temple in obedience to the Law of Moses. At last, Simeon could see with his own eyes the Christ: "Lord, now You are letting Your servant depart in peace, according to Your word; for my eyes have seen Your salvation" (Luke 2:29–30). What a unique blessing God granted to Simeon!

Often, we sing Simeon's song at the close of the Lord's Supper, where we receive Christ's true body and blood. We don't see Christ's body and blood "in, with, and under" (Small Catechism, Question 352) the earthly elements of bread and wine. But the Holy Spirit has given us *eyes of faith*, by which we know that we are receiving Christ's body and blood for the forgiveness of our sins. The same is true for Holy Baptism. As Luther states in his baptismal hymn, "all that the mortal eye beholds is water." But with the "eye of faith," we see God's power in working "His own pardon"—for the forgiveness of our sins, for the healing of our sin-induced ills. Thanks be to God for giving us eyes of faith!

"Christ Jesus brought this gift to me, my faithful Savior, whom You have made my eyes to see by Your favor. Now I know He is my life, my friend when I am dying." Amen. (LSB *938:2*)

OCTOBER 24

Today Your gate is open,
And all who enter in
Shall find a Father's welcome
And pardon for their sin.
The past shall be forgotten,
A present joy be giv'n,
A future grace be promised,
A glorious crown in
heav'n. (*LSB* 915:2)

JESUS' PARABLE OF THE PRODIGAL SON (LUKE 15:11–32) IS A beautiful illustration of God the Father's love and compassion for us. We are the children who presume to demand an inheritance from God, then receive His riches but squander them in unholy, sinful living. Essentially, we break the First Commandment by willfully having other gods. Like the son in the parable, we hit rock bottom at some point and return to the Father, hoping that He will allow us at least one of the lowest places in His household.

But then comes the great surprise. Our Father sees us "a long way off" (v. 20). He already knows our sins, and yet—in fatherly compassion and mercy—He comes out to meet and embrace us. He is the One who acts, not even waiting to hear our excuses and explanations. Moreover, He wants to *celebrate* our return and bestows on us yet more gifts from His riches, including a festive banquet!

The hymn writer places Jesus' words in beautiful perspective. God's gate is open to us, and we receive "a Father's welcome and pardon" for our sin. We are adorned in the most expensive clothing ever—the white robes earned for us by our crucified and risen Lord. Our sinful "past shall be forgotten" in favor of the "present joy" of sins forgiven and the future promise of "a glorious crown in heav'n." The compassionate Father does not dwell on the past but celebrates the return of the sinner.

He provides a banquet for us even here and now—the very body and blood of Jesus for the forgiveness of sins, a foretaste of that eternal banquet to come!

"Today our Father calls us; His Holy Spirit waits; His blessed angels gather around the heav'nly gates. No question will be asked us how often we have come; although we oft have wandered, it is our Father's home." Amen. (LSB *915:3*)

OCTOBER 25

What God ordains is always good:
His will is just and holy.
As He directs my life for me,
I follow meek and lowly.
My God indeed
In ev'ry need
Knows well how He will shield me;
To Him, then, I will yield me. (*LSB* 760:1)

EACH STANZA OF THIS HYMN BEGINS WITH THE CONFIDENT assertion "What God ordains is always good." There may be days when it is easy for us to agree with that statement—thanks be to God for such days! There may be other days when it is difficult for us to understand that what is happening in our lives is good. Times of illness, unemployment, or familial strife may cause us to wonder if, in fact, God is working for good in our lives.

The hymn writer acknowledges the troubles that will befall the child of God in this sinful world but always sees our loving God constantly caring for His children. God's hand may well send sadness, but in His own time and in His own way, He "will turn my tears to gladness" (st. 2). The Christian will experience grief, but "God gives relief, my heart with comfort filling and all my sorrow stilling" (st. 5).

But how can the hymn writer be confident? How can we be confident? We turn to God's Word: "For those who love God all things work together for good" (Romans 8:28). Nothing in all creation "will be able to separate us from the love of God in Christ Jesus our Lord" (v. 39). The Holy Spirit works faith in our hearts to believe these promises of God—promises that enable us to sing and pray "what God ordains is always good."

"What God ordains is always good: this truth remains unshaken. Though sorrow, need, or death be mine, I shall not be forsaken. I fear no harm, for with His arm He shall embrace and shield me; so to my God I yield me." Amen. (LSB *760:6*)

OCTOBER 26

When in the hour of deepest need
We know not where to look for aid;
When days and nights of anxious thought
No help or counsel yet have brought,

Then is our comfort this alone
That we may meet before Your throne;
To You, O faithful God, we cry
For rescue in our misery.
(*LSB* 615:1–2)

W*HEN ANXIETY LEADS TO SHEER MISERY, PERHAPS EVEN* despair, where do we turn in our deepest need? The hymn writer points us to the throne of our faithful God, where in prayer we may pour out all our troubles in life, our heartaches and disappointments, our deepest fears, and especially the sins that haunt us. God alone can rescue us from such ills, providing comfort and solace in the day-to-day struggles of life in a fallen world, and forgiveness for sins that trouble the conscience and thereby affect our daily lives: "For I know my transgressions, and my sin is ever before me" (Psalm 51:3).

In fact, our *deepest* need is forgiveness of sins. We come before God's throne in the name of Jesus, "our Savior and our advocate" (st. 3). We pray that through His "boundless grace" (st. 5) we would be absolved of our sins and freed from every ill. Christ's forgiveness wipes away our deepest fears and anguish and frees us to live lives of service to our neighbor. We don't spend our days in a fruitless attempt to figure out how we might make ourselves right with God, which is what Paul warned against: "Work out your own salvation with fear and trembling" (Philippians 2:12). No, it is God who works in us, who richly and daily meets our *deepest need* for full and free forgiveness. Thanks be to God!

"O from our sins, Lord, turn Your face; absolve us through Your boundless grace. Be with us in our anguish still; free us at last from ev'ry ill. So we with all our hearts each day to You our glad thanksgiving pay, then walk obedient to Your Word, and now and ever praise You, Lord." Amen. (LSB *615:5–6*)

OCTOBER 27

Who trusts in God
A strong abode
In heav'n and earth possesses;
Who looks in love
To Christ above,
No fear that heart oppresses.
In You alone,
Dear Lord, we own
Sweet hope and consolation,
Our shield from foes,
Our balm for woes,
Our great and sure
salvation. (*LSB* 714:1)

W***HEN JESUS WAS CRUCIFIED, THE CHIEF PRIESTS, SCRIBES,*** and elders mocked Him, saying, "He trusts in God; let God deliver Him now, if He desires Him. For He said, 'I am the Son of God'" (Matthew 27:43). Those who mocked Jesus knew their Scriptures—Psalm 37:5 says, "Commit your way to the LORD; trust in Him, and He will act." They may have reasoned that if Jesus was truly the Son of God, surely His trust in God would result in God taking action to save His Son. But God's plan for our salvation required the death of His beloved Son.

We place *our* trust in Jesus' atoning death and resurrection. With the hymn writer, we believe and proclaim that whoever trusts in Christ possesses a strong abode, both here and in heaven. We live without fear, for we know that in Christ we are kept safely from our foes, and we are granted balm for our woes in this world—whether sickness, suffering, economic want, or despair. Jesus is our consolation in all troubles, and our hope in all circumstances. Most of all, He is "our great and sure salvation." With the prophet Isaiah, we believe and confess, "Behold, God is my salvation; I will trust, and will not be afraid" (12:2). We do not fear, for "Your strength will never fail us" (st. 2) and nothing will ever "separate us from the love of God in Christ Jesus our Lord" (Romans 8:39).

"Though Satan's wrath beset our path and worldly scorn assail us, while You are near, we shall not fear; Your strength will never fail us. Your rod and staff will keep us safe and guide our steps forever; nor shades of death nor hell beneath our lives from You will sever." Amen. (LSB 714:2)

OCTOBER 28

Though devils all the world should fill,
All eager to devour us,
We tremble not, we fear no ill;
They shall not overpow'r us.
This world's prince may still
Scowl fierce as he will,
He can harm us none.
He's judged; the deed is done;
One little word can fell him. (*LSB* 656:3)

AFTER HIS BAPTISM, JESUS ENDURED A FORTY-DAY PERIOD OF fasting in the desert. When the devil came to Him, offering to turn stones into bread, that must have been a great temptation for a starving man. But our Lord answered the devil by pointing to something more sustaining than food: "It is written, 'Man shall not live by bread alone, but by every word that comes from the mouth of God'" (Matthew 4:4). In his hymn "A Mighty Fortress Is Our God," Luther also points us to the Word: "The Word they still shall let remain" (st. 4), the Word of God proclaiming the great truth that Jesus fights for us; He is "the valiant One, whom God Himself elected" (st. 2). On our own, we can't win the battle against sin, death, and the devil, but Jesus has won the victory for us.

Jesus tells us in no uncertain terms that the devil is real: "He is a liar and the father of lies" (John 8:44). In today's hymn, Luther also acknowledges the power of the devil in stanza 1 ("on earth is not his equal") but in stanza 3 observes that "one little word can fell him [the devil]." We want to know—what is that one little word? Elsewhere in his voluminous writings, Luther brands the devil a "liar," that one little word being precisely the same one Jesus used to label the devil.

Thanks be to God that Jesus "holds the field forever" (st. 2). "The Kingdom ours remaineth" (st. 4).

"With might of ours can naught be done, soon were our loss effected; but for us fights the valiant One, whom God Himself elected. Ask ye, Who is this? Jesus Christ it is, of Sabaoth Lord, and there's none other God; He holds the field forever." Amen. (LSB 656:2)

OCTOBER 29

**We are God's house of living stones,
Built for His own habitation.
He through baptismal grace us owns
Heirs of His wondrous salvation.
Were we but two his name to tell,
Yet He would deign with us to dwell
With all His grace and His favor.** (*LSB* 645:3)

IN TODAY'S HYMN, GOD'S CHILDREN ARE PICTURED AS LIVING STONES. And while we are not literal stones, we are truly a habitation. Yes, God's children are a holy habitation where the triune God dwells and gives us His blessed name and means of grace and lives in us. And it is those means that make us living stones. We are stones who love the habitation of God's house because we know He is there with His abundant gifts. "O Lord, I love the habitation of Your house and the place where Your glory dwells" (Psalm 26:8).

This is not about brick, mortar, and stained glass. Instead, this holy habitation is about Jesus' words: "I know My own and My own know Me" (John 10:14). Wherever two or more of His own are gathered in His name, He promises to be among them with His gifts of grace and favor. This is His Bride.

So, this hymn paints a picture of "the church" very different from how most think of church; yet this hymn's image is spot-on accurate and stunningly beautiful. For in this holy habitation, we taste and see that our Lord is good, see Him face to face, and then leave with His peace.

"Grant, then, O God, Your will be done, that, when the church bells are ringing, many in saving faith may come where Christ His message is bringing: 'I know My own; My own know Me. You, not the world, My face shall see. My peace I leave with you. Amen.'" (LSB 645:5)

OCTOBER 30

Here stands the font before our eyes,
Telling how God has received us.
The altar recalls Christ's sacrifice
And what His Supper here gives us.
Here sound the Scriptures that proclaim
Christ yesterday, today, the same,
And evermore, our Redeemer. (***LSB*** **645:4**)

IN A FEW WORDS, THE ABOVE HYMN STANZA TELLS THE COMPLETE picture of what we have been given as the baptized saints. This is an amazingly concise summary of what is important and who is doing it all. Here we see a stanza of true Gospel—His font, His Word, and His Supper all present and proclaiming Him, Jesus Christ, the same yesterday, today, tomorrow and always *for us*.

Often this marvelous stanza is lost in the big picture of rousing sung confession on Reformation Sunday. Yes, it is a gentle statement, especially compared to the typical rugged battle hymns sung that day. But a careful look shows a complete "means of grace" hymn stanza. Everything that the Reformation recovered for the church is right here—the Gospel. Behold a beautiful picture of the very means by which God has chosen to pour out His grace on His children.

As the church militant, we cannot endure life's ongoing battle against Satan and his treacherous ways without these gifts. "The Lord of hosts is with us; the God of Jacob is our fortress" (Psalm 46:11). They are armor in life's battle. They are the very means by which we live safely all our days on our way to becoming the church triumphant.

"All glory to the One who lavishes such love; the triune God in love assures our life above. His means of grace for us are gifts He loves to give; all thanks and praise for His great love by which we live!" Amen. (LSB 602:6)

OCTOBER 31

Preserve Your Word, O Savior,
To us this latter day,
And let Your kingdom flourish;
Enlarge Your Church, we pray.
O keep our faith from failing;
Keep hope's bright star aglow.
Let nothing from truth turn us
While living here
below. (*LSB* 658:1)

T***HERE MAY BE TIMES WHEN WE COMPLAIN ABOUT THE PRESENT*** state of the church. Beyond complaint, we may despair, wondering if our local congregations will even exist twenty or thirty years hence. The refrains are familiar—dwindling attendance, financial worries, a shortage of pastors. What are we to do? Today's hymn has an important answer: "Enlarge Your Church, we pray." The distinction is important—it is not our church but it is Christ's church. The solution is important—to pray. Our task is not to save Christ's church by our own efforts and innovative programs but rather to pray. Today's hymn teaches us how and what to pray on behalf of Christ's church on earth.

"Preserve Your Word and preaching, the truth that makes us whole" (st. 4). The Word of God—read, preached, sung—is truth. As Jesus prayed to His Father, "Sanctify them in the truth; Your word is truth" (John 17:17). Through the prophet Isaiah, God promises, "So shall My word be that goes out from My mouth; it shall not return to Me empty, but it shall accomplish that which I purpose, and shall succeed in the thing for which I sent it" (55:11). God's Word is truth, and it is all sufficient.

We also pray "keep our faith from failing; keep hope's bright star aglow." That is the antidote to complaint and despair. Jesus' clear words to Peter's confession that Jesus is "the Christ, the Son of the living God" (Matthew 16:16) will bolster us in faith and hope: "I will build My church, and the gates of hell shall not prevail against it" (v. 18).

"Preserve Your Word and preaching, the truth that makes us whole, the mirror of Your glory, the pow'r that saves the soul. Oh, may this living water, this dew of heav'nly grace, sustain us while here living until we see Your face." Amen. (LSB 658:4)

NOVEMBER 1

The golden evening brightens in the west;
Soon, soon to faithful warriors cometh rest;
Sweet is the calm of paradise the blest.
Alleluia! Alleluia!

But, lo, there breaks a yet more glorious day:
The saints triumphant rise in bright array;
The King of Glory passes on His way.
Alleluia! Alleluia! (***LSB*** **677:6–7)**

A GLORIOUS, GOLDEN SUNSET IN THE WESTERN SKY IS A BEAUTIFUL aspect of God's creation. Such a sunset ushers in the night and a time of sleep and rest. The hymn writer uses that picture as a way for us to understand what happens when "faithful warriors"—God's saints, our loved ones—die. The immortal soul of that saint is given a rest unlike anything we have ever experienced in this life—a rest in "the calm of paradise the blest." That is precisely what Jesus promised to the penitent man crucified next to Him: "Truly, I say to you, today you will be with Me in paradise" (Luke 23:43). We don't know exactly what that time of rest will be like—nor do we need to. We know that we will be in the presence of our Savior, and that is sufficient.

But as wonderful as that prospect is, the hymn writer tells us the rest of the story: "There breaks a yet more glorious day: The saints triumphant rise in bright array"! On the Last Day, when Jesus, "the King of Glory," returns, the saints will rise bodily from death. Glorified, perfect bodies will be reunited with the souls that already enjoyed the rest of paradise! Then, as the prophet Job once testified, "In my flesh I shall see God, whom I shall see for myself, and my eyes shall behold" (19:26–27). Then the great vision of "the countless host" (st. 8) will be fulfilled: "a great multitude that no one could number, from every nation, from all tribes and peoples and languages, standing before the throne and before the Lamb" (Revelation 7:9).

"From earth's wide bounds, from ocean's farthest coast, through gates of pearl streams in the countless host, singing to Father, Son, and Holy Ghost: Alleluia! Alleluia!" Amen. (LSB 677:8)

NOVEMBER 2

Behold a host, arrayed in white,
Like thousand snow-clad mountains bright!
With palms they stand;
Who is this band
Before the throne of light?
These are the saints of glorious fame,
Who from the great affliction came
And in the flood
Of Jesus' blood
Are cleansed from guilt and shame.
They now serve God both day and night;
They sing their songs in endless light.
Their anthems ring
As they all sing
With angels shining bright. (*LSB* 676:1)

IN THE BOOK OF REVELATION, WE ARE GRANTED A WONDERFUL AND comforting vision of a multitude of saints "that no one could number," gathered around the throne of God "and before the Lamb"—namely, Jesus (7:9–17). They are clothed in white robes—perfectly clean and spotless—because they have washed their robes in the purifying blood of the Lamb. The hymn writer adds yet another comparison to help us understand this grand vision of eternity: This great host of saints in white is "like thousand snow-clad mountains bright!" In our mind's eye, we can picture a soaring mountain peak so high that it is perpetually covered in white snow. Perhaps we could even picture adjacent peaks. But one thousand? As far as the eye can see, and beyond?

By faith, we grasp this grand vision of unnumbered saints before God's throne. By faith, we look more closely, and we see our departed loved ones who have gone before us to the paradise that Jesus promised from the cross. Yes, our loved ones are among those who have been "cleansed from guilt and shame." Our loved ones are part of that grand heavenly choir and "sing their songs in endless light." They are before the throne of God and the Lamb, in perpetual light, and they are *singing*—a heavenly music that one day we, too, shall join!

"Unnumbered choirs before the shining throne their joyful anthems raise till heaven's arches echo with the tone of that great hymn of praise. And all its host rejoices, and all its blessed throng unite their myriad voices in one eternal song." Amen. (LSB 674:4)

NOVEMBER 3

**Despised and scorned,
they sojourned here;
But now, how glorious
they appear!
Those martyrs stand,
A priestly band,
God's throne forever near.
On earth they wept
through bitter years;
Now God has wiped
away their tears,
Transformed their strife
To heav'nly life,
And freed them from their fears.
They now enjoy the
Sabbath rest,
The heav'nly banquet
of the blest;
The Lamb, their Lord,
At festive board
Himself is host and
guest.** (*LSB* 676:2)

I*N JOHN'S GREAT VISION OF THE SAINTS BEFORE GOD'S THRONE, HE* is told, "These are the ones coming out of the great tribulation" (Revelation 7:14). These saints may have been "despised and scorned" in their earthly lives, weeping "through bitter years." These saints are not only martyrs, some of whom may have died particularly gruesome deaths for their Christian faith. These saints before God's throne also include our loved ones, who, like Jesus, wept at the tomb of a loved one. Whether a spouse or parent who may have lived a long life, or a child taken after only a few years on this earth, the tears shed by our loved ones were a part of the "bitter years" that—at some point in life—affect all of us who live in this sinful, fallen world.

One of the most striking passages in all of Scripture is what John heard as part of this great revelation: "God will wipe away every tear from their eyes" (7:17). The saints who "now enjoy the Sabbath rest" of heaven no longer know fears or tears. They now enjoy "the heav'nly banquet of the blest," an eternity of happiness in the presence of Christ. We who are still walking this earthly life know with certainty that the day will come when God will wipe away every tear from our eyes as well. Come quickly, Lord Jesus!

"He lives to silence all my fears; He lives to wipe away my tears; He lives to calm my troubled heart; He lives all blessings to impart." Amen. (LSB 461:5)

NOVEMBER 4

Jerusalem the golden,
With milk and honey blest—
The promise of salvation,
The place of peace and rest—
We know not, oh, we know not
What joys await us there:
The radiancy of glory,
The bliss beyond compare!

Within those walls of Zion
Sounds forth the joyful song,
As saints join with the angels
And all the martyr throng.
The Prince is ever with them;
The daylight is serene;
The city of the blessed
Shines bright with glorious sheen. (*LSB* 672:1–2)

We don't know what joys await us in heaven, but, by faith, we believe that the glory and bliss of heaven will be "beyond compare." Jesus speaks of it simply as "paradise" (Luke 23:43). John, in Revelation, presents partial images from the full picture that will always elude us as time-bound mortals.

The light of heaven will be unlike anything we have ever encountered: "The city has no need of sun or moon to shine on it, for the glory of God gives it light, and its lamp is the Lamb" (Revelation 21:23). Jesus, the Lamb of God who redeemed us with His own blood, is ever-present there. The full presence of God provides light—a "glorious sheen" that defies our imagining.

Saints, angels, and martyrs all join in acclamations of glory to the God who saved us: "Blessing and glory and wisdom and thanksgiving and honor and power and might be to our God forever and ever" (Revelation 7:12). Our loved ones who died in the faith are now part of that great multitude of saints. And when we sing the Sanctus in the Divine Service, we—in a foretaste of the feast to come—join in that heavenly acclamation: "Holy, holy, holy!" We long for the day when we will sing before the throne of the Lamb and see Him face to face.

"Around the throne of David, the saints, from care released, raise loud their songs of triumph to celebrate the feast. They sing to Christ their leader, who conquered in the fight, who won for them forever their gleaming robes of white." Amen. (LSB *672:3*)

NOVEMBER 5

O sweet and blessed country,
The home of God's elect!
O sweet and blessed country
That faithful hearts expect!
In mercy, Jesus, bring us
To that eternal rest
With You and God the Father
And Spirit, ever blest. (*LSB* 672:4)

FAITHFUL HEARTS LONG FOR THEIR FUTURE HOME—"THE HOME of God's elect." Concerning their future, they believe and trust God's promises with all their heart, soul, and mind. These saints have set their minds on things above and do not doubt what is coming; theirs is a confident expectation.

Then, every year on All Saints' Sunday, these faithful hearts again hear and sing the joys of their future sweet and blessed country. On that day, all saints *love* singing about the joys of heaven. And they are reminded of their loved ones who have gone before and now dwell in the joy and rest of that sweet and blessed country. They can name many near and dear souls who now rest from their labors. And while they miss them, they cannot help but be overjoyed for the sublime peace and rest that is theirs. It is a day filled with many truths and emotions—a great day in the Church Year.

Here, the lives of loved ones may have been filled with hardship, suffering, and strife, but there is absolute confidence that God has now wiped away every tear from their eyes. On All Saints' Sunday, we are grateful and give the highest thanksgiving for the faithful witness of these blessed, dearly departed saints, now singing in the church triumphant!

"O happy day, O yet far happier hour, when will you come at last, when by my gracious Father's love and pow'r I see that portal vast? From heaven's shining regions to greet me gladly come Your blessed angel legions to bid me welcome home." Amen. (LSB 674:2)

NOVEMBER 6

Jerusalem, my happy home,
When shall I come to thee?
When shall my sorrows have an end?
Thy joys when shall I see?

O happy harbor of the saints,
O sweet and pleasant soil!
In thee no sorrow may be found,
No grief, no care, no toil. (*LSB* 673:1–2)

IMAGINE A PLACE WHERE WE EXPERIENCE NO SORROW, GRIEF, OR cares of this life. Imagine a place without sickness and without diseases of body or mind, a place where death has been eliminated. Imagine a place where toil and drudgery no longer play a role. Finally, imagine this place as the home for all the saints who have preceded us, a place where our loved ones now live anew in perfect, eternal peace. It is no wonder that our anonymous poet *longs* for the heavenly Jerusalem—as do we who pray and sing this hymn.

In the final two chapters of the book of Revelation, John gives us a picture of this heavenly Jerusalem. One of the most striking things he tells us is that this eternal city "has no need of sun or moon to shine on it, for the glory of God gives it light, and its lamp is the Lamb" (Revelation 21:23). When we dwell in the heavenly Jerusalem, we will live in the very presence of God the Father and of the Lamb—Jesus, who, through His death and resurrection, paid the price that brings us into this eternal heavenly city of unending bliss. Moreover, John adds, "They will see His face, and His name will be on their foreheads. And night will be no more" (22:4–5). Beholding God face to face is an extraordinary thought, but we don't have merely to *imagine* that, for in its closing pages God's Word gives us that promise. Thanks be to God for the blessed reality of eternal life in the light of God's face!

"O Christ, do Thou my soul prepare for that bright home of love that I may see Thee and adore with all Thy saints above." Amen. (LSB *673:6*)

NOVEMBER 7

O happy day, O yet far happier hour,
When will you come at last,
When by my gracious Father's love and pow'r
I see that portal vast?
From heaven's shining regions
To greet me gladly come
Your blessed angel legions
To bid me welcome home. (*LSB* 674:2)

PAUL WROTE IN *ROMANS* 8:19 THAT "*THE CREATION WAITS WITH* eager longing for the revealing of the sons of God," for that promised future of new and eternal life in heaven with Christ. With Paul and with the hymn writer, we long for eternal glory. The book of Revelation pictures the myriad throngs of heaven singing, "Salvation belongs to our God who sits on the throne, and to the Lamb!" (7:10). The Lamb of God, Jesus, won eternal life for us and has gone ahead to prepare a place for us, as He promises in John 14:3. That promise from our Savior is one to remember always as we journey through this life. No matter what comes our way, we remember that Jesus has already prepared a place for us!

The hymn writer stunningly pictures the believer's welcome to the heavenly home: accompanied by singing and music of such splendor and beauty that it is beyond our capability to imagine. Angels, patriarchs, prophets, all of Christ's followers constitute the heavenly choir singing "one eternal song" (st. 4) to God and to the Lamb. We yearn for that blessed day!

"The patriarchs' and prophets' noble train, with all Christ's foll'wers true, who washed their robes and cleansed sin's guilty stain, sing praises ever new! I see them shine forever, resplendent as the sun, in light diminished never, their glorious freedom won. Unnumbered choirs before the shining throne their joyful anthems raise till heaven's arches echo with the tone of that great hymn of praise. And all its host rejoices, and all its blessed throng unite their myriad voices in one eternal song." Amen. (LSB 674:3–4)

NOVEMBER 8

Saints, see the cloud of witnesses surround us;
Their lives of faith encourage and astound us.
Hear how the Master praised their faith so fervent:
"Well done, My servant!" (*LSB* 667:1)

O*NE OF THE REASONS* A*LL* S*AINTS*' S*UNDAY IS SO BELOVED BY* the faithful is that we each bring our own history to church. We walk in the door thinking of our fathers, mothers, children, or spouses—and we miss them. It is a tough day, but it is a good kind of difficult day. Yes, there may be more tears on this Sunday than on all other Sundays combined, but on this day, these tears are sadness and joy mixed in a happy combination as we sing together of what our loved ones now have.

As saints, a cloud of witnesses surrounds us, those who have gone before us, whose lives of faith continue to inspire and amaze us. On All Saints' Sunday, we come together to remember these faithful saints who have heard their Master say, "Well done, My servant!" And as we gather, we also look ahead, for we are still in our heavenly race, eagerly awaiting the day when we will leave behind the church militant, join the church triumphant, and hear our Lord's words of commendation.

The faith and lives of our cloud of witnesses, including Abel, Enoch, Noah, Abraham, Moses, and many others, are a source of great inspiration and encouragement on our pilgrimage. Their accounts, as told in Hebrews 11, continue to instruct and amaze us. They are now the glorious church triumphant, showing us our promised inheritance and future.

"O sweet and blessed country, the home of God's elect! O sweet and blessed country that faithful hearts expect! In mercy, Jesus, bring us to that eternal rest with You and God the Father and Spirit ever blest." Amen. (LSB 672:4)

NOVEMBER 9

These saints of old received God's commendation;
They lived as pilgrim-heirs of His salvation.
Through faith they conquered flame and sword and gallows,
God's name to hallow.

They call to us, "Your timid footsteps lengthen;
Throw off sin's weight, your halting weakness strengthen.
We kept the faith, we shed our blood, were martyred;
Our lives we bartered." (*LSB* 667:2–3)

T*HE CLOUD OF WITNESSES BEFORE TODAY'S FAITHFUL SAINTS IS* a vast and formidable assembly that stretches back to the earliest days of Christ's church. It certainly did not look like His apostles were conquering as they were being put to death by stones and swords, flayed and beheaded, burned at the stake, and crucified upside down or on an X-shaped cross. Yet that was what our Lord's first apostles willingly suffered as they hallowed His name. They were faithful disciples who took up their cross and followed their Master, not weighing the cost.

Discipleship in our Lord's kingdom is not easy, but it is a blessed road. "Blessed are those who are persecuted for righteousness' sake, for theirs is the kingdom of heaven" (Matthew 5:10). We have been told and firmly believe that the cost of discipleship is nothing compared to the reward; "Rejoice and be glad, for your reward is great in heaven, for so they persecuted the prophets who were before you" (Matthew 5:12). As today's faithful saints, we are pilgrims through this land with our eyes set on the great reward of heaven—and along the way, the finest food of Word and Sacraments sustains us well in our heavenly race.

"The patriarchs' and prophets' noble train, with all Christ's foll'wers true, who washed their robes and cleansed sin's guilty stain, sing praises ever new! I see them shine forever, resplendent as the sun, in light diminished never, their glorious freedom won." Amen. (LSB 674:3)

NOVEMBER 10

Come, let us fix our sight on Christ who suffered,
He faced the cross, His sinless life He offered;
He scorned the shame, He died, our death enduring,
Our hope securing. (*LSB* 667:4)

IN THE BLESSED KINGDOM OF OUR LORD JESUS CHRIST, THE FAITHFUL saints have eyes fixed on Him alone, "Looking to Jesus, the founder and perfecter of our faith, who for the joy that was set before Him endured the cross, despising the shame" (Hebrews 12:2). For He alone is the one who secured life, salvation, and hope through His sinless life, suffering, and death for His saints. Today's stanza delves into the wonders of what God, in His love, has done.

During the Lenten season, it is common for choirs to sing arrangements of the Lenten gradual verse, "O come, let us fix our eyes on Jesus" (*LSB Altar Book*, p. 579).This practice is appropriate and salutary in preparing hearts and minds to ponder the Passion of our Lord once again. Indeed, fixing our sight on Jesus Christ and His suffering for sinners rightly defines those most holy days.

Yet the saints, in their unwavering faith, keep their eyes fixed on Jesus—not only in Lent but all the days and seasons of each new year of grace—and their beautiful eyes of faith are focused on their heavenly home, where they eagerly anticipate living with their Savior forever. Meanwhile, their earthly days are filled with the hope and trust that He will bring them safely into His glorious church triumphant!

"Lord, when Your glory I shall see and taste Your kingdom's pleasure, Your blood my royal robe shall be, my joy beyond all measure! When I appear before Your throne, Your righteousness shall be my crown; with these I need not hide me. And there, in garments richly wrought, as Your own bride shall we be brought to stand in joy beside You." Amen. (LSB 438:4)

NOVEMBER 11

Lord, give us faith to walk where You are sending,
On paths unmarked, eyes blind as to their ending;
Not knowing where we go, but that You lead us—
With grace precede us. (*LSB* 667:5)

I*N THE HYMN THAT WE HAVE BEEN CONSIDERING THE PAST FEW* days, Pastor Stephen Starke provides a beautiful sung paraphrase of a well-loved prayer "for guidance in our calling" (*LSB*, p. 311). We acknowledge that we don't know what the future holds for each of us—our eyes are "blind" to what will happen today, tomorrow, and in all the days of our lives. The Lord does not present us with a detailed map or plan to reveal all that He has in store for us over a lifetime. What a blessing that is! We simply await His direction, His guidance through a lifetime that will bring both joys and sorrows. We don't know precisely where we will be going or what we will be doing, but we know that the Lord will lead us in the ways that He knows are best for us.

The closing poetic line of this hymn stanza is so important: "With grace precede us." When God's grace precedes, we may proceed in confidence. For we know that His grace is sufficient for us (2 Corinthians 12:9) and that it is His grace alone that takes care of our greatest need, forgiveness of sins. His grace alone opens the door to eternal life. Thus, we know our ultimate destination, and we pray for faith as we journey through life toward "the upward call of God in Christ Jesus" (Philippians 3:14).

As Pastor Starke states so beautifully, "our lives unfold, embraced within Your story" (st. 6). Our futures unfold according to our Lord's wisdom, the Lord who is "the same yesterday and today and forever" (Hebrews 13:8). Our lives are in His hands; He gives us "a future and a hope" (Jeremiah 29:11).

"You, Jesus, You alone deserve all glory! Our lives unfold, embraced within Your story; past, present, future—You, the same forever—You fail us never!" Amen. (LSB 667:6)

NOVEMBER 12

Sing with all the saints in glory,
Sing the resurrection song!
Death and sorrow, earth's dark story,
To the former days belong.
All around the clouds are breaking;
Soon the storms of time shall cease;
In God's likeness we awaken,
Knowing everlasting peace. (*LSB* 671:1)

God has promised, Christ prepares it; there on high our welcome waits" (st. 2). The hymn writer perfectly captures these most comforting words of Jesus: "And if I go and prepare a place for you, I will come again and will take you to Myself, that where I am you may be also" (John 14:3). When we die, we will be welcomed to our eternal home, which Christ won for us through His atoning death and resurrection. His resurrection will be our resurrection, His home our home, His life our life—forever. For that reason, we sing the resurrection song and shout for joy!

Before we sing the Sanctus ("Holy, holy, holy") in the Divine Service, we hear these remarkable words of the Proper Preface: "Therefore with angels and archangels and *with all the company of heaven* we laud and magnify Your glorious name, evermore praising You" (emphasis added). Thus, even here and now, while still on our earthly pilgrimage, we are privileged to join the saints in heaven in their ceaseless hymn of praise: "Holy, holy, holy, is the Lord God Almighty, who was and is and is to come!" (Revelation 4:8).

To sing the resurrection song is to sing of Jesus, "the resurrection and the life" (John 11:25). It is to sing of His saving acts that will ultimately consign death and sorrow to a long-forgotten past, never to be remembered or repeated in the joys of eternal life with Christ.

"Oh, what glory, far exceeding all that eye has yet perceived! Holiest hearts for ages pleading never that full joy conceived. God has promised, Christ prepares it; there on high our welcome waits. Ev'ry humble spirit shares it, Christ has passed the eternal gates." Amen. (LSB 671:2)

NOVEMBER 13

Our hope and expectation,
O Jesus, now appear;
Arise, O Sun so longed for,
O'er this benighted sphere.
With hearts and hands uplifted,
We plead, O Lord, to see
The day of earth's redemption
That sets Your people free! (*LSB* 515:4)

IN JESUS' PARABLE OF THE TEN VIRGINS* (*MATTHEW 25:1–13*), *THE Bridegroom is Christ Himself, and the wedding feast is eternal life in His presence, an unending feast of perfect bliss and happiness in heaven. As the ten virgins eagerly awaited the appearance of the bridegroom and the wedding feast, so also we eagerly await the second coming of Christ and the fullness of eternal life. In today's hymn, we pray that Jesus would appear again on earth; after all, He is "our hope and expectation," the one we long for! The hymn writer speaks of Jesus' second coming as "the day of earth's redemption that sets Your people free." On that Last Day, our resurrected bodies will be freed from the power of death; bodies and souls will be reunited, and with our very own eyes we will see our Redeemer in all His glory.

Through the Word of God, and by a Spirit-worked faith, we believe that there will be this Last Day when Christ comes again to take us to Himself. But do we *plead* for that day to arrive, do we *pray* that Jesus will come in final judgment and bring us into the eternal glory that is ours through His death and resurrection? When—by God's grace—our earthly lives are going along reasonably well, we may neglect to pray today's hymn-prayer. But we have only to think about "cross and suff'rings"—whether ours or those of our loved ones—to remind ourselves that, yes, we long to "live and reign forever when sorrow is no more" (st. 3). Come, Lord Jesus!

"The saints, who here in patience their cross and suff'rings bore, shall live and reign forever when sorrow is no more. Around the throne of glory the Lamb they shall behold; in triumph cast before Him their diadems of gold." Amen. (LSB *515:3*)

NOVEMBER 14

The clouds of judgment gather,
The time is growing late;
Be sober and be watchful,
Our judge is at the gate:
The judge who comes in mercy,
The judge who comes in might
To put an end to evil
And diadem the right. (*LSB* 513:1)

In the parable of the ten virgins, Jesus tells us to be like the five wise virgins—ready to meet the Bridegroom. "Watch therefore, for you know neither the day nor the hour" (Matthew 25:13). When Jesus, the Bridegroom, returns, He will separate believers and unbelievers (Matthew 25:31–46). Thus, the day of judgment is a terrible prospect for unbelievers. But for believers, it is the culmination of life in Christ; it is eternal life bestowed by Christ.

Jesus told us that there will be signs of the end times and "people fainting with fear and with foreboding of what is coming on the world" (Luke 21:26). That may sound scary, but what does our Savior tell us? "Now when these things begin to take place, straighten up and raise your heads, because your redemption is drawing near" (v. 28). Don't cower in fear; stand up straight and look to the heavens, where you will see "the Son of Man coming in a cloud" (v. 27). The Bridegroom is coming to claim His Bride, the church.

Judgment Day is our redemption day. As the hymn writer says, our Judge comes "in mercy"! Our Savior comes "to put an end to evil," to fulfill a new reality of eternal joy and peace in His presence. The hymn writer describes this new reality as our "home of fadeless splendor" (st. 3), of peace and calm, a home that is the sweetest and the best. The clouds of judgment here give way to the splendor of eternal light there!

"The home of fadeless splendor, of blooms that bear no thorn, where they shall dwell as children who here as exiles mourn; the peace of all the faithful, the calm of all the blest, inviolate, unfading, divinest, sweetest, best." Amen. (LSB *513:3*)

NOVEMBER 15

You are the way;
through You alone
Can we the Father find;
In You, O Christ, has
God revealed
His heart and will and mind.

You are the truth;
Your Word alone
True wisdom can impart;
You only can inform the mind
And purify the heart.

You are the life; the empty tomb
Proclaims Your conqu'ring arm,
And those who put
their trust in You
Not death nor hell shall
harm. (*LSB* 526:1–3)

IT MAY BE ONE OF JESUS' MOST MEMORABLE SAYINGS: "I AM THE way, and the truth, and the life. No one comes to the Father except through Me" (John 14:6). Today's hymn functions rather like the brief answers in Luther's Small Catechism: "What does this mean" that Jesus is the way, and the truth, and the life?

Jesus declares that He is the only *way* we come to God the Father. Jesus is the way God has "revealed His heart and will and mind." As Paul tells us, "He is the image of the invisible God" (Colossians 1:15). He is revealed to us through His perfect life, Passion, death, and resurrection, which provide us the only way to God.

Jesus is the *truth*, for His Word alone is true wisdom for our hearts and minds. In His High Priestly Prayer to the Father, Jesus shows His high regard for the truth of God's Word: "Sanctify them in the truth; Your word is truth" (John 17:17).

Jesus is the *life*, meaning that, through His work, He has given us eternal life. He defeated death on the cross and at the empty tomb. "Those who put their trust in You not death nor hell shall harm." Because Jesus is the life—our life—we are freed from death and hell and from any worry or fear about our life after death. Jesus has provided all we need.

"You are the way, the truth, the life; grant us that way to know, that truth to keep, that life to win whose joys eternal flow." Amen. (LSB 526:4)

NOVEMBER 16

Your hand, O Lord,
in days of old
Was strong to heal and save;
It triumphed over ills and death,
O'er darkness and the grave.
To You they came, the
blind, the mute,
The palsied and the lame,
The lepers in their misery,
The sick with fevered frame.

Your touch then, Lord,
brought life and health,
Gave speech and
strength and sight;
And youth renewed
and frenzy calmed
Revealed You, Lord of light.
And now, O Lord, be
near to bless,
Almighty as before,
In crowded street, by
beds of pain,
As by Gennes'ret's
shore. (*LSB* 846:1–2)

ALL FOUR OF THE GOSPEL WRITERS RECORD ACCOUNTS OF JESUS as healer. Luke, for example, wrote, "In that hour He healed many people of diseases and plagues and evil spirits, and on many who were blind He bestowed sight" (7:21). Perhaps we sometimes wish that Jesus walked our streets so that He could place His hands on us and our loved ones, granting healing from diseases that even modern medicine in all its sophistication and advancements cannot fully cure.

But in today's hymn-prayer we ask, "O Lord, be near to bless, almighty as before." In His great love for us, Jesus is still our healer. He hears our every plea for healing and works for our good according to His gracious will. He guides the hands of physicians and nurses, whose skills are gifts given to them—and to us—by His great love.

In addition, God has provided the ultimate healing that we so desperately need—forgiveness of sins. "By His wounds you have been healed" (1 Peter 2:24). Whether our lives be long or short, whether afflicted by pain or disease, we know with certainty God will grant us full healing in the perfection of resurrection and eternal life with Him.

"O be our great deliv'rer still, the Lord of life and death; restore and quicken, soothe and bless, with Your life-giving breath. To hands that work and eyes that see give wisdom's healing pow'r that whole and sick and weak and strong may praise You evermore." Amen. (LSB *846:3*)

NOVEMBER 17

Lord Jesus Christ, with us abide,
For round us falls the eventide.
O let Your Word, that saving light,
Shine forth undimmed into the night.

In these last days of great distress
Grant us, dear Lord, true steadfastness
That we keep pure till life is spent
Your holy Word and Sacrament. (*LSB* 585:1–2)

TODAY'S HYMN FOCUSES ON GOD'S WORD, EACH STANZA proclaiming some version of that means of grace: "Your Word," "Your holy Word," "Your mighty Word" (st. 4), or "Your truth" (st. 5). That kind of remarkable thematic consistency is appropriately applied to the priceless gift that is God's written Word for His people. "The word of God is living and active" (Hebrews 4:12), always accomplishing God's purposes and succeeding "in the thing for which I sent it" (Isaiah 55:11c).

In this hymn, we pray for ourselves. May God's Word abide with us as night approaches—not only the darkness of each evening but also the darkness caused by sin, fear, despair, illness, affliction, and trouble, as well as the darkness of death. God's Word is the "saving light" that will see us through all such darkness, giving us the assurance of God's redeeming love for us in Christ and His ultimate promise that "you will be with Me in paradise" (Luke 23:43).

In this hymn, we also pray for the church, that it would "be strong, bold, unified in act and song" (st. 4). When we pray that God's "Word of saving grace" would shine "into each dark and loveless place" (st. 3), we are praying that the church may always be found faithful in preaching God's Word, the Holy Spirit working powerfully—with God's promise that His Word "shall not return to Me empty" (Isaiah 55:11b).

"May glorious truths that we have heard, the bright sword of Your mighty Word, spurn Satan that Your Church be strong, bold, unified in act and song. Stay with us, Lord, and keep us true; preserve our faith our whole life through—Your Word alone our heart's defense, the Church's glorious confidence." Amen. (LSB 585:4, 6)

NOVEMBER 18

Lord Jesus Christ, be present now;
Our hearts in true devotion bow.
Your Spirit send with light divine,
And let Your truth within us shine.

Unseal our lips to sing Your praise
In endless hymns through all our days.
Increase our faith and light our minds;
And set us free from doubt that blinds. (*LSB* 902:1–2)

THIS SHORT HYMN PROVIDES A RICHNESS OF PETITIONS FOR DAILY prayer. We begin by pleading, "Lord Jesus Christ, be present now," for He has promised to be with us always, "to the end of the age" (Matthew 28:20). We ask further that He would send the Holy Spirit, who—He has promised—will guide us "into all the truth" (John 16:13). God's "word is truth" (John 17:17), showing us Jesus, who is "the light of the world" and "the light of life" (John 8:12).

For the great gift of Christ's presence—our light and life and salvation—it is right that we sing His praise and give thanks. But precisely there we must ask yet another petition—that the Holy Spirit would "unseal our lips." It is an important truth that we don't always think about; of our own accord we cannot praise God. Thus, with the psalmist, we must ask, "O Lord, open my lips, and my mouth will declare Your praise" (51:15).

In further petitions, we plead that God would "increase our faith" and "set us free from doubt." We ask that we might heed Jesus' words to the disciple Thomas: "Do not disbelieve, but believe" (John 20:27).

We pray these petitions both for our living and for our dying. For our living, that we may enjoy the fullness of Christ's presence and the gifts of the Holy Spirit throughout our lives. For our dying, that Jesus would bring us to that blessed place that He has prepared for us, that we may spend an eternity seeing our Savior face to face.

"Then shall we join the hosts that cry, 'O holy, holy Lord Most High!' And in the light of that blest place we then shall see You face to face." Amen. (LSB *902:3*)

NOVEMBER 19

O Holy Spirit, enter in,
And in our hearts
Your work begin,
Your dwelling place
now make us.
Sun of the soul, O Light divine,
Around and in us brightly shine,
To joy and gladness wake us
That we may be
Truly living,
To You giving
Prayer unceasing
And in love be still
increasing. (*LSB* 913:1)

When Jesus promised the Holy Spirit to His disciples, He spoke of Him as "the Helper, the Holy Spirit, whom the Father will send in My name, He will teach you all things and bring to your remembrance all that I have said to you" (John 14:26). We might well imagine that the disciples were relieved to hear this, for often they were slow to understand Jesus' teachings. The Spirit, who would teach them and help them to remember all that Jesus had told them, would be essential to their lives after Jesus would complete His redemptive work here and then return to His Father in heaven.

It is the same with us. We pray that the Holy Spirit would continue to teach us and help us to remember Jesus' life-giving words. As we confess in Luther's explanation of the Third Article of the Creed, it is the Holy Spirit who calls us by the Gospel, enlightens us with His gifts, and keeps us in the true faith. We cannot do any of this by our own choice or will. It is the Holy Spirit who works faith in our hearts through the power of God's Word.

Thus, we pray that the Holy Spirit, the "Source of life" (st. 3), would work through the Word to teach us true wisdom and keep us faithful unto death. May God grant it!

"O mighty Rock, O Source of life, let Your dear Word, in doubt and strife, in us be strongly burning that we be faithful unto death and live in love and holy faith, from You true wisdom learning. Your grace and peace on us shower; by Your power Christ confessing, let us see our Savior's blessing." Amen. (LSB *913:3*)

NOVEMBER 20

"Wake, awake, for night is flying,"
The watchmen on the heights are crying;
"Awake, Jerusalem, arise!"
Midnight hears the welcome voices
And at the thrilling cry rejoices:
"Oh, where are ye, ye virgins wise?
The Bridegroom comes, awake!
Your lamps with gladness take!
Alleluia!
With bridal care
Yourselves prepare
To meet the Bridegroom, who is near." (*LSB* 516:1)

MATTHEW 25 CALLS US YEARLY WITH ITS URGENT THEME, echoed here in this hymn by Philipp Nicolai: "With bridal care yourselves prepare." And how do we do that? How do we stay awake with enough oil as we await our Bridegroom, "who is near"? The answer is found in the definition of *oil*. Oil is the faith and love that Jesus wants to find in the hearts of those claiming to be His waiting Bride. Along the way, our patient and loving Bridegroom has promised to keep the faith and love of His dear Bride strong and healthy through His Word and Sacraments.

Jesus needs His whole church to be awake and dressed in the breastplate of faith and love at His return. And because all are not presently ready and dressed in this breastplate, our Lord is delaying His arrival. He is waiting and we are waiting, but this time of grace will have an end. And at midnight, a lack of oil will not be able to be fixed—it will be too late. Hence, the urgency of this Matthew 25 text and this hymn. "Awake, Jerusalem, arise!"

"Lord, when Your glory I shall see and taste Your kingdom's pleasure, Your blood my royal robe shall be, my joy beyond all measure! When I appear before Your throne, Your righteousness shall be my crown; with these I need not hide me. And there, in garments richly wrought, as Your own bride shall we be brought to stand in joy beside You." Amen. (LSB *438:4*)

NOVEMBER 21

Zion hears the watchmen singing,
And all her heart with joy is springing;
She wakes, she rises from her gloom.
For her Lord comes down all-glorious,
The strong in grace, in truth victorious;
Her star is ris'n, her light is come.
Now come, Thou Blessed One,
Lord Jesus, God's own Son,
Hail! Hosanna!
We enter all
The wedding hall
To eat the Supper at Thy call. (*LSB* 516:2)

THE BRIDE OF CHRIST IS DELIGHTED TO EAT THE SUPPER AT HIS call. She lives for it and desperately needs it, for in this Supper, her Bridegroom is bodily present for her. And there, He loves to shower His gracious gifts of forgiveness and health upon her. There, He "comes down all-glorious" for her as He lives in her, giving her life.

At the end of the Church Year, Christ's Bride sings of a present-tense Supper and a future-tense supper. Yes, He is coming "down all-glorious" now to a table, but on the Last Day, He will come not on a table in body and blood but on the clouds as the Bridegroom who carries His Bride to a feast that will never end.

The overall shape of today's hymn text is a chalice. While it is unknown if the author and composer Philipp Nicolai planned that his meter and text, when centered, would picture a chalice, it is, nevertheless, a beautiful and fitting reality that it does. Every year, Zion hears the watchmen singing yet again, and every year, she gladly readies herself for her Bridegroom to come. "Amen. Come, Lord Jesus!" (Revelation 22:20).

"Feast after feast thus comes and passes by, yet, passing, points to that glad feast above, giving sweet foretaste of the festal joy, the Lamb's great marriage feast of bliss and love." Amen. (LSB *631:7*)

NOVEMBER 22

Now let all the heav'ns adore Thee,
Let saints and angels sing before Thee
With harp and cymbals' clearest tone.
Of one pearl each shining portal,
Where, joining with the choir immortal,
We gather round Thy radiant throne.
No eye has seen the light,
No ear has heard the might
Of Thy glory;
Therefore will we
Eternally
Sing hymns of praise and joy to Thee! (*LSB* 516:3)

JOHANN SEBASTIAN BACH REGARDED PHILIPP NICOLAI'S CHORALE text and tune so highly that they are featured in his Cantata 140. Most of the world knows Nicolai's chorale through Bach's memorable musical settings of this cantata.

It is miraculous and providential that Pastor Nicolai, surrounded by crushing grief and sadness when he wrote this hymn, was inspired to let all the heavens, saints, and angels, with instruments, explode in such highest joyful adoration. It is almost as if, after writing these words at the end of stanza 2—"we enter all the wedding hall to eat the Supper at Thy call"—Nicolai wished to give the singing church a stanza that would provide them with a glorious foretaste of music at the banquet feast of the Lamb.

What Nicolai crafts in this magnificent third stanza gives saints on earth a taste of breathtaking heavenly music for their days of waiting and yearning for their Bridegroom's return. "Therefore will we eternally sing hymns of praise and joy to Thee!"

"What joy to know, when life is past, the Lord we love is first and last, the end and the beginning! He will one day, oh, glorious grace, transport us to that happy place beyond all tears and sinning! Amen! Amen! Come, Lord Jesus! Crown of gladness! We are yearning for the day of Your returning!" Amen. (LSB *395:6*)

NOVEMBER 23

Lord Jesus Christ, we humbly pray
That we may feast on You today;
Beneath these forms of bread and wine
Enrich us with Your grace divine.

Give us, who share this wondrous food,
Your body broken and Your blood,
The grateful peace of sins forgiv'n,
The certain joys of heirs of heav'n. (*LSB* 623:1–2)

B*EFORE HIS SUFFERINGS AND DEATH WOULD TAKE PLACE, JESUS* assured His disciples, "I will not leave you as orphans; I will come to you" (John 14:18). After His resurrection, He did indeed come to His disciples, appearing bodily to them and inviting them to "see My hands and My feet, that it is I Myself. Touch Me, and see" (Luke 24:39). Nor does Jesus leave us as orphans, for He says the same thing to us: "I will come to you," and so He does—in His Holy Supper, instituted on the night when He was betrayed, the night before He was crucified and died for our sins.

Jesus knew that His disciples—then and now—needed His continuing presence. In addition to promising "the Helper, the Holy Spirit" (John 14:26), Jesus provided the means by which He Himself would come to us most intimately—giving us His very body and blood "for the forgiveness of sins" (Matthew 26:28).

Today's hymn speaks of this—"the grateful peace of sins forgiv'n"—but also adds a corollary statement: "the certain joys of heirs of heav'n." The Lord's Supper is our "foretaste of the feast to come" (*LSB* 955). As forgiven sinners, we will have that great joy of being our Lord's "welcomed guest in heaven's high and holy feast" (*LSB* 623:5). Jesus promised, "I tell you I will not drink again of this fruit of the vine until that day when I drink it new with you in My Father's kingdom" (Matthew 26:29). As we await that great day, we pray, "Come, Lord Jesus."

"Lord Jesus Christ, we humbly pray: O keep us steadfast till that day when each will be Your welcomed guest in heaven's high and holy feast." Amen. (LSB *623:5*)

NOVEMBER 24

O Holy Spirit, grant us grace
That we our Lord and Savior
In faith and fervent
love embrace
And truly serve Him ever.
The hour of death
cannot bring loss
When we are sheltered
by the cross
That canceled our
transgressions.

Help us that we Thy
saving Word
In faithful hearts may treasure;
Let e'er that Bread of Life afford
New grace in richest measure.
O make us die to ev'ry sin,
Each day create new life within,
That fruits of faith may
flourish. (*LSB* 693:1–2)

IN TODAY'S HYMN, WE PRAY TO GOD THE HOLY SPIRIT: "EACH DAY create new life within." It is the Holy Spirit who works faith in our hearts, thus creating that new life in us. He works through God's saving Word and the Holy Sacraments of Baptism and the Lord's Supper. Thus, we pray in this hymn that we may *treasure* God's Word, making it our daily companion on our walk through this earthly life.

When we do so, two things happen. First, the "fruits of faith may flourish." Paul defines the fruit of the Spirit as "love, joy, peace, patience, kindness, goodness, faithfulness, gentleness, self-control" (Galatians 5:22–23). The Holy Spirit works in us to manifest these fruits in our service to the neighbor.

Second, the faith worked by the Holy Spirit brings us the confidence to believe that in the hour of our death, we are not lost forever—because the redemptive work of Jesus on the cross has "canceled our transgressions" and brought us to eternal life. Thus, we pray that the Holy Spirit's work in us would "continue till life's ending," when we "commend our souls into our Savior's hand, the crown of life obtaining" (st. 3).

With the psalmist, we pray, "Take not Your Holy Spirit from me" (51:11).

"And when our earthly race is run, death's bitter hour impending, then may Thy work in us begun continue till life's ending, until we gladly may commend our souls into our Savior's hand, the crown of life obtaining." Amen. (LSB *693:3*)

NOVEMBER 25

**Come, ye thankful
people, come;
Raise the song of harvest home.
All be safely gathered in
Ere the winter storms begin;
God, our maker, doth provide
For our wants to be supplied.
Come to God's own
temple, come;
Raise the song of harvest home.**

**All the world is God's own field,
Fruit unto His praise to yield;
Wheat and tares together sown,
Unto joy or sorrow grown.
First the blade and then the ear,
Then the full corn shall appear.
Lord of harvest, grant that we
Wholesome grain and pure
may be. (*LSB* 892:1–2)**

T*HIS BELOVED THANKSGIVING HYMN IS ALSO AN END TIMES HYMN* that sings of the "final harvest home" (st. 4). "The ransomed of the LORD shall return and come to Zion with singing; everlasting joy shall be upon their heads" (Isaiah 51:11). "Gather Thou Thy people in, free from sorrow, free from sin, there, forever purified, in Thy garner to abide" (st. 4).

And as an end times hymn, it also sings of the weeds, tares, and *evil* growing up and living together with wholesome grain until the final harvest. "Wheat and tares together sown, unto joy or sorrow grown." This is a sung version of our Lord's parable of the weeds.

As a Thanksgiving hymn, it joyfully speaks of our life filled with a cornucopia of abundance and overflowing plenty—all from the good and gracious hand of God, our Maker, giving beautiful voice to the First Article of the Apostles' Creed.

What perfect singing this is for the Bride of Christ as she gathers at the end of the Church Year!

"Even so, Lord, quickly come to Thy final harvest home; gather Thou Thy people in, free from sorrow, free from sin, there, forever purified, in Thy garner to abide: Come with all Thine angels, come, raise the glorious harvest home." Amen. (LSB 892:4)

NOVEMBER 26

Now thank we all our God
With hearts and hands and voices,
Who wondrous things has done,
In whom His world rejoices;
Who from our mothers' arms
Has blest us on our way
With countless gifts of love
And still is ours today. (*LSB* 895:1)

THIS HYMN IS A FAMILIAR, EVEN EXPECTED, CHOICE ON A DAY OF thanksgiving. We are right to thank God for gifts of harvest and abundant food at this time of year. But we may always pray this hymn and in so doing recognize the poet's larger sense of thankfulness.

We pray that "this bounteous God" may be near us throughout our life, and especially that He would "keep us in His grace" (st. 2). Christ's grace came to us in Holy Baptism when we "were baptized into His death" (Romans 6:3). Paul makes clear that "if we have been united with Him in a death like His, we shall certainly be united with Him in a resurrection like His" (Romans 6:5). As God keeps us in this baptismal grace, "joyful hearts and blessed peace" (st. 2) are among His highest gifts to us, for true peace and joy come only through His grace. In Christ, we are forgiven sinners—saints who will be united with our bounteous God in a resurrection like His.

As we live our earthly lives in communion with Christ, we pray that He would "guide us when perplexed" (st. 2), directing us always back into His living Word and sustaining us with His very body and blood in His Holy Supper. He has indeed done "wondrous things" for us, and His "countless gifts of love" not only sustain us in this world but bring us to the next world, where we will live forever in His presence. Thanks be to God!

"Oh, may this bounteous God through all our life be near us, with ever joyful hearts and blessed peace to cheer us and keep us in His grace and guide us when perplexed and free us from all ills in this world and the next!" Amen. (LSB 895:2)

NOVEMBER 27

The day is surely drawing near
When Jesus, God's anointed,
In all His power shall appear
As judge whom God appointed.
Then fright shall banish idle mirth,
And flames on flames shall ravage earth
As Scripture long has warned us. (*LSB* 508:1)

As we come to the end of the Church Year, our Scripture readings relate to the end times and the long-awaited return of Christ as judge of all. Hymn writers have focused on these same themes, providing us with sung and prayed poetry to teach and encourage us. But how are we to take encouragement from the first stanza of this hymn? We read of "fright" and "flames" that will "ravage earth." We might be excused for thinking that this is not exactly encouraging, consoling talk! Later the poet preaches the reality of God's Law: Woe to those who scorned the Lord and despised His precious Word, to those who placed earthly treasure and pleasure first.

But when we read on, the hymn writer gives us nothing but the healing balm of the Gospel. By His shed blood, Jesus has paid the price for our sins, and our names are written in the Book of Life. Satan cannot threaten us; we are free! "There is no condemnation!" (st. 5). Eternal life in the presence of Jesus is our reality. For this reason, we confidently pray, "O Jesus Christ, do not delay, but hasten our salvation" (st. 7). We long for Christ's return in glory, for He will take us to Himself, to that place He has prepared for us.

"My Savior paid the debt I owe and for my sin was smitten; within the Book of Life I know my name has now been written. I will not doubt, for I am free, and Satan cannot threaten me; there is no condemnation! May Christ our intercessor be and through His blood and merit read from His book that we are free with all who life inherit. Then we shall see Him face to face, with all His saints in that blest place which He has purchased for us." Amen. (LSB 508:5–6)

NOVEMBER 28

Lo! He comes with clouds descending,
Once for ev'ry sinner slain;
Thousand thousand saints attending
Swell the triumph of His train:
Alleluia, alleluia, alleluia!
Christ the Lord returns to reign. (*LSB* 336:1)

WHEN *JESUS* ASCENDED INTO HEAVEN, A CLOUD TOOK *HIM* OUT of the disciples' sight, and angels told them that one day Jesus would return "in the same way as you saw Him go into heaven" (Acts 1:11). In the revelation to John, the apostle also tells us that Jesus "is coming with the clouds, and every eye will see Him" (1:7). At His ascension, a cloud *obscured* Jesus from His disciples; surely, they had wished to follow His upward journey for as long as they possibly could. When, at the time appointed by His Father, Jesus returns on the Last Day for final judgment, clouds will not obscure Him but will *reveal* Him—in a glorious descent to earth never seen before or to be seen again.

The first time Jesus left His Father's throne was in the greatest humility—entering the womb of the virgin Mary to be born as a helpless baby. How unlike that will be His second coming! Jesus Himself tells us that we "will see the Son of Man coming on the clouds of heaven with power and great glory" (Matthew 24:30). But even as Jesus will be "robed in glorious majesty" (st. 2), simultaneously, "His dazzling body" will still bear "those dear tokens of His passion" (st. 3)—those wounds in Jesus' hands and side that Thomas demanded to see. Thus will it be clear to us the awful price that Jesus had to pay for our sins. His return in great glory is possible only because—through His suffering, death, and resurrection—He accomplished what the Father required of Him in order to balance the scales of divine justice.

Lord, come quickly on the clouds of glory!

"Those dear tokens of His passion still His dazzling body bears, cause of endless exultation to His ransomed worshipers. With what rapture . . . gaze we on those glorious scars!" Amen. (LSB *336:3*)

NOVEMBER 29

Christ is surely coming
Bringing His reward,
Alpha and Omega,
First and Last and Lord:
Root and Stem of David,
Brilliant Morning Star;
Meet your Judge and Savior,
Nations near and far! (*LSB* 509:1)

THE BOOK OF REVELATION IS FULL OF ENCOURAGEMENT FOR THE Christian. Here we receive assurance that Christ will return and will take us to our eternal home to live with Him forever.

In the last chapter of Revelation, Jesus names Himself as the "Alpha and the Omega"—"the first and the last, the beginning and the end"—and "the root and the descendant of David, the bright morning star" (22:13, 16). Jesus makes clear that although He suffered and died, being fully human, He is now exalted at the right hand of the Father, fully divine. He was first—at creation: "Let Us make man in Our image, after Our likeness" (Genesis 1:26). He was not only a descendant of David but also the root of David. He will also be last—bringing His earthly creation to a close at the end of time, before the promised reality of "new heavens and a new earth" (2 Peter 3:13).

In this final chapter of Revelation, John pictures us entering heaven! We are among the ones who have been washed from every sin by the blood of Christ. We enter heaven—the holy city—only by virtue of what Christ, the Alpha and the Omega, has done *for us*. We are the thirsty who desire to "take the water of life without price" (Revelation 22:17). Christ Himself paid the price so that we may have this lifegiving water forever. This is the precious gift that our God "loves to give" (st. 2). Thanks be to God!

"See the holy city! There they enter in, all by Christ made holy, washed from ev'ry sin: thirsty ones, desiring all He loves to give, come for living water, freely drink, and live!" Amen. (LSB *509:2*)

NOVEMBER 30

At the name of Jesus
Ev'ry knee shall bow,
Ev'ry tongue confess Him
King of glory now.
'Tis the Father's pleasure
We should call Him Lord,
Who from the beginning
Was the mighty Word. (*LSB* 512:1)

A*T THE TURNING POINT OF THE CHURCH YEAR, WE LOOK TO THE* end of time, when Jesus will return as judge of all. But simultaneously, we look to His incarnation—born as a human to live a life of perfect obedience to His Father's will, to His sacrificial death, His glorious resurrection, and His triumphant ascension to the Father. In today's hymn, the poet gives us words to sing of Jesus Christ, "the same yesterday and today and forever" (Hebrews 13:8).

From the beginning, Jesus was the eternal Word. Indeed, in His High Priestly Prayer to His Father, Jesus speaks of "the glory that I had with You before the world existed" (John 17:5). Jesus was present at the creation of the world: "At His voice creation sprang at once to sight" (st. 2). He was "humbled for a season" (st. 3) as He came to sinners to live the perfect life none of us could ever claim. In final victory, He rose from death and ascended "to the central height, to the throne of Godhead, to the Father's breast" (st. 4). There He prays for us—His beloved children—on a continual basis. Finally, the poet declares, "Christians, this Lord Jesus shall return again in His Father's glory, with His angel train" (st. 6).

We eagerly await this return of Jesus, the eternal one—from before the creation of the universe to the endless eternity He has planned for us, the perfect life He won for us and wishes to live with us. Thanks be to Jesus for His great love!

"Christians, this Lord Jesus shall return again in His Father's glory, with His angel train; for all wreaths of empire meet upon His brow, and our hearts confess Him King of glory now." Amen. (LSB *512:6*)

DECEMBER 1

The night will soon be ending;
The dawn cannot be far.
Let songs of praise ascending
Now greet the Morning Star!
All you whom darkness frightens
With guilt or grief or pain,
God's radiant Star now brightens
And bids you sing again. **(*LSB* 337:1)**

DARKNESS AND LIGHT. WE NOTICE THE RELATIVE PRESENCE OF each as our seasons turn, December bringing shorter times of daylight and longer nights in the Northern Hemisphere. Of course, we also use these two terms figuratively, the poet in today's hymn associating "darkness" with fear, guilt, grief, pain, and sadness. The child of God is not immune from any of these aspects of figurative darkness, for we are sinners living in a sin-infested world.

But thanks be to God, we have the Morning Star—Jesus (Revelation 22:16). Notice how the hymn writer characterizes the Morning Star: Jesus "brightens" our situation, easing our fears and freeing us from the guilt of our sins. Jesus bids us "sing again"—even in times of grief and sadness. From this Morning Star beam rays of light that pierce the night and conquer "sin's oppressive might" (st. 4). Jesus frees us from the darkness, as He promised us: "So if the Son sets you free, you will be free indeed" (John 8:36).

What might seem incongruous to the world is the fact that this Morning Star, present before the world even existed (John 17:5), and present at creation, is willing to enter this world in great humility—as a child, yet the child who "will save His people from their sins" (Matthew 1:21).

Even when we as sinners resist the brightness of God's redeeming light, God's grace is constant, claiming us as His children, redeemed and forgiven through the perfect life, death, and resurrection of Jesus, our bright Morning Star.

"Yet nights will bring their sadness and rob our hearts of peace, and sin in all its madness around us may increase. But now one Star is beaming whose rays have pierced the night: God comes for our redeeming from sin's oppressive might." Amen. (LSB *337:4*)

DECEMBER 2

Oh, brighter than
the rising morn
When Christ, victorious, rose
And left the lonesome
place of death
Despite the rage of foes.

Oh, brighter than that
glorious morn
Shall dawn upon our race
The day when Christ
in splendor comes
And we shall see His
face. (*LSB* 348:3–4)

O*NE OF OUR EASTER HYMNS BEGINS "ALL THE EARTH WITH JOY* is sounding: Christ has risen from the dead!" (*LSB* 462:1). Indeed, the joy and triumph that we sing of on Easter knows no bounds, for we know that Christ rose victorious in His defeat of death—on our behalf, for us.

The writer of today's hymn tells us that there is a glorious morning coming that will be even brighter than that first Easter morning. That brighter day will take place when Jesus returns to earth on Judgment Day. He will come in splendor as the King of kings and the Lord of lords, and we shall see His face! On that day, we, too, will rise from death, as Christ did before us. In his great resurrection chapter (1 Corinthians 15), Paul writes about the order of resurrection: "Christ the firstfruits, then at His coming those who belong to Christ" (v. 23).

This is what makes this final day one that we anticipate with great joy, for His resurrection will then be our resurrection. We—forgiven sinners—will see Him, and we will go to live with Him forever. On that day, "the King shall come when morning dawns and light triumphant breaks, when beauty gilds the eastern hills and life to joy awakes" (st. 1). Thanks be to our risen, ascended Lord, who will come again in glory to take us home to Himself forever!

"The King shall come when morning dawns and light and beauty brings. Hail, Christ the Lord! Your people pray: Come quickly, King of kings!" Amen. (LSB *348:5*)

DECEMBER 3

Sin's debt, that fearful burden,
Cannot His love erase;
Your guilt the Lord will pardon
And cover by His grace.
He comes, for you procuring
The peace of sin forgiv'n,
His children thus securing
Eternal life in heav'n.
(*LSB* 334:5)

"STIR UP YOUR POWER, O LORD, AND COME." THAT IS THE CHURCH'S recurring petition in the season of Advent. Why? "That we may be rescued from the threatening perils of our sins" (Collect for the First Sunday in Advent). As we begin the new Church Year, we focus on what is most important—the twin realities: our sins, and God's unfathomable, unending love for us lost and fallen creatures.

During Advent, we recognize that Christ came to us in human flesh—His incarnation, which we celebrate each year at Christmas. We also know that He will come again in glory and power to be our judge on the Last Day. But Lutheran pastor and hymn writer Paul Gerhardt points us to the fact that Jesus comes to us not just at one point in history—as a baby born in Bethlehem—and not only at an unknown point in the future—at the end of time. In fact, He comes to us now—every day—in His Word and Sacraments to pardon our guilt and cover our sins by His grace. Through His Word, the Holy Spirit works faith in our hearts (Romans 10:17). In Holy Baptism, that Word of God, in and with the water, works forgiveness of sins and rescues us from eternal death. And in His Holy Supper, Christ gives us His very body and blood for the forgiveness of our sins. Christ's advent—His coming—is our *daily* reality, providing us "the peace of sin forgiv'n."

Such blessings are ours due solely to God's great love for us. It is a "love beyond all telling" (st. 4), given to us freely by the One who Himself *is* love (1 John 4:8).

"Love caused Your incarnation; love brought You down to me. Your thirst for my salvation procured my liberty. Oh, love beyond all telling, that led You to embrace in love, all love excelling, our lost and fallen race." Amen. (LSB *334:4*)

DECEMBER 4

On Jordan's bank the Baptist's cry
Announces that the Lord is nigh;
Awake and hearken, for he brings
Glad tidings of the King of kings!

Then cleansed be ev'ry life from sin;
Make straight the way for God within,
And let us all our hearts prepare
For Christ to come and enter there. (*LSB* 344:1–2)

JOHN THE BAPTIST WAS THE PREACHER OF PREPARATION. Therefore, the character of Advent flows from his call to "repent, for the kingdom of heaven is at hand," recorded in Matthew 3:2 with parallel accounts in Mark and Luke. This unique wilderness preacher teaches how to prepare for the One who is coming, including "coming" in all its advent senses.

He would have us do this with clean hearts, made right, forgiven, and *ready*. "Repent" is his cry; we would all do well to let John the Baptist teach us this godly readiness. It must not be confused with the world's frantic attempt at readiness in the busy pre-Christmas days. But then, the world and the Bride have never been able to agree on very much, and the world will never understand how the church prepares for Christmas. So be it!

John's work on Jordan's banks also brings glad tidings of the King of kings. Wake up, listen up—this is important news! Prepare the way for this King to live in your hearts and your lives, for that is where He wants to enter, rule, and reign. He is your King and wants to set you free and eventually give you a crown. Yes, you have an Advent King!

"I lay in fetters, groaning; You came to set me free. I stood, my shame bemoaning; You came to honor me. A glorious crown You give me, a treasure safe on high that will not fail or leave me as earthly riches fly." Amen. (LSB *334:3*)

DECEMBER 5

We hail Thee as our Savior, Lord,
Our refuge and our great reward;
Without Thy grace we waste away
Like flow'rs that wither and decay.

Lay on the sick Thy healing hand
And make the fallen strong to stand;
Show us the glory of Thy face
Till beauty springs in ev'ry place. (*LSB* 344:3–4)

I ONCE SUFFERED SIGNIFICANT LOSS AND SADNESS DURING AN Adventtide. I returned to my home congregation after the funeral, and every Advent hymn that Sunday seemed to be written for me—in my need. Yes, singing hymns that day was difficult, but my eyes were more open to what these hymns proclaimed than ever before. I was genuinely grateful for how they ministered to me that Sunday. I have since viewed Advent hymnody with greater appreciation and will forever be thankful that my needy condition that day helped me see the depth and richness of Advent hymns.

Yes, Advent is about our Lord's coming, but it's also about our waiting. Waiting for the saints can be hard, especially in challenging times. While we wait, we often need a healing hand, a refuge, a shelter, and a comforter. Advent hymns help us to see our Savior standing there, ready to grant us a much-needed showering of His healing, comfort, and grace. He knows very well that we are poor and lowly and would "waste away like flow'rs that wither and decay" without His life-giving mercy and grace—and He is there for us.

"Enter now my waiting heart, glorious King and Lord most holy. Dwell in me and ne'er depart, though I am but poor and lowly. Ah, what riches will be mine when Thou art my guest divine! My hosannas and my palms graciously receive, I pray Thee; evermore, as best I can, Savior, I will homage pay Thee, and in faith I will embrace, Lord, Thy merit through Thy grace." Amen. (LSB *350:2–3*)

DECEMBER 6

See, the Lamb, so long expected,
Comes with pardon down from heav'n.
Let us haste, with tears of sorrow,
One and all, to be forgiv'n. (*LSB* 345:3)

THIS IS ONE OF THE MOST PROFOUNDLY BEAUTIFUL STANZAS IN Christian hymnody, with much of its beauty being its quiet simplicity. Yet, its leading beauty is the wondrous truth it proclaims—the Lamb of God has come to bring pardon for our sins. It is no small matter that to do this He had to come all the way down from heaven for us.

Many composers have set this text to music; without exception, they treat these words with great care, reverence, and awe. Therefore, the musical setting of these beloved words contrasts significantly with the rest of the composition, setting it apart as something extraordinary. And rightly so, for these words state the heart of the incarnation—God as the sacrificial Lamb for mankind.

Our cries of "Hosanna, save us, help us" are answered in the arrival of the long-expected Lamb. And the ongoing prayers of the Bride for intervention, rescue, mercy, and peace are here fully answered by God's own Son—as He comes to take away our sins. It is difficult for our mere mortal minds to take in that the very Son of God came to be a sacrificial Lamb! But because of that truth, our Adventtide can be filled with hope, peace, joy, and quiet expectation. Come, Lord Jesus, come.

"Behold the Lamb of God that bears the world's transgression, whose sacrifice removes the devil's dread oppression. Behold the Lamb of God, who takes away our sin, who for our peace and joy will full atonement win. O grant, dear Lord of love, that we receive, rejoicing, the word proclaimed by John, our true repentance voicing, that gladly we may walk upon our Savior's way until we live with Him in His eternal day." Amen. (LSB *346:3–4*)

DECEMBER 7

Savior of the nations, come,
Virgin's Son, make
here Your home!
Marvel now, O heav'n and earth,
That the Lord chose
such a birth.

Not by human flesh and blood,
By the Spirit of our God,
Was the Word of God
made flesh—
Woman's offspring, pure
and fresh. (*LSB* 332:1–2)

O*N THIS DAY, THE CHURCH COMMEMORATES THE FOURTH-*century theologian Ambrose of Milan, known especially for his Latin hymns. His hymn "Savior of the Nations, Come" is particularly well known; Luther translated it into German, and it has long been available to English-language singers, being commonly sung on the First Sunday in Advent.

When Mary asked the angel Gabriel how she would give birth to the Son of God, the angel told her that the child would be conceived by the power of the Holy Spirit—"not by human flesh and blood." Jesus was born as a human child from a human mother: "God of God, yet fully man," as Ambrose would write (st. 4). Simultaneously, Jesus was the "Word of God," the first verses of John's Gospel telling us that "the Word was with God, and the Word was God" (1:1) and "the Word became flesh and dwelt among us" (v. 14). Ambrose enables us to sing of the two natures of Christ—true God and true man, both necessary for the accomplishment of our salvation.

Mary's womb was, in the words of Ambrose, a "throne" for Jesus (st. 3), one that He willingly assumed—in great humility—as He began His saving work on our behalf. That work would take Him to a different kind of throne, when He hung on the cross for our sins. But ultimately, His glorious resurrection and defeat of death would lead Him, as Ambrose puts it, "back then to His throne and crown" in His Father's house (st. 5), where He waits to welcome us home.

"God the Father was His source, back to God He ran His course. Into hell His road went down, back then to His throne and crown." Amen. (LSB *332:5*)

DECEMBER 8

Startled at the solemn warning,
Let the earthbound soul arise;
Christ, its sun, all sloth dispelling,
Shines upon the morning skies.

So, when next He comes in glory
And the world is wrapped in fear,
He will shield us with His mercy
And with words of love draw near. (*LSB* 345:2, 4)

O*N THAT LAST DAY, CHRIST "WILL SEND OUT HIS ANGELS WITH* a loud trumpet call, and they will gather His elect from the four winds, from one end of heaven to the other" (Matthew 24:31). On that day, shining upon the morning skies will be our Advent King coming in splendid, magnificent, and inexpressible glory—*coming for us*! Come quickly, King of kings!

Yet, on that day, the world will be "wrapped in fear." Then the King will say to those on His right, His sheep, "Come, you who are blessed by My Father, inherit the kingdom prepared for you from the foundation of the world" (Matthew 25:34). Our Advent King's words here are beautiful words of tender mercy and boundless love spoken to us, His dear sheep. They are words we have longed to hear. However, the unbelieving world and the goats on the left will listen to three terrifying words: "Depart from Me" (v. 41).

Fear not, O precious little flock, for our Advent King "will shield us with His mercy and with words of love draw near": "Come, . . . inherit the kingdom." This is our certain and glorious future. Come quickly, King of kings!

"The King shall come when morning dawns and light triumphant breaks, when beauty gilds the eastern hills and life to joy awakes. The King shall come when morning dawns and light and beauty brings. Hail, Christ the Lord! Your people pray: Come quickly, King of kings!" Amen. (LSB *348:1, 5*)

DECEMBER 9

Hark! A thrilling voice is sounding!
"Christ is near," we hear it say.
"Cast away the works of darkness,
All you children of the day!" (*LSB* 345:1)

WHY IS JOHN THE BAPTIST'S VOICE "THRILLING"? WHY ARE we called to hark to its sound? The answer has nothing to do with the scruffy wilderness man going about preaching but is entirely about this man's message. John the Baptist had news to proclaim that was indeed thrilling, and that message was the reason he was born. While still in the womb, John had a vocation: preparing the way for Christ.

Pastor Stephen Starke's Benedictus hymn sums up John's vocation simply and eloquently:

> You, child, will go on before the Lord
> As prophet, His way preparing;
> To speak on behalf of God Most High,
> His counsel of truth declaring:
> Rich mercy and grace for all whereby
> Iniquity is forgiven. (*LSB* 936:3)

As John prepares the way for the Lord, he creates quite a stir: "And all the country of Judea and all Jerusalem were going out to him" (Mark 1:5). His message to them is about light and darkness. "Cast away the works of darkness, all you children of the day!" Or in the words of an ancient Advent chant, "O Dayspring, splendor of light everlasting: Come and enlighten those who sit in darkness and in the shadow of death" (*LSB* 357, "O" antiphon for December 21).

"Prepare the way before Him; prepare for Him the best. Cast out what would offend Him, this great, this heav'nly guest. Make straight, make plain the way: the lowly valleys raising, the heights of pride abasing, His path all even lay. Prepare my heart, Lord Jesus; turn not from me aside, and help me to receive You this blessed Adventtide. From stall and manger low come now to dwell within me; I'll sing Your praises gladly and forth Your glory show." Amen. (LSB 354:2, 4)

DECEMBER 10

When all the world was cursed
By Moses' condemnation,
Saint John the Baptist came
With words of consolation.
With true forerunner's zeal
The greater One he named,
And Him, as yet unknown,
As Savior he proclaimed.

Behold the Lamb of God
That bears the world's
transgression,
Whose sacrifice removes
The devil's dread oppression.
Behold the Lamb of God,
Who takes away our sin,
Who for our peace and joy
Will full atonement
win. (*LSB* 346:1, 3)

GOD SENT JOHN TO ANNOUNCE, "THE TRUE LIGHT, WHICH enlightens everyone, was coming into the world" (John 1:9). And then when John the Baptist saw Jesus coming toward him, he said, "Behold, the Lamb of God, who takes away the sin of the world!" (v. 29). With these glorious words, John the Baptist and John the evangelist reveal the depth and fullness of what the true light coming into the world meant for the world—forgiveness, life, salvation, peace, and joy!

"John the Baptist came with words of consolation." There can be no greater consolation than what the Lamb of God brought to this sin-soaked world. God's Son must become incarnate to bring that consolation to the children He loves so dearly. They desperately needed it and could not win it for themselves—for the Law condemned us, and there we sat in our transgression.

It is as the church sings in her Agnus Dei: "Lamb of God, You take away the sin of the world; have mercy on us. . . . Grant us peace" (*LSB*, p. 163). All that is left to say is amen.

"O grant, dear Lord of love, that we receive, rejoicing, the word proclaimed by John, our true repentance voicing, that gladly we may walk upon our Savior's way until we live with Him in His eternal day." Amen. (LSB *346:4*)

DECEMBER 11

Jesus came, the heav'ns adoring,
Came with peace from realms on high;
Jesus came to win redemption,
Lowly came on earth to die;
Alleluia! Alleluia!
Came in deep humility.

Jesus comes to hearts rejoicing,
Bringing news of sins forgiv'n;
Jesus comes with words of gladness,
Leading souls redeemed to heav'n.
Alleluia! Alleluia!
Hope to all the world is giv'n. (*LSB* 353:1, 3)

THE WORLD TO WHICH JESUS CAME COULD NOT BE MORE OPPOSITE from the one He willingly left. He left the peace of heaven, where He sits at the right hand of God the Father, in order to enter an often-chaotic world tainted by the sins of fallen creatures. To win redemption for us meant giving up the perfection of the heavenly realms and being born as a helpless human baby. Such lowliness, such humility was overshadowed by the cold fact that He came here for only one purpose—to die for us. His death was the price that had to be paid so that *we* could one day inhabit the peace of the heavenly realms, which He willingly gave up for a season.

Of great comfort to us, Jesus still comes today—in His Word and Sacraments. His Word is read, preached, and proclaimed in His church, and that Word declares that we are forgiven sinners by virtue of His redemptive work on the cross. His called pastors forgive the sins of penitent sinners, according to His command (John 20:23). Moreover, He comes to us again and again with His very body and blood in His Holy Supper—for the forgiveness of sins.

We know that He will come again in great glory and majesty; on that day, we, too, will share in His resurrection; and we, too, will be welcomed to His heavenly realms!

"Jesus comes in joy and sorrow, shares alike our hopes and fears; Jesus comes, whate'er befalls us, cheers our hearts and dries our tears; Alleluia! Alleluia! Comforts us in failing years." Amen. (LSB 353:4)

DECEMBER 12

Creator of the stars of night,
Thy people's everlasting Light:
O Christ, Redeemer, save us all
And hear Thy servants when they call.

Thou cam'st the Bridegroom of the bride,
As drew the world to eventide,
The spotless Victim all divine
Proceeding from a virgin shrine. (*LSB* 351:1, 3)

IT IS A STRIKING AND BEAUTIFUL IMAGE: JESUS IS THE BRIDEGROOM, and the church is His Bride. *We* are the Bride—loved and cherished by our Bridegroom, our Redeemer, Jesus.

In the Nicene Creed, we confess that Jesus was "begotten of His Father before all worlds." Thus, He was present at creation; He was indeed "Creator of the stars of night." But now we call on Him as our Redeemer, and we plead that He might "save us all" from the sin that has infected this world ever since the fall of our first parents in that perfect Garden of Eden God created for His beloved creatures—the crown of His creation.

In this Advent season we recall that Jesus came into this world to save us. He willingly was born of the virgin Mary. Though He was and remained "spotless," He willingly became the victim on our behalf, suffering and dying for us, paying the price for sins that He never committed, for the sins that continue to mark our days and lives. The Creator died to redeem His fallen creatures.

In this Advent season, we also confess, in the Creed, that Jesus "will come again with glory to judge both the living and the dead." For His second coming, the church—His Bride—continues to pray that short, fervent prayer, "Come, Lord Jesus!" (Revelation 22:20).

"O Thou, whose coming is with dread to judge the living and the dead, preserve us from the ancient foe while still we dwell on earth below. To God the Father and the Son and Holy Spirit, Three in One, praise, honor, might, and glory be from age to age eternally." Amen. (LSB 351:5–6)

DECEMBER 13

I lay in fetters, groaning;
You came to set me free.
I stood, my shame bemoaning;
You came to honor me.
A glorious crown You give me,
A treasure safe on high
That will not fail or leave me
As earthly riches fly. (*LSB* 334:3)

T*HE HYMN WRITER, PASTOR PAUL GERHARDT, PAINTS A GRAPHIC* picture of someone shackled and chained, groaning in misery. Clearly, this person—"me"—is in prison. But the Lord Jesus "came to set me free." He removed the shackles and chains that bound me as a captive, stretched out His hand to me, and told me to stand. I stood, but I still realized and bemoaned the shame of my sins, which were the just cause of my imprisonment.

But wonder of wonders, the Lord not only frees me from prison but He "came to honor me"! In a completely unexpected and totally unmerited way, He gave me a crown—a glorious crown, a crown of righteousness. My sins are forgiven, erased!

But my redemption was costly, and my crown of righteousness came at a very steep price. The Lord who honors me is the very Son of God, who, to win my freedom, had to become incarnate, live the perfect life that I could not, then suffer and die for *my* sins. And He did all this willingly, without complaint, out of sheer love for me. And all this He gladly suffered, as Pastor Gerhardt summarizes in another of his marvelous hymns (*LSB* 438:1).

Jesus gives each of us "a treasure safe on high"—namely, the promise of eternal life. That treasure will never fail us; it is sure and certain!

"O Lord, how shall I meet You, how welcome You aright? Your people long to greet You, my hope, my heart's delight! O kindle, Lord most holy, Your lamp within my breast to do in spirit lowly all that may please You best." Amen. (LSB *334:1*)

DECEMBER 14

Once He came in blessing,
All our sins redressing;
Came in likeness lowly,
Son of God most holy;
Bore the cross to save us;
Hope and freedom gave us. (*LSB* 333:1)

IT IS A CONTINUING THEME OF OUR ADVENT HYMNS THAT JESUS—the "Son of God most holy"—lowered Himself, humbled Himself, to enter our mortal world. He did so for one purpose only: to pay the price for all our sins. He "bore the cross to save us." He was born to die for us.

Through His redemptive work, Jesus gave us "hope and freedom." We experience that freedom every day. Because we are freed from the burden of trying to work out our own salvation from sin, we can live productive lives of service to our neighbors—parents, spouse, children, employers, all those who live and work in proximity to us. We are also freed from the burden of fear and worry about when we might die and what might happen after our death. God has given us hope—not some sort of wishful thinking about the future but a sure and certain hope of eternal life, "the hope laid up for you in heaven" (Colossians 1:5).

Such hope in Christ is nourished as He comes to us here and now, again and again, in His Holy Supper. He feeds us with His body and blood, "precious food from heaven," a "pledge of peace" in which our sins are forgiven (st. 2).

Hope and freedom, comfort and peace—these are the blessings on which we meditate during this season of Advent.

"Now He gently leads us; with Himself He feeds us precious food from heaven, pledge of peace here given, manna that will nourish souls that they may flourish." Amen. (LSB *333:2*)

DECEMBER 15

Soon will come that hour
When with mighty power
Christ will come in splendor
And will judgment render,
With the faithful sharing
Joy beyond comparing. (*LSB* 333:3)

D*URING THE SEASON OF ADVENT, WE PONDER THREE COMINGS* of Christ. In His first coming, His incarnation, He humbly took on human flesh to live a sinless life, suffer and die for our sins, and rise from the dead—His resurrection being the promise of our own resurrection to eternal life. Second, Christ continues to come to us in His Holy Supper, His bodily presence giving us forgiveness of sins, life, and salvation. Third, we look for His second coming at the end of time, when He will "judge both the living and the dead" (Nicene Creed) and take His redeemed children to live with Him forever.

Instead of coming in lowliness and humility, His second coming will be marked by "power and great glory. . . . Your redemption is drawing near" (Luke 21:27, 28). For all who believe in Him this second coming will bring "joy beyond comparing," as we enter an eternity where God Himself "will wipe away every tear from [our] eyes" (Revelation 7:17).

Thus, during the Advent season, we pray fervently for Christ's second coming, for the fulfillment of all that He has promised His redeemed children. We pray that the Holy Spirit will "keep our hearts believing" (st. 4) so that we continue to confess Jesus as our Savior from sin and death and, by His grace, live with Him forever.

"Come, then, O Lord Jesus, from our sins release us. Keep our hearts believing, that we, grace receiving, ever may confess You till in heav'n we bless You." Amen. (LSB *333:4*)

DECEMBER 16

O Savior, rend the heavens wide;
Come down, come down with mighty stride;
Unlock the gates, the doors break down;
Unbar the way to heaven's crown.

O Father, light from heaven send;
As morning dew, O Son, descend.
Drop down, you clouds, the life of spring:
To Jacob's line rain down the King. (*LSB* 355:1–2)

ISAIAH CRIES OUT, "*OH THAT YOU WOULD REND THE HEAVENS AND* come down" (64:1). Rend the heavens—tear the skies apart—so that we might more readily gain Your presence. Tear the skies apart—for we need Your help. Tear the skies apart—so that we here on earth might receive the crown of heaven. Come down to us! For You, Lord God, are our only hope. Isaiah's cry is an urgent plea for salvation.

We pray that same petition in this hymn, for we know that God alone can unlock the gates, unbar the way, and break down all the doors that are barriers to us who long for the crown of righteousness in heaven. Our sins constitute those locked gates and barred doorways to heaven, and we know that, on our own, we do not have the ability or means to atone for those sins and thereby unlock the door to heaven. We need a Savior, and that is our urgent Advent prayer.

We ask the Father to send light from heaven, and He responds by sending His Son: "The true light, which gives light to everyone, was coming into the world" (John 1:9). We plead for the Son to descend to us, and He does. He foregoes His heavenly throne, takes on human flesh, and dwells among us. Just as when Isaiah pleaded, He came down to us.

Christ continues to come down to us daily and richly through His Word and Sacraments. We meditate on His Word, and we eat and drink His body and blood in the Lord's Supper. His advent is His continued coming down from heaven—for us!

"O Fount of hope, how long, how long? When will You come with comfort strong? O come, O come, Your throne forego; console us in our vale of woe." Amen. (LSB *355:4*)

DECEMBER 17

O Morning Star, O radiant Sun,
When will our hearts
behold Your dawn?
O Sun, arise; without Your light
We grope in gloom
and dark of night.

Sin's dreadful doom
upon us lies;
Grim death looms fierce
before our eyes.
O come, lead us with
mighty hand
From exile to our promised
land. (*LSB* 355:5–6)

THROUGHOUT THE MONTH OF DECEMBER, WE MAY EXPERIENCE a certain disconnect between the church and the secular world regarding Christmas. The church's calendar provides a season that gives us the necessary context for Christmas—the incarnation of Jesus as Savior of the world. On the other hand, the world around us looks merely for an early winter holiday and immerses itself in the "feel-good" traditions of a secular holiday season, beginning in early November.

It would be jarring indeed for the secular world to hear as part of its holiday music the phrase "Sin's dreadful doom upon us lies; grim death looms fierce before our eyes." And yet that is precisely the reason for Christmas, for the incarnation of Jesus. He came into this world as the promised Messiah, the Christ, because we needed to be saved from the dreadful doom caused by our sin, which could only lead to our grim death—eternal separation from God.

We call on Jesus—the "morning star" (Revelation 22:16) and our "radiant Sun"—to dawn upon us and be the light we need, lest "we grope in gloom and dark of night," attempting to save ourselves. Jesus answers this call, declaring, "I am the light of the world. Whoever follows Me will not walk in darkness, but will have the light of life" (John 8:12). This blessed season of Advent teaches us why Jesus came to us at Christmas, thus providing the richest context for our great Christmas joy.

"There shall we all our praises bring and sing to You, our Savior King; there shall we laud You and adore forever and forevermore." Amen. (LSB *355:7*)

DECEMBER 18

O come, O come, Emmanuel,
And ransom captive Israel,
That mourns in lonely exile here
Until the Son of God appear.

O come, Thou Key of David, come,
And open wide our heav'nly home;
Make safe the way that leads on high,
And close the path to misery. (*LSB* 357:1, 5)

THE SEASON OF ADVENT IS ABOUT OUR WAITING AND HOPING FOR the Key of David to come and open wide the door to our heavenly home. And while we wait, we sing yet again with this centuries-old hymn, "O come, O come, Emmanuel, and ransom captive Israel."

Obviously, we are not waiting for Him to be born in Bethlehem, for by God's boundless grace, that already happened. And we are not waiting for Him to be present for us in His body and His blood on His altar, for by God's boundless grace, that feast is now an ongoing blessed reality. No, we are waiting for the Key of David to come and open wide the door to our heavenly home.

Only God the Father knows the day, the hour, and the moment when He will open the door to our heavenly home. Meanwhile, we wait as we implore Him to make safe the way that leads on high.

The blessed saints are pilgrims in exile here. This is not our home. So we wait and long for the promised land on the other side of that door. We live in hope and great expectation of the promised new heaven that will be ours at last. Amen! Come, Lord Jesus!

"Sin's dreadful doom upon us lies; grim death looms fierce before our eyes. O come, lead us with mighty hand from exile to our promised land. There shall we all our praises bring and sing to You, our Savior King; then shall we laud You and adore forever and forevermore." Amen. (LSB *355:6, 7*)

DECEMBER 19

O come, Thou Wisdom from on high,
Who ord'rest all things mightily;
To us the path of knowledge show,
And teach us in her ways to go.
Rejoice! Rejoice! Emmanuel
Shall come to thee, O Israel! (*LSB* 357:2)

THE HYMN "O COME, O COME, EMMANUEL" IS A STROPHIC (rhymed, poetic) form of the ancient seven "O" antiphons. Historically these antiphons were sung during worship in the final seven days of Advent. Each antiphon addresses Christ by a different title based on Old Testament prophecies.

"O Wisdom" is the first antiphon of the seven and the hymn's second stanza. The church here asks for divine help, for Wisdom. It is what David seeks in Psalm 25:4: "Make me to know Your ways, O LORD; teach me Your paths." The waiting church seeks this knowledge and truth "from on high."

Just as Jesus left His Supper to feed His people as we wait, He also leaves His Wisdom to show us "the path of knowledge" and teach us how to walk in those ways. God's Word and God's Son are that Wisdom. The more we learn of His paths, ways, and truths, the more we are filled with His Wisdom. And by that Wisdom, we are equipped for every day of our earthly pilgrimage. "For wisdom will come into your heart, and knowledge will be pleasant to your soul" (Proverbs 2:10).

Therefore, today's message is simple: Read and hear God's Word and let His Holy Spirit, the Spirit of Wisdom, fill you with precious truths and "Wisdom from on high."

"O Wisdom, proceeding from the mouth of the Most High, pervading and permeating all creation, mightily ordering all things: Come and teach us the way of prudence." Amen. (LSB *357, "O" antiphon for December 17*)

DECEMBER 20

O come, Thou Dayspring from on high,
And cheer us by Thy drawing nigh;
Disperse the gloomy clouds of night,
And death's dark shadows put to flight. (*LSB* 357:6)

THE CHURCH LOVES TO SING OF OUR BRIGHT AND SHINING Morning Star, of her "Dayspring from on high." Why? Because such singing fills our hearts with cheering hope as it allows us to confess what we believe our glorious and beautiful future to be.

Christ's first and second comings are brought together in these samples of churchly singing. Zechariah's prophecy sings of the Dayspring in his Benedictus: "Whereby the dayspring from on high hath visited us, to give light to them that sit in darkness and in the shadow of death" (Luke 1:78–79 KJV). The "O" antiphon for December 21 sings of the Dayspring this way: "O Dayspring, splendor of light everlasting: Come and enlighten those who sit in darkness and in the shadow of death." And the hymn "O Come, O Come, Emmanuel" sings, "O come, Thou Dayspring from on high, and cheer us by Thy drawing nigh."

"Dayspring" is the messianic title that signifies the rising of a dawn that overcomes the gloomy clouds of night. And oh, how we long for the gloomy clouds of night to be dispersed, to be wiped away, to be history for us. A new heaven and a new earth sound awfully good. Yes, the Bride could use some cheering up while she waits.

"I am the root and the descendant of David, the bright morning star" (Revelation 22:16). Amen! Come, Lord Jesus!

"Our hope and expectation, O Jesus, now appear; arise, O Sun so longed for, o'er this benighted sphere. With hearts and hands uplifted, we plead, O Lord, to see the day of earth's redemption that sets Your people free!" Amen. (LSB *515:4*)

DECEMBER 21

Bruise for me the serpent's head
That, set free from doubt and dread,
I may cling to You in faith,
Safely kept through life and death. (*LSB* 352:5)

We are poised with anticipation for the annual celebration of our Lord's nativity. In preparation, let us hear and ponder God's first announcement of the Gospel again: "I will put enmity between you and the woman, and between your offspring and her offspring: He shall bruise your head, and you shall bruise His heel" (Genesis 3:15).

Martin Luther shows the promise in this condemnation: "The human being's heel is in danger, but his head is safe and remains uninjured and undefeated. On the other hand, it is not the tail and not the belly of the serpent but the head itself, that is to be crushed and trodden underfoot by the Seed of the woman. But this victory will also be given to us a gift, as Christ clearly states" (*Luther's Works*, volume 1, p. 190).

Today's hymn presents the profound truths of God's promise in words that apply directly to us. God's children are set free! They are "free from doubt and dread." They are kept safe in this life and in death. They are free because of the Seed of the woman. They are free because the head of the serpent would be trampled and humbled. They are free because God, in His incarnation, is setting His Gospel promise in motion.

In faith, we cling to this in these final days of Advent—Gospel victory, freely given to us!

"Thou, grieving that the ancient curse should doom to death a universe, hast found the healing, full of grace, to cure and save our ruined race. To God, the Father and the Son and Holy Spirit, Three in One, praise, honor, might, and glory be from age to age eternally." Amen. (LSB *351:2, 6*)

DECEMBER 22

The angel Gabriel
from heaven came,
With wings as drifted
snow, with eyes as flame:
"All hail to thee, O
lowly maiden Mary,
Most highly favored lady."
Gloria!

"For know a blessed
mother thou shalt be,
All generations laud
and honor thee;
Thy son shall be Emmanuel,
by seers foretold,
Most highly favored lady."
Gloria! (*LSB* 356:1–2)

The angel Gabriel comes to a poor, lowly young maiden who does housework and tends cattle. But it is to be her womb that will be highly favored as it will surround God's Son. This is even greater than Simeon physically holding God in his arms. This was Mary holding God in her body for nine months until—wonder of wonders—she gave birth to God.

What God is doing here with this young maiden is so incomprehensible that there have always been doubters who ask, "How can this be?" But in faith, Mary does not doubt; she believes and she sings in the Magnificat, "For the Mighty One has done great things to me, and holy is His name" (*LSB*, p. 231). Mary's faith sings as she witnesses the reality of what God is doing in and with her life. Yes, Mary is indeed a highly favored lady.

What starts privately between Gabriel and Mary does not stay private, for all peoples and all generations have forever remembered this most blessed exchange.

"My soul rejoices, my spirit voices—sing the greatness of the Lord! For God my Savior has shown me favor—sing the greatness of the Lord! With praise and blessing, join in confessing God, who is solely mighty and holy—O sing the greatness of God the Lord! His mercy surely shall rest securely on all who fear Him, love and revere Him—O sing the greatness of God the Lord!" Amen. (LSB *933:1*)

DECEMBER 23

Then gentle Mary meekly bowed her head;
"To me be as it pleaseth God," she said.
"My soul shall laud and magnify God's holy name."
Most highly favored lady, Gloria!

Of her, Emmanuel, the Christ, was born
In Bethlehem all on a Christmas morn,
And Christian folk throughout the world will ever say:
"Most highly favored lady."
Gloria! (*LSB* 356:3–4)

MARY BOWED HER HEAD AND, IN FAITH, WAS OPEN AND receptive to God's will for her, which included great things beyond her thought—beyond all thought! She humbly says, "Behold, I am the servant of the Lord; let it be to me according to your word" (Luke 1:38).

> A maiden, in her lowly place,
> Became, in ways beyond all thought,
> The chosen vessel of His grace. (*LSB* 385:3)

Blessed Mary, the most highly favored lady, was the chosen vessel of God's grace. And Christian folk throughout the world will rightly ever sing of her, her faith, and her role in God's plan to save this world—the role as mother of God's Son!

Starting tomorrow, the name of Mary will be in the readings, in the preaching, and in all the joyous singing of Christmas and its season because of the important role God gave her in His plan to save the world. But the name above all names is the name of her Son, our Lord and Savior, Jesus Christ. Gloria!

"Oh, that birth forever blessed, when the virgin, full of grace, by the Holy Ghost conceiving, bore the Savior of our race, and the babe, the world's Redeemer, first revealed His sacred face evermore and evermore." Amen. (LSB *384:2*)

DECEMBER 24

Once in royal David's city
Stood a lowly cattle shed,
Where a mother laid her baby
In a manger for His bed:
Mary was that mother mild,
Jesus Christ her little child. (*LSB* 376:1)

THE TRADITION OF BEGINNING THE CHRISTMAS EVE SERVICE AT King's College, Cambridge, with the first stanza of "Once in Royal David's City" sung by a single boy's voice started in 1918. The first broadcast was in 1928, and it is now heard annually by millions, making this carol a part of Christmas Eve celebrations worldwide.

The admirable goal of the carol's author, Cecil F. Alexander, was to help catechize the young through hymns. In this hymn, she portrays our Lord's incarnation in picturesque terms that a child can imagine and understand. She does the same with our Lord's suffering and death in the hymn "There Is a Green Hill Far Away."

However, the unique characteristic of her beloved carol is how it ends: "And He leads His children on to the place where He is gone" (st. 4). As Christmas Eve worshipers sing the last two stanzas, they are transported from baby Jesus in a lowly manger to the ascended Jesus, now set at God's right hand on high. And He is leading us there!

Very few carols take the singers to the end of their own life. But it is a masterful way to show children—and us—the grand and glorious purpose for the Christ Child's coming to earth on that first Christmas. Alexander's carol jumps to the end of the story in God's plan to save us. And it is a magnificent end!

"Not in that poor, lowly stable with the oxen standing by shall we see Him, but in heaven, set at God's right hand on high. Then like stars His children, crowned, all in white, His praise will sound!" Amen. (LSB *376:5*)

DECEMBER 25

All my heart again rejoices
As I hear
Far and near
Sweetest angel voices.
"Christ is born!" their choirs are singing
Till the air
Ev'rywhere
Now with joy is ringing. (*LSB* 360:1)

S*HEPHERDS HEARD THE AIR FILLED WITH THE SWEETEST ANGEL* voices on the night of Jesus' birth. Such a sound is far beyond our imagination, but it was an explosion of joy. Nothing like it had ever happened or will ever happen again. Oh, that we were there! Oh, to hear the singing that night!

And yet, the angels had to be puzzled by what God was doing by coming so far down. However, if they were puzzled, there was no hint in their singing, for it loudly and joyously confessed that God's Son had been born in human flesh! In a way, their song still fills the earth, but now from our lips in worship when we repeat their words: "Glory to God in the highest, and peace to His people on earth" (*LSB*, p. 154).

It is hard for anyone to grasp that God took on the weakness of our flesh when He became incarnate. How can this be? God is taking on frail human flesh that will weep at the grave of Lazarus and sweat blood in the Garden of Gethsemane. This was the miracle of miracles: God came down and joined us in our weakness. "How greatly God must love" us! (*LSB* 372:4).

"Ah, dearest Jesus, holy Child, prepare a bed, soft, undefiled, a quiet chamber set apart for You to dwell within my heart. Glory to God in highest heav'n, who unto us His Son has giv'n! While angels sing with pious mirth a glad new year to all the earth." Amen. (LSB *358:13, 15*)

DECEMBER 26

Praise for the first of martyrs
Who saw You ready stand
To help in time of torment,
To plead at God's right hand.
Like You, our suff'ring Savior,
His enemies he blessed,
With "Lord, receive my spirit,"
His faith, by death, confessed. (***LSB*** **517:7)**

TODAY WE REMEMBER THE CHRISTIAN MARTYR STEPHEN, WHO IS known for his forgiving spirit and Christlike words, "Lord, do not hold this sin against them," as he was being stoned to death (Acts 7:60). Stephen is a towering witness to the church for blessing enemies while they are torturing you, even killing you. Stephen receives a high place of honor, for when the early church chose a day to celebrate the memory of St. Stephen's death, they chose the day nearest Jesus' birthday.

In our human frailty, we ask, "How can we possibly forgive as Stephen did?" This can only be possible as the love of Christ lives in us and leads us to treat the hate of an enemy as He would.

As blessed saints, we walk all our days living in the state of forgiveness won for us and forgiveness that we are now to show to our neighbor. Along the way, blessed Stephen and many others model for us what that state of forgiveness looks like. Yet we cannot help but sing, "Saints their watch are keeping; their cry goes up, 'How long?' And soon the night of weeping shall be the morn of song" (*LSB* 644:3).

"*Amen, Lord Jesus, grant our prayer; Great Captain, now Thine arm make bare, fight for us once again! So shall Thy saints and martyrs raise a mighty chorus to Thy praise forevermore. Amen.*" (LSB 666:4)

DECEMBER 27

For Your belov'd disciple
Exiled to Patmos' shore,
And for his faithful record,
We praise You evermore.
Praise for the mystic vision
Through him to us revealed;
May we, in patience waiting,
With Your elect be sealed. (*LSB* 517:8)

TODAY WE REMEMBER *JOHN*, THE BELOVED APOSTLE AND evangelist who, in his "faithful record," gives Jesus in the truest and most memorable ways: "I am the light of the world" (8:12); "I am the way, and the truth, and the life" (14:6); "I am the resurrection" (11:25); "I am the door" (10:9); "I am the good shepherd" (10:11, 14). This, together with John's account of the Word becoming flesh in Jesus, is how most people know Jesus.

We praise and thank God for this towering gift to His beloved church in John's writing and witness! Yes, John was the disciple "whom Jesus loved" (13:23), but we, the church, love and treasure him too. For John alone is able to see the complete picture, the unbelievable vision from the beginning to the end of all things, and he wants us to see it—and he wants to bring us along. The breadth of John's picture is truly extraordinary!

"Of the Father's love begotten ere the worlds began to be, He is Alpha and Omega, He the source, the ending He, of the things that are, that have been, and that future years shall see evermore and evermore" (*LSB* 384:1). John's writing gives us a mature and complete picture of what the church has even now by faith. It shows us that through His Spirit, Jesus Christ lives fully and richly in His beloved church even now and forevermore.

"Now in the manger we may see God's Son from eternity, the gift from God's eternal throne here clothed in our poor flesh and bone. Alleluia! The very Son of God sublime entered into earthly time to lead us from this world of cares to heaven's courts as blessed heirs. Alleluia!" Amen. (LSB *382:2, 5*)

DECEMBER 28

First victims for the incarnate Lord,
A tender flock to feel the sword;
Beside the altar's ruddy ray,
With palm and crown, you seemed to play. (*LSB* 969:2)

THE TWELVE-DAY CELEBRATION OF THE INCARNATION HAS BARELY begun when the church is suddenly plunged into the horrific slaughter of baby boys. It's hard to imagine a more "tender flock" feeling Herod's wrath and terrible sword. However, we had better steel ourselves, for what we see here is the beginning of precious blood flowing due to our Lord's coming to earth to save us. This incarnation is going to be bloody!

Today we remember the holy innocents, those young martyrs, with the hymn "Sweet Flowerets of the Martyr Band" by Prudentius Clemens. It has two pictures: One is very hard to view, and the other is easy and helps explain what is happening according to God's plan, "with palm and crown, you seemed to play." These boys are fine—in fact, they are more than fine!

The hard part to view in this picture is the bloodbath released by Herod's fear that another king is lurking. But where is he? Since Herod does not know, his fear turns to anger, then to action full of hate. Herod is king; there cannot be another king in his land! In jealousy, he sends a decree, causing an unthinkable slaughter.

The easy part of the Prudentius picture is beautifully depicted in a mural by artist Edward Riojas. In it, saints from all ages are joyously moving toward Jesus on the Last Day. In this grand procession of saints, toddlers are waving palm branches as they run toward the Lamb. Here, we see what God meant for those butchered babies, and there is pure *joy* in their faces. Baby boys are the first martyrs of the incarnate God, a tender flock swiftly going home to be with their Lord.

"All praise for infant martyrs, whom Your mysterious love called early from their warfare to share Your home above. O Rachel, cease your weeping; they rest from earthly cares! Lord, grant us crowns as brilliant and faith as sure as theirs." Amen. (LSB *517:9*)

DECEMBER 29

Praise the Almighty, my soul, adore Him!
Yes, I will laud Him until death;
With songs and anthems I come before Him
As long as He allows me breath.
From Him my life and all things came;
Bless, O my soul, His holy name.
Alleluia, alleluia! (*LSB* 797:1)

God said, "I have found David, My servant; with My holy oil I have anointed him. . . . And I will make him the firstborn, the highest of the kings of the earth" (Psalm 89:20, 27). Yes, King David is a crucial figure in God's salvation story, but David is also a key figure in establishing *how* God's people will sing of Him. On this day, the church remembers the shepherd boy, the king, and the musician who taught the church to sing of Christ.

Johann Walter, the first Lutheran kantor, wrote this of David's foundational role:

> When David came to royal power,
> He brought the art to fullest flower.
> Thus many kinds of music mark
> The progress of the golden ark. . . .
> Worship's praise and music's sound
> Are in the Psalms together bound.
> (*Johann Walter: First Cantor of the Lutheran Church*, [Concordia Publishing House, 1992], 17–18)

Regarding the church's song, King David set the stage for Luther, "the Nightingale of Wittenberg," and Luther set the stage for Bach, "The Fifth Evangelist." And in this glorious procession, God blessed His beloved church with towering composers like Michael Praetorius, Heinrich Schütz, Felix Mendelssohn, and many others. But David started it all and was the chief architect of praise on earth by always having saints sing about God and what He has done. So, while his psalms voice our laments, anguish, and fears, they always show God's solution to our problems. Therefore, David's formula is simple: Sing the Gospel!

"Praise God, from whom all blessings flow; praise Him, all creatures here below; praise Him above, ye heav'nly host: Praise Father, Son, and Holy Ghost. Amen." (LSB 805)

DECEMBER 30

O sing of Christ, whose birth made known
The kindness of the Lord,
Eternal Word made flesh and bone
So we could be restored.
Upon our frail humanity
God's finger chose to trace
The fullness of His deity,
The icon of His grace. (*LSB* 362:1)

"The kindness of the Lord" and "the icon of His grace"—this profoundly beautiful hymn by Pastor Stephen Starke provides glorious truths of the faith in sparkling, fresh, and memorable ways.

Yes, Jesus' birth shows an extreme kindness that is pure compassion and reveals the heart of the one born in Bethlehem, the one who wants us to share His wealth and His name for all eternity. Such kindness and generous gifts are difficult, even impossible, to imagine or believe—without faith.

This hymn makes real for all ages what happened on that night long ago and proclaims clearly the true purpose of Christmas, without any myth or fluff. What God is doing here must be made clear to everyone: God is with us, "Emmanuel, to bring this holy birth" (st. 4).

There is no doubt about it—we are frail and very needy. But the Lord of all has come to this earth to join us in our poverty as He brings with Him all that we will ever need to meet our every need for all eternity—wonder of wonders! Jesus loves us, and His coming to earth makes these days of Christmas joyous!

"Lord Jesus Christ, You deigned to dwell among us here on earth as God with us, Emmanuel, to bring this holy birth. Though rich, You willingly became one with our poverty, that we might share Your wealth and name for all eternity!" Amen. (LSB *362:4*)

DECEMBER 31

The ancient Law departs,
And all its fears remove,
For Jesus makes with faithful hearts
A covenant of love.

His infant body now
Begins the cross to feel;
Those precious drops of blood that flow
For death the victim seal.

Today the name is Thine
At which we bend the knee.
They call Thee Jesus, child divine;
Our Jesus deign to be. (*LSB* 898:1, 3–4)

O*UR LORD JESUS CHRIST FULFILLED THE ENTIRE OLD TESTAMENT* for us. On His eighth day, this astonishing fulfillment manifests in His circumcision, where He sheds His first blood to fulfill the ancient Law. And with His circumcision, "the ancient Law departs."

The ancient Law departs because the infant Jesus has represented all humanity! This means all are circumcised once and for all in our Lord's circumcision—making circumcision a freedom. Paul writes, "In Him also you were circumcised with a circumcision made without hands, by putting off the body of the flesh, by the circumcision of Christ, having been buried with Him in baptism, in which you were also raised with Him through faith in the powerful working of God, who raised Him from the dead" (Colossians 2:11–12).

"Joy, O joy, beyond all gladness, Christ has done away with sadness! Hence, all sorrow and repining, for the Sun of Grace is shining!" (*LSB* 897:Refrain).

"Remember now the Son of God and how He shed His infant blood. . . . This Jesus came to end sin's war; this Name of names for us He bore. . . . His love abundant far exceeds the volume of a whole year's needs. Rejoice! Rejoice! With thanks embrace another year of grace." Amen. (LSB 896:2–4)

PALM SUNDAY (SUNDAY OF THE PASSION)

Ride on, ride on in majesty!
In lowly pomp ride on to die.
O Christ, Thy triumphs now begin
O'er captive death and conquered sin. (*LSB* 441:2)

At the beginning of each Holy Week, we recall the triumphal entry of Jesus into Jerusalem. As He rode into Jerusalem on a donkey, the crowds cut palm branches and even placed their outer garments on the road—all to adorn His path and welcome Him. Unlike the victorious commander of a Roman legion, Jesus did not ride into the city on a proud stallion fitted with military regalia, nor with disciplined ranks of troops following. As Zechariah had prophesied, "Behold, your king is coming to you; righteous and having salvation is He, humble and mounted on a donkey" (9:9). The hymn writer gets it exactly right: Jesus entered Jerusalem not in triumph but in "lowly pomp" for one purpose only—to die for the sins of the world.

The members of the crowd could scarcely have imagined that in six short days, Jesus would be crucified as a common criminal. But Jesus knew that this triumphal entry was actually the beginning of mortal pain unknown before or since. That it began with "lowly pomp" was part of Jesus' work as the humble servant: "He humbled Himself by becoming obedient to the point of death, even death on a cross" (Philippians 2:8). Zechariah tells us that "your king is coming to you; righteous and having *salvation*" (emphasis added). The "lowly pomp" of Palm Sunday led to Jesus' death on the cross *for our salvation* and then to His glorious resurrection victory over death and sin *for our salvation*. Jesus' triumphal victory provides for our entry into heaven, where we will live forever in His presence! Thanks be to God!

"Ride on, ride on in majesty! In lowly pomp ride on to die. Bow Thy meek head to mortal pain, then take, O God, Thy pow'r and reign." Amen. (LSB 441:5)

MONDAY IN HOLY WEEK

A Lamb goes
uncomplaining forth,
The guilt of sinners bearing
And, laden with the sins of earth,
None else the burden sharing;
Goes patient on, grows
weak and faint,
To slaughter led
without complaint,
That spotless life to offer,
He bears the stripes, the
wounds, the lies,
The mockery, and yet replies,
"All this I gladly
suffer." (*LSB* 438:1)

On Palm Sunday, the crowds welcomed Jesus as He entered Jerusalem, exclaiming, "Hosanna to the Son of David! Blessed is He who comes in the name of the Lord! Hosanna in the highest!" (Matthew 21:9). But in a few short days, those shouts of acclamation would turn to shouts of derision: "Crucify Him!" (Luke 23:21). The triumphant Palm Sunday procession would give way to a different kind of procession, captured so well by Pastor Paul Gerhardt in today's hymn.

That procession sees the Son of God go to the cross as the sacrificial Lamb given for our sins and offenses. Though He lived a sinless, spotless life on our behalf, He is the one who faces death by crucifixion. No one else could bear such a heavy burden—all the sins of all the people who ever lived or would live on this earth, including our own. He goes forth without complaint—patiently, willingly bearing the physical wounds and pain inflicted by scourging and the deeply spiritual pain inflicted by the lies and mockery coming from the very creatures for whom He is dying. "All this I gladly suffer"—for you.

This procession is unlike any other in the history of the world. Jesus, the Lamb of God, goes uncomplaining forth, and He does so purely out of great love for us, so that "with His wounds we are healed" (Isaiah 53:5).

"'Yes, Father, yes, most willingly I'll bear what You command Me. My will conforms to Your decree, I'll do what You have asked Me.' O wondrous Love, what have You done! The Father offers up His Son, desiring our salvation. O Love, how strong You are to save! You lay the One into the grave who built the earth's foundation." Amen. (LSB 438:3)

TUESDAY IN HOLY WEEK

Jesus, I will ponder now
On Your holy passion;
With Your Spirit me endow
For such meditation.
Grant that I in love and faith
May the image cherish
Of Your suff'ring,
pain, and death
That I may not perish.

Make me see Your great distress,
Anguish, and affliction,
Bonds and stripes and
wretchedness
And Your crucifixion;
Make me see how
scourge and rod,
Spear and nails did wound You,
How for them You died, O God,
Who with thorns had crowned
You. (*LSB* 440:1–2)

IN TODAY'S HYMN, WE PRAY THAT WE MAY PONDER THE AWFUL PRICE that Jesus had to pay for our redemption. Even more, the hymn writer asks that we "cherish" images of Jesus' suffering, pain, and death. He names some of those images: how the crown of thorns, the scourging rod, the spear, and nails afflicted our Savior with enormous bodily pain and suffering. Crucifixion was a truly painful means of execution, and the hymn writer does not shy away from noting the "great distress, anguish, and affliction," the "wretchedness" of Jesus' death. While focusing on these aspects of the Passion may offend our sensibilities, we dare not turn away from the reality of what our sins caused our Savior to suffer.

But God never lets our sins have the last word. So too our hymn writer turns to the comforting results of Jesus' sufferings: His cross disarms our fears and gives the conscience peace! His holy Passion brings forgiveness of sins. If for us God "slays His Son, God must have compassion!" (st. 5). While we confess that we deserve God's punishment, in Holy Absolution, our sins are forgiven for the sake of Jesus Christ. Thus, we may also cherish the image of our sins being blotted out through Jesus' blood, given into death for us.

"If my sins give me alarm and my conscience grieve me, let Your cross my fear disarm; peace of conscience give me. Help me see forgiveness won by Your holy passion. If for me He slays His Son, God must have compassion!" Amen. (LSB 440:5)

WEDNESDAY IN HOLY WEEK

**O dearest Jesus, what
law hast Thou broken
That such sharp sentence
should on Thee be spoken?
Of what great crime hast
Thou to make confession,
What dark transgression?**

**Whence come these sorrows,
whence this mortal anguish?
It is my sins for which Thou,
Lord, must languish;
Yea, all the wrath, the
woe, Thou dost inherit,
This I do merit.** (***LSB*** **439:1, 3)**

OUR HYMN WRITER POSES TWO QUESTIONS DIRECTLY TO JESUS. What law have You broken? What crime did You commit? From everything observable—the crown of thorns, the scourging, the mocking, the crucifixion—laws must have been broken and crimes committed. Of course, the hymn writer knows the answers to the questions, as do we. Jesus is the sinless Son of God; we are the sinners for whom He suffered. "It is *my sins* for which Thou, Lord, must languish" (emphasis added). We broke God's laws; we committed the crimes.

This is what is known as the great exchange: In His incarnation, Jesus takes on our humanity and in turn gives us His heaven and His glory. Today's hymn shows the culmination of that exchange: "The Shepherd dies for sheep that loved to wander; the Master pays the debt His servants owe Him" (st. 4). It defies all human logic. We should be made to pay our debts, to pay the penalties for our crimes. But in fact, we could never do so—our human nature is so innately and constantly sinful that we could never pay that price. Though Jesus broke no laws, His great love for us caused His incarnation, His death by crucifixion, and His life-giving resurrection.

During this Holy Week, we continue to ponder all that our Savior did to win for us an eternity with Him.

"What punishment so strange is suffered yonder! The Shepherd dies for sheep that loved to wander; the Master pays the debt His servants owe Him, who would not know Him. The sinless Son of God must die in sadness; the sinful child of man may live in gladness; man forfeited his life and is acquitted; God is committed." Amen. (LSB *439:4–5*)

HOLY THURSDAY

When You woke that
Thursday morning,
Savior, teacher, faithful friend,
Thoughts of self and
safety scorning,
Knowing how the
day would end;
Lamb of God, foretold for ages,
Now at last the hour had come
When but One could
pay sin's wages:
You assumed their dreadful sum.

What was there that You
could give them
That would never be outspent,
What great gift that
would outlive them,
What last will and testament?
"Show Me and the
world you love Me,
Know Me as the Lamb of God:
Do this in remembrance of Me,
Eat this body, drink this
blood." (*LSB* 445:1, 3)

O*ur Lord Jesus Christ, on the night when He was betrayed* . . ." (*LSB*, Divine Service, Setting Four). When we hear these words spoken before Communion, we remember that consequential Thursday *evening*. Today's hymn imagines what Jesus contemplated as He woke up that *morning*. He knew what was coming. Jesus desired one last meal with His disciples—to teach them, to care for them, to show them that He would always be with them.

As He washed His disciples' feet, He showed them the kind of sacrificial love that He would manifest even more fully the next day as He willingly went to the cross. But there was yet another gift that evening—one that would "outlive" those disciples, one that would "never be outspent." How the disciples must have been amazed at the Savior's words: "Take, eat; this is My body. . . . Drink of it, all of you, for this is My blood" (Matthew 26:26, 27–28). Jesus gave them—and us—a gift beyond anything we ever could have imagined. By instituting this Sacrament, Jesus established beyond any doubt that He is with us always, giving us His very body and blood in His Holy Supper for the forgiveness of our sins. This is truly our foretaste of the eternal feast to come!

"One day all the Church will capture that bright vision glorious, and Your saints will know the rapture that Your heart desired for us, when the longed-for peace and union of the Greatest and the least meet in joyous, blest communion in Your never-ending feast." Amen. (LSB 445:5)

GOOD FRIDAY

Upon the cross extended
See, world, your Lord suspended.
Your Savior yields His breath.
The Prince of Life from heaven
Himself has freely given
To shame and blows and bitter death. (*LSB* 453:1)

GOOD FRIDAY BRINGS US FACE TO FACE WITH THE STARK REALITY of our sins and what it cost our Savior to redeem us. Each Good Friday confronts us with this jarring, disturbing, but necessary picture: the Son of God, Creator of the universe, suspended on a cross—between the earth that He created and the heaven that He willingly surrendered to save us from our sins. The hymn writer invites us to "come, see these things and ponder" (st. 2). In fact, we *must* do so if we are to understand fully the joy of the resurrection on the third day.

But when we ponder Good Friday, we are confronted with yet another jarring, disturbing picture: *We* are the ones who caused it all. Jesus is suspended on the cross because of our sins. The hymn writer states it plainly: "I caused your grief and sighing. . . . I caused the woes unnumbered" (st. 4). Indeed, our sins are "as countless as the sands" (st. 4). And yet the Son of God willingly took the sins of the whole world—all who would ever live on this earth—and bore the punishment in the place of His fallen creatures so that they might live forever in the perfection of the paradise that He surrendered for a time.

When we ponder Good Friday, we are simply overwhelmed by God's love for us. This love is unlike anything we ever could have imagined; indeed, such love is possible only from the God who *is love* (1 John 4:8–10). His love—poured out while suspended on the cross—is for you.

"Your soul in griefs unbounded, Your head with thorns surrounded, You died to ransom me. The cross for me enduring, the crown for me securing, You healed my wounds and set me free." Amen. (LSB 453:5)

HOLY SATURDAY

What language shall I borrow
To thank Thee, dearest Friend,
For this Thy dying sorrow,
Thy pity without end?
O make me Thine forever!
And should I fainting be,
Lord, let me never, never
Outlive my love for
Thee. (*LSB* 450:5)

I*T IS NOT DIFFICULT TO IMAGINE THAT ALL WHO WITNESSED THE* crucifixion and death of Jesus on Friday must have spent the next days mentally recalling and pondering details of the extraordinary event that had taken place in Jerusalem. For while crucifixions occurred with some regularity at Golgotha ("Place of a Skull"), this was no ordinary event. First, the religious leaders had to rile up the crowds to demand that the Roman governor free a known criminal but sentence to death Jesus of Nazareth—with no evidence of wrongdoing on His part. And then there were the amazing words spoken by Jesus as He hung on the cross. For those who crucified Him, He prayed, "Father, forgive them, for they know not what they do" (Luke 23:34). To one crucified alongside Him, He said, "Today you will be with Me in paradise" (v. 43). This was no ordinary event, and it invites our sustained contemplation.

Pastor Paul Gerhardt translated portions of a medieval Latin hymn into German, which then became the basis of the hymn we know as "O Sacred Head, Now Wounded." In this hymn, Gerhardt helps us not only to recall the events of Christ's Passion but also to reflect on their meaning for us, both in our life and in our death. May Jesus' death for us kindle our deep love for Him. Most important, may His death for us be our consolation at the time of our own death. "Who dieth thus dies well" (st. 7).

"My Savior, be Thou near me when death is at my door; then let Thy presence cheer me, forsake me nevermore! When soul and body languish, O leave me not alone, but take away mine anguish by virtue of Thine own! Be Thou my consolation, my shield, when I must die; remind me of Thy passion when my last hour draws nigh. Mine eyes shall then behold Thee, upon Thy cross shall dwell, my heart by faith enfold Thee. Who dieth thus dies well." Amen. (LSB 450:6–7)

EASTER DAY

Christ Jesus lay in
death's strong bands
For our offenses given;
But now at God's right
hand He stands
And brings us life from heaven.
Therefore let us joyful be
And sing to God right thankfully
Loud songs of alleluia!
Alleluia!

No son of man could
conquer death,
Such ruin sin had wrought us.
No innocence was
found on earth,
And therefore death
had brought us
Into bondage from of old
And ever grew more
strong and bold
And held us as its captive.
Alleluia! (*LSB* 458:1–2)

In his great Easter hymn, Luther states it clearly: Death is a strong enemy, one that no human can conquer. Death is the result of our offenses, the sins that hold each of us captive. Jesus' death was real—He did not escape "death's strong bands." He could not if He was to pay the full price for our sins by dying the death we deserve.

But then in the fourth line of the hymn comes the Gospel: Jesus did not remain in the strong bands of death. He stands at God's right hand—even now—and brings us life, eternal life from heaven! In a brilliant demonstration of poetic and theological concision, Luther needs only the first four lines of this seven-stanza hymn to bring us face to face with both Law and Gospel. And he tells us how to respond to this good news: Let us be joyful and *sing* to God in thanksgiving! Because Jesus defeated death, our strong archenemy will not have the last word! We will not escape death, but the strong bands of death have been forever defeated by Christ. Those strong bands could not hold Christ, and they will not hold us. For us, death is only temporary, and on the Last Day, it will give way to a joyful resurrection to life forever in the presence of our Savior, who broke death's strong bands for us.

"Christ Jesus, God's own Son, came down, His people to deliver; destroying sin, He took the crown from death's pale brow forever: stripped of pow'r, no more it reigns; an empty form alone remains; its sting is lost forever. Alleluia!" Amen. (LSB *458:3*)

EASTER MONDAY

It was a strange and dreadful strife
When life and death contended;
The victory remained with life,
The reign of death was ended.
Holy Scripture plainly saith
That death is swallowed up by death,
Its sting is lost forever.
Alleluia!

Here our true Paschal Lamb we see,
Whom God so freely gave us;
He died on the accursed tree—
So strong His love—to save us.
See, His blood now marks our door;
Faith points to it; death passes o'er,
And Satan cannot harm us.
Alleluia! (*LSB* 458:4–5)

S*o that Christians might sing and pray of Christ's Easter* victory over death, Martin Luther draws on Holy Scripture in his great Easter hymn. First, he quotes from the prophet Isaiah: "He will swallow up death forever" (25:8). Paul would subsequently quote this prophecy to conclude his great resurrection chapter (1 Corinthians 15): "Death is swallowed up in victory," before mocking death by asking derisively, "O death, where is your victory? O death, where is your sting?" (vv. 54–55). With Luther, we, too, proclaim the demise of death's power: "Its sting is lost forever. Alleluia!"

Yet again, Luther draws on Scripture to proclaim the defeat of death. Just as at the Passover, where the blood of a lamb applied to a doorpost would spare a household from death (Exodus 12), so also the blood of Christ metaphorically "marks our door" and spares us from the eternal death that our sins demand. In Christ, God gave us the Lamb of God, the substitute whose blood saves us. In His Holy Supper, Christ continues to feed us with His body and gives us to drink of that saving blood "shed for you for the forgiveness of sins" (*LSB*, Divine Service, Setting Two). In Luther's concluding words, "He is our meat and drink indeed; faith lives upon no other! Alleluia!" (st. 7).

"So let us keep the festival to which the Lord invites us; Christ is Himself the joy of all, the sun that warms and lights us. Now His grace to us imparts eternal sunshine to our hearts; the night of sin is ended. Alleluia!" Amen. (LSB 458:6)

EASTER TUESDAY

All the earth with joy is sounding:
Christ has risen from the dead!
He, the greater Jonah, bounding
From the grave, His three-day bed,
Wins the prize:
Death's demise—
Songs of triumph fill the skies. (***LSB*** **462:1**)

THE FIRST TWO LINES OF TODAY'S HYMN DESCRIBE EASTERTIDE— joy abounds! At Jesus' gentle and humble birth, the heavens were filled with joy and glorious singing from those who alone knew what had happened on earth—the angels. Now, it is the earth's turn to explode with joy, for Christ has risen from the dead! And now, the whole world knows of God's plan for life and salvation for all, and it resounds with its earthly version of the angel's "Gloria!" "Songs of triumph fill the skies"!

In Matthew 12:41, Jesus announces, "Something greater than Jonah is here." And in this hymn by Pastor Stephen Starke, we sing of Christ, the one who is greater—"the greater Jonah, bounding from the grave, His three-day bed." Christ it is who won the prize with death's demise. It is no wonder this marvelous news is filling the earth with joy!

This victorious message is the same throughout the ages, but we are blessed to ponder that message in new ways with hymns like this one, where fresh vocabulary helps our Eastertide joy sparkle anew.

"This joyful Eastertide away with sin and sorrow! My love, the Crucified, has sprung to life this morrow: Had Christ, who once was slain, not burst His three-day prison, our faith had been in vain: But now has Christ arisen, arisen, arisen; but now has Christ arisen!" Amen. (LSB 482:1)

EASTER WEDNESDAY

Christ, the devil's
might unwinding,
Leaves behind His
borrowed tomb.
Stronger He, the strong
man binding,
Takes, disarms his
house of doom;
In the rout
Casting out
Pow'rs of darkness,
sin, and doubt.

Jesus, author of salvation,
Shared in our humanity;
Crowned with radiant
exaltation,
Now He shares His victory!
From His face
Shines the grace
Meant for all our fallen
race. (*LSB* 462:2–3)

F*OR MANY, EASTER WEEK IS THEIR FAVORITE, FULL OF BRIGHTNESS,* supernal gladness, and the festive loud singing of alleluias. Of course, why not? It is a high celebration week that is fitting as our King is crowned with radiant exaltation and now shares His victory with us. But it is more; it is a victory *for us.*

Some may think this is the highest week of the Church Year calendar as it explodes in the Gospel's good news. But is it? This week is the result of last week, Holy Week, and that is where and when the pure Gospel was given to the world as God acted to save each of us in stakes He already laid out in Genesis 3:15. The words "It is finished" (John 19:30) ended the devil's house of doom and darkness, sin and doubt, evil and death—that's over! Our King has disarmed the strong man, and he has been cast out!

And our King erased the curse, triumphed over death, and opened paradise! Alleluia! He is the author of our salvation, and as such, now His face shines grace upon grace, mercy upon mercy, gift upon gift, as He leaves us with and in His peace forever. Alleluia!

"Now let the heav'ns be joyful, let earth its song begin, let all the world keep triumph and all that is therein. Let all things, seen and unseen, their notes of gladness blend; for Christ the Lord has risen, our joy that has no end!" Amen. (LSB 478:3)

EASTER THURSDAY

Praise the Lord, His reign commences,
Reign of life and liberty—
Paschal Lamb, for our offenses,
Slain and raised to set us free!
Evermore
Bow before
Christ, the Lord of Life adore! (*LSB* 462:4)

TRUMPETS, LILIES, AND LITURGICAL COLORS OF GOLD AND WHITE draped everywhere signal an extraordinary event and week—one resplendent with ubiquitous alleluias, regal hymns, and grand shouts of praise filling churches throughout the world as voices and hearts together burst forth with joy and the radiant gladness of Eastertide.

Eastertide will last fifty days, leading the Bride of Christ on to the Feast of Pentecost. These fifty days of Easter are sometimes called the "queen of seasons," in which the Bride celebrates and adores her Lord of Life, Christus Victor, who won for her life, liberty, and blessed freedom from all her offenses. Alleluia! Yes, the highest praise is in order for what God's slain Paschal Lamb won for, and now showers upon, all who believe in Him.

On the cover of *Lutheran Service Book*, the hymnal from which nearly all of these hymn texts are taken, is a prominent cross surrounded by eight embossed squares. This rich, symbolic art is a visual reminder of our Lord's resurrection on Sunday, which could be understood as the eighth day of creation. For us, it is the beginning of a new creation that is ours through our Baptism into the death and resurrection of Christ. This day is eternal—it never ends!

This is why baptismal fonts are often eight-sided. Baptismal life is ours, made possible by our Lord's resurrection on the eighth day, the day of new creation when His reign commences and never ends. Alleluia!

"Then sing your hosannas and raise your glad voice; proclaim the blest tidings that all may rejoice. Laud, honor, and praise to the Lamb that was slain: With Father and Spirit He ever shall reign." Amen. (LSB 480:5)

EASTER FRIDAY

Awake, my heart, with gladness,
See what today is done;
Now, after gloom and sadness,
Comes forth the glorious sun.
My Savior there was laid
Where our bed must be made
When to the realms of light
Our spirit wings its flight. (*LSB* 467:1)

PAUL GERHARDT'S HYMNS ARE MARVELOUS MEDITATIONS ON what God has done for us. They were initially written as devotions for his congregation, and his hymns often had ten to twenty stanzas for this meditative purpose.

Today's hymn stanza, part of Pastor Gerhardt's Easter meditation for his parish, proclaims abundant confidence and understanding in what the risen Christ did for us. As a devotional hymn, it points to the saint in first-person writing, such as "my heart," "my Savior," "my soul," "I am safe" (st. 4), "I follow Him," I "cling" to Him (st. 6), and "He brings me to the portal" (st. 7). Pastor Gerhardt makes this life-changing event much more than a historical narrative and brings it close to home so that it has meaning for us.

Thus, the second half of our stanza today tells each of us that because my Savior was laid in a tomb for me, one day when I am laid in a tomb, my spirit will wing its flight to be with Him. And while the body will remain in the earth until the Last Day, the soul will immediately go to peace in our risen Lord's presence. This is pastoral teaching of what Easter means *for us.*

"Now I will cling forever to Christ, my Savior true; my Lord will leave me never, whate'er He passes through. He rends death's iron chain; He breaks through sin and pain; He shatters hell's grim thrall; I follow Him through all." Amen. (LSB 467:6)

EASTER SATURDAY

The day of resurrection!
Earth, tell it out abroad,
The passover of gladness,
The passover of God.
From death to life eternal,
From sin's dominion free,
Our Christ has brought us over
With hymns of victory.

Now let the heav'ns be joyful,
Let earth its song begin,
Let all the world keep triumph
And all that is therein.
Let all things, seen and unseen,
Their notes of gladness blend;
For Christ the Lord has risen,
Our joy that has no
end! (***LSB*** **478:1, 3)**

A ***DARKENED SANCTUARY BECOMES FULLY LIT; SILENCE AND*** quietness move to "This Is the Feast" with full organ and trumpets; sadness and gloom are left behind for joy and gladness. This stunning progression in last week's Easter Vigil from darkness to light and from a serene, hushed beginning to a full-voiced acclamation of "Alleluia! Christ is risen! He is risen indeed! Alleluia!" is perhaps the most dramatic moment of the entire liturgical year. What can compare to that second in time when the gathered saints hear yet again the loud shout from their pastor that their Savior lives?

Today's hymn, by John of Damascus, would make a fine soundtrack for the death-to-life progression just described as the turning point in the Easter Vigil. "Let earth its song begin"! "Earth, tell it out abroad"! Yes, the heavens and all the earth are radiant with pure joy over this "passover of gladness, the passover of God" and have given voice in striking kingly texts such as this early Greek hymn. "Now let the heav'ns be joyful, let earth its song begin"! "Let all things, seen and unseen, their notes of gladness blend"! Alleluia! Amen!

"Let hearts be purged of evil that we may see aright the Lord in rays eternal of resurrection light and, list'ning to His accents, may hear, so calm and plain, His own 'All hail!' and, hearing, may raise the victor strain." Amen. (LSB *478:2*)

SECOND SUNDAY OF EASTER

When Thomas first the tidings heard
That they had seen the risen Lord,
He doubted the disciples' word.
Alleluia! (*LSB* 471:5)

***O*N SUNDAY EVENING OF THE RESURRECTION, JESUS APPEARED** to His disciples, but Thomas was absent. How fortunate for us was his absence, for then we could hear Thomas tell his fellow disciples, "Unless I see . . . I will never believe" (John 20:25). Such a statement could be ours as well, a response that proceeds from elevating human reason over the truth of God's Word. But by His undeserved love that comes to us purely through God's grace, Jesus changed Thomas's unbelief to belief. Thomas did not do this on his own; Jesus did it for him. The same is true for us.

Among Martin Luther's most memorable writings is his explanation of the Third Article of the Creed: "I believe that I cannot by my own reason or strength believe in Jesus Christ, my Lord, or come to Him; but the Holy Spirit has called me by the Gospel" (Small Catechism). Unbelief is changed to belief by the grace of God through the action of the Holy Spirit, working faith in our lives through means—the power of the Word in Holy Baptism, and the preaching of the Word in His church.

The verses of John's Gospel immediately following the account of Thomas attest to the purpose of God's Word: "But these are written so that you may believe that Jesus is the Christ, the Son of God, and that by believing you may have life in His name" (John 20:31). Jesus changed Thomas's unbelief to belief so that he might "have life and have it abundantly" (John 10:10). Thanks be to God that He does the same for us!

"Jesus lives! To Him the throne high above all things is given. I shall go where He is gone, live and reign with Him in heaven. God is faithful; doubtings, hence! This shall be my confidence." Amen. (LSB 490:2)

ACKNOWLEDGMENTS

The authors thank the following for permission to use their work:

"Break Forth, O Beauteous Heavenly Light" © 1973 Openbook Publishers. All rights reserved. Used by permission.

"By All Your Saints in Warfare," stanza 14 © Gregory J. Wismar. All rights reserved. Used by permission.

"Christ Is Surely Coming" © 1975 Jubilate (admin, Hope Publishing Company).

"Christ Mighty Savior" © 1982 United Methodist Publishing House. All rights reserved. Used by permission.

"Christ, the Lord of Hosts, Unshaken" © Peter M. Prange. All rights reserved. Used by permission.

"Eternal Spirit of the Living Christ." Words: Frank von Christierson © 1974 The Hymn Society (admin. Hope Publishing Company, www.hopepublishing.com). All rights reserved. Used by permission.

"Evening and Morning," stanzas 3–4 © Augsburg Publishing. All rights reserved. Used by permission.

"For All the Faithful Women," stanza 8 text© 1993, 1997, 2003 GIA Publications, Inc. All rights reserved. Used by permission.

"Fruitful Trees, the Spirit's Sowing." Words: Timothy Dudley-Smith © 1984 Hope Publishing Company, www.hopepublishing.com. All rights reserved. Used by permission.

"God's Own Child" © 1991 Robert E. Voelker. All rights reserved. Used by permission.

"O Darkest Woe" © Joseph Herl.

INDEX OF HYMNS

A

B

C

D

E

F

G

H

I

J

L

M

N

O

P

R

S

T

U

W

Y